The
BORGIAS

ALSO BY PAUL STRATHERN

Mendeleyev's Dream

Dr Strangelove's Game

The Medici

Napoleon in Egypt

The Artist, the Philosopher and the Warrior

Death in Florence

The Spirit of Venice

The Venetians

The
BORGIAS

Power and Fortune

PAUL STRATHERN

PEGASUS BOOKS

NEW YORK LONDON

THE BORGIAS

Pegasus Books Ltd.
148 West 37th Street, 13th Floor
New York, NY 10018

First Pegasus Books hardcover edition August 2019

Map artwork by Jeff Edwards

ISBN: 978-1-64313-083-5

10 9 8 7 6 5 4 3 2 1

Printed in the United States of America
Distributed by W. W. Norton & Company, Inc.

To
Julian Alexander
agent extraordinaire

CONTENTS

Maps   ix
Abbreviated Borgia Family Tree   xi
Dramatis Personae   xiii
Prologue: The Crowning Moment   1

1   Origins of a Dynasty   17
2   The Young Rodrigo   33
3   Cardinal Rodrigo Borgia Emerges in His True Colours   53
4   The Way to the Top   73
5   A New Pope in a New Era   89
6   'The Scourge of God'   107
7   The Best of Plans . . .   123
8   A Crucial Realignment   139
9   A Royal Connection   155
10   Il Valentino's Campaign   177
11   Biding Time   195
12   The Second Romagna Campaign   209
13   The Borgias *in excelsis*   223
14   Cesare Strikes Out   241
15   Changing Fortunes   257
16   Cesare Survives   275
17   Borgia's 'Reconciliation'   289
18   Lucrezia in Ferrara   307
19   The Unforeseen   313
20   Desperate Fortune   329

Epilogue   339
Acknowledgements   342
Sources   343
Illustrations   363
Index   365

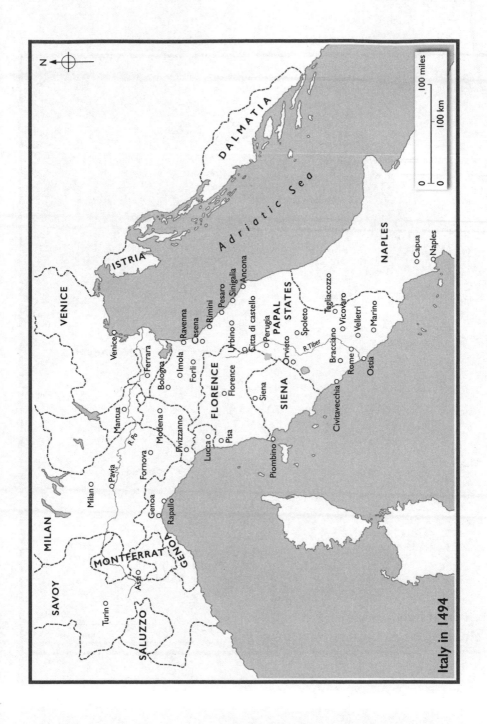

Italy in 1494

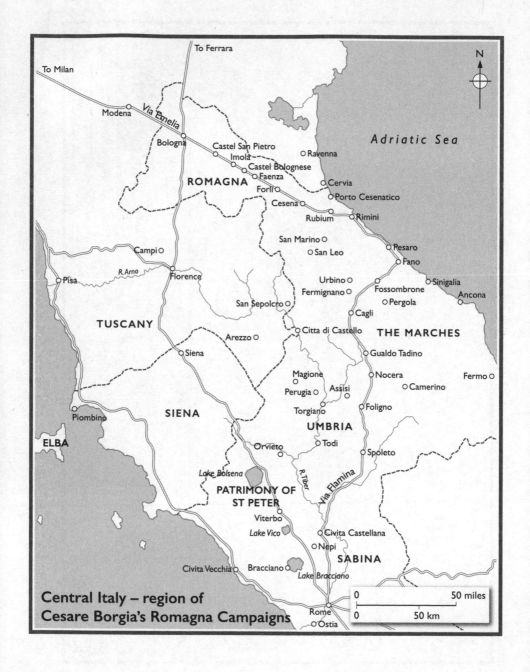

Central Italy – region of
Cesare Borgia's Romagna Campaigns

ABBREVIATED BORGIA FAMILY TREE

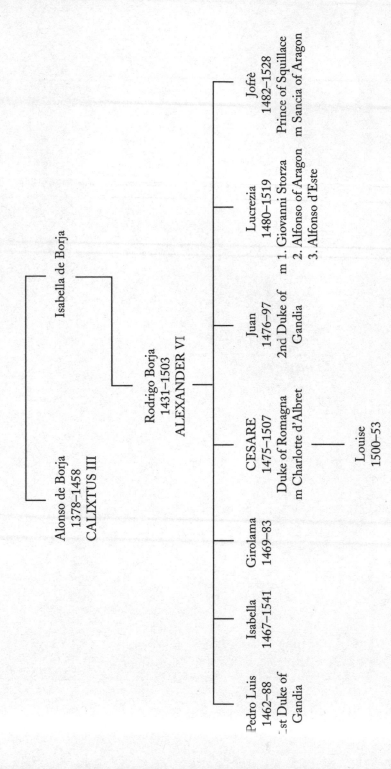

Alonso de Borja
1378–1458
CALIXTUS III

Isabella de Borja

Rodrigo Borja
1431–1503
ALEXANDER VI

Pedro Luis
1462–88
1st Duke of
Gandia

Isabella
1467–1541

Girolama
1469–83

CESARE
1475–1507
Duke of Romagna
m Charlotte d'Albret

Juan
1476–97
2nd Duke of
Gandia

Lucrezia
1480–1519
m 1. Giovanni Storza
2. Alfonso of Aragon
3. Alfonso d'Este

Jofrè
1482–1528
Prince of Squillace
m Sancia of Aragon

Louise
1500–53

DRAMATIS PERSONAE

This list is not exhaustive. If any names you are looking for do not appear, try looking up the page of their first entry in the Index.

Alexander VI Born Rodrigo Borgia, he rose during the papacy of his uncle, who became Pope Callixtus III.

Alfonso II Son of King Ferrante I of Naples, whom he succeeded as short-lived King of Naples.

King Alfonso of Aragon Made controversial heir to the throne of Naples by Joanna II. The future Callixtus III became his secretary.

Georges d'Amboise Archbishop of Rouen and a powerful influence at the French royal court.

Alfonso of Aragon, Duke of Bisceglie Illegitimate son of King Alfonso II of Naples, whose father was Ferrante I. Alfonso became Lucrezia's beloved second husband.

Sancia of Aragon Spirited childhood friend of Lucrezia Borgia, who fell in and out of favour with Alexander VI.

Cardinal Basilios Bessarion Greek scholar who was at one time a candidate for the papacy.

Pietro Bembo Venetian poet who wrote sonnets to Lucrezia Borgia when she was living in Ferrara and married to the Duke of Ferrara.

Alonso de Borja See Callixtus III.

Cesare Borgia Oldest son of Vanozza de' Cattanei and Cardinal Rodrigo Borgia, the future Alexander VI.

Giovanni Borgia Known as the *Infans Romanus*; the child who appeared in the Borgia family, whose parentage became a source of scandalous speculation.

Isabella Borgia Sister of Callixtus III, mother of Rodrigo, who became Alexander VI.

Juan Borgia Younger brother of Cesare Borgia, who much resented him.

Jofrè Borgia Fourth child of Rodrigo Borgia by Vanozza de' Cattanei.

Lucrezia Borgia Daughter of Alexander VI, who married her off several times in pursuance of his political goals.

Pedro Luis Borgia Nephew of the man who would become Callixtus III, appointed by his uncle as Captain-General of the Papal Forces.

Cardinal Rodrigo Borgia See Alexander VI.

Pedro Calderon Nicknamed 'Perotto', who was Alexander VI's unfortunate chamberlain.

Callixtus III, born Alfonso de Borja, the first Borgia Pope, who gave his nephew Rodrigo Borgia the all-important post of Vice-Chancellor.

Cardinal Angelo Capranica Loyal friend to Callixtus III.

Vanozza de' Cattanei Mistress of Cardinal Rodrigo Borgia (Alexander VI) and mother of Cesare, Juan, Lucrezia and Jofrè.

Charles VIII The young King of France who invaded Italy.

Miguel da Corella Known as 'the strangler', one of Cesare Borgia's closest Spanish commanders.

Alfonso d'Este Son of Ercole I d'Este, was ruler of Ferrara, became third husband of Lucrezia Borgia.

Ercole I d'Este Military leader, Duke of Ferrara, who grudgingly allowed his son to marry Lucrezia Borgia.

Isabella d'Este Cultured Marquesa of Mantua, who disliked Lucrezia Borgia. Had her portrait sketched by Leonardo.

Fiammetta de' Michaelis The renowned Roman courtesan whom Cesare took as his mistress during the summer of 1500.

Giulia Farnese Sixteen-year-old who became mistress to the fifty-eight-year-old Alexander VI.

Ferrante I The long-lived King of Naples, whose death triggered the invasion of Italy by Charles VIII of France.

Francesco Gonzaga Duke of Mantua and husband to Isabella d'Este.

Francesco Guicciardini A contemporary historian and friend of Machiavelli.

Innocent VIII The Pope who preceded Alexander VI.

Joanna of Aragon At twenty-three became the second wife of the ageing King Ferrante I, and thus became Queen of Naples. Not to be mistaken for the earlier Queen Joanna II of Naples (see below) who had died before she was born.

Queen Joanna II of Naples Aged ruler of Naples who made Alfonso of Aragon her heir, thus antagonizing French claimants to the throne.

Ramiro da Lorqua Cesare Borgia's most trusted Spanish commander.

Louis XII Formerly Louis of Orléans, who succeeded to the French throne after Charles VIII.

Cardinal Giovanni de' Medici Son of Lorenzo de' Medici, who would became a cardinal aged thirteen, but fled Rome when Alexander VI became pope.

Lorenzo de' Medici Also known as 'the Magnificent', the ruler of Florence.

Niccolò Machiavelli Notorious author of *The Prince*, contemporary historian and emissary for Florence to Cesare Borgia.

Federigo da Montefeltro Renowned condottiere who transformed Urbino into a Renaissance city.

Guidobaldo da Montefeltro Son of Federigo, who became a sworn enemy of Cesare Borgia.

Oliverotto da Fermo Originally a loyal commander of Cesare Borgia's army in the Romagna.

Cardinal Giambattista Orsini Senior member of the Orsini clan who became a friend of Alexander VI.

Giulio Orsini Condottiere who together with his brother Paolo joined up with Cesare Borgia in the Romagna campaigns.

Paolo Orsini See previous entry.

Riario family Genoese relatives of the della Rovere family.

Francesco della Rovere The young ruler of Sinigalia

Cardinal Giuliano della Rovere Sworn enemy of Alexander VI, continually plotting against him.

Sancia See Sancia of Aragon.

Antonio di Monte Sansovino Humanist scholar appointed by Cesare Borgia as governor of his Romagna territories.

Gian Carlo Scalona Mantuan ambassador in Rome.

Cardinal Ascanio Sforza Influential cleric from Milan whose vote ensured Rodrigo Borgia would become Alexander VI.

Giovanni Sforza Lord of Pesaro and Lucrezia Borgia's first husband.

Caterina Sforza Countess of Forli, who was taken prisoner by Cesare Borgia and Sixtus IV.

Gaspar Torella Cesare Borgia's Spanish personal physician, who became an expert on syphilis.

Cardinal Giovanni Zeno Extremely wealthy Venetian cleric who lived in Rome. On his death Alexander VI took charge of his fortune.

THE CROWNING MOMENT

IN THE SUMMER OF 1492, amidst the stifling, malaria-infested heat of Rome, Pope Innocent VIII became unwell, and it was soon clear that he was seriously ill. He began suffering from stomach pains, and his digestion was severely affected. The Pope's personal physicians proved for the most part unwilling to take any responsible role in administering to a patient who was so evidently close to death. This was understandable in an age where medicine remained primitive and suspicions of poisoning were rife, with punishments for such misdemeanours proving drastic in the extreme. Indeed, doing nothing was often less likely to harm the patient than administering the usual accepted treatments. However, amongst the Pope's personal physicians was a Jewish doctor called Giacomo di San Genesio, who favoured his own advanced methods of medical treatment above the more medieval practices then current. Excessive bleeding with leeches was commonplace, and usually only served to weaken the patient. Similarly archaic was the administering of 'elixirs of life' containing gold or ground pearl or other exotic ingredients, whose sheer expense encouraged the expectation of efficacy. Instead, San Genesio was all for radical and experimental treatments, several of which would later be adopted by orthodox contemporary medicine. Unfortunately, many of these treat-ments had yet to evolve the modern refinements which accounted for their curative, rather than their hazardous properties. In order to cure Innocent VIII, Giacomo di San Genesio decided to perform 'the world's first blood transfusion'. This involved him bleeding the Pope, whilst at the same time inducing him to drink draughts of freshly drawn youthful blood, a treatment which would result in the death of three ten-year-old boys, before San Genesio was persuaded to desist. By then Innocent VIII had become so weak that he was able 'to take for nourishment no more than a few drops of milk from the breast of a young woman'.

At the time, Italy was in the midst of what seemed to many like a golden age. According to the contemporary historian Francesco Guicciardini:

> Since the fall of the Roman Empire, Italy has not experienced such peace and prosperity. The entire land has become adorned with magnificent princes and beautiful cities filled with noble minds learned in every branch of study and skilled in every branch of the arts.

This may have been a somewhat rosy view, but there was no denying that something momentous was taking place in Italy. The Renaissance, centred on Florence, was coming into its own, with the rebirth of classical learning, art and architecture inspiring the likes of Botticelli and Leonardo da Vinci. A new era of practical humanism was beginning to emerge, with its emphasis on the values and philosophical attitude adopted by an individual human being during the course of his or her life. This replaced the otherworldly preoccupations of the Middle Ages, during which our life on earth was seen as a necessary ordeal. After death, we would be judged and rewarded with a life in paradise or otherwise, dependent upon the good or evil which we had manifested during our earthly life. Put simply, during the Renaissance humanity was beginning to undergo a sea change. This marked an entirely new attitude towards life: one whose effects are still with us to this day.

Despite such advances, Innocent VIII retained a more medieval cast of mind, allied to a largely ineffective and corrupt character. Of part-Greek origin, it was said of him that he 'begat eight boys and just as many girls, so that Rome might justly call him Father'. His eight-year reign had become a byword for corruption. His speciality had been the selling of pardons and indulgencies, allowing sinners to buy reductions in their time suffering the punishments of Purgatory, where their sins were purged, before their ascent into Paradise. When questioned on this matter, Innocent VIII replied, 'Rather than the death of a sinner, God wills that he should live – and pay.' One of the more notable features of his reign was his approval of the notorious Dominican friar Tomás de Torquemada as Grand Inquisitor of the Spanish Inquisition. Another contribution came as a result of the Little Ice Age that had blighted crops and brought famine to northern Europe. Innocent VIII ascribed this to occult powers, and issued a bull authorizing the persecution of all witches and sorcerers as heretics, a move that led to widespread denunciations of personal enemies, settlings of old scores, as well as the judicial murders of 'old wives' and other defenceless women.

As knowledge concerning the illness of the Pope became more widespread, this gradually led to a breakdown of public order within his domains. Crime and civil unrest increased in Rome, where 'hardly a day passed without a murder somewhere'. Meanwhile, in the city of Cesena, in the Papal States 150 miles to the north, there was an open revolt. In April news reached Rome that Lorenzo the Magnificent, the Medici ruler of Florence, had died at the age of forty-three. Innocent VIII had both admired and relied upon Lorenzo, and had even persuaded him to allow his eldest son to marry Lorenzo's illegitimate daughter. In return for this favour, Innocent VIII had made Lorenzo's thirteen-year-old son Giovanni de' Medici a cardinal.[*] The charismatic Lorenzo the Magnificent was described by Innocent VIII as 'the needle of the Italian compass', in grateful recognition of his diplomatic skill in guiding the fortunes of Italy safely through the stormy seas of its turbulent politics.

---

[*] Twenty-four years later Cardinal Giovanni de' Medici would become Pope Leo X.

This entailed maintaining the balance of power in the peninsula, whose territory was mainly divided between the powerful and contentious city states of Venice, Milan, Florence, Rome and Naples. Now, with Lorenzo de' Medici gone, and Innocent VIII dying, there appeared to be nothing to restrain each of these states from scheming to follow their self-interest at the expense of the others, a situation which would inevitably lead to a further bout of internecine wars.

Along with the death of Lorenzo the Magnificent, there also came news from Florence of disturbing prophecies which had been made by the fiery fundamentalist priest Girolamo Savonarola. He had seen apocalyptic visions of 'a black cross which stretched out its arms to cover the whole of the earth, upon which were inscribed the words: "The Cross of the Wrath of God"', and he prophesied that 'all mankind shall suffer the scourge of God'. More pertinently, some weeks earlier he had specifically 'prophesied that Lorenzo the Magnificent, Pope Innocent VIII and King Ferrante of Naples would all soon die'. Lorenzo had now died, Pope Innocent appeared to be dying, and the sixty-nine-year-old King Ferrante, the paranoid tyrant of Naples, was said to be in failing health. The advent of the Renaissance was undermining many of the old certainties, and people throughout Italy were becoming bewildered by this age of change: Savonarola's hellfire sermons harked back to an earlier age of primitive, unquestioned belief, while his visions seemed to fulfil the people's forebodings of divine retribution. More and more of those who crowded to hear his sermons in Florence, the very epicentre of the Renaissance, were beginning to regress to the beliefs of the previous era.

As the long hot summer progressed, Innocent VIII gradually became weaker. Rumours swept Rome of the Pope's more unorthodox medical treatment by di San Genesio, fuelling anti-Semitism. More substantial reports by the Mantuan ambassador Gian Carlo Scalona spoke of an angry shouting match in the dying pope's bedchamber between two of the assembled senior cardinals. This had involved Cardinal Rodrigo Borgia, the papal Vice-Chancellor, a wily, bullish figure, whose vigour belied his sixty-one years. Borgia's adversary in this unseemly row had been his sworn, long-term enemy Cardinal Giuliano della Rovere, who, despite his comparative youth, had emerged at the age of forty-eight as the most powerful figure amongst the College of Cardinals during the largely ineffective papacy of Innocent VIII. Whereas the Vice-Chancellor may be seen as the chief administrator of the Holy See (whose supreme ruler was, of course, the Pope), the College of Cardinals acted in the capacity of an advisory body to the pontiff.

In the course of Innocent VIII's eight-year reign, he had incurred considerable disapproval for his distribution of papal offices amongst his family, as well as the selling of benefices and ecclesiastical privileges to the highest bidders. Such nepotism and simony had become an increasing feature of papal rule, though Innocent VIII's behaviour in this regard had been regarded as excessive. However, on his deathbed Innocent VIII excelled even himself by declaring as his dying wish that the entire contents of the Vatican's financial reserves be distributed amongst his relatives. This was estimated be worth around 47,000 ducats.* Such a pronouncement proved too much for Cardinal Borgia, much of whose efforts had gone into accumulating these reserves. Unable to contain himself, Cardinal Borgia chose to express his disapproval of this move in the presence of the Pope and his assembled cardinals. However, Cardinal della Rovere, in order to retain his favour with the Pope, had in fact ensured that the College of Cardinals agreed to Innocent VIII's dying wish. Outraged at Cardinal Borgia's disrespectful attitude, Cardinal della Rovere responded strongly, alluding in a contemptuous fashion to Cardinal Borgia's Spanish origins. Cardinal Borgia, as Vice-Chancellor, was second only to the Pope himself in terms of administrative power; remaining as vigorous mentally as he was physically during his long years of office, he had grown unaccustomed to being contradicted, let alone insulted in such a fashion. Aggressively advancing towards della Rovere, Borgia informed him that if they had not been in the presence of the Pope himself, he would have taken matters into his own hands. Della Rovere stood his ground. In an effort to prevent an unholy brawl in the papal bedchamber, their colleagues

---

* At the time, an artisan would have been lucky to earn twenty-five ducats in a year. An adolescent female Caucasian slave could be bought for six ducats

had rushed forward, restraining the two cardinals in their revered scarlet robes from coming to blows.

Cardinal Rodrigo Borgia was particularly sensitive concerning his Spanish origins, of which he remained intensely proud. Anyone who cast aspersions on this proud heritage was noted – a target for future revenge. Cardinal Rodrigo Borgia would never forgive, let alone forget, any insult or act of betrayal. Indeed, second only to his driving ambition was his powerful and vindictive impulse to revenge. He might wait, often for years, but any disloyalty would eventually be avenged. As we shall see, this was a trait which ran more or less strongly through the entire Borgia family.

Innocent VIII finally died on 25 July, and on 6 August members of the College of Cardinals gathered for the conclave to elect the next pope. 'They were twenty-three in number.' Only four cardinals remained absent: the ones in Jerusalem, Bordeaux and Toledo, as well as Cardinal Borgia's cousin Cardinal Luis Juan del Milà, who refused to attend, being averse to the heat of Rome.*

The conclave of 1492 was the first to be held in the Sistine Chapel, which had been restored by (and received its name from) della Rovere's uncle Pope Sixtus IV†. By this time the high walls of the chapel had already been adorned with frescoes by the likes of Botticelli and Ghirlandaio, though Michelangelo's ceiling would not be painted until some two decades later. Throughout the conclave the participating cardinals would be locked inside the chapel, in order to isolate them from outside influences. Conditions were oppressive, with the high windows boarded up and the inner chapel reduced to an oppressive gloom, illuminated only by candles. At night the cardinals shared plain wooden cells, sleeping on simple uncomfortable palliasses. Meals were carried to the chapel and passed through a hatchway by trusted janitors, the dishes meticulously inspected for hidden messages by the guards. These dishes consisted of

---

* Cardinal del Milà had attended his first conclave as early as 1458, but had found the Roman climate intolerable. The prospect of such discomfort would cause him to decline invitations to attend the six ensuing conclaves which took place during his lifetime.

† *Sisto* is a variant on the Italian *sesto* for 'sixth'.

frugal fare, in keeping with the oaths of poverty, chastity and obedience once taken by the clerical participants. However, this austere regime was not imposed to accord with priestly vows, but to encourage the conclave of wealthy cardinals unused to enduring such privation to reach a conclusion as hastily as possible.

After their tiring, uncomfortable nights, the candidates were free to wander up and down the dim confines of the chapel. Here the leading contenders and their supporters would engage in whispered conversation, bargaining, arm-twisting, attempting to gain sufficient votes. A two-thirds majority was needed before a successful candidate could be declared. This often required several votes. When an insufficient majority was obtained, the ballot papers would be burned, emitting black smoke from the chapel chimney – a sign recognized by the large, expectant crowds waiting outside. (When a successful candidate emerged, the ballot papers were burned with an added chemical – today, potassium chlorate – which produced the celebrated white smoke.) Following an unsuccessful vote, more urgent bargaining would ensue. The most serious deals were made when leading cardinals unobtrusively retired to the latrines – which remained unsluiced throughout the conclave, their pervasive stench adding further incentive for the cardinals to conclude their business.

Cardinal Borgia was well practised in the secretive procedures of the conclaves, having already attended those that elected Pius II, Paul II, Sixtus IV and Innocent VIII – whereas Cardinal della Rovere had only attended the previous conclave, which elected Innocent VIII. Even so, he had proved himself highly adept at the politicking involved. In the previous conclave, Cardinal Borgia had felt certain that he held sufficient votes to ensure his election, but a number of the Spanish cardinals (who could have been guaranteed to support their countryman) had failed to arrive at Rome in time. Cardinal della Rovere had mustered his followers to block Borgia, who had been forced to accept the compromise candidate suggested by della Rovere, who became Innocent VIII. It was this move which had given della Rovere such influence with Innocent VIII.

But now that Innocent VIII was dead, Borgia was determined that this time there would be no mistake. He well realized that at the age of sixty-one this was almost certainly his last chance of becoming pope. Despite his age, Borgia retained many of the qualities of his youth, when he had been described as 'handsome, of a pleasant and cheerful countenance, with a sweet and persuasive manner'. Now, in late middle age, he appeared a rotund jovial character, but retained much of the menace which underlay the vigour of his younger years. However, this contradictory personality was not without his skills; the contemporary historian Guicciardini noted that he 'possessed singular cunning and sagacity, excellent judgement, a marvellous efficacy in persuading, and an incredible dexterity and attentiveness when dealing with weighty matters'. These had been put to good use during his years as Vice-Chancellor, in the course of which he had accumulated all manner of papal offices, including 'numerous abbeys in Italy and Spain, and his three bishoprics of Valencia, Porto and Cartagena'. According to Roman diarist Jacopo da Volterra, writing some years earlier: 'He possesses more gold and riches of every kind than all the other cardinals combined, excepting only d'Estouteville."

However, as the Florentine historian Guicciardini noted, Borgia's great riches, magnetic charm and administrative skills were not all that he possessed:

> these qualities were far outweighed by his vices: the most obscene behaviour, insincerity, shamelessness, lying, faithlessness, impiety, insatiable avarice, immoderate ambition [and] a cruelty more than barbaric.

Borgia's gross sensuality had quickly become evident. Even during his early years as Bishop of Valencia (a city he seldom visited), his degenerate lifestyle had attracted the attention of his superiors. Hearing of his 'unbecoming behaviour at an entertainment given at Siena', Pope Pius II

---

* Cardinal d'Estouteville, Bishop of Rouen, became a byword for vast wealth after he survived a serious outbreak of the Black Death in France, consequently declaring himself the possessor of the many bishoprics and benefices which had fallen vacant following the death of their incumbents.

had written to him: 'Our displeasure is unspeakable,' remonstrating that Borgia's exploits were so scandalous that they brought disgrace upon the entire Church. Such warnings had been ignored. Around 1472 Cardinal Borgia had taken as his mistress a married Roman woman called Vanozza de' Cattanei, by whom he had fathered four children. And now, some three decades later, at the approach of old age, his eye had fallen on the sixteen-year-old bride Giulia Farnese. Her husband Orsino Orsini may have been a member of one of the most powerful families in Rome, but he has been variously described in terms such as 'squint-eyed and devoid of any meaningful self-confidence'. When he was persuaded to leave Rome on a pilgrimage, his wife, too, would become Borgia's mistress; on Orsino's return, he would take up residence in one of the family castles at Basanello, some fifty miles north of Rome.

Yet Borgia had never allowed such behaviour to interfere with his hold on power or his ultimate ambition. By the time of Innocent VIII's death, it was thirty-six years since Cardinal Borgia's uncle Pope Callixtus III had appointed him Vice-Chancellor, and according to Borgia's secretary, 'during that time he never missed a single consistory unless prevented by illness from attending, which very seldom happened'.*

Borgia considered that he had two serious rivals for the papacy. His main rival, Cardinal della Rovere, had the backing of King Charles VIII of France, at the time the richest and most powerful nation in Europe. Charles VIII had provided della Rovere with 200,000 ducats to garner votes amongst the 'neutral' cardinals. On top of this, the wealthy maritime republic of Genoa, della Rovere's birthplace, had provided a further 100,000 ducats to his cause. Della Rovere also knew that he could count on the backing of King Ferrante of Naples. The divisions within the College of Cardinals mirrored the increasing tensions within Italy,

---

* The consistory was the formal committee of cardinals which regularly met to advise the Pope. The Vice-Chancellor was its senior member. The consistory was made up of the limited amount of cardinals resident in Rome at the time, as distinct from the College of Cardinals, which included all cardinals, many of whom were resident in France, Spain, the German states or other more distant territories of Christendom.

with the result that this bloc was opposed by Cardinal Ascanio Sforza, the uncle of the ruler of Milan, who had every reason to be suspicious of his near-neighbour France, and was well aware of the antagonism of King Ferrante of Naples.

Such were the two favourites for the papacy: this time no one but Borgia himself felt that he was a serious candidate. The Spanish interloper was widely reviled. In the first vote, Cardinal Borgia and his supporters duly supported the candidacy of Cardinal Ascanio Sforza, thus blocking Cardinal della Rovere. As the voting continued, it quickly became clear that a compromise candidate would have to be considered, if anyone was to gain the necessary two-thirds majority. But after four days and three votes the situation remained in stalemate. Then, quite unexpectedly, during the night of 10–11 August, a dramatic change took place. Just before dawn on 11 August, with the sky of Rome illuminated by flickers of summer lightning, the doors of the Sistine Chapel were unlocked and it was announced that Cardinal Borgia had been elected as the next pope.

This had come about because Cardinal Sforza had suddenly decided to cast his vote, and those of his supporters, for Cardinal Borgia. Cardinal Sforza had apparently decided that he had no chance of getting himself elected, and Cardinal Borgia had assured him that if he were elected he would appoint Cardinal Sforza as his vice-chancellor. Such was almost certainly the case; but it seems that this may not have been the entire story. The contemporary Roman writer Stefano Infessura recorded in his diary that during the hours of darkness on 10–11 August 'the Vice-Chancellor [Borgia] sent four mules laden with silver to the palazzo of [Cardinal Sforza]'. The evidence of Guicciardini would seem to confirm this:

> Primarily [Borgia's] election was due to the fact that he had openly bought many of the cardinals' votes in a manner unheard of in those times, partly with money and partly with promises of offices and benefices of his own, which were considerable.[*]

---

[*] Upon assuming office, a pope was required to divest himself of all his bishoprics, benefices and other appointments.

Although doubt has been cast on the colourful story of the overnight mule train, the financial dealings to which it alludes would seem to be supported by the fact that during these days the withdrawals from the Spannocchi Bank in Rome, where Cardinal Borgia deposited his money, were so massive that the bank almost went under.

There had been bargaining, arm-twisting and horse-trading during the course of previous conclaves, but this was the first time that the papacy had simply been bought outright. As the twentieth-century historian Marion Johnson observed: 'It was a measure of the times that this could happen.' Borgia decided to take as his papal name Alexander VI. This was widely seen as an allusion to Alexander the Great, rather than St Alexander, the second-century martyr, for Borgia had already blatantly named his son Cesare after Julius Caesar. Even before the white smoke had appeared from the Sistine chimney, the waiting crowd already knew the result. Scraps of paper had been thrown down from the Sistine Chapel windows containing the words: 'We have for Pope Alexander VI, Rodrigo Borgia.' When the newly appointed pope was presented to the public, it was customary for him to acknowledge his appointment modestly with the word 'volo' ('if this is what you wish'). Instead, when Alexander VI appeared at the window of the Old St Peter's he could not restrain himself from crying out exultantly: 'I am pope! I am pope!'

The effect of Alexander VI's election was immediate and dramatic. The young Cardinal de' Medici was filled with alarm and exclaimed, 'Flee, we are in the clutches of the wolf!' before rushing back home to Florence. Meanwhile, Cardinal della Rovere fled to a fortress on the coast at Ostia, from where he would eventually set sail to France and live under the protection of Charles VIII.

Yet over the coming weeks the citizens of Rome, and beyond, gradually began to see a different picture. In the brief period between Innocent VIII's final illness and the coronation of Alexander VI, no less than 220 murders had been recorded in Rome: now, the papal guards were despatched and order returned to the streets. Every Thursday Alexander VI would hold an audience, at which petitioners could place before him their grievances. Some even began to doubt the tales of his scandalous personal behaviour when they learned of the austere regime he had imposed on the papal household: expenditure was limited to just 20–30 ducats a day, while all dinners served at the papal table were to consist of just one course. Alexander VI announced that his declared aim for Italy was peace, and a unification of the Christian states to oppose the Ottoman Empire, which was continuing to expand through the Balkans and threaten Eastern Europe. At last, it seemed, the vast papal income – some 300,000 ducats in annual dues, collected throughout Western Christendom, whose varying limits extended from Greenland to Sicily, from Cadiz to Vienna – was to be put to good use.

This news was received with suspicion by the Venetians, but was welcomed by the Florentines. Even King Ferrante of Naples, who had harboured reservations concerning Borgia's candidature, assured the new pope that he would behave towards him 'as a good and obedient son'. At the same time, Ludovico Sforza of Milan rejoiced that his brother Ascanio was now the Pope's right-hand man. For the first time in living memory Rome finally had a strong pope with a clear vision for the future.

The full extent of this vision – audacious in the extreme and far exceeding the imagination of any but Alexander VI himself – would only gradually become clear as his reign unfolded. For some, the Borgias have become a byword for utter depravity and ruthlessness. And their Spanish inclination towards superstition, particularly evident in Alexander VI, would prove a further alienating factor. Others have attempted to mitigate this picture, with mixed success. However, it would be the Florentine historian and diplomat Niccolò Machiavelli, a contemporary of the Borgias, who would grasp the heart of the matter. In the course of his work as a diplomat, Machiavelli would have intimate dealings with the Borgias; and it was this experience that gave him a crucial insight into their intentions. The stories of lurid depravity, ruthlessness and sadism served as little more than a smokescreen for their more dangerous ideas, as well as a warning to their enemies. There was so much more to the Borgias than mere self-aggrandizement and corrupt hedonism. They would stop at nothing: the main driving power behind the family was ambition. No considerations of morality or loyalty would be allowed to stand in their way. And the family's ultimate ambitions were far more sensational than all the rumours concerning their behaviour. Indeed, when revealed they take one's breath away.

So what were these fantastic ambitions which Alexander VI harboured in his heart at the time he became pope? No less than a united Italy: a return to the glories of Ancient Rome, ruled over by a hereditary Borgia 'Prince'. On Alexander VI's death, his son Cesare was to take over the papal powers, becoming in effect a hereditary pope. Years later, Machiavelli would write his notorious work *The Prince*, whose amorality gained him infamy throughout Europe. In this short work Machiavelli would set down, with chilling frankness, the methods by which a 'prince' (in effect, any ruler) could gain power – and, perhaps more importantly, retain this power. He gives a number of historical examples, illustrating the success or otherwise of their methods. One of his chief examples would be Cesare Borgia, whose chillingly brutal methods would best illustrate Machiavelli's main requirements for success.

Machiavelli's examples were devoid of gloss, morality or any other than personal justification. He distilled such harsh reality into the maxim: 'Virtù e Fortuna'. This saying is open to widespread interpretation, from the more judicious 'Power and Fortune', to the informal, rule-of-thumb 'Strength and Luck'. Machiavelli's use of 'Virtù' has many connotations. Its original roots hark back to 'vir' (man), as well as 'vis' (strength), with connotations of 'virility'. Though it also implies 'virtue'. But this should not be mistaken for the Christian or even classical virtues of good, justice, compassion, prudent restraint and the like. If anything, it is more akin to the idea which would emerge several centuries after Machiavelli, with Nietzsche's 'will to power' and his 'Superman', who operated 'beyond good and evil'. The meaning of 'fortuna' is more evident: fate, luck, chance or destiny are the most appropriate echoes. Yet it also contains an element of occasion or opportunity (to be seized). On the other hand, 'Power and Fortune' can be more crassly seen as 'Guts and Luck', and there would be times when the Borgias' fortunes hung upon just such brash and dangerous opportunism and chance.

However, Alexander VI's vision of a strong united Italy, under the power of Rome, was but the first stage in his ambitious strategy. Borgia's predecessor, after whom he had named himself, was Alexander the Great. The man who had conquered Ancient Greece had not stopped at the borders of his early conquest. And Borgia, too, had a greater dream. One which would, perhaps, owing to his age, only be fully approached by his aptly named son Cesare. If successful, this dream would eventually have extended to a great empire, stretching from the Atlantic coast of the Borgias' native Spain to the shores of the Eastern Mediterranean and the Holy Land. This would have to be backed with military might sufficient to retake Byzantium and sweep the Ottoman Empire from the Levant – not such an unthinkable task, as we shall see. Here, in the mind of the new pope Alexander VI, was the embryonic dream of a new Roman Empire, a Renaissance realm echoing its classical predecessor.

Impossible? Implausible? Hindsight may reveal such ideas as a chimera. But it is important to bear in mind that these and similar dreams had long been in the air. Machiavelli's writings would merely articulate this vision. Versions of such ideas would certainly not have been foreign to the crusaders of the previous centuries. And as the historian Machiavelli would have well understood, the precedent for the evolution of a great Roman Empire, well established in ancient history, was already a resurgent idea in fifteenth-century Italy. At the time, Florence was regarded by many as the new Athens. And as with the original Athens, the cultural innovations of Florence had grown up amidst a territory of squabbling city states. In the classical era, the cultural revolution of Athens and the Greek city states had given way to the military might and civil innovations of the great empire ruled from Ancient Rome. The 'eternal city' could well rise again. It is worth bearing in mind the existence of such dreams during the era we are about to describe.

The Renaissance had begun in Florence in the middle of the preceding century; this transformation of art, architecture and thought had now evolved and was beginning to spread north from Italy across the Alps into Germany and France. A spectacular unforeseen transformation of the western world had begun. The Renaissance may have been, in part at least, a rebirth of classical ideas, but it would also grow to include its own unique elements. Western Europe was developing a new, recognizably modern culture. Who could predict how this might evolve?

At the same time other events, of profound but unrealized significance, were already taking place. Again, with hindsight, we can see that the ascent of a ruthless Borgia to the papal throne in 1492 was but one of these events. In Spain, the last of the Muslim rulers surrendered to King Ferdinand of Aragon and Queen Isabella of Castile in January 1492. By October of the same year, Columbus had made landfall in the New World. Europe appeared poised to enter a new age where anything was possible. And Alexander VI was determined that the Borgias should play a leading role in any such historical development.

CHAPTER 1

ORIGINS OF A DYNASTY

THE BORJA FAMILY (AS they were known in Spain) originated from the remote hill town of Borja, some 150 miles west of Barcelona in the Kingdom of Aragon. This occupied the large wedge of eastern Spain south of the Pyrenees, including Catalonia. As we have seen, the first Borgia pope was Callixtus III, of whom it has been said: 'The election to the papacy of Alonso de Borja as Callixtus III was little more than an accident, yet without it, there might never have been such a phenomenon as the Borgia Age.'

Alonso de Borja was born in 1378 near Valencia. During the early life of Alonso the fortunes of the Kingdom of Aragon would wax and wane. Even during its lesser periods it would be an important regional kingdom. In its glory days it would be the major power of the western Mediterranean, its territory extending to Corsica and Sardinia, as well as Sicily and the Kingdom of Naples. The latter occupied almost the entire southern half of Italy, while its ancient capital city – Naples – would become the third largest city in Europe and an important centre of the Renaissance. The population of Naples was at this time around 100,000, just below that of Venice and Milan.

According to long-standing family tradition, the Borjas had royal blood, being descended from eleventh-century King Ramiro I of Aragon. Although there is little evidence to support this, it is impossible to over-emphasize its importance in the self-conception of those members of the Borgia family who will play the leading roles in this history. In their eyes, the Borgias were the descendants of kings and were destined to become kings once more. Ironically, an exception to this driving psychological myth was Alonso de Borja. In some histories of the popes he is regarded as a nonentity before he ascended to the papal throne in his mid-seventies, and little better afterwards during his brief four-year reign. Such belittlement is not born out by the facts.

Alonso de Borja was the only son of an estate-owner outside Valencia. He evidently exhibited an early gift for learning, and was sent to the nearby University of Lerida, the third oldest such institution in the country, having been founded in 1300.* Here Alonso studied law, which he later went on to teach at Lerida, at the same time taking minor holy orders to become canon of the local cathedral. Entering the Church was unusual for an only son, who would have been expected to inherit and run the family estate. However, it must have become evident to his father that Alonso was neither suited, nor equipped for such a task. Alonso exhibited spiritual qualities which matched his intellectual abilities. He led an ascetic life and devoted himself to his studies. His academic distinction eventually brought him to the notice of the charismatic and ambitious twenty-one-year-old King Alfonso of Aragon, one of the first humanist leaders in Spain. King Alfonso is credited with the saying: 'Old wood to burn, old wine to drink, old friends to trust, old books to read'; although this admirable contemporary attitude does not appear to have been reflected in his somewhat archaic attitude towards women: 'Happy marriage requires that the wife be blind and the husband deaf.' Despite this attitude, King Alfonso would so charm the ageing and childless Queen Joanna II of Naples that she he would later adopt him as her heir, much to the annoyance of the French claimant to the throne. The

---

* That is, around the same time as the founding of the Sorbonne in Paris, but twenty-six years earlier than the University of Oxford.

fulfilment of Queen Joanna II's promise would involve great diplomatic tact, and it was here that Alonso de Borja's clear-headed advice would prove invaluable.

At the age of thirty-eight Alonso de Borja was appointed to the influential and trusted post of secretary to the king. Apart from overseeing His Majesty's affairs and duties, he was also required to undertake diplomatic missions involving considerable skill. At the time, western Christendom was split between two popes. The so-called Avignon line, with its stronghold in southern France, was represented by the 'anti-pope' Clement VIII; while the 'true' pope, elected by conclave in Italy, was Martin V. King Alfonso of Aragon had initially supported Clement VIII, but in order to strengthen his claim to the Kingdom of Naples, in 1428 he decided to switch sides. The tricky diplomatic task of leading the diplomatic mission to persuade Clement VIII to resign in favour of Martin V fell to Alonso de Borja. By now Borja was fifty years old, but neither the travelling involved, nor the authority of his opposition appeared to daunt him, and within a year Clement VIII had been persuaded to resign. This put an end to the schism which had divided the Church since the previous century. Martin V was so filled with gratitude that he made Alonso de Borja Bishop of Valencia. By 1442 King Alfonso had also become King of Naples, which title included King of Sicily and Jerusalem (this last being a purely nominal title, a hangover from the time of the crusades). King Alfonso now moved, along with his court, to southern Italy.

This displeased the new Pope Eugenius IV, who as pope remained officially – though in title alone – liege lord of the Kingdom of Naples, receiving an annual small symbolic payment of dues. Protocol dictated that King Alfonso should at least have 'consulted' the Pope on taking up residence in Naples. King Alfonso once again despatched Borja to effect a reconciliation, acknowledging the Pope as his liege lord. The success of these negotiations so delighted Pope Eugenius IV that he made Bishop Alonso Borja a cardinal.

Some sources claim that both of these negotiations were something of a foregone conclusion, requiring little expertise on behalf of the new Cardinal Alonso de Borja, Bishop of Valencia, yet there is no denying the importance of their outcomes. It was some time during this period that Alonso de Borja was despatched back to Spain on another important mission. He was instructed to educate King Alfonso's adolescent illegitimate son Ferrante, schooling him in the Classics, courtly manners, and a smattering of the new humanist learning. King Alfonso then married off Ferrante to Isabelle of Clermont, the daughter of a high-ranking French aristocrat, whose family had links with the Orsini in Rome and large estates in southern Italy, as well as being a distant descendant of an earlier Queen of Naples. The illegitimate Ferrante was then declared to be King Alfonso's legitimate heir.

Shortly after returning to Naples from his mission to educate Ferrante, Cardinal de Borja retired from the court of King Alfonso. His wish was to take up residence in Rome and spend his final years in the Holy City; but this was no simple matter, even for a cardinal. By this time, Rome was a shadow of its former glory. One and a half millennia previously, at the height of the Roman Empire, the city had supported a population of more than a million, its great buildings, triumphal arches and monuments the envy of Europe. With the decline and fall of the Empire, accompanied by various sackings by Vandals, Visigoths and similar barbarian tribes, its population had become seriously depleted, and so it had remained during the ensuing centuries. By the fifteenth century the population had sunk to less than 20,000, living amongst the crumbling ruins of the eternal city. Such was the lawlessness of this diminished citizenry that during the Avignon schism the so-called 'Roman pope', mindful of his safety, had frequently chosen to live elsewhere. Pilgrims were liable to be robbed, or worse, by the thieves and cutpurses who frequented the low taverns and bordellos. Officially the city was ruled by a governor, but in practice virtual anarchy prevailed. The aristocratic families lived in their fortress-palaces, guarded by their own liveried soldiers. These escorted their masters through the streets when they left for their more hospitable castles in the countryside during the hot summer months. The impoverished Roman population lived in makeshift shacks, often constructed with stones pillaged from the ancient ruins.

Cattle grazed in the once-sacred Forum and wandered at will down the triumphal avenues; pigs rooted for sustenance where they would; the beautiful gardens became small, inefficient farms, while street after street of empty houses decayed, forming breeding grounds for plague and lairs for bandits.

With the ending of the Avignon Schism, Pope Martin V attempted to take up residence in Rome, but this proved too insecure and he spent much of his papacy in Florence. It was not until after Eugenius IV was elected pope in 1431 that the situation changed. The turning point came after Eugenius IV was forced to flee down the Tiber in a boat, being pelted with stones and refuse by citizens lining either bank. Thereupon he appointed Bishop Ludovico Trevisano as Captain-General of the Papal Forces. A bullish, hard-faced aggressive character, Trevisano quickly gained the nickname 'Scarampo' (the Scrapper). After restoring order to the streets of Rome with punitive thoroughness, Bishop Trevisano led the Papal Forces north to subdue the Papal States. In theory at least, the Papal States stretched north across the Apennine Mountains to the Adriatic Coast, then further north across the badlands of the Romagna as far as Bologna. In practice, Bishop Trevisano's campaign was little more than an incursion into this territory, inflicting damage and acting as a warning to the local tyrants and warlords. During the course of his campaign, Bishop Trevisano made a point of seizing as much booty as he could. This not only prevented his defeated enemies from hiring mercenaries to regain their territory, but also meant that he returned to Rome one of the richest bishops of his time. In gratitude, Eugenius IV made him a cardinal, whose benefices added further to his riches.

Yet these military exercises served their purpose by enabling Eugenius IV to take up permanent residence in the crumbling quarters of St Peter's, which would be linked to the nearby impregnable Castel Sant'Angelo by a discreet passage for use in case of emergency. From this time on, the city of Rome would gradually return to the fold of civilized Italy. In practice, this meant that pilgrims were now fleeced, rather than mugged or murdered. But it also meant that the locals from aristocrats and cardinals to the common people – were able to live a semblance of normal life. Riots were limited to occasions when the authorities incurred popular displeasure. Such was the new Rome to which Cardinal Alonso de Borja retired in 1445, after leaving the service of King Alfonso of Naples.

By the time Eugenius IV died in 1447 the influence of the Florentine Renaissance had begun to spread to Rome. At the accession of the next pope, Nicholas V, a number of new churches were under construction, though the Pope himself often appeared more interested in his own fortune than that of the Church. During his eight-year reign, Nicholas V built up an extensive collection of ancient books, manuscripts and paintings. The aristocratic families, too, began to flourish, adorning their palazzi with treasures and works of art. Despite this cultural re-awakening, Cardinal Alonso de Borja continued to live a modest, reclusive life, regularly attending the Church of Santi Quattro Coronati, which had been entrusted to him along with his cardinal's hat. And it was during this period that Cardinal de Borja became known as Cardinal Borgia, the Latinized form of his name.

In March 1455 Nicholas V died, necessitating a conclave of all available cardinals. 'By the time of the conclave of April 1455 [Cardinal Alonso de Borgia] was living in Rome, an austere, modest and increasingly gouty old man in his late seventies.' On this occasion fifteen cardinals assembled for the conclave. The obvious choice for pope was Cardinal Basilios Bessarion, 'by far the most intelligent and cultivated churchman in Rome'. Added to this was the fact that he had once been a metropolitan bishop of the Orthodox Church in Constantinople (modern-day Istanbul). This had been the capital of the eastern realm of Christendom, which some 400 years previously had split from the western realm, thus accounting for the latter being known as the Roman Catholic Church. Prior to the fall of Constantinople to the Ottoman Turks in 1453, Bessarion and a stream of Orthodox monks had fled west, bringing with them much treasure and many ancient classical works (especially by Plato), which had long since vanished from western Europe. In time, these works would be translated from the Ancient Greek (which remained barely understood in Western Christendom) and have a transformative effect on Christian doctrine, giving its faith a basic intellectual underpinning in Platonism. As a Metropolitan Bishop, Cardinal Bessarion also retained some authority and respect in the realms of the Orthodox Church, which was still holding out against the Ottomans in Serbia, northern Anatolia (modern-day Turkey) and the Greek Peloponnese (where a new Byzantine capital had been established at Mystras).* Bessarion was the obvious man to bring about the ultimate reconciliation between the Roman Catholic Church and its Orthodox counterpart during its time of need, indeed when the latter was fighting for its very survival.

Common sense may have dictated that the conclave should vote in Cardinal Bessarion as the next pope, but this was not to be. Bessarion remained deeply resented for his superior learning, but most of all because he was Greek, and even continued to dress like an Orthodox priest, growing a long beard, beneath which he wore an Orthodox cross.† Many thought his election might even suggest that the Catholic cardinals considered the Orthodox Church to be in some way superior. Even so, there was no denying that he was the best equipped candidate for the job. So in order to teach him a lesson in humility, it was decided that Bessarion should be made to wait. Instead, the conclave chose to vote in the obscure and ailing Cardinal Alonso de Borgia, who was 'in such poor health that it was doubted that he would survive the arduous ceremonies of his coronation'. These were undoubtedly something of an endurance test – involving days of slow, lengthy processions past the crowds lining the sweltering streets of Rome, punctuated by the even more arduous task of having to conduct a series of lengthy services in churches throughout the city. A distinctly gruelling induction, which had so exhausted several previous (younger) candidates that they had been forced to retire to their bed for several days afterwards.

As it happened, the people of Rome were outraged that a 'Catalan' had been elected pope, and Callixtus III's triumphal processions through

---

* This small hillside city, just outside Sparta, remains to this day an almost perfectly preserved Byzantine relic.

† As distinct from the Catholic cross with its longer lower vertical arm, the Greek Orthodox cross has arms of equal length.

the streets of Rome were roughed up several times by gangs of Orsini and Colonna thugs. On one occasion they even broke through the protective line of papal soldiers, almost dislodging Callixtus III from his horse.

The main part of the celebrations involved the new pope and his entourage of cardinals, dignitaries and protective soldiers making their way in procession down the long route through the centre of Rome. This started from the papal residence at St Peter's, crossed the Tiber, proceeded past the dwarfing ruins of the Colosseum and the church of San Clemente, ending up three miles later at the Lateran (Basilica of San Giovanni in Laterano) close to the western city wall. Here at the Lateran, the ceremony of the Pope's official enthronement would take place, in the church he inherited as Bishop of Rome. This church was at the time arguably the most sacred site in Rome, being the repository of a large number of ancient holy relics, including no less than 'the wooden table where Christ ate with his Apostles, about three *braccia* square'.*

At a certain point in the Pope's enthronement procession it was customary for him either to avert his eyes, dismount or make a detour to avoid encountering a particularly notorious statue just past San Clemente. Numerous pilgrims (including Luther himself) record that this statue portrayed the notorious female Pope Joan, who is said to have reigned for two years until 1099, when she died giving birth to a child. Despite the fact that most historians now discount 'Pope Joan' as a purely legendary figure, the statue itself was certainly real and was said to have been erected at the very spot where she died in childbirth. It is known to have been destroyed in 1600.

Possibly as a consequence of Pope Joan, legendary or otherwise, each new pope, during the course of his enthronement at the Lateran would be required to take part in an intimate ceremony. During this, he 'is seated in a chair of porphyry, which is pierced for this purpose, that one of the younger cardinals may make proof of his sex'. The young cardinal would reach up through the hole in order to establish that the new pope had

---

* The medieval term of measurement known as a *braccia* was taken from an arm's length. It varied from time to time and place to place, and was usually between 26 and 28 inches, though it could on occasion be only 18 inches long.

testicles, before proclaiming: '*Duos habet et bene pedentes*' ('He has two and they dangle well').

Callixtus III would turn out to be made of much sterner stuff than his electors had bargained for, and, despite his surprise at being elected, he quickly began leaving his stamp on the Holy See. One of the new pope's first demands was to see the account books. These he scrutinized, and was horrified at the extravagances they revealed. Why, his predecessor Nicholas V had, during his eight-year reign, run up debts of no less than 70,432 florins.* 'See how the treasures of the Church have been wasted!' Callixtus III exclaimed on entering the Vatican Library for the first time. Such a treasury of rare manuscripts, books and works of art he regarded as superfluous to the offices and purposes of the Holy See. Callixtus III may have been a man of great spiritual refinement, but he had little regard for art. This did not mean that he was a philistine, more that his aesthetic taste was limited. Fortunately, in this field he had come to rely upon the advice of his favourite sister Isabella, the mother of Rodrigo Borgia. Isabella ensured that despite the new pope's restriction on funds, the building of a number of Renaissance-style churches in Rome continued. Having suffered from years of neglect during the Great Schism with Avignon, Rome was desperately in need of some modern Christian grandeur amongst the rubble and towering ruins of pagan Ancient Rome. Isabella also persuaded Callixtus III to use Spanish artists. Most notable of these was Juan Rexach, whose modern influence stemmed from the Flemish School. These artists were the first to propagate the use of oil paint, which would in turn have a transformative effect on Renaissance art. Characteristically, Callixtus III was more concerned with the newly expanding city itself and improving its urban conditions. It was during his reign that the Campo de' Fiori ('Field of Flowers'), across the Tiber a mile or so south of the Vatican, was paved over to

---

* The golden florin (*fiorino d'oro*) was the first currency to be widely accepted throughout European trading centres. The gold ducat, which was minted in Venice, was directly modelled upon the florin. Their values fluctuated against each other, but as a rule of thumb one can view their value as approximately equal during this period.

become a piazza. This led to a regeneration of a neglected part of the city, and the piazza itself would soon become renowned for the aristocratic palaces built around its edges.

Even so, the reign of Callixtus III would be characterized by an absence of the usual ostentatious display. At the same time many papal treasures would be sold off, and this income put to good use. None would be exempt from this new austerity, even the Pope himself. An example would be set: the papal household would cut out all public extravagances. (As we have seen, his nephew Rodrigo Borgia, the future Pope Alexander VI, would quickly grasp the propaganda value of such a gesture amongst his more deprived flock in the city of Rome, and beyond, as word of the Pope's priestly frugality spread. However, consistent observance of such niceties would prove another matter where Alexander VI was concerned, as we shall see.)

Despite Callixtus III's insistence upon austerity, this was not to be his overriding concern:

Deeply pious, dry as dust and crippled by gout,* Callixtus devoted himself to two consuming ambitions. The first was to organize a European crusade that would deliver Constantinople from the Turks; the second was to advance the fortunes of his family and compatriots.

---

* This often excruciating arthritis particularly attacked the leg joints and the toes. In a traditional saying, which dates back to at least medieval times, it has been known as 'the disease of kings, and the king of diseases'. It was prevalent amongst the upper classes, and was often ascribed to overindulgence, particularly in forti- fied wines. This was not the case with Callixtus III (or indeed the Medici family of Florence, who were widely known to suffer from this disease). At this time, when fruit and fresh vegetables were largely unavailable in winter, the lower classes were reduced to surviving on root vegetables such as turnips and the like. These were regarded as little better than cattle fodder by the upper classes. However, such vegetables did in fact produce some semblance of a balanced diet. Meanwhile, the upper classes confined themselves to succulent meats and other delicacies freshly killed from the hunt. The lack of vegetables (and associated vitamins) led to a build-up of uric acid, which formed painful, needle-like crystals on the joints and toes, even afflicting an ascetic such as Callixtus III.

Callixtus III was the first Spanish pope of the Roman Catholic Church, and as such was deeply resented by the leading aristocratic families of Rome, such as the Orsini and the Colonna, from amongst whom the popes were frequently elected. Not only did these families have a xenophobic distaste for this 'Catalan', but they were determined to do what they could to obstruct (or even to disobey) his wishes, anticipating that his reign would soon be over. Only by appointing loyal Spaniards to senior posts around him could Callixtus III be sure that his orders would be followed. Unlike so many previous popes of the period, he had remained faithful to his vow of chastity, and thus had no immediate family, no illegitimate sons upon whom he could rely by appointing them to positions of power. So instead he was forced to turn to his cousins, nephews and other Spanish relatives he knew he could trust.

Rodrigo's elder brother Pedro Luis Borgia was made Duke of Spoleto, Captain-General of the Papal Forces, and governor of the formidable Castel Sant'Angelo. This was the fortress which guarded the strategic Ponte Sant'Angelo across the Tiber from historic Rome to the district of Trastevere (Trans-Tiber). Much of Trastevere was occupied by the Vatican, which nonetheless remained within the protection of the ancient city walls. With Pedro Luis Borgia ensuring the loyalty of the Papal Forces, this served to secure Callixtus III against any menace from personal forces owned or hired by the antagonistic aristocratic families of Rome, such as the Orsini, the Savelli and the Colonna.

Upon ascending to the papal throne, Callixtus III had of course been required to divest himself of all his previous posts, including the important and lucrative bishopric of Valencia. This he passed on to his nephew Rodrigo Borgia, whose intelligence and social skills had already come to the Pope's notice. The twenty-four-year-old Rodrigo Borgia had by now exhibited 'an appreciation for the arts and sciences and an immense amount of respect for the Church'. He had also become highly regarded during his law studies at the University of Bologna. Rodrigo Borgia would quickly make himself invaluable in the Vatican, carrying out his uncle's orders and many of his administrative duties, especially when the ailing pontiff was incapacitated with gout.

Although Callixtus III was hardly in rude health, and well knew that his reign would be short, he was determined to leave his mark by setting the Church back on its way to recovery. The fall of Constantinople, just two years previously, to the twenty-one-year-old Sultan Mehmed the Conqueror, had wrought a traumatic effect throughout western Christendom. For over a thousand years Constantinople had been the capital of the Byzantine Empire (Eastern Orthodox Christendom). But now the world had changed. The whole of Europe stood under threat from the energetic and ambitious Mehmed the Conqueror, whose Ottoman army continued to press on through the Balkans, moving ever closer to Italy. Callixtus III realized that an immediate response was required. Utilizing monies gained from selling off some of the Vatican treasures, 'he built galleys in the boatyards of the Tiber, despatched preachers across the continent to sell indulgencies and imposed swingeing taxes throughout Western Christendom'. Venice was worried: the Ottoman advance was having a disastrous effect on the eastern Mediterranean trade upon which it relied, while its imperial possessions, such as Corfu, Crete and several strategic Aegean islands, all lay exposed. Likewise, Hungary felt threatened by the Ottoman advance west from Constantinople.

Others, however, both amongst the city states of Italy and further afield throughout Europe, were less inclined to join forces for a crusade to confront the advancing Ottoman army. Quite simply, Europe was now tired after mounting three centuries of crusades against the 'infidel'. Countries were more concerned with their own affairs: France was still recovering from the Hundred Years War against England, while the scattered German states of the Holy Roman Empire remained in disarray.

Nonetheless, Callixtus III managed to collect 70,000 ducats, which enabled him to assemble on the Tiber a fleet of twenty-seven galleys, manned by 1,000 sailors and 5,000 soldiers, armed with 300 canons. This he placed under the command of Cardinal Trevisano, ordering him to sail and join up with the forces of King Alfonso at Naples. Here, despite Cardinal Trevisano's outrage, King Alfonso refused to allow his fleet to join in the crusade against the Ottomans. In fact, he refused to recognize that his former 'secretary' was now his liege lord. King Alfonso was not only the rightful king of Naples, which occupied the whole of southern Italy, but also ruled Sicily, Sardinia and Aragon. Pope Callixtus III, on the other hand, was barely tolerated in Rome and had but a precarious hold on the Papal States to the north.

In retaliation against King Alfonso's betrayal, Callixtus III declared that he would refuse to ratify King Alfonso's illegitimate son Ferrante as his rightful heir. At the same time he wrote to King Alfonso, threatening: 'Your Majesty should know that a pope can depose kings.' King Alfonso responded angrily: 'Your Holiness should know that, should we wish, we shall find a way of deposing a pope.'

Meanwhile, Callixtus III had ordered that all monies collected throughout Europe for the new crusade should be directed to the Hungarian commander János Hunyadi, allowing him to assemble a formidable force. In the summer of 1456 Hunyadi marched south into the Balkans, and on 22 July managed to relieve the Serbian capital Belgrade, where the Orthodox population was under siege from the Ottomans. Had Belgrade fallen, the whole of Eastern Europe, and even Venice itself, would have been under threat. But Hunyadi did much more than relieve the siege, he then chased after the Ottoman army, which was retreating in disarray, and even managed to inflict a wound on Sultan Mehmed the Conqueror. This was the greatest defeat that Sultan Mehmed would ever receive, and when news of Hunyadi's victory reached Rome, Callixtus III decreed that a miracle had taken place. He ordered 22 July to be celebrated annually as a permanent feature of the liturgical calendar.

By now Cardinal Trevisano had sailed from Naples and set up base in Rhodes. From here he launched a series of attacks throughout the Aegean, capturing Corinth and even taking the Acropolis in Athens. He then began advancing through the Aegean Islands, before he encountered the Ottoman fleet off Lesbos. Here he successfully outman-oeuvered the Turks, inflicting a damaging, though not fatal, defeat on the Ottoman navy.

Unfortunately, neither Hunyadi nor Trevisano had sufficient resources to follow up on their victories. Callixtus III's appeals to western

Christendom continued to fall on deaf ears, and the Ottomans prevented any serious threat to Constantinople. But Callixtus III had at least demonstrated one important lesson to his young nephew Rodrigo Borgia: the Ottomans may have presented a distinct threat, but they were far from being invincible. Given sufficient unity, it was not beyond the bounds of possibility that one day the combined forces of western Christianity could retake Constantinople and drive the Ottomans from their empire in the Levant. Rodrigo Borgia would certainly have discussed such matters with his uncle, and indeed, according to a rumour heard by Antonio da Trezzo, a Milanese diplomat: 'I believe . . . the Pope has created his nephew Pedro Luis the Emperor of Constantinople.' Adding, lest his master Francesco Sforza of Milan did not grasp the seriousness of his news: 'This is not a joke.' Such rumours may have been more than a little premature, but there is no doubting the fact that they sowed the seeds of an idea in the mind of the young, and still impressionable, Rodrigo Borgia.

In early 1456 Callixtus III appointed three new Spanish cardinals, one of which was his talented, twenty-five-year-old nephew Rodrigo Borgia. This incurred considerable opposition amongst the Italian and French members of the College of Cardinals. But Callixtus III was a determined man and a year later he made Cardinal Rodrigo Borgia Vice-Chancellor of the College of Cardinals. This important administrative post had in fact been vacant since 1453, its decisions evidently taken either by the Pope himself or a senior member of the Curia, the papal administration. Yet by now Callixtus III was ageing fast and all but permanently confined to his bed. He needed to delegate some of his authority, so that he could concentrate on his main objective. And this he remained as determined as ever to fulfil, pressing hard for a full-scale European crusade against the Ottoman Turks. Nothing was to be spared in order to finance this endeavour: 'Jewels, table services, church vessels and other precious objects from the papal treasure were sold.' On seeing Nicholas V's silver salt cellars, Callixtus gave the order, 'Sell them for the crusade, earthenware is good enough for me.' Despite his youth and inexperience Cardinal Rodrigo Borgia proved highly effective at organizing Callixtus III's fundraising for his crusade, as well as following his uncle's orders to appoint Spanish clerics to important posts within the Vatican. This was by no means an easy task, meeting much local resistance. As a result, Callixtus III's Catalans succeeded in gaining only a foothold in the Curia, with around one fifth of its staff being Spanish. On the other hand, the Catalans quickly took over almost all the important posts in the papal household: the chief secretary, controller of the household, papal doctors, chief treasurer, even the cook and the like, all soon became Spanish.

At the end of June 1458 news arrived from Naples that King Alfonso had unexpectedly died at the age of sixty-two. Callixtus III immediately seized his opportunity: he may have been well into his late seventies, and with all the outward appearances of piety, but as we have seen in his attempts to raise troops for his crusade, he had his determined side. And when this was thwarted he could be ruthless towards anyone he held responsible – most notably towards his former mentor King Alfonso of Naples. According to a report written by envoy Antonio de Pistoia to his master in Milan:

The Pope shows signs of being pleased at the death of the king [Alfonso of Naples] and of being resentful of his behaviour while he lived. For, the moment the news [of his death] arrived, he sent a soldier to the house of the king's ambassador with orders to arrest him and take him to Castel Sant'Angelo. But the said ambassador, who had news of the death of the king earlier and fortunately had been informed of the Pope's intentions, had left immediately, leaving most of his possessions, which Callixtus III then seized.

These assets would not have been seized for personal gain, but would have been added to the exchequer for funding the crusade. But Callixtus III was not content with such small fry. Shortly afterwards, he signed a papal bull declaring that as King Alfonso had died without leaving a legitimate heir, the Kingdom of Naples therefore reverted to its liege lord: it was now Papal Territory. It was rumoured that Callixtus III intended to name his nephew Pedro Luis Borgia, the Captain General of the Papal

Forces, as the new king of Naples. Meanwhile, in Naples itself, King Alfonso's illegitimate son, the thirty-eight-year-old Ferrante, declared himself king. By now the ageing Callixtus III was frailer than ever, worn down by his efforts to galvanize Europe into a crusade, and at the same time battling those who opposed his attempts to further Spanish influence within the Vatican. Before he could take action against Ferrante in Naples, Callixtus III died on 6 August 1458 at the age of seventy-nine.

Upon hearing this news, the citizens of Rome flooded the streets, chanting with glee against the hated 'Catalans', whose hold on the papacy now appeared to be over. Sensing which way the wind was blowing, Pedro Luis Borgia fled the Castel Sant'Angelo and took refuge in the fortress at the port city of Civitavecchia, some fifty miles to the north-west of Rome. The newly appointed Vice-Chancellor Cardinal Rodrigo Borgia was now left on his own, his only allies the despised clique of 'Catalans' who had been infiltrated into the Vatican.

CHAPTER 2

THE YOUNG RODRIGO

T HE ALL-BUT-ACCIDENTAL, YET IN the event very decisive, papacy
of Callixtus III opened the eyes of young Rodrigo Borgia as to
what *could* be done. Besides providing him with a blueprint for future
dreams of empire, it had also raised him to such a senior position that
there was even a possibility he might himself one day fulfil such dreams.
Yet who precisely was this young man within whom there hatched such
overweening ambition?

Rodrigo de Borja was born on 1 January 1431 in the small town of
Xàtiva near Valencia, in the Kingdom of Aragon. As we know, his mother
was Isabella de Borja, Callixtus III's trusted younger sister. Isabella in fact
married her cousin Jofrè de Borja,* thus enabling a male Borja to take
over the family estate which Callixtus III would have inherited had he
not entered the Church. It is possible that this genetic proximity played
a part in Rodrigo de Borja's preternaturally close relationship with his

---

* At the time, he was known as Jofrè de Llançol, and Rodrigo himself may well
have retained this name until his uncle became Callixtus III. For the sake of clarity,
I have followed the course adopted by many commentators, referring to him as
Borgia or Borja from the outset.

offspring, and indeed the singular psychology of several of his children. (He was to have no less than eight acknowledged children, by three different women.)

Little is known about Rodrigo Borgia's early life, apart from the fact that his father died when he was just six. Even the exhaustive researches of his hagiographer Peter de Roo can only come up with the recorded anecdote that 'when eight years old, the boy was often seen riding a pony through the streets of Xàtiva'. Soon after this Rodrigo travelled with his mother and the family to Valencia, where they moved into no less than the episcopal palace. By this stage, Uncle Alonso (the future Callixtus III) was Bishop of Valencia, but had been obliged to move to Naples in the service of King Alfonso of Aragon, who had now also become King of Naples. Here Rodrigo and his older brother Pedro Luis were given a classical education by a private tutor.

Uncle Alonso soon began to take a serious interest in the education of his nephews: Rodrigo, Pedro Luis and their cousin Luis Juan de Milà. According to Borgia biographer G. J. Meyer:

> Vatican records show Rodrigo and Luis Juan being singled out, as early as the reign of [Pope] Eugenius IV, for benefices, offices generating ecclesiastical income, that would have been unimaginable without the intervention of a patron who had access to the Pope's ear and the King of Aragon's as well.

Thus, while Rodrigo was still a schoolboy he began receiving benefices, first a post at his birthplace Xàtiva, and then from the cathedrals of Barcelona and Valencia. Such benefices were virtual sinecures and did not in this case require their holders to be inducted into the Church.

By the time Rodrigo was eighteen his Uncle Alonso had become a cardinal and had retired from King Alonso's service, moving from Naples to Rome. Cardinal Alonso may have been a man of high spiritual demeanour, but he was determined that his protégés – Rodrigo, Pedro Luis and Luis Juan de Milà – should receive a first-class university education. But at this time the best universities were all in Italy, while his protégés were confined to Spain. The trouble was, if Rodrigo, or the others, left Spain they would immediately forfeit the income from their Spanish benefices. In Rome, Cardinal Alonso had a word with his new friend Pope Nicholas V, who then issued a papal bull* allowing the three young Borgias to travel to Italy without forfeiting any income they were receiving in Spain. Rodrigo and his two young relatives now travelled together to Italy, to study at the University of Bologna.

Bologna was at the time a papal fiefdom; though unlike Naples this strategic city state was more closely under papal control. Its university was founded in 1088 and claims to be the oldest in the world. It even coined the word 'universitas' and its crest contained the first use of the term 'alma mater' in its modern sense. Traditionally it was noted for the teaching of canon and civil law. (At the time, canon law was applied by the ecclesiastical authorities to those within the Church. Civil law was quite separate in its statutes and its courts, which applied exclusively to the lay members of the population.) The poets Dante and Petrarch had studied here prior to Rodrigo Borgia's arrival. And in the immediate years after he left, the great humanist Erasmus of Amsterdam; the astronomer Copernicus, who first proposed that the Earth travelled around the Sun; and the maverick physician Paracelsus, who became a pioneer of modern medicine, would all study here. This gives an indication of the academic excellence of Bologna, and makes even more impressive the fact that Borgia was judged by a contemporary as 'the most eminent and judicious jurisprudent'. Yet it would hardly be accurate to judge that Rodrigo Borgia's student years were all work and no play. For a start, his Spanish benefices would have made him and his cousins as wealthy as any fellow students from the nobility. The three young Borgias would certainly have lived in some style. According to the contemporary commentator Gaspare da Verona, '[Rodrigo Borgia] is handsome, of a pleasant and cheerful countenance . . . With a single glance he can fascinate women, and attract them to himself more strongly than a magnet draws iron.' However, as the papal historian John Julius Norwich observes, drawing on the same

---

* Such a bull, issued by the Pope, overrode all laws, customs and practices in the particular instance to which it referred.

source: 'What he lacked was the slightest glimmer of religious feeling.'
Rodrigo Borgia also made it abundantly clear from the very outset 'that
he was in the Church for what he could get out of it'.

As we have seen, in 1455 Rodrigo Borgia's uncle Alonso ascended
the papal throne to become Callixtus III. In line with precedent, he
divested himself of all his previous offices; consequently his favourite
protégés, the three young Borgia cousins, soon 'inherited' many of his
high offices. Within months of Callixtus III's accession, the oldest,
Luis Juan de Milà, was made a cardinal and papal legate to the city of
Bologna. In effect this made him governor of the city, which occupied
the northerly part of the Papal States. Cardinal de Milà would in time
become so attached to his city that after attending one conclave, he
would turn down his next invitation to Rome for such a gathering,
much to the irritation of his cousin Rodrigo Borgia. However, Cardinal
de Milà's attachment to Bologna cannot have been that strong, for after
a number of years 'he seems to have preferred a quiet life in Spain'.
From here, there was no hope of tempting him to any further conclaves
in Rome.

Again, as we have seen, Rodrigo Borgia's older brother, the 'handsome
. . . arrogant and energetic' Pedro Luis was made Captain-General of the
Papal Forces and commandant of the Castel Sant'Angelo. This, however,
proved to be no simple matter. The contemporary incumbent, Giorgio
di Saluzzo, Bishop of Lausanne, was initially reluctant to hand over the
keys to his young successor. But frail and old though Callixtus III may
have been, he remained a man of considerable determination. The bishop
was immediately threatened with excommunication, whereupon he
changed his mind and Pedro Luis Borgia took over his post. The military
was the traditional choice for an older brother, especially if he showed
suitable qualities; but it seems that appearances may have been deceptive
where Pedro Luis was concerned. As we shall see, despite his apparent
overweening fortitude he was in fact prone to being stricken down with
serious illness.

Like his older cousin Luis Juan de Milà, the twenty-five-year-old
Rodrigo Borgia was also appointed a cardinal, with the titular church

of San Nicola in Carcere.* Within months of his appointment, Cardinal Rodrigo Borgia was despatched on his first important mission. He was appointed papal legate to the March of Ancona, the Papal Territory south of the Romagna, which had recently overthrown papal rule. Rodrigo's brief was to lead a papal force across the Apennines and restore papal rule. As the papal troops approached the port city of Ancona, they threatened to lay siege to the town of Ascoli, which at once surrendered. From then on, his mission proved more diplomatic and tactical, with little use of force required. Through sheer force of character, a blend of threat and charm, Cardinal Borgia managed to resolve this potentially hazardous state of affairs by means of negotiation and decisive appointments. As the contemporary historian Guicciardini (no admirer of Borgia) would concede: 'in him were combined rare prudence and vigilance, mature reflection, marvellous power of persuasion, skill and capacity for the conduct of the most difficult affairs'.

Cardinal Rodrigo Borgia's success in Ancona proved more than just good news for Callixtus III himself. It vindicated his controversial nepotism, forestalling what might have proved some difficult recriminations from his other cardinals. Some months after Callixtus III's election

---

* As far as it is possible to judge from contemporary sources, it was not until this late date that Rodrigo Borgia and his cousin Luis Juan de Milà actually took holy orders, becoming priests and obliging them to live a life of 'poverty, chastity and obedience'. Their previous appointments (benefices) had been as canons, and later deacons, which made them subject to ecclesiastical law, but did not require them to take up holy orders. However, when Callixtus III ascended the papal throne in April 1455 Rodrigo Borgia 'inherited' his uncle's title, Bishop of Valencia. Although this was not officially announced – and was indeed resisted by King Alfonso in his capacity as ruler of Aragon – there is some evidence to suggest that for around a year the Bishop of Valencia was not even a priest. This anomaly can only be resolved by the technicality that perhaps Rodrigo Borgia had not yet been 'confirmed' in his post. On the other hand, several reliable sources agree with Mallet, who insists that 'Rodrigo did not take holy orders until 1468.' Thus, he would have been a cardinal and a bishop for more than a *decade* without being a priest. An unusual distinction, even during this era. Although, as Mallet points out, in holding such high offices 'he was just as much bound by the rules of chastity as was a priest'. From what we shall see, this was hardly the case.

as pope, he had summoned a secret consistory of the relatively few cardinals remaining in Rome at the time. During the course of this he had
browbeaten the dozen cardinals present into allowing him to appoint his
two Borgia nephews to their high office. This was not only transparent
nepotism, but also highly irregular with regard to their ages – less than
half that of almost all previous cardinals. As a concession, Callixtus III
had been forced to agree that these appointments should not be publicly
announced. However, he insisted that if a conclave were called (in the
event of his death), the two young Borgias should have their appointments made public, thus qualifying them to take part, and cast their votes
for the next pope. The cardinals were forced to agree to this, on threat
of excommunication. Callixtus III must have ensured that the cardinals
were shown a papal bull to this effect, already dated, which could be
released in case of disobedience to his wishes. However, according to
Aeneas Piccolomini, who would become a cardinal shortly after this:

> the other cardinals hoped to deceive the Pope, who they thought
> would die soon, but in the end it was the Pope who deceived the
> cardinals for, that summer, when there was only one cardinal left
> in Rome, he made the creation public.

Having bested the opposition, Callixtus III now decided to reward
Cardinal Rodrigo Borgia for his work in Ancona by appointing him
Vice-Chancellor. Callixtus III must have had supreme confidence in his
nephew. Cardinal Borgia was still just twenty-six, and Vice-Chancellor
of the Church was not only one of the most prestigious posts (rewarded
with an annual income of some 6,000 ducats), but it was also one of the
most powerful. The Vice-Chancellor was to all intents and purposes in
charge of the day-to-day running of the Curia, the papal government. At
the same time, all new appointments passed through his office, offering
a supreme opportunity for the extraction of 'gifts' or other payments
from the grateful appointees. Such rewards were regarded as common
practice at the time, rather than corruption. Cardinal Borgia now enjoyed
the prospect of great power and great riches. Yet as he well knew, this

good fortune could only last as long as his uncle was pope. Such high position, especially gained by one so young, and through family influence, inevitably attracted all manner of envy and powerful enemies. Especially amongst the influential aristocratic families of Rome. And these might even strike before his uncle died.

Cardinal Rodrigo Borgia knew that if he was to survive and thrive as Vice-Chancellor he needed to utilize his renowned charm to make new friends beyond his family circle and the unpopular 'Catalans'. As it happened, one of his first 'new friends' would be the recently appointed Cardinal Aeneas Piccolomini, a forty-three-year-old Sienese from an impoverished aristocratic family who had gained a widespread reputation for his intellectual brilliance. Before the age of thirty, when he took holy orders, Piccolomini had shown such literary promise that he was considered one of the finest poets in the land, famed for the penning of romances, which with hindsight we can see echoed episodes in his own life. However, the popularity of his works had not always stemmed from their purely literary qualities, for they also included 'not only a quantity of mildly pornographic poetry, but also a novel in much the same vein'. His winning personality and evident abilities had proved attractive to the earlier pope Eugenius IV, as well as several senior cardinals. Consequently he had been entrusted with a number of important diplomatic missions taking him all over Europe. Yet his winning ways had proved attractive to more than senior men of the Church. Whilst on a mission to Scotland, he had fathered a child. And several years later, whilst in Strasbourg, there had been a similar episode. In both cases the children died in infancy. In the event, neither these incidents nor his pornographic poems had proved an impediment to him taking holy orders. Nor, according to widespread gossip, had it prevented him from becoming involved in a number of similar indiscretions, and continuing to pen a wide variety of poetry.

Yet Piccolomini had a further side to his multi-faceted character. Surprisingly, this was his faith and his determination. On occasion, his diplomatic missions had placed him in perilous circumstances. In particular, on his 1435 mission to Scotland, when his boat crossing the North

Sea from Bruges ran into two violent gales. As Piccolomini described it in his memoirs (where he refers to himself in the third person) one of these storms 'kept them in fear of death for fourteen hours', while the other drove them off course towards Norway, and 'pounded the ship for two days and a night, so that she sprung a leak'. On stepping safely ashore, Piccolomini vowed that he would walk in his bare feet to the nearest shrine to the Virgin Mary, in gratitude for his salvation. This proved somewhat further than he had bargained. The fulfilment of his vow would involve a ten-mile trek through snow and across ice in the midst of a harsh Scottish winter, where daylight was 'not more than four hours long'. The frostbite he suffered in the process was so severe that for the rest of his life he would walk with a limp and suffer intermittent bouts of incapacitating pain in his foot. As we have seen, Callixtus III later made Piccolomini a cardinal and even Bishop of Siena. Here was a man whose intellectual tastes and determination chimed perfectly with those of the young Cardinal Rodrigo Borgia.

As if Callixtus III did not have enough to concern him, especially with regards to the assembling of his crusade, in October 1457 Pedro Luis Borgia, the Captain-General of the Papal Forces, was suddenly stricken with a serious illness, which rendered him incapable of fulfilling his duties. With typical disregard for the usual rules and precedents, Callixtus III unhesitatingly appointed Cardinal Rodrigo Borgia as replacement Captain-General. Here, even the accomplished Rodrigo Borgia suddenly found himself out of his depth. Previously, he had only acted as commander of the small force he led into the Ancona March, relying heavily for tactics upon his military second-in-command, a career soldier. In this instance, Borgia's chief role had been as a negotiator. Even after this single experience, he would have known little of military matters, apart from the writings of Herodotus, Caesar and the like, whom he would have studied in the course of his classical education. However, this experience of being plunged in at the deep end would certainly have added to his expertise. Later, as his dream of empire blossomed, he would undeniably have needed to understand the rudiments of military strategy. And as we shall see, there is good evidence that he was not lacking in a knowledge of the practicalities of campaigning. These he may well have gained in military exercises during his tenure as Captain-General. However, a few months later Pedro Luis would recover from his illness, enabling the young cardinal to resume full attention to his vital role as Vice-Chancellor.

Rome itself had now regained its prestige as the eternal city. Once more it had become a centre of pilgrimage, attracting a large influx of outsiders from all over Europe. This new popularity had begun a few years back, when Pope Nicholas V had declared that 1450 would be a holy year, celebrating the Jubilee of Christ's birth. A description from around this time gives an idea of the sheer chaos this influx of pilgrims involved, as well as indicating that these pilgrimages were not limited to the warm summer months:

> There were so many people in Rome that there was not enough accommodation for them all, even though every house became an inn. The pilgrims offered to pay generously and pleaded, for the love of God, to be taken in, but in vain, and they had to sleep outside where many died of the cold. It was terrible to witness. And so many came that the city itself starved.

Worse still, the entire purpose of their visit was often thwarted:

> You could not get to St Peter's because of the enormous crowds on the streets, and San Paolo Fuore le Mura, San Giovanni in Laterano and Santa Maria Maggiore were full of people praying. Rome was so full that it was impossible to get around. When the Pope gave his benediction at St Peter's the whole area was densely packed with pilgrims, and they even filled the orchards where it was possible to see [down on] the benediction loggia.

It comes as no surprise that such conditions invariably brought with them disease. Rome was notorious for its malaria, which in those days was thought to be brought on by *mal aria* ('bad air'). This caused many pilgrims to lull themselves into a false sense of security by using nosegays of sweet-smelling flowers held under their nostrils. It would take centuries before medical science discovered that the disease was spread by malarial mosquitoes, which infested the entire Pontine Marshes region south-east of Rome, and would spread to standing water in the city itself, especially during the hot summer months.

Worse still were the recurrent outbreaks of the plague. There was an outbreak in 1450, and yet another in 1451. In the late summer of 1456, during the reign of Callixtus III, there was a further outbreak. The following contemporary description, by the chronicler Giovanni Inghirami, is in fact of the 1450 outbreak, but could serve to describe any of these disastrous epidemics:

> That evening in the church of San Celso there were 176 corpses, men and women, but mostly women . . . They say many more have fallen into the Tiber, including those who climbed on to the parapets to escape and those who were thrown in. Many who escaped had their clothes ripped off their backs and they were running about, some in their hose, others in shirts, some even naked, and the women all dishevelled, looking for their companions who they feared had died. By midnight San Celso was full of the dead; some found a father, others a mother, a brother or a son, and their cries deafened the city.

At the onset of the 1456 outbreak, anyone who could fled the city. This included all the cardinals, apart from a certain Cardinal Domenico Capranica – and Callixtus III himself. It was on this occasion that he called a one-cardinal Consistory, following which he publicly announced the appointment of his young nephew Rodrigo as a cardinal. However, after just over a year of his reign, it became evident that all was not well with the seventy-seven-year-old Callixtus III. In early October 1456 the ambassador for Milan went so far as to write home that the Pope had been confined to his bed with what appeared to be a mortal illness, and 'his condition is such that he might die at any moment'.

Over the coming years, there would be more than a dozen such reports, but still Callixtus III hung on, doing his best to collect troops for the crusade, venting his anger on King Alfonso of Naples for his lack of support:

> You traitorously used our money to betray us. God and the Holy See will bring retribution down on you! Alfonso, King of Aragon, aid Pope Callixtus, because if you do not God will surely punish you.

He insisted on trying to create three new cardinals, in order to bolster the Spanish contingent, but, according to Cardinal Piccolomini:

> There was a bitter argument in the consistory, because the Pope wanted to create cardinals, but was opposed by the college [of cardinals]. First they argued that there were too many cardinals already and then poured scorn on the men he nominated, arguing vociferously against all of them. Callixtus, however, got the better of the college, especially thanks to the vigorous assistance of those three cardinals he had already created and made it clear to the college that he was in charge, as was fitting.

Cardinal Rodrigo Borgia certainly backed his uncle in this meeting. He was already beginning to flex his muscles and discover the power of politicking. He had helped Callixtus III regain Papal Territory; he had also witnessed his uncle threaten to depose a king, as well as impose his will on a reluctant College of Cardinals. This was what a strong-minded pope could do, even when he was old and frail and all but confined to his bed.

Yet finally, on Sunday, 6 August 1458, the inevitable came about. The Milanese ambassador reported home:

> The Pope died today at nightfall; the Catalans have all fled, and those who are harbouring them are so detested that it will go

badly for them if they are found out before the election of a new pope.

As we have seen, Pedro Luis Borgia, the Captain-General of the Papal Forces, fled the city – in fact, on the Sunday morning before the Pope was actually dead. However, this was not quite the act of cowardice it might at first appear. Initially, he had informed his younger brother Cardinal Rodrigo Borgia that he intended to hold on to his post, so that during the conclave his very presence, along with his troops in the nearby Castel Sant'Angelo, might be used to induce the cardinals to vote for a candidate who was favourable to him retaining his post. Unexpectedly, it was his brother Cardinal Rodrigo Borgia who dissuaded his brother from adopting this bold but reckless plan. Cardinal Rodrigo was beginning to grasp the ways of politicking within the Curia. He understood that the result of the conclave would lie in manipulating the College of Cardinals from within, rather than simply threatening its members from without. He even managed to persuade Pedro Luis to surrender the Castel Sant'Angelo and all the papal troops to the command of the College of Cardinals. Cardinal Rodrigo Borgia ensured that for this gesture Pedro Luis received 22,000 ducats. Only then did Pedro Luis flee to the port of Ostia, where he was more than disappointed to discover that there was no sign of the galley he had ordered to transport him to the safety of Spain. He was thus obliged to take refuge in the fortress at Civitavecchia, some forty miles up the coast.

In the customary manner, the conclave to elect a new pope would be held within the confines of St Peter's, beginning on 16 August. The cardinals who had retired to their estates outside Rome on account of the summer heat and rumours of a further outbreak of the plague, quickly made their way back to the eternal city. Meanwhile Cardinal Luis Juan del Milà arrived post-haste from Bologna, covering the 200 miles across the Apennines from Bologna in just three days to arrive on 11 August, the same day as Cardinal Aeneas Piccolomini arrived from Viterbo, some sixty miles north of Rome. Three days later, on the very eve of the conclave, a sensational development took place. Cardinal Domenico

Capranica, the only member of the college who had loyally remained in Rome with Callixtus III during the previous outbreak of the plague, and who was widely regarded as one of the favourites to win the election, took ill and suddenly died. According to Gerard Noel, the historian of the Renaissance popes: 'This meant the loss to the Renaissance papacy of an outstanding humanist and potential reformer.'

On 16 August eighteen cardinals were gathered within the Vatican's small chapel of San Niccolò (with dining and sleeping areas nearby in a larger chapel). This conclave consisted of eight Italians, no less than five Spaniards (whereas at the previous conclave there had been but one), one Portuguese (also appointed by Callixtus III), two Frenchmen and two Greeks (one of whom was Cardinal Bessarion, who had suffered such disappointment in the previous conclave). Cardinal Rodrigo Borgia was well aware that he stood no chance of winning the vote himself: all Catalans were despised in Rome, and a large majority of the cardinals present shared this view. Also, he was simply too young. His only slight hope was to try and cling on to his post as vice-chancellor.

Two days after assembling, the first vote took place. This revealed that two Italian candidates had received the most votes: five for Cardinal Calandrini, Bishop of Bologna and half-brother of the earlier pope Nicholas V, and five for the newly elected Cardinal Piccolomini, Bishop of Siena. Yet both were well short of the necessary two-thirds majority of twelve votes. This was just the opening move: only now did the real bargaining begin.

This is the earliest conclave where we have a first-hand account of the secret proceedings. Not surprisingly, these appear in the secret memoirs of the literary Aeneas Piccolomini, who refers to himself in the third person, and with some confidence: 'It was common talk that Aeneas, Cardinal of Siena would be pope, since no one was held in higher esteem.' He devotes eight pages to describing in some detail the machinations which took place in the conclave. Most of these centred on the fabulously rich Guillaume d'Estouteville, Cardinal of Rouen and a cousin of the king of France, who saw himself as the obvious choice for the papal throne. Where the Frenchman was concerned, no deceit was too low, no trick too blatant, to ensure his victory. After the next vote, the ballot papers were tipped on to a table in the centre of the room:

> Then they read out the ballots one after another and noted down the names written on them. And there was not a single cardinal who did not likewise make notes of those named, that there might be no possibility of trickery.

The following passages (in italics in the translated edition) had been censored in previous editions:

> *This proved to be to Aeneas's advantage, for when the votes were counted and the teller, Rouen, announced that Aeneas had eight, though the rest said nothing about another man's loss, Aeneas did not allow himself to be defrauded. 'Look more carefully at the ballots,' he said to the teller, 'for I have nine votes.' The others agreed with him. Rouen said nothing, as if he had merely made a mistake.*

From now on things began in earnest:

> *Many cardinals met in the privies as being in a secluded and retired place. Here they agreed as to how they might elect Guillaume [d'Estouteville] pope, and they bound themselves by written pledges and by oath. Guillaume was presently promising benefices and prefer-ment and dividing provinces among them. A fit place for such a pope to be elected!*

But Aeneas Piccolomini ensured that one of his spies secreted himself in the latrines, so that he could eavesdrop on these proceedings. As the historian of the Renaissance Popes, Gerard Noel surmises: 'This may have been Cardinal Calindrini. No one knows, as this part of the scenario was only pieced together from evidence emerging later.'

Through his spy, Piccolomini learned: '*Not a few were won over by Rouen's splendid promises and were caught like flies by their gluttony.*'

Even Cardinal Rodrigo Borgia said he would give d'Estouteville his vote, after he was promised that he would retain his post as vice-chancellor. On the night before the final voting, Borgia sought out his friend Piccolomini, urging him to vote for d'Estouteville, as he was bound to win. Borgia's defence of his decision is revealing: '*It is not for my advantage to remain with a small minority out of favour with a new pope. I am joining the majority and I have looked after my own interests.*' Borgia revealed that he had been promised he would retain the vice-chancellorship. But Piccolomini berated him: '*You young fool! Will you put an enemy of your nation in the Apostle's chair?*' He informed Borgia that he had been tricked: Piccolomini knew d'Estouteville had already promised the vice-chancellorship to the Bishop of Avignon. Borgia was left to brood on this dumbfounding news, as Piccolomini moved on to visit other cardinals with similar revelations.

Next morning, following the celebration of Mass (in order that God could guide the cardinals in their choice) the voting began. As d'Estouteville had so blatantly tried to rig the ballot papers, it was decided that each cardinal should cast his vote by verbal accession, so that all could see who had voted, and for whom, when each cardinal cast his vote. At this point the atmosphere in the chapel became charged in the extreme. 'All sat pale and silent in their places, as if entranced. For some time no one spoke, no one moved any part of his body except the eyes which kept glancing all about. Then Rodrigo, the Vice-Chancellor, rose and said, "I accede to the Cardinal of Siena," *an utterance which was like a dagger in Rouen's heart, so pale did he turn.*'

Voting continued, with many cardinals breaking their promises to d'Estouteville and deciding to cast their vote for Piccolomini.

Aeneas now lacked but one vote. Realizing this, Cardinal Prospero Colonna thought that he must get for himself the glory of announcing the Pope. *He rose and was about to pronounce this vote when he was seized by the Cardinals of Nicaea* [Bessarion] *and Rouen ...*

The two cardinals attempted to silence him, shouting at him, trying to drag him from the room. But just in time Cardinal Colonna managed to call out: 'I too accede to the Cardinal of Siena and I make him pope.'

In the words of Gerard Noel: 'This shocking scene was immediately followed by a scene that could have happened nowhere but at a late medieval papal conclave.' Immediately all those present, including the 'panting dishevelled cardinals', flung themselves to their feet and prostrated themselves before the new pope. 'Such was the magnetic power of a pope, instantly operative from the moment of his election.' The Pope remained the direct descendant of St Peter, and as such was God's representative on earth.

Piccolomini had won, and took the papal name Pius II. His election was greeted with cheers and rejoicing from the crowds waiting outside. One of his first moves was to confirm Cardinal Rodrigo Borgia as vice-chancellor, in recognition for his role in getting him elected pope.

Pius II was still only fifty-three. He had already distinguished himself as a papal envoy, as a poet and a writer, and as 'the father of several bastards'. Even so, he was determined to take seriously his role as St Peter's successor. Despite his comparative youth, he was by then badly afflicted by gout, as well as the recurrent problem with his feet. Indeed, the reason he had been at Viterbo when Callixtus III died was because he had been taking the famous curative waters, whose powers had been renowned since before Roman times. However, although he strove so hard to overcome the problem of his feet, he was philosophical about the outcome of his gout, 'because this illness, once it has become chronic and firmly rooted, is only ended by death'. He vowed to mend his ways:

I do not deny my past. I have been a great wanderer from what is right, but at least I know it and hope that the knowledge has not come too late.

Cardinal Rodrigo Borgia was now very much in favour, and worked closely with Pius II, as his right-hand man. But this was not without its difficulties. Cardinal Rodrigo Borgia was forced to travel to Civitavecchia, where his task was to persuade his brother Pedro Luis to renounce formally his post as Captain-General of the Papal Forces, and also to divest himself of the various titles bestowed upon him by Callixtus III. These latter mainly involved posts as 'lord' or governor of various cities in the Romagna, which Pius II wished to take back, as these cities belonged to the Papal States. Somehow Cardinal Rodrigo managed to persuade his brother to give up all of these titles. This was almost certainly because his brother had once more lapsed into serious illness, for within a month he would die, almost certainly of malaria. This now left the post of Captain-General of the Papal Forces free for Pius II to award to a member of the Colonna family, in recognition of Cardinal Prospero Colonna's casting vote in the conclave.

Having retained his post as vice-chancellor, Cardinal Rodrigo Borgia was now able to consolidate his hold over the Curia, as well as the Rota, the Church's supreme court. It was the vice-chancellor who received all communications to the Pope. As we have seen, apart from diplomatic matters, this also included notification of important benefices which had fallen vacant all over Europe on the death of the incumbent. A number of these the vice-chancellor chose to bestow upon himself. Favours, such as 'recommendations' for benefices, required financial inducements to the vice-chancellor. As well as accumulating considerable power to himself, Cardinal Rodrigo Borgia was now becoming exceedingly wealthy. In consequence he would begin to cast aside some of the restraint he had showed during the reign of his ascetic uncle Callixtus III. As a demonstration of his status, over the coming years Cardinal Rodrigo Borgia would build himself an extravagant palace on the wide main street which ran east–west across Rome from the Vatican to the Lateran (part of which had once formed Ancient Rome's Sacred Way, the traditional path of triumphal processions into the city). The new Borgia residence was described by a contemporary: 'The palace is splendidly decorated; the walls of the great entrance hall are hung with tapestries depicting various scenes.' He goes on to describe 'a sumptuous day bed upholstered in red satin with a canopy over it, and a chest on which was laid out a vast and beautiful collection of gold and silver plate . . . a couch covered with cloth of gold' and so on. The exterior was equally imposing. In the centre of the palace was a large courtyard overlooked by three-storey loggias with slender, octagonal columns, indicating a Renaissance influence. This palace Cardinal Rodrigo used as his residence, as well as his chancellery. It dominated the district and towered over the main street passing outside its gates. This street was not only used for papal inaugurations, but also other important processions, when it would be lined by large crowds. Whilst leading one of these processions, Pius II would note that Borgia's palace was bedecked with a sumptuousness whose decorations outshone all the other palaces along the route, including those of the old aristocratic Roman families and the senior cardinals who resided in Rome.

As the Borgia historian G. J. Meyer remarks: 'Anyone who used this great office [the vice-chancellorship] skilfully could make himself one of the most important men in Europe. No one would ever use it more skilfully than Rodrigo Borgia.' But he also had other skills to learn, and this instruction would begin at the side of Pius II. The new pope found himself facing a number of serious problems. First there was the Kingdom of Naples. France, now by far the most powerful nation in Europe, began re-insisting that it had a claim to this throne. When Queen Joanna II had died, she had no right to leave the kingdom to King Alfonso, when her nearest rightful successor belonged to the Royal House of Anjou, from which the king of France was descended. Then came another claim, this time from the Kingdom of Aragon in Spain. The present King Ferrante had only been the illegitimate son of the previous King Alfonso, and there were legitimate Spanish claimants who had been overlooked. Pius II, advised by Rodrigo Borgia, contacted the powerful Francesco I Sforza, Duke of Milan, suggesting to him that for the good of Italy it would be best if both the French and the Spanish were kept out of Naples. Reversing the policy of his predecessor, Pius II decided to give his blessing to King Ferrante of Naples. When the House of Anjou mounted a naval invasion of Naples, Sforza and Pius II sent a combined force to repel the invaders. Despite an uprising of barons loyal to the legitimate royal line and against Ferrante, the joint papal and Milanese forces held out. Ferrante remained on the throne, at least for the time being.

Pius II now found himself facing a second, even more important threat. This came from the expansion of the Ottoman Empire to the east. In a highly symbolic victory, the forces of Mehmed the Conqueror overran Athens in 1458, with Mehmed himself decreeing that the Parthenon be turned into a mosque. The founding city of western classical culture had fallen to the infidels, and now the whole of Greece lay at their mercy. It was only a matter of time before the new Byzantine capital at Mystras was conquered. Pius II understood the pressing need to carry on the work of his predecessor and oppose the Ottoman threat. The new pope wrote to the crowned heads of all Europe, inviting them to meet in the summer of 1459 at Mantua. Pius II was determined to mount the crusade that remained Callixtus III's unfinished task. This called for drastic measures. Pius II let it be known that he planned to impose a levy on every church and holder of any ecclesiastical post throughout western Christendom. Together with further material and manpower support from all European leaders, a vast army would be raised, ready to mount a two-pronged attack – one force-marching east overland, and the other setting sail for the shores of the eastern Mediterranean. The Ottomans were becoming a threat not only to Italy, but also to western Christendom itself. It was in everyone's interests that this scourge be defeated.

In January 1459 Pius II set off with high hopes for the congress of European leaders he had called at Mantua. He was accompanied by a large entourage which included all available cardinals. This, of course, included Cardinal Rodrigo Borgia, who had the difficult task of liaising with Rome in his capacity as vice-chancellor, and also ensuring that the city remained in some semblance of order. When so many of the grandees were out of town, the authorities often found it difficult to restrain the local populace from any breakdown of civil order and excesses of unruly behaviour. Likewise, the affairs of the chancery remained central to the functioning of the papacy itself, and were thus far too important to be delegated to a functionary in the Vatican during the Pope's absence. The vice-chancellor would maintain a constant string of couriers, riding post-haste to and from Rome during the many months of the Pope's absence.

Despite Pius II's high hopes for his congress, it was several months before he and his entourage finally made it to Mantua. It soon became clear that not all was going according to plan. For months the Pope waited, but no one of any importance turned up. During the long hot summer, Pius II and his cardinals endured the humid heat, disease and indifferent cuisine. Cardinal Borgia found himself housed in uncomfortably close proximity to his master in a small city filled with gossips, and was thus forced to behave himself, adopting an uncharacteristically abstemious and frugal way of life. Dealing with consistory business, consulting with Pius II, and replying to the messages from Rome became a necessary distraction. Meanwhile summer passed into autumn, then winter.

Finally, in January 1460 Pius II's patience came to an end. He issued two papal bulls. The first of these optimistically announced that the crusade would go ahead regardless. The second, on the other hand, opened with the word *Execrabilis*, and went on to express Pius II's disgust at the outcome of the Congress of Mantua. Thereupon the Pope and his entourage departed for Rome.

CHAPTER 3

CARDINAL RODRIGO BORGIA EMERGES IN HIS TRUE COLOURS

THE POPE'S PROCESSION BACK to Rome seems to have taken him as long as his journey out to Mantua. Despite this tardiness, Italy was now descending into an ever-deeper crisis. Anjou forces had once again attacked Naples, where its barons had once again risen against King Ferrante, whose position was looking increasingly precarious. It was now beginning to look as if Pius II's decision to support Ferrante might prove a dangerous diplomatic blunder. And then news came through that there was serious trouble in the Papal States, notably in the Romagna. Here Sigismondo Pandolfo Malatesta, lord of Rimini and a former commander of the Papal Forces, had risen in revolt. History presents a distinctly two-sided picture of Malatesta. On the one hand, he was regarded as a nobleman, patron of the arts, a Renaissance man and a brilliant military commander of the Venetian forces against the Turks. And now reports were coming through of his 'trussing up a papal emissary, the fifteen-year-old Bishop of Fano, and publicly sodomising him before

the applauding army in the main square of Rimini'. This incident would
earn him excommunication by Pius II, who contacted Sforza of Milan,
a known enemy of Malatesta, and Federigo da Montefeltro, a powerful
condottiere* based in Urbino. Italy had to be rid of this dangerous usurper,
or there was no telling where such disorder would end. Indeed there was
not, for reports now reaching Pius II suggested that in his absence from
Rome the populace were becoming increasingly restless, and there was
even a conspiracy to expel the Pope and declare the city a republic.

As if all this was not a bad enough reflection on the political and moral
state of contemporary Italy, a report now reached Pius II concerning
the behaviour of his trusted right-hand man, Cardinal Rodrigo Borgia.
During the long journey south from Mantua, Cardinal Borgia had
separated from the papal entourage, which was now in Tuscany, at Bagni,
where the Pope was taking the waters to relieve his gout and his painful
foot. Meanwhile, Cardinal Rodrigo Borgia, accompanied by Cardinal
d'Estouteville, arrived in Siena, free at last from the watchful eye of
their master. Here the two senior cardinals were invited to become joint
godparents at the baptism of the child of a local nobleman, Giovanni de
Bichis, who had also been a close friend of Pius II during his period as
Bishop of Siena. Following the baptism ceremony, there was a party in
the gardens of the de Bichis residence. It was not long before rumours of
what had taken place at this 'party' began reaching the Pope's ears. On 11
June 1460 Pius II wrote to Cardinal Rodrigo Borgia:

> We have learned that three days ago a considerable number of
> women, adorned with all worldly vanity, were assembled in the
> gardens of our well-beloved son Giovanni de Bichis, and that you,
> in contempt of the dignity of your position, remained with them
> for five hours during the afternoon. Also, that you had with you
> another cardinal, who in the light of his advanced age, if not the
> honour of the Holy See, should have recalled his duty. We are
> told that the dances were immodest and the seductions of love

---

* A mercenary general, with his own army for hire.

beyond bounds, so that you behaved as if you were one of the most vulgar young men of your time. Modesty forbids me from giving a full account of what I am told took place. Not only these things themselves, but the mere mention of them, is a disgrace to the office you hold. Husbands, fathers, brothers and other relatives who accompanied the young women were forbidden to enter so that you could be free to enjoy yourself. You two, along with a handful of servants, organized and directed the dancing. They say that in Siena at the moment there is no talk of anything else, and that you are the laughing stock of the city . . . it gives a pretext to those who accuse us of using our wealth and our high office in order to indulge in orgies . . . We are more angry than we can say . . . We leave it to your own judgement to say if this befits your high office: to pay compliments to women, to be sending them fruit, to drink a mouthful of wine and then have the glass carried to the woman who pleases you most . . .

According to the authoritative papal historian Ludwig von Pastor, this was 'the first light thrown upon Rodrigo's immorality'. He implies that previously such behaviour had been conducted more discreetly, in such locations as his palace in Rome, more than a mile away across the Tiber from the papal residence in the Vatican. Some sources, in defence of Borgia, claim that he had not yet been ordained a priest (as discussed previously). Others claim that this letter is a forgery, pointing to occasional lapses in 'the usual polish of [Pius II's] Latin prose'. Such an argument has its plausibility; the Pope was, after all, highly regarded for his literary works. But on this occasion it seems that his anger got the better of his style. As we shall see, it is difficult to doubt the authenticity of the letter per se. Its contents are another matter. Even Pius II himself implies ('I have been told . . .') that the letter was a combination of rumour, gossip and hearsay. Evidence of exaggeration would seem likely for various reasons. Not least of these, the implausibility of this particular 'orgy'. Would the 'husbands, fathers, brothers and other relatives' of such women have permitted themselves 'to be barred entry' to this party in the garden of a nobleman's house? Something evidently took place, but its indiscretions seem to have been blown out of all proportion. All this is put into perspective by the letter Pius II wrote to Cardinal Rodrigo Borgia some days later:

> We have received your letter and take note of the explanations which you give. What you have done, beloved son, is not without blame, even if it is perhaps less grave than I was at first led to believe. We grant you the pardon you ask . . . Be assured that as long as you mend your ways, and live discreetly and modestly, you will have in me a father and protector.

Pius II may be at the same time warm, affectionate and forgiving, but one cannot escape the element of warning in the letter. It is as if he knows Borgia's character, yet prefers not to know. From this time on, Cardinal Borgia would try to remain more circumspect in his conduct. On the other hand, as we shall see, he would continue to indulge in unbridled behaviour on a regular basis.

The Pope now continued his slow journey south towards Rome, passing through southern Tuscany. However, upon reaching his birthplace Corsignano (modern Pienza), Pius II 'fell seriously ill, the moisture spreading downward from his head and so weakening his chest, arms and entire body that he could not stir without assistance and seemed on the point of death'. This lasted twelve days, and served as a warning sign to Cardinal Rodrigo Borgia that his fifty-five-year-old 'father and protector' was unlikely to reach the venerable age attained by his predecessor in this role, namely Callixtus III. The Pope then resumed on his way to Rome, carried in a chair by members of his bodyguard. As he crossed the countryside on the last stretch of his journey, he was met by a delegation of citizens urging his speedy return, to restore the city to order. By this stage Rome was in a state of virtual anarchy, with gangs defying the authorities, committing mayhem, and even murder, on the streets.

As Pius II came close to the city walls, 'the fields were full of people coming to meet and greet the Pope'. Amongst these were some of the young thugs who had been calling for a revolution. When they offered to carry the Pope's chair, the Pope's bodyguard warned him that he could not trust these people. Pius II laughed at this and, determined to call the young men's bluff, summoned them to him and asked them to carry his chair. Awed by the papal presence, this was precisely what they did. The Pope and his chair-bearers were greeted by cheering crowds as they entered the Holy City.

Other problems proved less easy to resolve. In response to the continuing disgraceful news from Rimini, Pius II held a public ceremony where the image of Sigismondo Pandolfo Malatesta was burned. The Pope himself then 'canonized Malatesta to Hell with a curse' (i.e. damned him to serve the devil as the very opposite of a saint). He then ordered the condottiere general da Montefeltro to march on Rimini. Over a period of months Malatesta's forces were eventually driven back into the refuge of Rimini, where they would have surrendered but for the sudden and unexpected intervention of the Venetians. Rimini was a strategic city on the Adriatic, and the Venetians were keen to retain allies along their main shipping route to the Mediterranean – a vital lifeline for the powerful city state's trade and armed fleets. But at least the majority of the Romagna remained nominally under papal control, for the time being.

Despite remaining in close attendance on the Pope, Cardinal Rodrigo Borgia once again found himself in a difficult predicament. He had, as ordered by Pius II, been 'living discreetly'; however, this had not curtailed his determinedly licentious behaviour. It was during these years that he fathered his first child, by a mistress whose name remains unknown. This unwanted addition to the cardinal's household was a son, who would be christened Pedro Luis, after Rodrigo's older brother who had died just a few years previously. Naturally this event, and the circumstances surrounding it, were cloaked in secrecy. Indeed, even the precise year of Pedro Luis Borgia's birth remains unclear. Some sources place it as early as 1462, implying that Pedro Luis had been conceived in the very year following Pius II's outrage, and wary forgiveness, concerning the events in Siena. Despite the lack of detail surrounding Pedro Luis Borgia's birth, it is known that Cardinal Borgia soon despatched his son to Spain, where he would be brought up by Borja relatives in his home town of Xàtiva.

In 1464, following upon the effective end of Malatesta's revolt in the Romagna, Pius II ordered Montefeltro and his mercenary army to join up with the Duke of Milan's troops and march upon Naples. Here King Ferrante's forces had been defeated by Réné Count of Anjou in a battle just south of Vesuvius. King Ferrante had barely managed to escape from the field with his life, and fled back to Naples. However, the tables were turned with the arrival of the Papal Forces, backed by Montefeltro and the Duke of Milan. Here, too, the will of Pius II had now prevailed. Throughout all these difficulties, Cardinal Rodrigo Borgia was at Pius II's side, learning the essentials of papal strategy first hand.

Pius II now decided to turn his full attention once more to mounting his crusade. The situation with regard to the Ottomans was more perilous than ever. In 1460 the new capital of the Byzantine Empire at Mystras had fallen to Mehmed the Conqueror, whose forces had soon overrun the rest of the Peloponnese, apart from a number of Venetian islands and outposts. Then in 1461 the news came through that the last Byzantine stronghold, on the eastern Black Sea at Trabzon, had also fallen to Ottoman forces. When Pius II announced that despite his frail health he intended to lead his crusade personally, Cardinal Rodrigo Borgia immediately gave his support, even going so far as to mortgage his sumptuous palace to help raise money for Pius II's pet project. This move was not entirely selfless. Pius II had recently held a secret consistory, at which he had berated his cardinals in no uncertain manner:

> The priesthood is derided by many. They say we live too comfortably, acquire undeserved wealth, pursue ambitions before all else . . . spend nothing on defending Christendom. They are not wrong: many of the cardinals do just this and, it seems to me, that the extravagance and arrogance of our court is excessive.

Cardinal Rodrigo Borgia had certainly understood that these words were at least in part directed at him. By mortgaging his palace, he intended to demonstrate his remorse for his behaviour. But Pius II was not so easily appeased. Although he had refrained from dismissing his close and by now vitally supportive friend, he announced a measure that would considerably restrain the vice-chancellor's powers. In order to raise even more funds for the crusade, Pius II decided to appoint a College of Abbreviators to the chancellery, as added fundraisers. Cardinal Rodrigo Borgia protested that the new college would severely limit his ability to do his job properly, but Pius II was adamant. It was all for the good of the crusade.

Despite this setback, Borgia would soon find himself deeply involved in the Pope's affairs. In the summer of 1464 the Pope announced that despite his ill-health he would travel to Ancona to take charge of the crusade, bringing with him his vice-chancellor and senior cardinals. This involved a taxing journey of over a hundred miles across the Apennines. Upon arrival in Ancona, Pius II was confronted by scenes of chaos as the troops were at last being assembled ready for shipment east to take on the Ottomans. The Papal Forces consisted of a mixed bunch. Although European leaders had for the most part ignored Pius II's call to arms, the people had not. From pulpits as far afield as Germany and the Low Countries, Spain, France and even Scotland, local priests had loyally supported Pius II's crusade, calling for volunteers. By now Ancona was not only teeming with the assembled papal troops, but also 'amateur crusaders from all over Europe'.

The Venetians, who had been unable to form an alliance with the Turks, had reluctantly decided to support Pius II's crusade by sending a fleet to transport the assembled troops. But the papal party arrived in Ancona to find that there was no sign of the Venetian fleet. Ancona was by now overrun: such a small city was unable to support an entire crusader army, and amidst the sweltering heat of a hot southern Italian summer, food, drink and accommodation were by now running out. Meanwhile, the ill Pius II sat propped up in his bed gazing out of the window at the horizon, impatiently awaiting any sign of the Venetian galleys. Then rumours began to spread of an outbreak of bubonic plague in the port, and soon troops were beginning to melt away. Cardinal Rodrigo Borgia, too, seems to have lost his enthusiasm for the crusade – turning his interest to his more usual amorous pursuits. This contact with female members of the local citizenry brought about a dramatic development. According to the Mantuan ambassador's report home on 10 August:

> The vice-chancellor is sick with a disease, and I can confirm the truth of this. He has pain in one of his ears and also under the arm on the same side ... the doctor who first saw him said he has little hope, as he has not been alone in his bed.

Cardinal Borgia had evidently caught the plague from one of his female companions.*

While the Pope and his vice-chancellor both lay in their sickbeds, as well as a number of other cardinals who were stricken with the plague in varying degrees, the Venetian fleet finally arrived on 14 August. By this stage it was obvious to all in attendance on Pius II that he was at death's door, and the following day he died. After consulting with those cardinals in a fit state to receive him, the commander of the Venetian fleet decided to head back home. There would be no crusade.

A few days later, those cardinals in good health accompanied the body of Pope Pius II back to Rome. Astonishingly, Cardinal Rodrigo Borgia was able to undertake this same journey, despite his parlous state. There is no doubting his motive for risking his life in this fashion: he was determined to attend the coming conclave. This duly began in Rome on 28 August, with Cardinal Rodrigo Borgia making a dramatic appearance, his head wrapped in bandages. Owing to Pius II's propensity for appointing fellow Italians as cardinals, there were now ten Italians amongst the nineteen cardinals in attendance, the first time there had been an Italian majority for several centuries.

The first 'scrutiny' (vote) took place two days later. Despite the fact that Cardinal Bessarion was generally considered the favourite to win the papacy, Cardinal Rodrigo Borgia well understood which way things were likely to unfold. For some time now, he had gone to great trouble

---

* It has been suggested that the vice-chancellor's disease was in fact syphilis; but this could not have been the case, as the modern outbreak of syphilis would not arrive in western Europe until 1493.

cultivating a friendship with Cardinal Pietro Barbo, a worldly Italian who cared more for his own comfort than his spiritual calling. The son of a wealthy Venetian merchant, Barbo, too, had trained as a merchant, but had entered the Church after seeing the success of his uncle, who had been elected Pope Eugenius IV. Consequently, Pietro Barbo had been assured a rapid rise through the ranks – and benefices – becoming a cardinal at the tender age of twenty-three (two years younger even than Cardinal Rodrigo Borgia). His love of finery and lavish generosity had made him a popular figure, and he had let it be known that if elected pope he would reward any cardinal who had voted for him with a fine villa in the country, so that he could escape the summer heat of Rome. Under such circumstances, Cardinal Rodrigo Borgia had gambled on the fact that the Greek Cardinal Bessarion was unlikely to win the votes of all the Italian cardinals, and would only win if there was a deadlock between Barbo and another candidate. Cardinal Rodrigo Borgia thus made it clear that at first scrutiny his vote would be cast with the Italians, encouraging the three other Spanish cardinals to follow suit. This galvanized the Italians to unite behind Barbo, ensuring that on the first scrutiny Cardinal Barbo received a clear two-thirds majority of fourteen. The delighted new pope announced that he would take on the name Paul II. He was just forty-seven years old, and it was thus expected that his rule would a long one.

On 4 September the Mantuan ambassador reported home that Cardinal Rodrigo Borgia was 'in high standing' with the newly elected pope. By now, Cardinal Rodrigo Borgia had been a cardinal for eight years, and on the elevation of Barbo to the papal chair he became the senior member of the College of Cardinals. He was still only thirty-three years old. As such, he should have received the honour of crowning the new pope with his papal tiara. But by the time of the ceremony, which took place on 16 September, Borgia was once again too ill to stir from his bed. The effort to attend the conclave had evidently drained him, but this effort was certainly appreciated by his friend Paul II. The new pope not only confirmed his friend in the important position of vice-chancellor, but also went one step further by abolishing the College of Abbreviators which had curbed his power. This heartening news had its effect on the gratified vice-chancellor, who gradually began to recover from his illness. By 9 October the ever-vigilant Mantuan ambassador was reporting, 'Yesterday [Cardinal Rodrigo Borgia] was seen out, even though the scar left by the plague is not yet healed.'

Prior to the conclave at which Cardinal Barbo became Pope Paul II, the College of Cardinals (without Cardinal Rodrigo Borgia in attendance) decided to impose a series of restrictions upon papal power. Pius II's obsession with personally leading the crusade had worried many: apart from the several dangers of such a move, it would leave a power vacuum in Rome, with the Church exposed to political power throughout Europe. So the College of Cardinals decided that from now on whoever was elected pope would be forbidden to leave Rome without their majority consent. And if he wished to leave Italy, he would need the unanimous consent of the college. It was also decided that from now on the College of Cardinals should not exceed twenty-four members, while at the same time a pope would only be permitted to appoint one 'nephew-cardinal' (or, in Latin, *cardinalis nepos*, from which the word nepotism is derived).

Paul II's love of finery and extravagant dressing up had long been evident to those close to him, who were also aware of his homosexual inclinations. His extravagance, if not his homosexuality, quickly became evident to all when he appeared at the 1465 Easter Mass wearing a new papal tiara. This he had designed himself, ensuring that it was encrusted with jewels. The ambassador for Milan estimated this new papal tiara to be worth 60,000 ducats. (Other contemporary estimates went as high as double this price.) But this was just the beginning. Since the late 1450s, the young Cardinal Barbo had begun building himself a lavish palace overlooking the Piazza San Marco in central Rome. And in 1466, just two years into his office, he took the unprecedented step of making this his official papal residence, abandoning the papal quarters in the Vatican. The Palazzo San Marco* was sumptuously furnished with his accumulated treasures, including:

---

* Over the centuries this palace would become known as the Palazzo Venezia, until in the 1930s it acted as the residence of Mussolini, who was in the habit of delivering his grandiose, posturing speeches from the balcony.

his extensive collections of Flemish tapestries, Byzantine icons, paintings, statues, bronzes, mosaics, coins, medals and innumerable antiques.

Paul II particularly enjoyed dressing up in all his finery, and watching the processions pass below his grand balcony. However, despite Paul II's passion for collecting antiquities, he was no Renaissance man and certainly not a humanist. Indeed, one of his main reasons for dissolving the College of Abbreviators was that it had become filled with humanist scholars, quickly multiplying to a membership of seventy. After Paul II's dissolution of the college, their aggrieved leader Bartolomeo Platina led the abbreviators and a large crowd of their supporters to besiege the papal residence. After this 'republican insurrection' was quickly put down, Platina was flung into the notorious dungeons of the Castel Sant'Angelo, which were 'dark and damp, and infested with spiders, snakes and rats'. From then on, Paul II forbade all teaching of humanism and the ancient classics, condemning them as heretical. However, Platina would have the last word, when, many years later, he wrote his *Lives of the Popes*, in which Paul II is described as 'a monster of cruelty and sexual depravity'.

There is more than an element of truth in this characterization, though in the words of papal historian John Julius Norwich, Paul II was best known for 'his two weaknesses – for good-looking young men, and for melons'. Indeed he devoted so much of his daily life to such pastimes that he often took little interest in his papal duties, leaving these to be dealt with by his loyal vice-chancellor. Paul II was also renowned for his obsessive vanity. He usually had a mirror carried by an attendant, into which he would frequently gaze. On occasion he even wore lipstick, which was particularly conspicuous on his pale-skinned, podgy face. His original choice for a papal name had been Formosus II ('handsome'), but he was dissuaded from this by his fellow cardinals after the conclave.[*]

---

[*] Pope Formosus I ruled at the end of the ninth century. He is best remembered for the fact that his body was exhumed and clad in his papal vestments, so that he could face charges at the so-called Cadaver Synod, where he was belatedly found to have been 'unworthy of the pontificate'.

Under Pius II, Cardinal Rodrigo Borgia had gained knowledge of how the papacy was run, now he was gaining actual experience of the job itself. Meanwhile, despite the insurrection, Paul II did his best to encourage his popularity amongst the citizenry. He indulged to the full his love of displays and public occasions. The traditional carnival season, which took place before Lent, was extended. During this period, Paul II particularly enjoyed watching the traditional horse races. These ran from the Arch of Domitian to the Church of San Marco, finishing under his balcony. As Platina himself described it: 'After the boys' race he gave a coin to each entrant, even though they were all covered in mud.'

In 1467 Cardinal Rodrigo Borgia would father a second illegitimate child, this time a daughter, who was named Isabella after her grand-mother. A third child, a daughter named Girolama, would be born two years later. There are indications that all three of these children had the same mother, whose name remains uncertain. What is certain is that these children were either born in Spain or were quickly despatched there, where they were entrusted to the Borja family in Xàtiva.

In a further effort to bolster his popularity with the citizens of Rome, Paul II announced that from now on the Jubilee (of the birth of Christ) would be celebrated every twenty-five years, rather than every fifty years as was previously the custom. The people of Rome rejoiced, as this would bring more pilgrims to the Holy City; the income of the citizenry was almost entirely dependent upon such visitors. Meanwhile, Paul II antici-pated with pleasure presiding over the great round of festivities which would be held to mark the Jubilee of 1475. But this was not to be. On the morning of 26 July 1471 Paul II attended an unusually long and exhausting consistory. After this, he dined in the Vatican Gardens, where, at the age of just fifty-four, he died of an 'apoplexy'. This vague medical term was frequently used as a euphemism, and this is no exception. The unpalatable truth was that 'after an immoderate feasting on melons, he expired from the excessive effect of being sodomized by one of his favourite boys'.

Cardinal Rodrigo Borgia now found himself faced with his third conclave. This was attended by eighteen cardinals, fifteen of whom were Italian. Only Borgia, d'Estouteville and the ageing Bessarion were foreigners. Once again, Borgia well understood that he had no chance of gaining the two-thirds majority he would need to be elected pope. However, he did attract one backer, the twenty-seven-year-old Cardinal Francesco Gonzaga, a well-educated and serious young aristocrat who had been appointed a cardinal at the age of just seventeen. Francesco was a member of the influential and well-connected House of Gonzaga, the rulers of Mantua. Pius II had appointed him a cardinal in gratitude for the hospitality he had received in the city during the ill-fated Congress of Mantua. Cardinal Gonzaga had been impressed by the effective and experienced way in which Cardinal Rodrigo Borgia had used his vice-chancellorship to maintain the papacy during Paul II's negligence. But Cardinal Rodrigo Borgia persuaded Cardinal Gonzaga that he should join him in voting for Cardinal Francesco della Rovere.* This apparently selfless gesture had helped swing the Italian votes in favour of della Rovere, who thus became the next pope, taking the name Sixtus IV. The grateful Sixtus IV confirmed Cardinal Rodrigo Borgia as vice-chancellor, a post he had now held under no less than four papacies.

Sixtus IV had been born the son of a Genoese fisherman some fifty-seven years previously. At an early age he had joined the Franciscan order, where he had shown such intellectual quality that he had quickly risen through the ranks, becoming head of the order at the age of fifty. Three years later he had been created a cardinal by Paul II. His pious reputation, along with his exceptional intellectual powers, had played a large part in attracting the votes of the Italian cardinals, once Borgia's move had indicated that he was a likely candidate for the papacy. However, Sixtus IV's unexpected election had left him feeling insecure in such high office. So, in order to bolster his position, he embarked upon an unprecedented bout of nepotism. The 'only one nephew-cardinal' decree was simply ignored as he appointed a stream of nephews and cousins to bishoprics and the College of Cardinals, until the della Rovere family emerged as a leading power within the hierarchy. But Sixtus IV was also a man of

---

* Not to be mistaken for his nephew Cardinal Giuliano della Rovere, who would later become Cardinal Rodrigo Borgia's sworn enemy.

some discernment, who would reverse the anti-humanist policy of his predecessor. It was Sixtus IV who first imported early Renaissance artists and architects from Florence to Rome, and his name would forever be immortalized in the building of the Sistine Chapel,* where he employed Botticelli to paint murals. Sixtus IV would also create the Vatican Library, appointing the humanist Francesco Platina as first librarian. It was now that Platina would write his *Lives of the Popes*, which so castigated Paul II and in which Sixtus IV would play an exemplary role. Platina had arrived in Rome as a tutor in the retinue of the young Cardinal Gonzaga, and would also be renowned for writing the first printed cookbook, 'a monument of medieval cuisine in humanist trappings', which also contained the first recorded use of cannabis in a recipe.

In the year following the election of Sixtus IV, Cardinal Rodrigo Borgia travelled to Spain, officially in his capacity as Archbishop of Valencia. The city laid on a rapturous reception for their compatriot, who had risen so high in Rome. He also found time to visit his family, and see his three children. His oldest son Pedro Luis was now ten years old, though Borgia's mother Isabella had died four years previously. However, the real reason behind the cardinal's visit was not self-aggrandizement or even paternal love. Sixtus IV had entrusted Cardinal Rodrigo Borgia with a mission of considerable importance. He was to visit the court of King Juan of Aragon, who was known to be a difficult character. King Juan was the younger brother of King Alfonso of Aragon and Naples, who had fallen out so disastrously with Callixtus III and was thus no friend of the Borgias. Despite this, Cardinal Borgia had been chosen by Sixtus IV because of his long experience as vice-chancellor, and because he was Spanish.

Three years earlier King Juan had taken the astute decision to marry his seventeen-year-old son and heir Ferdinand to the King of Castile's eighteen-year-old half-sister and heir, Isabella. In this way, when the young couple each came into their separate inheritances, their marriage would unite the kingdoms of Aragon and Castile to form the beginnings

---

* Originally known as the Capella Magna, the name of the original chapel it replaced on this site. The chapel would only receive its present name, in honour of Sixtus IV, after his death.

of a larger Spain. The couple were in fact cousins, several times over, owing to the persistent tradition of marriage between members of the royal families of Aragon and Castile – even so, it was not certain that Isabella would inherit the throne of Castile. On top of this, King Juan had assured the world that the marriage was legitimate by producing a forged papal bull to this effect. Cardinal Rodrigo Borgia had been entrusted with the tricky task of assessing whether a genuine papal dispensation should be granted for the marriage. In return, Sixtus IV would insist that King Juan should commit himself to support the Pope in his attempt to raise forces for a crusade against the ever-increasing threat of the Ottomans. Cardinal Rodrigo Borgia quickly understood that such support was unlikely as long as King Juan continued to face internal problems. Three years previously, the Catalan capital of Barcelona had risen against Aragonese rule. King Juan had immediately laid siege to the city, but this had resulted in a stalemate. If Borgia could overcome this difficulty to the satisfaction of King Juan, then the king would back Sixtus IV's efforts to launch a crusade – efforts which had involved the Pope sending envoys all over Europe, not just Borgia to Spain.

In a bold move, Cardinal Rodrigo Borgia asked the king for permission to visit Barcelona and attempt to negotiate a resolution of this problem. Permission was granted and the cardinal travelled to Barcelona, where he held talks with the Catalan leaders. But the Catalans remained obdurate and the cardinal was forced leave empty-handed. However, on further consideration of what the cardinal had told them, the Catalan leaders sent word that they were willing to negotiate with King Juan. As a result, a peace was agreed, with honour on both sides – a direct result of Cardinal Rodrigo Borgia's intervention. As Meyer remarks:

> No account of how he accomplished this exists, but the engaging frankness he brought to all his relationships . . . must surely have been a factor . . . As we shall see, his life story is studded with instances in which his ability to connect even with adversaries affected the course of history.

This was perhaps the first major instance in which Cardinal Rodrigo Borgia would charm his way into achieving such a feat. As an encouragement to King Juan, the cardinal now handed him the signed papal dispensation which had been given to him by Sixtus IV: the marriage between Ferdinand and Isabella was legitimized. But Cardinal Rodrigo Borgia still had one more important obstacle to overcome: the problem of whether Isabella would in fact be recognized as the heir to the throne of Castile.

In an attempt to resolve this issue, Cardinal Rodrigo Borgia travelled to Madrid, to the court of King Enrique IV of Castile. Here he found the nobility split between those who favoured Isabella as the rightful heir, and those who backed the king's putative daughter Joana, whom the opposition believed had in fact been fathered by the Duke of Albuquerque. (King Enrique was widely known as 'Enrique the Impotent', but may well have been homosexual.) Without any resolution, this squabble was liable to erupt into civil war on the death of the weak and ailing King Enrique IV, and any hope of a united Spain would be out of the question.

Cardinal Rodrigo Borgia began a series of negotiations with King Enrique IV, and soon understood that the king would be willing to recognize Isabella as his heir if his favourite bishop, Pedro González de Mendoza, Bishop of Sigüenza, was given a cardinal's hat by Sixtus IV. Cardinal Rodrigo Borgia agreed to this request, on behalf of Sixtus IV.

By sheer talent and force of character, Cardinal Rodrigo Borgia had achieved a near miracle of diplomacy, which would have a lasting effect over the coming decades, when a united Spain would emerge as the richest country in Europe. He had also used his charm to make a number of influential friends. Not least of these was the young Ferdinand of Aragon, the man set to become king of the united kingdoms of Castile and Aragon, who had been won over by the magnetic cardinal's avuncular charms and enjoyment of life.

Yet we now come to an example of the 'Virtù e Fortuna' prescription which the perceptive Machiavelli would use to characterize the events that govern humanity. Cardinal Rodrigo Borgia had certainly demonstrated his Virtù – his strength, his ability – to the utmost. Yet he still remained at the mercy of 'Fortuna'. In late September 1473 Cardinal Rodrigo Borgia, accompanied by his large papal retinue – swelled by many Spanish clerics (including three bishops) wishing to seek favour from the Pope in Rome – gathered at Valencia. Here they boarded two large Venetian galleys and set off – by oar and by sail – on the 600-mile voyage across the Mediterranean to Ostia. On 10 October, as they approached the coast of Tuscany:

> A fearful storm arose at sea and chased the vessels towards land. The one that carried [Borgia] early veered from the rockbound coast and remained afloat, although tossed about, with a shattered stern and constantly in danger of submersion. The other galley, less prudent, was repeatedly hurled against the rocks, during a whole night and part of the day, till at last it broke up and sank.

Fortuna had been kind to Cardinal Rodrigo Borgia, who was lucky to escape with his life. The captain of his galley eventually managed to run his badly damaged vessel aground on the sandy beach near Livorno. An idea of the scale of this tragedy can be seen from the fact that almost 200 lives were lost, including the three bishops, as well as property and gold in the region of 30,000 ducats.

After recovering in nearby Pisa, a chastened Cardinal Rodrigo Borgia travelled to Rome, where he received a genuinely heartfelt welcome from Sixtus IV. Here Borgia learned that of all the missions which Sixtus IV had sent out to win support for his crusade against the Ottomans, his alone had been successful. The ageing Cardinal Bessarion had been sent to France. Here he had been flatly turned down and even subjected to insults by the French king Louis XI, a public humiliation which is said to have contributed to the Greek cardinal's death on the return journey. Cardinal Angelo Capranica (the younger brother of Callixtus III's faithful friend) had been equally unsuccessful on his round of the Italian courts, the exhaustion of his travels and negotiations causing him to retire to his bed on his return to Rome. At the same time, Cardinal Marco Barbo (one of the many cousins promoted by Paul II) had been rebuffed by one eastern European monarch after another. Despite such setbacks, Sixtus IV had managed to despatch a combined Neapolitan–Venetian fleet under the Neapolitan Cardinal Oliviero Carafa into the eastern Mediterranean. Here they had inflicted defeats on several Ottoman squadrons, before capturing and burning to the ground the Anatolian port of Smyrna (modern Izmir). However, relations between the Venetians and the Neapolitans had then ruptured to such an extant that the fleet split in two, with its separate parties sailing home in opposite directions.

Only Cardinal Rodrigo Borgia's mission had achieved success of lasting value and Sixtus IV would not forget this. The extent of Borgia's success can be seen in the fact that when Ferdinand and Isabella produced their first son, they would ask their friend the cardinal to be his godfather.

During Cardinal Rodrigo Borgia's fourteen-month visit to Spain he appears to have been on his best behaviour. The papal legate provoked not a hint of scandal – apart from his visit to his three illegitimate children in Xàtiva, which was passed off as a purely familial visit to see his 'nephews'. However, on his return to Italy, the vice-chancellor quickly became involved in a relationship with a striking red-headed thirty-two-year-old called Vanozza de' Cattanei. According to one story, during his recuperation in Pisa following the shipwreck, he was invited as a guest of honour to a banquet. Most contemporary commentators agree that Vanozza was a courtesan, born of the numerous families of minor nobility who had fallen on hard times during this period. For an unmarried (or 'fallen') daughter, opportunities were stark: the nunnery, or spinsterhood as a virtual servant in the family. In Vanozza's case it appears she was previously married, but her husband died. As a widow, her choice to become a discreet courtesan would not have been so difficult. At any rate, her beauty and intelligence appear to have fascinated the forty-three-year-old cardinal – to such an extent that he quickly became close to her. This is no euphemism. Beside the evident sexual attraction, Cardinal Rodrigo Borgia soon began to feel a deep emotional attachment to Vanozza. Indeed, their relationship would eventually become as close to a marriage as his position permitted. He quickly instructed his trusted legal adviser and confidant Camillo Beneimbene to arrange for

Vanozza to be married to an elderly lawyer named Domenico di Rignano, who would have been fully cognizant of the situation, being handsomely rewarded for his tact and complaisance. Cardinal Rodrigo Borgia would even go so far as to attend the wedding ceremony: the most striking figure present in the full panoply of his scarlet cardinal's robes and hat.

The following year, Vanozza would give birth to a son, who was named Cesare. An indication of Sixtus IV's closeness to his vice-chancellor can be seen in the fact that five years later he would legitimize Cesare in an official document which explicitly stated that Cesare was 'the son of a cardinal and a married woman'. It now emerges that some years previously Sixtus IV had also legitimized Cardinal Rodrigo Borgia's oldest son Pedro Luis. This generosity on Sixtus IV's behalf would prove of vital significance in the years to come. For a start, it meant that Pedro Luis and Cesare were now free to enter the Church, if their father so wished it. And there is no doubting that Cardinal Rodrigo Borgia already had ambitions for his sons.

Sources indicate that Vanozza's husband soon died, but this did not prevent the widow from producing three more children: Juan in 1476, Lucrezia in 1480 and Jofrè in 1482. Vanozza's children would from the outset be Cardinal Rodrigo Borgia's favourites, held in far higher regard than his previous three children. It is also known that he publicly acknowledged them as his own, though it is uncertain as to when precisely this took place. Cardinal Borgia ensured that Vanozza was set up in some comfort in her own apartments in Rome, as well as purchasing for her a plot of land close to the ancient Baths of Diocletian, where she would build a house of her own. Later, Vanozza is known to have acquired three of Rome's finest hostelries, accommodation for visiting minor foreign dignitaries on their pilgrimages to the eternal city. In this way, she also became a woman of means in her own right, while Cardinal Rodrigo Borgia obtained for her another suitably aged, complaisant husband. In time, a third husband would be required to fill this post – a certain Carlo Canale, who was appointed a governor of the city gaol known as Torre Nuova.

When these four Borgia children grew beyond infancy, they were removed from the care of their mother Vanozza and placed under the charge of Cardinal Rodrigo Borgia's cousin Adriana de Milà. She was the niece of his cousin Cardinal Luis Juan del Milà (who had now, of course, long since removed himself permanently to Spain). Adriana de Milà was married into the powerful Roman aristocratic Orsini family, providing a useful alliance for Cardinal Rodrigo Borgia. Evidently, Vanozza was not considered capable of providing a suitable upbringing for the positions Cardinal Rodrigo Borgia had in mind for his favourite children. The full extent of these sensational filial ambitions remained, for the time being, confined to the vice-chancellor's mind alone.

CHAPTER 4

THE WAY TO THE TOP

I N 1474 IT BECAME clear that Sixtus IV had ambitions for further
expanding his papal power. By now he had created no less than six
'nephew cardinals' amongst the della Rovere family and the closely related
Riario family. In the summer he ordered his nephew Cardinal Giuliano
della Rovere to lead the Papal Forces into the Papal States and reassert
papal control over the towns of Todi and Spoleto, some eighty miles north
of Rome. And in October he announced that Giovanni della Rovere,
the younger brother of Cardinal Giuliano, was betrothed to Giovanna,
daughter of the powerful condottiere Federigo da Montefeltro, whom he
created Duke of Urbino.

The new-style Jubilee year in 1475 (which Paul II had so hoped to
celebrate) opened with a visit to Rome by King Ferrante of Naples. Sixtus
IV despatched Cardinal Rodrigo Borgia and Cardinal Giuliano della
Rovere to greet the king as he entered Papal Territory at Terracina, some
fifty miles south-east of Rome, and then to escort the royal procession to
the Holy City. This was a signal honour for Cardinal Rodrigo Borgia, but
also suggested that Borgia was no longer regarded as the senior cardinal
amongst the College of Cardinals. Instead, he would be expected to share

this role with the Pope's nephew Cardinal Giuliano della Rovere. King Ferrante brought with him a 'brilliant suite' consisting of his knights and leading attendants. According to Pastor, 'the number of falcons which the Neapolitans brought with them completely cleared the City and all the neighbourhood of owls'. Ferrante's visit was to cement relations between the Pope and his powerful southern neighbour; but Sixtus IV also held secret talks with Ferrante, with the aim of establishing a league of Italian and European powers, and calling for a council to decide on action against the Ottomans. Yet, as ever, this idea failed to attract much support, especially amongst the European powers. 'The wars in France, Burgundy, Germany, Hungary, Poland and Spain, and other countries were . . . the reason why so few people came.'

Despite the growing della Rovere family power, Sixtus IV made sure that Cardinal Rodrigo Borgia was still accorded the importance that was his due. In 1477 the Pope entrusted his vice-chancellor with the important task of acting as papal legate to Naples. This was hardly surprising, as Cardinal Rodrigo Borgia had gone out of his way to charm King Ferrante during his visit to Rome – to such an extent that the fifty-four-year-old king had personally requested the Pope to send him as papal legate to Naples to officiate at his marriage to his twenty-two-year-old first cousin Joanna of Aragon.* Thus in August Cardinal Rodrigo Borgia travelled to Naples in suitable pomp, where he not only married the royal couple, but was honoured with the task of conducting the coronation of Queen Joanna. Later, Ferrante would name Cardinal Rodrigo Borgia as the godfather of the royal couple's first son: Juan, Prince of Asturias. The Vice-Chancellor was forging a close personal alliance with Naples.

Such is the history as it appears. On the other hand, a good indication of the real daily dealings in Italy of the period is given by the following extended story, garnered from the papal records by Peter de Roo. King Ferrante may have been well disposed towards his friend Cardinal Rodrigo Borgia, but there were limits to his generosity when it came to more tangible matters. Owing to 'the scarcity of bread in the city of

---

* Ferrante's first wife had died twelve years earlier.

Rome at the time', Sixtus IV had entrusted his legate with the delicate task of persuading King Ferrante to allow Naples to export wheat to Rome. This was a perennial problem. Since the ancient Roman era, the city of Rome itself had always been nothing more than a centre of power: it actually produced nothing. Everything had to be imported: from food to commodities, as well as materials of all kinds.

King Ferrante assured his friend Cardinal Borgia that he would export the required wheat. But this promise proved empty. In increasing desperation, Sixtus IV would write to Ferrante no less than three times, but nothing happened. At last, when Cardinal Borgia was finally leaving Naples, Ferrante conveyed to the Pope 'that he had given orders to transport the cereals to the City straightway'. Yet when Borgia arrived back in Rome, he found that:

> No wheat came in sight, food grew ever scarcer in Rome and the prices rose in such a manner that the Pope was obliged to exhaust his treasury and to contract heavy debts in order to keep his people alive.

With the treasury empty, Sixtus IV was forced to borrow 25,000 gold ducats from Cardinal d'Estouteville, pledging him the 'rights and revenues' for the castles of Frascati and other localities. Sixtus IV also called upon Cardinal Rodrigo Borgia for assistance, involving 'all that the latter could afford, namely, in two instalments, the sum of fifteen thousand gold ducats'. In return, the Pope mortgaged to Borgia the city of Nepi, as well as other nearby properties and castles in the papal territories – on condition that Borgia spent 2,500 florins repairing and equipping these fortresses. Fortunately, during his long years as vice-chancellor, Cardinal Rodrigo Borgia had developed an eagle eye where the accounts were concerned. This meant that when the Pope came to repay his debt to his loyal friend, 'A mistake in the calculation was . . . discovered.' Although the Pope had borrowed the money from Borgia in gold florins, he was paying it back in 'baiocchi' (copper florins).

The College of Cardinals begged the Pope to make some compensation for this loss of their colleague, but the destitute Pontiff, unable to find any means to do so, resolved to grant him Nepi and the other cities for the whole of his lifetime.

All this gives but a glimpse of the difficulties encountered – and created – by Italian leaders of the period, as well as how they dealt with them. Such circumstances should be borne in mind as a constant background to the more plain facts which describe the surface history.

At this point, possibly in an attempt to relieve his financial situation, Sixtus IV became involved in a daring plan which would shock the entire Italian peninsula. Florence was officially a republic, but for the last thirty-five years its de facto rulers had been the powerful Medici banking family, whose head was now Lorenzo de' Medici (known as 'the Magnificent'). For half a century or so, the Medici Bank, with its branches all over western Europe, had acted as the papal bankers, facilitating the transfer of papal dues, benefices and other assets to Rome in the form of bankable money. This could prove a complex undertaking, yet one which allowed for considerable profit. For instance, at one point the Greenland bishopric had paid its papal dues to the Bruges branch of the Medici bank in the form of sealskins. The bank would estimate the worth of these items and transmit a receipt to its Rome branch, ordering payment of this amount into the papal account. On top of this, the bank also made money on the various and varying exchange rates, e.g. the Florentine florin was at this time worth around four pence more in Florence than it was in London.

However, four years previously Sixtus IV had transferred the lucrative papal bank account to the rival Salviati Bank in Florence, when the Medici Bank refused to grant him a loan of 40,000 ducats to purchase the town of Imola. This small Romagna city happened to be a vital link in the trade route from Florence across the Apennines to the Adriatic Coast, and the Medici were correctly suspicious of Sixtus IV's motives. Since then the Salviati Bank, led by the powerful Pazzi family in Florence, had sought means of trying to overthrow the Medici rulers. In this they had been covertly backed by Sixtus IV.

The excuse for the Pazzi to strike was provided by Lorenzo de' Medici, when he refused to let Sixtus IV's new appointment as Archbishop of Pisa,* his relative Francesco Salviati Riario, from entering Florentine territory to take up his post. Under normal circumstances, the Medici knew that in time of trouble they could always hire the nearby army of Federigo da Montefeltro to defend the Republic, and their position as its rulers. However, there had been a subtle shift of allegiances here, now that Sixtus IV had familial ties by marriage with Montefeltro, and had also declared him Duke of Urbino. Word was secretly passed by the Pazzi conspirators to Montefeltro that he should surreptitiously send his troops to the western border of Urbino, ready to march into Florentine territory. Such was the clandestine nature of this move that conclusive evidence of it only came to light as late as 2004 with the discovery of a coded letter. Whether or not this word was passed by the Pazzi conspirators, or possibly through the indirect orders of Sixtus IV himself, remains unknown. For centuries the accepted version has been that the Pazzi conspirators approached Sixtus IV with their plan to assassinate Lorenzo the Magnificent and topple the Medici, but were informed that as pope he could not sanction the taking of life. On the other hand: 'he was content to give all favour and the support of troops or whatever else might be necessary to attain our ends'.

In this instance, Sixtus IV did not take his vice-chancellor into his confidence, for he knew that Cardinal Rodrigo Borgia and Lorenzo the Magnificent had formed a close friendship. Lorenzo the Magnificent had recently endowed the University of Pisa, with the aim of educating his son Giovanni there, prior to him taking high office in the Church. Cardinal Rodrigo Borgia, knowing his son Cesare to be the same age as Giovanni, and also having great ambitions for his son in the Church, had written to Lorenzo the Magnificent that he wished to send his son to the University of Pisa as a 'pledge of the great love' he felt for the Medici family, and so that Cesare would be under Lorenzo's 'wing and protection'. There could

---

* Pisa was the Florentine Republic's second city, and its main coastal port.

be no question of Cardinal Rodrigo Borgia suspecting the slightest hint of any plot against the Medici.

On 26 April 1478 the Pazzi conspirators launched their daring plot to assassinate Lorenzo de' Medici and members of his family, then take over Florence. In the event, the plot went disastrously wrong when Lorenzo de' Medici managed to elude his assassins – though his beloved brother Giuliano was less fortunate, being stabbed to death in Florence Cathedral. In the aftermath, chaos reigned throughout the city. Cardinal Raffaele Riario, the Pope's cousin, who happened to be passing through the city that day, was lucky to be merely arrested by the authorities. Francesco Salviati Riario, the Pope's appointee as Archbishop of Pisa, had no such luck. Having secretly made his way into Florence in an attempt to aid the plotters, he was taken captive by a mob of Medici supporters. Dressed in the full panoply of his archbishop's robes, he was publicly hanged from a widow of the Palazzo Vecchio (the Old Palace, Florence's town hall), while the mobbed cheered below.

Although Sixtus IV publicly denied all knowledge of the plot, there was no doubting his outrage at the treatment of his two relatives, both senior officers of the Church. The imprisonment of a cardinal and the lynching of an archbishop – in his full ceremonial robes, no less – were not to be forgiven. This was nothing less than sacrilege! Sixtus IV forthwith excommunicated the entire population of Florence and declared war upon the city state, urging his ally King Ferrante of Naples to invade.

The following year, the Neapolitan army, under Ferrante's son Alphonse, Duke of Calabria, defeated the Florentine forces at Poggio Imperiale. Consequently, Lorenzo de' Medici decided to make a move of foolhardy daring: he would travel to Naples and visit Ferrante, to see if they could sort out their differences. In the event, Ferrante was so impressed at Lorenzo's brave gesture that he made peace with Florence.

Sixtus IV's ventures into foreign policy had been – and would prove to be – disastrous. Suffice to say that his complex finagling eventually caused the main Italian powers to unite against him, forcing him to embark upon a policy of peace, rather than interference. His reign would also be notorious for the issue of two significant papal bulls. In November

1478 he published the bull which established the Spanish Inquisition in Castile – though admittedly he was later to be alarmed by the excesses of this institution which he had set in motion. Secondly, in 1481 he would grant the Portuguese the right to buy slaves along the West African coast.

However, the 1480s would also see a more sensational development, heralding a potential disaster for western Christendom. In the summer of 1480 the whole of Italy had been shocked by the news that 120 ships of the Ottoman navy had launched a surprise attack on the port city of Otranto, on the heel of Italy just fifty miles across the Adriatic from the Balkan territory taken by Mehmed the Conqueror. After a short siege, 20,000 Turks had occupied the city, slaughtering 12,000 of its inhabitants, and shipping off 5,000 women and children into slavery. The Ottoman commander Gedik Ahmed Pasha had ordered the local bishop and military commander to be publicly sawn in half before the remaining population. This was evidently a prelude to a larger invasion of the Italian peninsula. King Ferrante despatched troops from Naples in an attempt to retake Otranto, laying siege to the city in May 1481. Then, just as suddenly as the Ottoman invasion had begun, it was over. News had reached Gedik Pasha from Istanbul that Mehmed the Conqueror had unexpectedly died at the age of just forty-nine. (According to Mehmed's biographer, Colin Heywood: 'There is substantial evidence that Mehmed was poisoned, possibly at the behest of his eldest son and successor Bayezid.') Gedik Pasha at once withdrew from Otranto. Italy had escaped by a miracle.

One of Sixtus IV's sole successes lay in his aggressive policy in the Romagna and the Marches. These territories had once been Papal Territory, and Sixtus IV's attempts to recover them began laying the foundations for a unified Papal Territory. Many of the small city states, run by unsavoury petty tyrants such as Malatesta, were taken back under papal rule, with Sixtus IV appointing relatives as their rulers. Rome now came to be regarded as a significant player on the Italian political scene – in line with, if not quite equal to, Naples, Venice and the like.

Cardinal Rodrigo Borgia may not have featured directly in the events previously described, but he would certainly learn lessons from Sixtus

IV's mistakes. He would also learn from Sixtus IV's attempts to bolster
the power and territory of the papacy. Such events would prove formative
when the time came for Borgia himself to face these same problems.

Sixtus IV would also leave a considerable cultural legacy: a foundation for glories to come. The Sistine Chapel, the Vatican Library, the
introduction to Rome of Renaissance artists such as Botticelli and
Ghirlandaio (to whom Michelangelo would be apprenticed), all represented a considerable heritage. He also built a second bridge across the
Tiber, the Ponte Sisto, replacing the Ancient Roman Ponte Aurelius,
which had been destroyed during the eighth century when the Lombards
overran the city. Here in solid form was a symbol of the growing rebirth
of ancient classical culture. Also indicative of the Renaissance was Sixtus
IV's papal bull issued to all bishops allowing the corpses of executed
criminals to be used for artistic and scientific purposes. A direct result
of this would be Renaissance artists such as Leonardo da Vinci and
Michelangelo exploring human anatomy first-hand; in the scientific field
it would lead eventually to the first complete modern work on anatomy
by the great Flemish physician Vesalius. Here was a genuine advance
in human knowledge, extending Renaissance understanding beyond
the classical 'authorities'. Prior to this, physicians had relied upon the
anatomy of the second-century Greek physician Galen, whose human
anatomical treatises mistakenly included various organs which had been
based on his dissections of monkeys and pigs.

In 1483 the redoubtable Cardinal d'Estouteville would die at the age
of seventy-one, leaving Cardinal Rodrigo Borgia as the wealthiest member
of the College of Cardinals. However, by now a majority of the college
were cardinals appointed by Sixtus IV. By this stage the Pope himself had
been ill for some time, beset by gout and a host of other ailments. Thus
it came as little surprise when he finally died, in the following year, at the
age of sixty. This left two major figures in contention for the next papacy:
Sixtus IV's nephew Cardinal Giuliano della Rovere, and the ever-present
vice-chancellor Cardinal Rodrigo Borgia. For the first time, Borgia knew
that he had a realistic chance of becoming pope.

Following the death of Sixtus IV Rome was swept with an outbreak of anarchy and rioting, as the long-suffering people of the city went on the rampage, venting their murderous fury on all in authority, settling old scores and so forth. Such a state of affairs was becoming a regular occurrence during the interregnum, when at least technically no one was in ultimate charge of the city. However this occasion was more than usually violent, on account of Sixtus IV's unpopularity amongst the people, who had watched his lavish spending on such costly projects as the Sistine Chapel, and the consequent neglect of their needs. Cardinal Rodrigo Borgia had taken the precaution of hiring troops to guard his palace, as did Cardinal Giuliano della Rovere, who was so afraid to venture out that he even missed his uncle's funeral. An indication of the chaotic conditions in the Holy City can be seen in the fact that troops loyal to Caterina Sforza seized the papal fortress, the Castel Sant'Angelo, in the name of her husband Girolamo Riario, who had been appointed by Sixtus IV as Lord of Imola and other estates in the papal territories. The situation would only be restored when the College of Cardinals bought back the fortress for 8,000 ducats, so that it could remain under the control of whoever was elected the next pope.

Meanwhile, in preparation for the conclave, Cardinal Rodrigo Borgia began, in the words of the ambassador for Ferrara, 'working hard for support'. In practice, this involved, according to the ambassador to Florence: 'trying to corrupt the world, some with money, some with jobs, others with benefices'. At the same time, Cardinal Giuliano della Rovere busied himself with similar lobbying tactics. The conclave itself opened on 26 August 1484 with twenty-five cardinals present. After several rounds of tactical voting, as well as widespread 'promises' from Cardinal Giuliano della Rovere and Cardinal Rodrigo Borgia, it soon became clear that neither could attain the necessary two-thirds majority. In the words of John Julius Norwich: 'And so, rivals as they were, they worked together to ensure that . . . the cardinals' choice should fall on some second-rate puppet whom they could dominate.'

The man who fitted this role was the fifty-two-year-old Cardinal Giovanni Cibo, whose father came from a well-known Genoese family, and whose mother was of Greek origin. Cibo's early years had been spent in the court at Naples, where his father had been appointed viceroy during the difficult years before Ferrante I's ascension to the throne. These formative years appear to have induced in Cibo a Neapolitan penchant for extreme superstition, a trait which would increase with age. Later he would live in Rome, where his father became a senator under Callixtus III, and here Cibo was encouraged to enter the Church, his father ensuring that he joined the retinue of a distinguished cardinal. From then on, nepotism enabled him to rise through the ranks, becoming a bishop at the age of thirty-five, and a cardinal six years later through the influence of his avuncular mentor Cardinal Giuliano della Rovere. By this time, he had also managed to father several illegitimate children, as well as indulging in his penchant for good-looking young men. But all this activity seems to have taken its toll. In the words of papal historian Noel,

> He slept almost continuously, waking to gorge himself on gargantuan meals. That he did not drink heavily has enabled respectable historians to describe him as 'abstemious'. He grew grossly fat and increasingly inert.

If Cardinal Rodrigo Borgia and Cardinal Giuliano della Rovere could agree on little else, they certainly agreed that this was just the man they were looking for as their papal choice. Such a lifestyle would undoubtedly ensure him an early death. Giovanni Cibo took on the papal name of Innocent VIII.

Cardinal Giuliano della Rovere naturally assumed that he would be the power behind the throne, after all the assistance he had given Cibo in his earlier years. However, Cardinal Rodrigo Borgia was now so practised in his role as vice-chancellor that his services had become indispensable to any pope, let alone one as indolent as the present incumbent. Consequently, Innocent VIII soon found himself dithering between two sources of contrary advice, earning himself the popular nickname 'The Rabbit'. And so things continued, with the new pope showing no signs of dying, despite his increasing bouts of lassitude. Indeed, despite regular input from his two close advisors, his papacy gradually began to

take on a distinct character of its own – featuring nepotism, greed, inept-
itude and ever-increasing superstition. As we have already seen, this last
trait would result in two notorious bulls: one appointing Torquemada as
Grand Inquisitor of the Spanish Inquisition, and the other resulting in
the mass burning of 'witches' throughout the German states.

However, it was Innocent VIII's greed and lavish spending habits
which were to inspire his most ingenious decision. Though some
commentators have suggested that this ingenuity bears the hallmark of
his money-raising vice-chancellor. Either way, Innocent VIII pronounced
that from now on indulgences could be purchased not only for oneself,
but also for friends and relatives who were already dead, so that they too
could gain remission for their time in Purgatory. This proved a resounding
success – for, as the papal historian Christopher Lascelles has observed:
'Who would not make sacrifices if they knew that they could shorten the
suffering of their mothers, fathers, siblings, cousins and even friends.'

It can hardly be claimed that Innocent VIII emulated Nero in fiddling
while Rome burned, yet his lack of interest in the state of the city and
its inhabitants would have a similar effect. Virtual anarchy continued to
reign in the streets, with the more distinguished aristocrats and cardinals
forced to fortify their palazzi and maintain ever-increasing private armies
for their personal protection. Meanwhile, the whole of Italy too might
have fallen into a similar state, but for the Florentine ruler Lorenzo the
Magnificent, to whom Innocent VIII virtually delegated his diplomatic
powers.

The influence of Lorenzo the Magnificent on the Italian political
arena during this period was masterly, and is difficult to underestimate.
As we have seen, Florence had for some time maintained no permanent
army of its own, and had been reliant upon using its considerable riches
(mainly accumulated by the Medici Bank) to hire the finest condottieri
to fight its battles. But the fallacy of this policy had been exposed during
the Pazzi conspiracy and Lorenzo's subsequent daring dash to Naples,
placing himself at the mercy of King Ferrante. Instead, Lorenzo the
Magnificent decided to try a different tack. From now on, he sought to
establish a network of interlocking alliances, thus achieving a balance of

power which brought about a period of unusual peace throughout the Italian peninsula. Venice, Milan, Naples, Rome, and lesser allied states such as Genoa and Ferrara, were all persuaded that it was in their interests to maintain the status quo. Lorenzo the Magnificent's influence was reinforced by his exploitation of the one commodity in which Florence excelled. Namely, its culture. As the birthplace of the Renaissance, the superiority of Florence's artists, sculptors and architects was undisputed. Consequently, Lorenzo the Magnificent's diplomatic skills were reinforced by his lending out Florence's best-known artists and architects to other states. These creators added kudos and distinction to the cities where they created their works, gifts which not only engendered good will, but also the spread of Renaissance culture. This policy would result in the likes of Michelangelo travelling to Rome, and Leonardo da Vinci to Milan. In later years it would also encourage Umbrian artists such as Perugino and Raphael to work in Rome, bestowing on the ruined classical city a Renaissance splendour second only to that of Florence.

As we have seen, in recognition of Lorenzo the Magnificent's supreme diplomatic skills Innocent VIII would characterize him as 'the needle of the Italian compass' – guiding the nation through the potentially hazardous seas of internecine rivalry between its major city states. Here, too, the highly experienced papal vice-chancellor found himself understanding further skills. Though in this case, as we shall see, the success of Lorenzo the Magnificent's diplomacy only served to blind Cardinal Rodrigo Borgia to its essential precariousness. Worse still, it also sowed the seeds of far greater ambitions in Borgia's mind. This peace was achieved within Italy through diplomacy, intermarriage between leading families in separate city states, and the delicate maintenance of a balance of power blocs: in particular, through the continuation of the Milan–Florence–Naples axis. However, such a policy was very much limited to this particular time and place in history. Any attempt to extend such methods beyond the Italian peninsula, where different circumstances prevailed, was untried. Meanwhile, Cardinal Rodrigo Borgia continued to build up his immense wealth, while also ingratiating himself with Innocent VIII, who came to rely increasingly upon the services of his loyal and demonstrably capable vice-chancellor.

At the same time, there is no denying that Cardinal Rodrigo Borgia continued with his characteristic secular pursuits. Though, as Pastor remarks:

> Of the worldly cardinals, Ascanio Sforza, Riario, Orsini . . . Giuliano della Rovere . . . and Rodrigo Borgia were the most prominent. All of these were directly infected with the corruption which prevailed in Italy amongst the upper classes in the age of the Renaissance. Surrounded in their splendid palaces, with all the most refined luxury of a highly developed civilization, these cardinals lived the lives of secular princes, and seemed to regard their ecclesiastical garb simply as one of the adornments of their rank. They hunted, gambled, gave sumptuous banquets and entertainments, joined in all the rollicking merriment of the carnival-tide, and allowed themselves the utmost license in morals; this was especially the case with Rodrigo Borgia.

Pastor was writing in the Wilhelmine period (Germany's equivalent of Britain's Victorian age) and certainly reflected its moral conservatism. He makes no bones about the fact that he abhorred Cardinal Rodrigo Borgia. Yet there is no mistaking the fact that many of Borgia's fellow cardinals behaved in a similar fashion. Likewise, the examples set by the popes under whom he served as vice-chancellor would, if anything, appear even worse. Cardinal Rodrigo Borgia may have exemplified the louche behaviour of his time, but there is – as yet – little to suggest that he was exceptional in this sphere. And he certainly did not let his indulgence in worldly pleasures in any way interfere with his duties as vice-chancellor. That these were onerous (as well as being financially rewarding) is beyond dispute. His appointment to this position by no less than five popes over thirty-six years indicates his exceptional abilities in the role. In this context it is worth repeating the claim of his secretary, Sigismondo de' Conti, that during Borgia's long reign as vice-chancellor, 'he never missed a single consistory unless prevented by illness from attending, which very seldom happened'. Furthermore: 'Throughout the reigns of

Pius II, Paul II, Sixtus IV and Innocent VIII he was always an important personage; he had been Legate in Spain and in Italy. Few people understood etiquette so well as he did.'

De' Conti was undoubtedly a loyal secretary, and somewhat dazzled by his master. Even so, the disapproving Pastor still finds it worthwhile to include de' Conti's rounded characterization of his master:

> He knew how to make the most of himself, and took pains to shine in conversation and to be dignified in his manners. In the latter point his majestic stature gave him an advantage. Also, he was just at the age, about sixty, at which Aristotle says men are wisest; robust in body and vigorous in mind . . . He was tall and powerfully built; though he had blinking eyes, they were penetrating and lively; in conversation he was extremely affable; he understood money matters thoroughly.

Though Pastor cannot refrain from appending that 'his portraits . . . all agree in giving him a crooked nose'. Thus was the man on the brink of ascending to the papal throne.

To the exasperation of both Cardinal Rodrigo Borgia and Cardinal Giuliano della Rovere, Innocent VIII, their stopgap pope, the 'second-rate puppet whom they could dominate', took an unconscionable long time dying. Although Innocent VIII was never in good health, it is not precisely clear when the period during which 'he slept almost continuously', rising only to consume vast meals, passed from lassitude into genuine bedridden illness. However, by the summer of 1492 it became clear that the end was approaching. Contrary to their customary practice, the senior cardinals did not flee the stifling heat of Rome for their country villas. Instead, they were in regular attendance at the Pope's bedside, each assessing the likely length of his survival. Yet as we have seen, even at the end, Innocent VIII still remained in sufficient control of his faculties to order the distribution amongst his relatives of the 47,000 ducats remaining in the papal coffers. This was the act that provoked Cardinal Rodrigo Borgia and Cardinal Giuliano della Rovere to reveal their true

colours: their near brawl over the dying pope's bed was but the prelude to
the bitter struggle which would dominate the coming conclave. On 25 July
1492 Innocent VIII finally died at the age of sixty, after eight years on the
papal throne. His only lasting monument was the Villa Belvedere, built
on the cool slopes overlooking the Vatican, the Tiber and the rooftops of
Rome, towards the distant hills. This would cost 60,000 ducats (almost a
quarter of the entire annual papal income at the time) and was the work
of the Florentine Renaissance artist and architect Antonio del Pollaiuolo.
It was the first villa built in Rome since ancient times.

Thirteen days later would begin the most notorious conclave the
Vatican had ever witnessed, featuring two of the most skilled, devious
and powerful operators in the College of Cardinals.

CHAPTER 5

A NEW POPE IN A NEW ERA

JUST BEFORE DAWN ON 11 August 1492, with the hot Roman night lit by flickers of lightning and distant rumbles of thunder, Cardinal Rodrigo Borgia emerged through the doors of the Sistine Chapel as Pope Alexander VI. Unable to contain his triumphant joy, he raised his arms and declared to the flickering, flare-lit faces of the waiting crowd: 'I am pope! I am pope!'

The crowd acclaimed his election with cheers. The new pope had long established himself as a popular figure amongst the Roman populace. They had warmed to his charms, his public displays of benevolence, as well as his evident enjoyment of life. And within no time he would further gain their respect. In the thirty-six days following the death of Innocent VIII and Alexander VI's accession as pope, the customary interregnum mayhem in the streets had resulted in no less than 220 murders within the walls of the city. Within days of gaining a new pope, Rome would be transformed: all mercenaries and private armies were expelled from the city and a new armed City Watch was created. This was a considerable force, which even extended to squads of armed men charged with guarding the bridges across the Tiber. By 3 September the two most powerful criminals, the del Rosso brothers, had been hunted down, publicly hanged and their family house bludgeoned to rubble. Lesser known criminals were simply rounded up and flung into the dungeons of the Castel Sant'Angelo. At the same time the city justice system was completely overhauled. New judges were appointed to try malefactors and hear civil complaints; more important still, they were paid a sufficient salary to enable them to resist bribes, while they and their houses were protected by the new constabulary.

Such moves hardly endeared Alexander VI to the aristocratic families of Rome, in particular the Orsini, who had previously regarded themselves as friends of the new pope. They had also commanded feudal respect amongst their favoured citizens and prided themselves on their company of armed, liveried retainers. Now, instead of queuing up outside the grand palazzi of the aristocrats to beg favours, the citizens were free to register their complaints to newly appointed magistrates, for the most part educated men who had studied law. And on Tuesdays, every week, even the Pope himself was available for any man or woman to petition. Such practices were unprecedented in the entire history of the papacy. Yet Alexander VI was fully conscious of the deeper historical precedent for what he was doing. As he wrote at the time: 'The town which gave Law to the world, should be prepared to give laws to itself.'

However, if Alexander VI was to live up to his classical predecessors, the inhabitants of the eternal city expected more than laws. Another tradition harking back to classical times was the provision of entertainments: the famous *pane e circo* ('bread and circuses'). And here too the new pope would not disappoint. His coronation would prove a spectacular event:

> Alexander VI . . . rode through Rome in a resplendent ceremony
> to take possession of the Lateran, attended by thirteen squadrons
> of cavalry, twenty-one cardinals, each with a retinue of twelve,
> and ambassadors and noble dignitaries vying in the magnificence
> of their garments and equestrian draperies. Streets were decorated
> with garlands of flowers, triumphal arches, living statues formed

by gilded naked youths and flags displaying the Borgia arms, a rather apt red bull rampant on a field of gold.

Although it is said that the intense summer heat, heavy robes and sheer oppressiveness of the cheering crowds lining the route caused the normally robust Alexander VI to faint, he soon recovered. And he would prove his usual ebullient self when it came to presiding over the entertainments laid on during the following days. Most spectacularly, these included a series of public bullfights in the piazza in front of St Peter's. Here the Borgia flags flying the 'red bull rampant' proved even more apt. There was no mistaking Alexander VI's message: the Spanish had arrived. And for the most part, even Alexander VI's detractors were grudgingly impressed. The contemporary Roman diarist Stefano Infessura was forced to concede that Alexander VI's reign 'began most admirably'.

A more controversial note was introduced by Alexander VI's decision to move his family into the Vatican apartments. Once again, such action was unprecedented. Yet it could be argued that this was proof of positive qualities in Alexander VI. Previous popes had kept their women, children or handsome young men under wraps, so to speak. No matter that their existence was common knowledge. Alexander VI was merely being open and honest, even if the behaviour so revealed was hardly in keeping with the highest office in the Church. To say nothing of the example which it set. Yet it could be argued that he was also exhibiting a quality which struck a chord with many Italians. Namely, love of family. Indeed, he seems to have preferred stable, uxorious relationships – apart from the odd sensational episode, which usually occurred after a period when he was obliged to observe priestly standards. All this is hardly exceptional, especially when judged by the standards of many of his predecessors in this office, as well as the general upper-class morality of the period.

Even so, there was no denying that the disparity between the sixty-year-old pope's age and that of his new 'bride' – the eighteen-year-old Giulia Farnese – caused something of a scandal. And then there was the fact that she was now to all intents and purposes his third 'wife'

– following his long relationships with his two previous 'wives'. Firstly, the unknown woman who had given birth to his three oldest children: Pedro Luis, Isabella and Girolama; and then Vanozza de' Cattanei, who had given birth to his four favourite children: Cesare, Juan, Lucrezia and Jofrè; and now a teenager . . .

Alexander VI had fallen in love with Giulia Farnese some two years previously. She was widely known as '*Giulia la bella*' on account of her radiant beauty, and contemporary descriptions reinforce this view. According to a letter written by her brother-in-law Puccio Pucci, Giulia was 'a most beautiful creature. She let her hair down before me and had it dressed; it reached down to her feet; never have I seen anything like it.' Another source speaks of her as having 'dark colouring, black eyes, round face and a particular ardour'.

Initially, despite being married off to the hapless Orsino Orsini, Giulia had moved into the Palazzo Santa Maria, residence of her lover's cousin Adriana de Milà, which was in the Portico district, beside the grand steps which led up to St Peter's. But it is now that the complications in this arrangement become apparent. Besides being Cardinal Rodrigo Borgia's cousin, Adriana de Milà also happened to be the mother of Guilia Farnese's official husband Orsino Orsini. And on top of this, Adriana was also looking after the cardinal's young daughter by his previous mistress Vanozza Cattanei – namely his beloved twelve-year-old Lucrezia.

When Cardinal Borgia became pope, both Giulia and Lucrezia were moved into the Vatican, whereupon Giulia was dubbed by the Roman public 'The Bride of Christ'. All the indications are that the teenage Giulia and the adolescent Lucrezia, after an initial wariness and jealousy, soon developed a fond, sisterly relationship. Surprisingly, it was Alexander VI who now developed feelings of jealousy. Whether in her innocence or out of some remnant feelings of marital orthodoxy, Giulia Farnese now took to visiting her husband at his twelfth-century castle in Basanello, some fifty miles north of Rome. On one occasion Alexander VI wrote:

We have heard that you have again refused to return to us [from Basanello] without Orsini's consent. We know the evil of your soul and of the man who guides you, but would never have thought it possible for you to break your solemn oath not to go near Orsino. But you have done so . . . to give yourself once more to that stallion. We order you, under pain of eternal damnation, never again to go to Basanello.

From this it would appear that Giulia was far from being cowed by the imposing preeminence of her lover. Indeed, this evidence suggests that she was possessed of the carefree wilfulness of youth. As well as a certain naivety. At least in her eyes, her marriage to Orsini was not the sham that was intended. Alexander VI's characterization of Orsini as 'that stallion' is undeniably at odds with other contemporary descriptions mentioned earlier ('devoid of meaningful self-confidence', etc.). Though in this instance, the Pope's words could well have been prompted by the intense jealousy of an older man.

On the other hand, there was soon to be an even more inexplicable complication. In 1492 Giulia Farnese gave birth to a daughter, who was named Laura. It has been widely assumed that Alexander VI was the father of Laura, but there is convincing evidence that this was not the case. In the words of Mallet: 'Alexander showed no interest in the child during his lifetime,' and later Laura would marry into none other than the della Rovere family, the sworn enemies of the Borgias. Whatever the truth of this matter, Alexander VI certainly forgave his beloved young Giulia, who even managed to persuade the Pope to promise that he would award a cardinalate to her twenty-five-year-old brother Alessandro in the coming year.* Giulia Farnese would retain Alexander VI's fond affections for some years to come, though to his irritation she refused to remain constantly at his side in the Vatican. In 1494 she would set off for Capodimonte, on the shores of Lake Bolsano, some sixty miles north-west of Rome, where she would spend some months attending the bedside of her fatally ill brother Angelo.

---

* This favour would in time take on some significance: forty years later, Cardinal Alessandro Farnese would become Pope Paul III.

At the same time as Lucrezia Borgia and Giulia Farnese moved into the papal apartments, Alexander VI's three sons by Vanozza de' Cattanei – the seventeen-year-old Cesare, sixteen-year-old Juan,* and the eleven-year-old Jofrè – would also take up residence in the Vatican. Alexander VI had long had great futures in mind for his sons. From the outset, Cesare had been groomed for high office in the Church. As we have seen, this had been made possible when Cardinal Rodrigo Borgia had managed to persuade his friend Sixtus IV to issue a bull legitimizing the five-year-old Cesare, without which he would not have been able to assume any official position in the Church. Ten years later, the vice-chancellor had seen to it that Cesare was appointed to the Spanish bishopric of Pamplona, and other benefices had soon followed. Upon Alexander VI's ascension to the papal throne, he had ceded his major post as Archbishop of Valencia to his son Cesare. And as we shall see, in the following year he would appoint Cesare a cardinal. Despite such efforts on behalf of Cesare, it seems that Alexander VI's real favourite was the younger Juan, in whom he placed his greatest hopes. One of his first acts on ascending the papal throne had been to issue a bull legitimizing Juan, and he would also make him Captain-General of the Papal Forces. In view of Alexander VI's as yet unrevealed territorial ambitions, this latter was in fact a much more significant appointment than all those accorded to the older Cesare. It so happened that Juan had also succeeded to the title which had previously been held by Alexander VI's first son (by the unknown mother) Pedro Luis, who had been born in 1462. Whilst Alexander VI had been vice-chancellor, he had managed to persuade his friend King Ferdinand of Aragon to appoint his firstborn Pedro Luis to a newly created Spanish title: Duke of Gandia. At the time, the title of duke was an honour usually reserved for members of the royal family; significantly, this dukedom also included the familial Borgia estates in Spain. In order to consolidate the standing in Spain of Pedro Luis, 1st Duke of Gandia, in 1485 his father had organized for him to become betrothed to Maria Enriquez, the first cousin of King Ferdinand of Aragon. Unfortunately, all this had come to nothing when Pedro Luis had died in

---

* Sometimes known by the Italian version of his name, Giovanni.

1488. But the far-sighted Cardinal Rodrigo Borgia had prepared Pedro Luis for such an eventuality. In his will Pedro Luis had bequeathed his title to his nine-year-old half-brother Juan Borgia, as well as 10,000 ducats to be set aside as a dowry for his half-sister Lucrezia. In this way, Juan Borgia became 2nd Duke of Gandia. And on top of this he also inherited his older brother's Spanish fiancée Maria Enriquez, whom he was now set to marry in Barcelona, in the presence of King Ferdinand of Aragon and his wife Queen Isabella of Castile. Meanwhile, Alexander VI's youngest son, the eleven-year-old Jofrè, was likewise included in his dynastic plans: he was betrothed to Sancia of Aragon, the illegitimate granddaughter of King Ferrante of Naples, who rewarded young Jofrè with the Neapolitan royal title Prince of Squillace.

Alexander VI's relations with Milan were already cordial, thanks to Cardinal Ascanio Sforza, the man who had finally been persuaded to sway the conclave in his favour. As we have seen, Cardinal Sforza had received handsome financial compensation for his vote. On top of this, the grateful Alexander VI also appointed Cardinal Sforza to his old job as vice-chancellor, at the same time gifting him the luxurious palazzo which he had made his residence and chancellery headquarters. In return, Cardinal Ascanio Sforza arranged through his brother Ludovico Sforza, the de facto ruler of Milan, for Alexander VI's beloved thirteen-year-old Lucrezia to be married by proxy to the twenty-five-year-old Giovanni Sforza, Lord of Pesaro, a widower who was an illegitimate descendant of the ruling Milanese family. Giovanni Sforza also held the added advantage that he was a skilled condottiere, whose domain on the north Adriatic Coast was allied to both Milan and Venice.

Four months later the actual marriage took place, when the couple met for the first time in Rome. This was to be but the first of many grand occasions staged during the reign of Alexander VI, and would last over several days. On 9 June, to the acclaim of the Roman crowds, Giovanni Sforza entered the city through the Porto Santa Maria del Popolo. He rode at the head of a large train, which included forty laden pack animals accompanied by no less than 280 flamboyantly liveried attendants on horseback. From here he was escorted past the cheering multitude to the Vatican, where he ceremonially kissed the Pope's foot. After a series of festivities, the actual marriage ceremony took place on 12 June, when Lucrezia's brother Juan gave away the bride. The scene was described in some detail by Johann Burchard, the Pope's master of ceremonies:

> The great hall, known as the Sala Reale, and other rooms were covered abundantly with tapestry and velvet hangings. At the end of the Sala Reale, to the right of the entrance, a throne approached by four steps was set up for the Pope . . . On the orders of the Pope, Don Juan Borgia, Duke of Gandia, son of the Pope and brother of the bride, escorted his sister . . . through the rooms, Don Juan on the left of his sister, whose robe had a long train carried by a young black girl . . .
>
> After her came Giulia Farnese, the concubine of the Pope, followed by some 150 Roman ladies, who proceeded past the Pope on his throne. Despite my strict instructions, none of these ladies genuflected before the Pope, apart from his daughter and one or two others who were near to her . . . His Holiness was dressed in his official vestments and a crimson hood. On either side of his throne he was attended by ten cardinals, five priests on his right, five deacons on his left. Then the Duke of Gandia approached with his sister to kiss the Pope's foot, and they were followed by all the ladies. On the Pope's left, by the wall, stood Don Cesare Borgia, the Bishop-Elect of Valencia.

At this point the editor of Burchard's diaries, Geoffrey Parker, interjects the telling point that: 'As only an ecclesiastic, Cesare had very definitely a secondary rank at this wedding, where his brother Don Juan was the leading figure.' He also mentions how other diplomats observed that Cesare was hardly noticeable amongst all the cardinals and clergy, 'and was necessarily far outshone by his younger brother'. There was no doubt that Cesare felt himself humiliated, and 'jealous of Juan's rank and opportunities'.

The ceremonies continued: 'When all the ladies had kissed the Pope's foot, Don Giovanni with Donna Lucrezia on his left, knelt on two cushions before the Pope.' The official wedding ceremony, along with the exchange of vows, now took place, presided over by 'Don Leonello, the Bishop of Concordia', who eventually placed the rings on the fingers of the bride and groom. Afterwards, the bridal feast was staged in the Sale Reale.

> An assortment of all kinds of sweets, marzipans, crystalized fruits and wines were served . . . over 200 dishes were carried in by the stewards and squires, each with a napkin over his shoulder, offering them first to the Pope and his cardinals, then to the bridal couple, and lastly the guests. Finally they flung what was left out of the window to the crowds of people below in such abundance that I believe more than 100 pounds of sweetmeats were crushed and trampled underfoot.

That evening a grand dinner was staged. After the more faint-hearted guests had retired, this developed into a boisterous and bawdy affair, where, according to gossip retailed to the diarist Infessura: 'all the guests were at the same table and each cardinal had a young lady next to him'. As more wine was taken, the male guests 'threw sweetmeats into the cleavages of many ladies, especially the good-looking ones'. This was followed by 'a series of entertainments', which, according to Burchard, included a comedy which was acted with 'such elegance that everyone loudly applauded'. On the other hand, Infessura insists that 'the meal went on until long after midnight', when 'lascivious comedies and tragedies were performed which provoked much laughter in the audience'. Afterwards, Alexander VI personally accompanied the bride and groom to the next-door Palazzo Santa Maria, where, according to Infessura, 'the groom took marital possession of his bride'. Such public witnessing of the first conjugal intimacy was traditional in Italy at the time, as well as elsewhere in Europe. Indeed, Geoffrey Parker insists that this quaint custom was 'to ensure that legal requirements for completing the ceremony of marriage were fulfilled'. Consequently a bloodied sheet was frequently exhibited to demonstrate for all to see that intercourse had taken place, as well as the fact that the bride had been a virgin. As we shall see, Alexander VI's 'witnessing' (which almost certainly did not include a bloodied sheet) would take on a crucial significance in the marriage of Don Giovanni and his bride Donna Lucrezia. Whether or not Alexander VI then returned to the party is not stated. However, by this stage its guests – in all likelihood aided and abetted by Cesare Borgia – appear to have resorted to their own entertainments, for as Infessura reports: 'I could tell you many other things, but I will not recount them because some are not true and those that are, are anyway unbelievable.'

Some two months later, Alexander VI took a further step to consolidate his position. Cesare Borgia, as well as Alessandro Farnese, were just two of the unprecedented twelve cardinals which the Pope appointed in September 1493. Although Sixtus IV and Innocent VIII had both ignored the ban on appointing more than one nephew-cardinal on their accession, neither had dared to appoint more than eight new members to the College of Cardinals.

However, Alexander VI's controversial move was not prompted so much by nepotism as by his diplomatic plans. Apart from his son and his mistress's brother, 'the rest were candidates for the rulers of Europe and the Italian states, with the marked exception of King Ferrante'. But then, as we have seen, he had favoured King Ferrante by marrying his young son Jofrè to the king's illegitimate daughter.

It is not difficult to determine Alexander VI's ulterior motives behind all this diplomatic manipulation. Just over four months prior to his election, Lorenzo the Magnificent, 'the needle of the Italian compass', had died in Florence, succumbing to the family curse of gout at the age of just forty-nine. Alexander VI was striving to take over where Lorenzo had left off, continuing the policy of peace between the competing city states of the Italian peninsula. But it is evident that he wished to extend his own influence beyond Italy, too: hence the links with Spain. He had also covertly put out feelers with the aim of establishing links with France. At the same time, fortune had delivered a timely gift into his hands, which considerably lessened the threat from the Ottomans in the east.

When Sultan Bayezid had ascended the Ottoman throne in 1481, after the 'untimely' death of his father Mehmed the Conqueror, his younger half-brother Cem had attempted to rally support for his own right to the throne. Eventually, Cem was defeated and fled for protection to the island of Rhodes, which was at the time ruled by the Knights of St John. Not wishing to antagonize the Ottomans, the Knights had contacted Sultan Bayezid II. Sultan Bayezid II had agreed to pay Cem's captors an annual stipend of 45,000 ducats as long as they promised to detain Cem under house arrest. Subsequently Cem had been shipped to France and had eventually ended up in Rome, under the charge of the Pope. Sultan Bayezid II had then sent gifts to the Pope, at the same time continuing to pay the annual stipend to whoever held Cem captive. As far as Alexander VI was concerned, this not only provided a useful source of income, but as he understood from the Sultan in Istanbul it also ensured that the Ottomans would launch no further attacks on Italy. This freed his hand to pursue his diplomacy, seeking alliances with western powers such as France and Spain.

In March 1493 Columbus arrived back in Spain with the sensational news that he had discovered lands on the western side of the Atlantic, which he assumed to be Cathay (China) or part of the Indies. 'He brought back parrots, gold and several indigenous people from the lands he had visited.' Alexander VI was quick to grasp the possibilities and dangers which this discovery presented to Christendom. Portuguese sailors, under the inspiration of Prince Henry the Navigator, had already laid claim to the mid-Atlantic Azores and Cape Verde Islands. From here they had pressed on to West Africa, where they had embarked upon the slave trade, which, as we have seen, received the blessing of Sixtus IV. Meanwhile, in 1488 Bartholomew Diaz had rounded the Cape of Good Hope.

However, Columbus's discovery opened up the prospect of competition, and even war, between two major Catholic countries – namely, Spain and Portugal. In order to avert this clash, Alexander VI hastily issued a papal bull, which would become incorporated in 1494 into the Treaty of Tordesillas. This would divide the world beyond Europe between Spain and Portugal. In order to achieve this division, Alexander VI drew a line on a map down the middle of the Atlantic, along the north–south meridian some 370 leagues* to the west of the Cape Verde Islands. All land discovered to the east of this line could be claimed by the Portuguese; all land to the west could be claimed by the Kingdom of Castile (effectively Spain.) This was seen as having favoured King Ferdinand of Aragon, further strengthening his ties with Alexander VI.

The Treaty of Tordesillas was intended to gift what became known as America to Spain, with Portugal being gifted Africa, and the prospect of trade with India. Unfortunately, owing to the lack of knowledge of the coastline of South America at this time, the Pope's line sliced through the eastern protuberance of the sub-continent. A lasting legacy of this mistake is that while most of South America is Spanish-speaking, its easternmost country, Brazil, speaks Portuguese. In the years to come, as Alexander VI's legacy became more and more blackened by his enemies, the Treaty of Tordesillas would continue to be seen as his greatest and most lasting legacy. With this, he had incontestably left his mark upon the world.

Despite all Alexander VI's diplomatic efforts to befriend each of the major city states and unite Italy in peace, there was no doubting the fact that he had lasting enemies. As we have seen, immediately after Alexander VI's election in August 1492 his rival Cardinal Guiliano della Rovere had fled to the fortress of Ostia. Eight months later, Cardinal della Rovere had slipped away and taken ship for France. Here he soon made contact with his backer in the election, King Charles VIII, and began scheming against Alexander VI. The other well-connected cardinal who had fled Rome after the election of Alexander VI was Cardinal Giovanni de' Medici, the second son of Lorenzo the Magnificent. The seventeen-year-old cardinal had taken up residence in Florence, where his older brother Piero de' Medici had succeeded his father as ruler of the republic. The twenty-year-old Piero de' Medici (who was to gain the nickname 'Piero the Unfortunate') was

---

* Approximately 1,110 miles.

highly unsuited to his new role. Piero had been spoilt as a child and has been justly characterized as 'impatient, arrogant and spiteful'. Such qualities were hardly aided by his tendency to sloth and his impatience with administrative details, which he largely handed on to his secretary. Meanwhile, to add to these difficulties, Florence itself was now in a state of increasing ferment, owing to the fire and brimstone sermons being delivered by the fundamentalist priest Girolamo Savonarola. As previously mentioned, Savonarola had famously prophesied the death of Lorenzo the Magnificent and Innocent VIII, as well as that of King Ferrante of Naples. Ferrante was now approaching his seventies, with his rule becoming increasingly tyrannical and paranoid. His mental state had barely been stable at the best of times. According to Burckhardt's celebrated characterization of Ferrante: 'Besides hunting, which he practised regardless of all rights of property, his pleasures were of two kinds: he liked to have his opponents near him, either alive in well-guarded prisons, or dead and embalmed, dressed in the costume which they wore in their lifetime.' One of his favourite habits was to take his guests on a guided tour of this 'museum of mummies'. It was now becoming evident to all, both from Ferrante's behaviour and his physical health, that it would not be long before Savonarola's third prophecy was fulfilled.

Another of Savonarola's prophecies spoke of how he had seen 'the Sword of the Lord [suspended] over the Earth', and he had now taken to cowing his fearful congregations with apocalyptic prophecies that 'a new Cyrus* would cross the mountains to act as God's scourge and destroy everything in his path'. Without naming the Medici rulers, he also began excoriating 'the rich' and 'great lords' for their extravagant decadence, as opposed to the poverty and simple way of life advocated by Jesus Christ.

Alexander VI's policy of uniting Italy and establishing good relations with neighbouring foreign powers such as Spain and France had in fact achieved a certain success. But although his diplomatic dealings were an astute blend of guile and wisdom, knowing precisely how to play the

---

* The great sixth-century king of the Medes and the Persians, who had launched a fearsome conquest of the Middle East, and, in freeing the Israelites from Babylon, came to be seen as an unwitting instrument of God.

weaknesses and strengths of the leaders with whom he dwelt, the same cannot be said for his dealings with his children. Here, his undoubted love for them appears to have completely blinded him to their faults and frailties. As a result, the dynastic marriages he had arranged on their behalf soon proved not only unsuitable mismatches, but soon began to unravel under disastrous circumstances.

The marriage of the twelve-year-old Lucrezia Borgia to Giovanni Sforza began to fall apart almost before it had begun. During the weeks following the somewhat excessive marriage ceremony, Sforza became increasingly dissatisfied with what he described as his 'white marriage' to his adolescent bride. It seems that the young girl had not in fact submitted to her bridegroom's sexual demands, even on their wedding night, despite the claims of the witnesses to the contrary. This is hardly surprising, given the protected and privileged upbringing the innocent bride-to-be had received in the palazzo of her aunt Adriana de Milà. From her earlier years, any romantic girlhood dreams of marriage which Lucrezia may have harboured had suffered a severe setback owing to the treatment of her beloved father, and his duplicitous political ambitions for his daughter.

When Lucrezia was just ten years old, her father had promised her in marriage to the well-connected Spanish nobleman Querubí Joan de Centelles, Lord of Val d'Ayora, in an attempt to reinforce his standing in Spain. This had been a purely formal arrangement, performed by proxy, without requiring Lucrezia to leave the Roman palazzo of her guardian Adriana de Milà. Even so, Lucrezia must have harboured some secret expectations of the aristocratic Spanish lord whom she expected would one day become her husband. But she was to be disappointed. Within months, Lucrezia's proposed bridegroom had broken the arrangement by marrying someone else. Yet her father was not to be put off, and just a year later Lucrezia had been betrothed once more to a Spanish grandee, this time to Don Gaspar de Procida, son of the Count of Almeira and Avisa. Again, the innocent young Lucrezia must have built up her hopes. But a year later her father had become Alexander VI and his ambitions for his daughter had changed a further time. As Lucrezia's biographer Sarah Bradford put it:

The new pope no longer saw his daughter's future in Spain. As Alexander trod the difficult path of endeavouring to preserve the independence of the papacy between conflicting interests, Lucrezia would be the victim of his shifting pattern of alliances.

It was hardly surprising that the thirteen-year-old Lucrezia was wary of her third fiancé, Giovanni Sforza. He was already a divorcee, and she had been married to him within months of their sudden and unexpected engagement. Even so, these traumatic manipulations by her father would prove to be only the beginning of her psychological problems.

The marriage of Lucrezia's older brother, the seventeen-year-old Juan, had if anything proved even more disastrous. As we have seen, Juan Borgia had now become the 2nd Duke of Gandia after the death of his older half-brother Pedro Luis, at the same time also inheriting his nineteen-year-old fiancée Maria Enriquez. During his adolescence, Juan had taken full advantage of his father's power and wealth as vice-chancellor to lord it over his peers. Even at this early age he had quickly gained a reputation as a roisterer in the taverns and a womanizer. When news of this behaviour reached his father's ears, the Pope decided it was time his young son took up his responsibilities. 'Juan, Duke of Gandia . . . had been sent off to Spain in the care of a guardian appointed by Alexander and under a deluge of papal admonitions to behave himself.' It was here that he was to marry Maria Enriquez in Barcelona Cathedral, deemed to be an occasion of such import that it would be graced by the attendance of King Ferdinand and Queen Isabella. If Alexander VI imagined that his worries over Juan were now a thing of the past he was to be much mistaken.

Reports of Juan's continuing misbehaviour soon began arriving at the Vatican. Worse was to come at his marriage, where,

His tactless arrogance had offended the king and queen, and immediately after this wedding he went off on such a wild spree of drinking, gambling and whoring that it was said to be improbable that he had bothered to consummate the marriage.

Far from strengthening relations with Spain, the 2nd Duke of Gandia's behaviour appeared to be on the point of wrecking them.

As for the marriage of Alexander VI's youngest son Jofrè, this too was to prove an embarrassment, which would in time lead to even greater consequences. Jofrè had been just twelve years old when he married Sancia of Aragon, the sixteen-year-old illegitimate granddaughter of King Ferrante of Naples. As we have seen, her dowry to young Jofrè had been the gift of the royal princedom of Squillace, making Alexander's son a princely member of the Neapolitan ruling dynasty; however, in return for this over-lavish gift, the ageing King Ferrante had extracted a promise from the Pope that on the king's death the Pope would recognize as king of Naples his son Alfonso, the father of Sancia by one of his mistresses. In the light of previous claims to this throne by the Royal French House of Anjou during the time of Pius II some thirty-five years earlier, Alexander VI should have been wary of making such a promise. But in his estimation such matters were now all a thing of the distant past. Likewise, he had hardly foreseen the treatment which would be meted out to his innocent young son Jofrè. His bride Sancia, growing up amidst the louche and unnerving surroundings of King Ferrante's Neapolitan court, had already established a reputation as a tempestuous and wilful young lady, who was hardly impressed by the courtly, reserved manners of the somewhat overawed, pubescent Jofrè. Here was yet a third Borgia marriage whose consummation would require further encouragement.

On the other hand, no such encouragement was needed where the sexual exploits of Alexander VI's older son Cesare was concerned. By now Cesare Borgia had grown into 'the handsomest man in Italy'. During his university days at Pisa he had excelled, and even the contemporary historian Paolo Giovio, no friend of the Borgias, had been forced to concede: 'he had gained such profit [from his studies] that, with ardent mind, he discussed learnedly the questions put to him both in canon and civil law'. However, Cesare's intended friendship with Giovanni de' Medici, so encouraged by both their fathers, failed to materialize. The young Cesare Borgia may have been Bishop of Pamplona, but Giovanni de' Medici had already become a cardinal. Both were the same age and both were gifted with exceptional intellectual talent, but the competitive Cesare was evidently determined to outshine his fellow student in all departments. Cesare cut a striking figure: fashionably dressed, sporting a red-tinged beard, his long dark hair flowing about his shoulders. And just like his father he had an animal magnetism for women – a talent he put to a use hardly becoming for the Bishop of Pamplona. Cardinal Giovanni, on the other hand, was a podgy youth, less assured in his public manner, yet secretly convinced of his own superiority. As Cesare Borgia's biographer Sarah Bradford puts it:

> Giovanni, legitimate son of one of the great families of Italy, probably secretly despised and resented the bastard son of the Catalan Borgia as an upstart, and possibly Cesare sensed this, for the two young men were never friends.

This assessment reveals but half the truth. Cardinal Giovanni de' Medici may well have despised the Borgias, but when he left Pisa and took up his position at the College of Cardinals in Rome he quickly learned to fear them. As we have seen, when Alexander VI became pope, Cardinal Giovanni de' Medici fled for Florence: the break between the Borgias and the Medici was now plain for all to see. And while Cardinal Giovanni de' Medici attempted to bolster the weak regime of his older brother Piero de' Medici, Cesare inherited his father's title of Archbishop of Valencia, and moved across to Trastevere to take up residence at the Vatican. A description of Cesare Borgia by a friend, dating from this period, is particularly revealing:

> The day before yesterday I went to find Cesare at his house in Trastevere. He was on the point of going out for the hunt; he was wearing a worldly garment of silk and had his sword at his side . . . . He possesses marked genius and a charming personality. He has the manners of a son of a great prince; above all, he is lively and merry and fond of society. [He] has never had any inclination for the priesthood.

The following year, his appointment by his father Alexander VI as a cardinal would provoke consternation. It is said that when Alexander VI's unforgiving rival Cardinal Giuliano della Rovere heard of Cesare's elevation he emitted 'a loud exclamation' and was overcome with such apoplectic rage that he was obliged to retire to his bed for several days. Typically, the news of his appointment reached Cesare Borgia when he was on holiday with his mother Vanozza de' Cattanei in the country-side north of Rome. Here he was engaged in an angry dispute with the governors of Siena, who had disqualified his horse from winning the famous Palio because he had instructed his jockey to cheat. In fact, this would turn out to be more than just an outbreak of petulant arrogance on Cesare's behalf. By now the race had been awarded to Francesco Gonzaga, the Marquis of Mantua, and Cesare Borgia's intemperate letters to the marquis threatened to have serious diplomatic consequences. Alexander VI's political strategy required Gonzaga to be a reliable ally. This would be the first serious indication that Cesare Borgia would not always be amenable to his father's wishes.

CHAPTER 6

'THE SCOURGE OF GOD'

ON 22 JANUARY 1494 the aged King Ferrante of Naples was stricken by a fainting fit as he was dismounting from his horse. For two days he lay near to death, angrily waving away the priest in attendance to take his last confession. On 25 January he finally died, thus fulfilling Savonarola's third prophecy. But this was not the only supernatural portent to be fulfilled at the opening of this fateful year. According to the generally sober words of the contemporary historian Guicciardini:

> Those who professed to tell the future, either by science or by divination, all claimed that the omens foretold that great changes and terrible events were about to happen. Strange things happened in all parts of Italy, giving rise to rumours. Three suns were seen one night in Puglia, surrounded by clouds and loud thunder and lightning. Near Arezzo soldiers on horseback were seen in the sky, accompanied by loud drumming and trumpeting. Sacred statues started to sweat in many places and monstrous births took place, filling the people with fear and dread.

King Ferrante's throne was now claimed by his son Alfonso II. But 'the greatest peace and tranquility [which] reigned everywhere' in Italy was already beginning to fall apart. Prior to his death, King Ferrante had fallen out with Ludovico Sforza, ruler of Milan. In retaliation, Sforza took the unprecedented step of asking the French king Charles VIII to march into Italy and invade Naples, reminding Charles VIII that under the ancient Anjou claim to the throne he was the rightful heir. This claim was further encouraged by Cardinal Giulio della Rovere, who well understood the danger posed to Alexander VI by a French army marching through Italy on its way to Naples. As it happened, the twenty-four-year-old French king needed little encouragement on this score.

Charles VIII had been something of an oddity since childhood. During his minority, a regency had run the country, while tutors had attempted unsuccessfully to instill in him the rudiments of literacy. Instead, he had been reading – and inspired by – tales of chivalry. Charles VIII longed to emulate such noble deeds, though his physical attributes were hardly suited to this purpose. Short, hunchbacked, with flapping, oversized feet (each with six toes), he suffered from the inbreeding which had begun to afflict the French royal family in its attempt to retain its familial power. Charles VIII's appearance was matched by his behaviour. He had a habit of muttering ominously to himself, instilling fear in his attendants; while all who encountered him were struck by his ugliness: 'he seemed more like a monster than a man'. Another observed: 'His prodigious sexual appetite was accompanied by an overweening ambition that bordered on megalomania.' It suited Charles's guardians to leave him to his own devices, but by the time he attained his majority and ascended to the throne, there was little they could do. Any prospect of modifying his behaviour, or indeed reforming his character, appeared long lost. Charles VIII would remain an awkward blend of ignorance, naivety and ambition. (The apparent normality of his official portrait is a masterly fiction.)

On hearing that King Ferrante had died, Charles VIII decided it was time to live out his childhood dreams of chivalry. He would lead the French army over the Alps into Italy, and then have himself crowned king of Naples. But this was just the beginning. From Naples he would sail east with a huge fleet to launch a crusade in the Holy Land, and here he would retake Jerusalem.* The French court and his powerful former guardians were in many ways only too pleased to have him out of the way, and acquiesced to his plans.

France was at the time the most powerful country in Europe, and its army of 30,000 men appeared unstoppable as it poured over the Alps into Italy. In Milan, Charles VIII was warily welcomed by Ludovico Sforza, who was beginning to have misgivings about what he had set in motion. From Milan, Charles VIII continued south towards Florence. It looked as if Savonarola's apocalyptic prophecy about 'the scourge of God who would cross the mountains and destroy everything in his path' was coming true.

Catastrophe upon catastrophe now followed in rapid succession. As Charles VIII's massive army swept south, approaching Florentine terri-tory, the young Piero de' Medici rashly decided to try and emulate his father – who had staked his life and the future of Florence on his brave dash south to meet King Ferrante of Naples. Only Piero de' Medici was no Lorenzo the Magnificent, and his impetuous ride across the mountains to meet Charles VIII only served to emphasize Piero's weakness. On arriving at the French king's camp he found himself overawed. Immediately he agreed to all Charles VIII's demands that his French army be allowed to march down the Italian peninsula unopposed. Defensive castles were to be surrendered and Florentine territory would be violated with impunity. On Piero de' Medici's return to Florence the population erupted in fury, forcing him and his brother Cardinal Giovanni de' Medici to flee the city. Whereupon the mob broke into the Palazzo Medici and ransacked its treasures. A republican government, heavily influenced by Savonarola, now assumed control of the city, which would soon succumb to a funda-mentalist Christian rule.

Alexander VI watched impotently from Rome as Charles VIII

---

* Ironically, there was more than a grain of justification in this particular instance of Charles VIII's megalomania. As we have already seen, amongst several titles which came with 'King of Naples' was also the ancient title 'King of Jerusalem'.

continued his march south towards the Holy City. Was Rome to suffer the same fate as Florence? Would Charles VIII simply depose the Pope, in line with the calls of Cardinal della Rovere? Alexander VI now faced the supreme test of his political and diplomatic skills. Both the Orsini and the Colonna families fled, defecting to the French. The Colonna seized the fortress at Ostia, and French troops took Civitavecchia. Rome was now cut off from the sea, its main supply route. Worse was to follow. French troops moving south through the countryside near Viterbo, some fifty miles north of Rome, surprised a party of noble ladies travelling south towards the capital. It soon became clear that amongst these were Giulia Farnese and Adriana de Milà, the Pope's young mistress and his sister, returning from a visit to the Farnese castle at Capodimonte. Fortunately for Alexander VI, their captor was willing to accept a ransom for the safe return of the ladies to Rome. Meanwhile, the French army continued its march south.

Alexander VI understood that armed resistance was futile, and despatched his few remaining forces south to Naples, personally retiring into the Castel Sant'Angelo. On 14 December 1494 the French army entered Rome unopposed, marching in through the northern gate, the Porta del Popolo. The crowds lining the streets watched aghast as the army marched into the city. It would take from three o'clock in the afternoon until nine o'clock at night for the columns of French foot soldiers, Swiss and other mercenaries, as well as squadrons of cavalry, to pass through the city gate – finally followed by the thunder of thirty-six huge cannon dragged across the cobbles by lines of carthorses. To the surprise of all, Charles VIII himself held back from entering the city: 'Charles delayed his own entry until New Year's Eve, a day approved by his astrologers.'

The following day Charles VIII lined up his cannon outside the Castel Sant'Angelo and ordered the Pope to come out and meet him. Alexander VI chose to remain put. But after one shot from a French cannon caused a large section of the ancient medieval walls to crumble in a cloud of dust, Alexander VI capitulated.

But it was at this point that Alexander VI played his masterstroke. After suitable negotiations through intermediaries, it was arranged that

Alexander VI and Charles VIII should stage a formal meeting in the Vatican gardens. Alexander VI emerged from the papal residence clad in the full panoply of his papal regalia, his demeanour embodying his sacred authority. Here was the spiritual ruler of all Christendom, Christ's vicar on earth through his divine succession from St Peter. The naive young Charles VIII was more than impressed. As he approached the Pope, the French king sank to his knees, attempting to kiss the pontiff's foot. With gracious benevolence Alexander VI raised the awkward young king to his feet. He welcomed him as a son and pronounced on him a blessing. It immediately became clear to Cardinal Giuliano della Rovere that there would be no question of deposing the Pope.

Even so, Charles VIII's troops now occupied the Holy City; and his military commissioners advised him to insist that Alexander VI should contribute from the papal coffers towards the expense of the last stage of the French army's journey to Naples. Alexander VI was obliged to agree to this demand. Then Charles VIII expressed his wish that the Pope should surrender Cem, the brother of the Ottoman sultan who was being held captive by the Pope. Charles VIII was mindful of using Cem as a bargaining tool against the Ottomans, when he eventually set out on his crusade to take Jerusalem. Cem remained 'a valuable hostage and a potent symbol of resistance to the sultan's rule'. With a characteristic sleight of hand, Alexander VI agreed to surrender Cem to Charles VIII, but only on condition that the annual 45,000 ducats paid by Sultan Bayezid continued to be paid into the papal coffers. This proved but a small victory, yet a victory nonetheless; it also gave Alexander VI further insight into Charles VIII's attitude. Money appeared not to be of fundamental importance to the king. Acting out his naive chivalric dream was his prime concern. Why, he had even brought along with him the legendary symbol of his nation's greatness: Charlemagne's sword.*

Despite Alexander VI's psychological insight into the unworldly character of Charles VIII, there was no denying that the French king

---

* Charlemagne ('Charles the Great') was the ninth-century Frankish king, ruler of the Carolingian Empire which emerged during the Dark Ages to cover much of western Europe, in what many regarded as a second Roman Empire.

retained a distinctly down-to-earth attitude towards the practicalities of supporting his large army. The price for him leaving the Holy City would be costly indeed. Along with the French army went a 'contribution' Alexander VI had been required to donate. This took the form of a train of no less than nineteen mules laden with boxes of jewels, gold plate and other treasures (almost five times as many as it had taken him to purchase the papacy). And as a show of good will, Alexander VI was asked to appoint his son Cardinal Cesare Borgia as papal legate to accompany the king. This meant that to all intents and purposes the Pope's son was a hostage, held to prevent Alexander VI from entering into negotiations with any power which might be opposed to Charles VIII's presence in Italy. This was a humiliation indeed for Cardinal Cesare Borgia, who remained averse to even the slightest affront to his dignity. And to make matters worse, on the second evening of their march south, the French king and his entourage (which naturally included the papal legate) were received at the city of Velletri by the local bishop, a post occupied by Cardinal Giuliano della Rovere. Yet it was now that Cardinal Cesare Borgia showed his true mettle. In the words of the Pope's master-of-ceremonies Johann Burchard, who remained back in Rome:

On 30 January [1495] news arrived that Cardinal Cesare Borgia had eluded the grasp of the French king and escaped from Velletri disguised as a groom from the royal stables, and that he had travelled so swiftly that he slept that night in Rome.

In order to elude any pursuers, and to avoid embroiling his father, Cardinal Cesare Borgia slipped out of the city when the gates opened at dawn. Further insult was added to Cardinal Giuliano della Rovere's hospitality when it was discovered that Cardinal Cesare Borgia had also engineered the escape of nine mules from the treasure train. On inspection, it was found that beneath the coverings in the boxes on the remaining mules there was nothing but stones and earth.

When Charles VIII was informed of the news that he had been outwitted in such a fashion, he was overcome with a violent rage.

According to those present, he yelled: 'All these Italians are filthy curs and none is worse than their Holy Father!' The French king was probably mistaken in his guess that Alexander VI was behind this escapade. In fact, Alexander VI even sent an apology to the king for his son's behaviour, realizing that it was in his best interests to keep on the right side of Charles VIII, at least for the time being. This entire incident bears all the hallmarks which would come to be associated with Cardinal Cesare Borgia: deception, daring, avoidance of humiliation – and, lastly, vicious revenge for any possible insult (especially where the women in his family were concerned).

This last particular trait is best exemplified by an earlier episode, retribution for which would only come at a later date. The details are simple enough. When Charles VIII had despatched his forward troops to take Rome, all soldiers had been under the strictest instructions to respect the inhabitants of the Holy City and their property. In order to make this abundantly clear, the French king had instructed his commanders to erect gallows in the public squares, where any soldier who disobeyed the order banning all looting and pillage could be hanged as an example. However, such good intentions had been impossible to maintain in practice. Burchard records how:

> On their way into the city the French troops forced an entrance into houses on either side of the road, throwing out their owners, horses and other goods, setting fire to wooden articles and eating and drinking whatever they found without paying anything.

A few days later he records how 'even the house of Donna Vanozza Cattanei, the mother of Cardinal Cesare Borgia, did not escape'. To add insult to injury, the looters also 'robbed her of 800 ducats and other possessions of value'. Cardinal Cesare Borgia could only watch impotently from the Castel Sant'Angelo, where he had taken refuge with his father. Yet he would not forget this insult to his mother.

After escaping from the clutches of Charles VIII at Velletri and riding post-haste through Rome, Cardinal Cesare Borgia had taken refuge in the countryside some seventy miles north of the city at the papal stronghold of Spoleto. Here he had lain low for two months before quietly slipping back into Rome. Some days after his return, a troop of Swiss mercenaries belonging to the French force occupying the city were on patrol and happened to march into St Peter's Square. Whereupon they found themselves surrounded by 200 armed Spanish soldiers, who immediately set upon them. After the ensuing melee, twenty-four Swiss soldiers lay dead, with many more severely wounded. It was Swiss soldiers who had been responsible for ransacking the house of Vanozza de' Cattanei, and Cardinal Cesare Borgia had taken particular note of this. Cardinal Cesare Borgia may have been a prince of the Church, but where lay matters were concerned he settled scores with military efficiency. Alexander VI may have been impressed, but he was also aware that once again his son had acted far beyond the limits of his father's wishes.

By now Alexander VI was maintaining a difficult, if duplicitous balance requiring all the diplomatic skills he had learned as vice-chancellor. Prior to Charles VIII leaving Rome, the Pope had been forced to issue a public statement confirming his friendship with the French king, and Rome itself had remained garrisoned by a French force. At the same time, Alexander VI had opened up secret negotiations with the ambassadors of Milan, Venice and Spain, with the aim of forming an alliance to drive the French from Italy. Ludovico Sforza of Milan had realized that inviting Charles VIII into Italy had been a colossal mistake, and was even willing to make amends by allying with Milan's traditional enemy Venice. At the same time, King Ferdinand of Aragon was determined to thwart Charles VIII's declared aim of deposing the Aragonese ruler of Naples, Alfonso II. Naples had traditionally been within the Spanish sphere of influence, and he had no wish to cede this to France.

Yet there had been no stopping the French army as it marched south towards Naples, sweeping all before it. Fortresses were overrun and their garrisons put to the slaughter. Meanwhile in Naples the populace, along with a section of the nobility, were soon in open rebellion against their hated Aragonese masters. Sizing up the situation, the new king Alfonso II decided to abdicate in favour of his son Ferrantino.

Taking his treasures with him, [Alfonso II] set sail for the island of Sicily and, in the city of Mazara, retired to a monastery of Olivetans, devoted himself to Christian penance, and died on 19th of November of that same year.

As the French came even closer, the new King Ferrantino also decided to flee, first to the offshore island of Ischia, and then to Sicily. He was accompanied by his loyal entourage, which included Alexander VI's thirteen-year-old son Jofrè and his tempestuous bride Sancia of Aragon. On 22 February 1495 Charles VIII entered Naples in triumph, with Cem, the half-brother of Sultan Bayezid, at his side. This was intended to emphasize that capturing the city was but the first step in his crusade to retake Jerusalem.

As we have seen, by ancient right the Kingdom of Naples remained under the suzerainty of the Pope, with any new ruler requiring his blessing. Indeed, it was customary for the Pope to conduct the coronation of the king of Naples, and Charles VIII was eager to take part in this noble, ancient ceremony, which appealed to his sense of chivalry. In an attempt to persuade Alexander VI into recognizing him as ruler of Naples, Charles VIII now offered the Pope the generous sum of 150,000 ducats, followed by an annual tribute of 40,000 ducats. To the disappointment of Charles VIII, his new friend Alexander VI failed to respond. But this was just a minor setback. Charles VIII had been welcomed into Naples, for, according to Guicciardini: 'The reputation of the last two kings was so odious among all the people and almost all the nobles, and there was much eagerness for the French regime.' Here Charles VIII found what he called 'an earthly paradise', where he was able to indulge his prodigious sexual appetite to the full. Contemporary sources claim that he was given a book filled with pictures of Neapolitan ladies, which he would slaver over in anticipation of their favours. Other sources provide a variant on this characteristic picture. Despite his obsession with copulation, Charles VIII is said to have insisted upon the novelty of never having the same woman twice.

In the midst of his idyll, Charles VIII was to receive some bad news. Bayezid II's half-brother Cem was found to have died in his sleep. He was just thirty-six years old. Inevitably, poison was suspected, with Alexander VI being seen as responsible. According to Guicciardini and others, Alexander VI had Cem poisoned 'with a white powder' – a conjecture which has persisted through the ages. This is unlikely on several counts. Firstly, the Pope would have found difficulty in hiring an assassin in the French court; and secondly, Alexander VI was in favour of Charles VIII continuing on his crusade to Jerusalem, which was the purpose of Cem's presence in his entourage. On top of this, the death of Cem meant the end of Sultan Bayezid II's annual stipend of 45,000 ducats which the Pope was receiving. On the other hand, as we have seen, and shall see on many future occasions, the notion of revenge was firmly engrained in the Borgia family nature, and often overrode even their most carefully planned strategies. Putting an end to Charles VIII's cherished dream of conquering Jerusalem was just the kind of revenge which Alexander VI would have sought, following the public humiliation he had recently suffered in Rome at the hands of the gauche young French king, together with his troops which had so despoiled the Holy City. And indeed, following the death of Cem, even Charles VIII would gradually come to understand the impossibility of achieving his transcendent chivalric feat – without Cem as a hostage against the Turks, it was simply too dangerous to risk launching his crusade so that he could be crowned King of Jerusalem in Christendom's other Holy City.

Perhaps inevitably, the French army which had taken Naples soon began emulating the conduct of its commander-in-chief. Although initially welcomed by the Neapolitan populace, their behaviour soon brought about a reversal of this attitude. As the Venetian ambassador recorded:

The French were stupid, dirty and dissolute people; they were constantly chasing women. Their table manners were disgusting and whenever they moved into a house they always took the best rooms and sent the master of the house to sleep in the worst.

They stole wine and grain and sold them in the market place. They raped the women, regardless of their status, then robbed them, pulling off their rings. If any resisted, they cut off their fingers to get the rings. Even so, they spent much of their time in church, praying.

The last mentioned quirk of behaviour was not due to superstition or an unlikely religiosity amongst the soldiery – who, being mercenaries, included a wide range of backgrounds and behaviours.* No, such addiction to prayer was hardly surprising in the light of the latest event in the city: it was during this period that syphilis first began to spread through Naples. The soldiers who flooded the churches were all praying to St George, the traditional protector against the plague, leprosy – and, by extension, this similar new malady.

It is generally held that syphilis had arrived in western Europe some two years previously, brought from the New World by sailors returning with Columbus on his first voyage of discovery. From Spain it eventually spread to Naples, where it soon reached the epidemic proportions of a modern plague, largely through the behaviour of the French army. The new plague became known as *le mal de Napoli* by the French, and as the *morbo gallico* ('French disease') by the Italians, who blamed its presence on the French.† However, although its origins may have been disputed, there was no mistaking its hideous symptoms. According to Guicciardini:

---

* The French army at this time included foreign mercenaries recruited from Scotland to Switzerland, from Flemish Brabant to Spanish Aragon. The Swiss were generally reckoned to be the toughest warriors, a reputation which led to them initially being hired as papal guards by Pope Sixtus IV, though not until well into the reign of Alexander VI did they become a permanent feature. The Swiss Guards, with their pikestaffs, colourful medieval uniforms and distinctive helmets, remain to this day the ceremonial guards of the Vatican, appearing much as they would have done during the time of Alexander VI.
† Not until 1530 would it receive the name 'syphilis' from the Italian physician and poet Girolamo Fracastro, who named it in his medical poem *Syphilis or the French Disease*, where Syphilis features as a shepherd, stricken with the disease by the angry god Apollo.

This illness, which was unknown here before those times, is so terrible that it must be regarded as another plague which has arrived among us. It manifested itself with hideous boils, which then developed into incurable ulcers, along with very severe pains in the joints and nerves. Because the doctors had no previous knowledge of this disease they used remedies which often made the patient even more ill. This disease killed men and women of all ages, others becoming deformed and suffering almost continuous pain, and many of those who seemed at first to be cured, would then relapse and die.

Meanwhile, Alexander VI's attempts to negotiate a united force to drive the French from Italy were coming to fruition. The Pope had influence throughout Europe, and was determined to use this. 'Even in faraway England, King Henry VII was prepared to contribute to keeping France from growing stronger than it already was.' Likewise, the Holy Roman Emperor Maximilian of Hapsburg, whose territories ranged from the Netherlands through to Austria, was also determined to protect his empire from the growing power of France. Maximilian held a 'deep personal grudge dating from the time when Charles had simultaneously jilted his daughter and stolen his fiancée, depriving him of the great duchy of Brittany'. However, as even Alexander VI's most favourable commentator Peter de Roo concedes:

It took time to establish the articles of a definite and formal league, binding each one of them to gather soldiers and to submit to heavy expenses for the protection of one another.

Even in Italy there remained those who opposed such a league. In Florence, Savonarola still believed that Charles VIII was the 'scourge of God', come to purify Italy and rid the Church of corruption, heralding a new age of fundamentalist Christianity. On the other hand, Ferrara was implacably opposed to joining any treaty which involved its powerful neighbour Venice. And nearby Bologna was 'resolved to place [itself] on the most promising side'. These three states may not have been as powerful as their neighbours on the peninsula, but they occupied a strategic wedge of territory stretching from coast to coast. However, even these states eventually began to see the necessity of such an alliance; and in March representatives of all those in favour of an alliance congregated in Venice to sign a treaty. This was a personal triumph for Alexander VI and is indicative of his supreme diplomatic abilities; consequently the treaty 'was called the Holy League, because it was undertaken principally for the defence of the papacy, and was headed by His Holiness, Pope Alexander VI'.

Back in Naples, Charles VIII decided to go ahead with his coronation, despite the absence of the Pope. A formal ceremony was held in Naples Cathedral, where Charles VIII 'crowned himself as monarch of Il Regno and "Emperor of the East"'* before his sycophantic commanders and such of their mercenaries as were deemed presentable. Despite this defiant gesture, it was gradually becoming clear even to Charles VIII that all was not going according to plan. The crusade was definitively abandoned when it was realized there were not enough ships to transport his army across the sea to the Holy Land. Worse still, as his commanders persisted in pointing out, the overland lines of supply and communication between the French army in Naples and their homeland in France were to all intents and purposes severed. Communication could still be maintained by sea, but if Charles VIII ever wished to return to France with his large army intact there was no choice but to march back north through Italy. Yet such a course was increasingly under threat from the forces of the Holy League which his deceitful friend Alexander VI was said to be assembling.

With reluctance, Charles VIII put away his picture book of Neapolitan ladies and prepared to lead his army on the gruelling 500-mile march up

---

* This was a reference to the external Aragonese territories, which, at least in theory, belonged to Naples at the time – including Sicily, as well as Sardinia and Corsica. And, of course, the kingdom of Jerusalem, which in Charles VIII's fantasy was to be 'the capital city of the East'.

through Italy back to France. Their route would take them north, then across the Apennines and the Lombardy plain, before finally reaching the foothills of the Alps. Prior to setting out, Charles VIII wrote to Alexander VI suggesting that they should meet in Rome, for the purpose of renewing their friendship. This time, Charles VIII promised, he would ensure that his troops behaved themselves in Rome, and no Swiss mercenaries would be permitted to enter through the gates to the Holy City. In the words of Borgia historian G. J. Meyer: 'Alexander, however, thought it a mistake to receive the king again, seeing no way to do so without arousing suspicion among the other members of the Holy League.' This sentence speaks volumes for the trust in which Alexander VI was held by the fellow members of his alliance. Skilled diplomat he may have been, but all knew better than to take him at his word. His ultimate strategy would always be for his own ends, and as yet the full magnitude of these remained unknown – apart from his evident wish to extend the power of his papacy.

On 20 May 1495 Charles VIII marched out of Naples with the remains of his massive army. Syphilis, desertion and casualties had whittled down his forces to just over half their former strength, with around 15,000 fighting men. Even so, this still far outnumbered any force which had yet been assembled in Italy to meet them. Behind the marching mercenaries trailed a long guarded convoy consisting of several hundred mules laden down with booty and treasures looted from the cities through which the French army had passed. And drawing up the rear came the usual ragged train of camp followers – cooks, prostitutes, scavengers and the like.

By the first day of June the French army had reached the gates of Rome, where Charles VIII still optimistically expected to meet the Pope. But Alexander VI and most of his cardinals were already fleeing north from Rome, under the protection of the papal troops. Cardinal Pallavicini, an intellectual member of the Sforza family, had been delegated the task of greeting Charles VIII, informing him that the Pope had just left for Orvieto. Charles VIII immediately despatched a troop of fast cavalry to catch up with the Pope and bring him back; but when they reached Orvieto they learned that Alexander VI had already left for Perugia, well off the route which the French army was taking on its way north. Alexander VI had learned that Charles VIII was planning to meet up with the army of his cousin Louis of Orléans at Asti, in territory belonging to Milan. By now the forces of the Holy League were belatedly assembling in the Lombardy plain, waiting for the French army to emerge from the Apennine passes. The hastily assembled army of the Holy League consisted mainly of Venetian forces, along with detachments of Stradiots (mercenaries from the Balkans), all under the command of the youthful but experienced twenty-nine-year-old condottiere Francesco Gonzaga, Marquis of Mantua.

Back in Rome Charles VIII decide that speed was of the essence and began leading his army into the Apennines in the hope of linking up with Louis of Orléans. Gonzaga made the mistake of letting the French army emerge from the passes and assemble in battle formation on the Lombardy plain, where the two armies confronted each other on the banks of the river Taro at Fornovo. The battle was fought amidst driving rain and mud, rendering cavalry all but useless. Gonzaga initially held the upper hand, but made a number of tactical blunders, in the midst of which his Stradiots spotted the lightly guarded French mule train of treasures, causing them to withdraw from the main action in their eagerness to snatch large quantities of booty. The remaining forces of the Holy League stood their ground, but from this point on the French cannons played a decisive role, inflicting heavy casualties, with over 4,000 soldiers of the Holy League losing their lives. At the same time, there were just 600 French deaths. Afterwards both sides claimed victory. The French had lost all their treasure, including Charles VIII's prized Sword of Charlemagne, but the forces of the Holy League were unable to prevent the vast French army from continuing on its march north back to France. The 'Scourge of God' had passed out of Italy, leaving a trail of syphilis in the cities through which it had passed.

CHAPTER 7

THE BEST OF PLANS . . .

I N Florence Savonarola was left bitterly disappointed that his 'Scourge of God' had failed to rid Italy of corruption and bring about the beginning of a new fundamentalist Christian era. In his sermons, Savonarola railed against Charles VIII:

> You have incurred the wrath of God by neglecting that work of reforming the Church which, by my mouth, he charged you to undertake and to which he called you by so many unmistakable signs.

Indeed, he even went so far as to prophesy that if Charles VIII did not fulfil the duty given him by God, he would die. (In fact, Savonarola refrained from actually naming Charles VIII, though the subject of his prophecy was plain to all who heard him.)

From this stage on, Savonarola would play down his apocalyptic prophecies and instead concentrate his sermons on the venality and vice of the citizens of Florence. It was now that he would begin his annual 'Bonfire of the Vanities', when all manner of luxuries, including jewellery, secular paintings, books and clothes would be heaped up in the city's central piazza and burned. At the same time, his sermons began calling down the wrath of God on the corruption of the Church. Alexander VI was already furious that Florence had been so reluctant to join the Holy League, and he responded to these sermons (which never actually named him either) by issuing a papal brief banning Savonarola from preaching. Savonarola chose to reply to this brief by sending a letter to Alexander VI arguing the theological justification for his words and actions. So Alexander VI decided to try a different tack. This time he would exercise his charm and attempt to flatter Savonarola. He sent a further brief to Florence, inviting Savonarola to Rome 'to discourse with you, so that we may gain from you a greater understanding of what is agreeable to God, and put this into practice'. But this appeal to Savonarola's personal vanity did not work. Savonarola was well aware of what would happen to him in Rome once he fell into the clutches of Alexander VI, so he sent a letter to Alexander VI explaining that he could not travel:

> firstly, because my body has been weakened by illness, and I am suffering from fever and dysentery. Secondly, my constant exertions on behalf of the welfare of the state of Florence have caused me to suffer from a constant agitation, in both my body and my mind . . .

The game of cat and mouse continued. Savonarola was well aware of Alexander VI's power, so he decided to preach his 'last sermon' in the cathedral, before retiring to his cell at the Dominican monastery of San Marco in Florence. Both would now bide their time.

Alexander VI had problems closer to home. In the first week of December 1495 Rome was suddenly struck by a flood of almost biblical proportions. For three days there was a continuous downpour, and the waters of the Tiber rose to become a raging torrent. Indeed, this had soon risen so high that the cardinals returning from a consistory in Trastevere to the main city were hardly able to cross the Ponte Sant'Angelo before the streets around the fortress itself were awash. By the time the floods had subsided, it was estimated that several thousand people had been washed away or drowned. In all, the damage was put at around 300,000 ducats – a colossal sum equivalent to the entire papal income for that year. According to an eyewitness:

> By yesterday morning the floods had subsided, but the courtyards and cellars are full of dead animals and rubbish, which will take months to clear. The damage to Rome is terrible and will take decades to clear. The boats on the Tiber, the mills and the houses on the banks are gone, and all the horses have drowned in their stables. With the mills gone there will be no bread.

He goes on to recount how one evening they found a poor man clinging to a tree trunk by the wharves who had been swept from his village eleven miles upstream. Prisoners had drowned in the dungeons of Castel Sant'Angelo, and its protective moats were overflowing with water. Vital repairs to the Pope's ancient fortress would cost Alexander VI 80,000 ducats over the coming year.

With the retreat of Charles VIII and his army from Italy back over the Alps, the Holy League to all intents and purposes fell apart. This allowed the Orsini and Colonna families to remain loyal to Charles VIII, even going so far as to fly the French flag from the battlements of their castles. They were aware that the French king was making covert plans to launch another invasion, and that even Savonarola remained in secret correspondence with him. But most threatening of all for Alexander VI was the fact that the Orsini and the Colonna now controlled the main roads to the north and south of Rome.

In February 1496 Alexander VI 'announced in consistory that Virginio Orsini and the others were declared rebels, and confiscated their estates because they had disobeyed him by taking pay from the French'. This was, in fact, no more than an ineffective threat. The Orisini, the Colonna and others now occupied much of the Papal Territories, and despite Alexander VI going so far as to excommunicate these enemies, there appeared little else he could do. These were difficult times for Alexander VI, and a low ebb in his papacy. Even when Charles VIII had humiliated him, passing through Rome, he had retained a certain power. And with the aid of his bold son Cardinal Cesare Borgia he had succeeded in retaining sufficient wealth and credibility to appeal throughout Europe for a Holy League. Now this had fallen apart, and the two most powerful aristocratic Roman families, along with their allies, had virtually confined him within the Holy City. In his time of need, the sixty-four-year-old Alexander VI began gathering his family about him.

As we have seen, the Pope's second son Cardinal Cesare Borgia had remained at his side. The twenty-one-year-old Cesare still cut a striking figure in his fashionable doublet and hose, with a sword hanging at his side. He also occupied a luxurious apartment on the second floor of the Vatican, directly above that of his father. The two apartments were connected by an inner winding staircase, and were unlike any other in the Vatican. These were flamboyantly decorated in Spanish style, but with an unmistakable Borgia touch: 'covering walls and ceiling in an almost megalomaniac repetition, are the two Borgia devices'. These were the royal Aragonese double crown, a reference to the Borgia's claimed descent from the ruling house of Spain, and the red bull of the original Borja arms (now in rampant form, following Alexander VI's ascent to the papal throne). In contrast to Italian custom, the rooms had tiled floors, and the walls were adorned with symmetrical patterns similar to those found in Moorish Granada.*

---

* Between 1492–4 Alexander VI added a six-storey tower abutting the main Vatican building. This was called the Torre Borgia and its interior was in the Spanish Borgia style. The main walls of the six-room Borgia apartments were decorated with large murals depicting standard religious themes, painted by the forty-year-old Perugian artist Pinturicchio and his assistants, who had helped decorate the walls of the Sistine Chapel some years previously. Interestingly, when *The Resurrection* was recently cleaned it revealed the figure of a Native American, painted in 1494, i.e. just a year after Columbus returned from his first voyage of discovery to the New World with some captive Native Americans on board. This is believed to be the first depiction of a Native American figure in European painting, though how (or if) he arrived in Rome remains a mystery. For centuries after the death of Alexander VI these apartments would remain abandoned. This was partly due to the notorious legends which clung to the Borgia name. In fact, the Borgia apartments were mostly used as reception rooms, and the family mainly lived in other apartments. The Torre Borgia exists to this day, and is now part of the Vatican Library.

Cesare maintained a close relationship with his father, who kept him informed of much of his day-to-day business, to the point where the Pope came increasingly to rely upon his son. But it was more than closeness to his father which enabled such a youthful character to establish a position where he was 'widely recognized as the most powerful cardinal in the college [of cardinals] and as the most unscrupulous'. In the latter aspect, he was very much his father's son. Cesare dominated by sheer force of personality, aided by the ability to overcome his enemies in the most ruthless fashion. And the more people knew this, the stronger he became. As Cesare Borgia's biographer observes: 'Without Giuliano [della Rovere] the College of Cardinals, packed with friendly or uncommitted cardinals, was an amenable body which Alexander and his son could manipulate more or less as they liked.' Though for the moment, with the Pope's fortunes in abeyance, the effects of this power were somewhat restricted.

The first member of Alexander VI's family which he summoned to be at his side in Rome during his time of need was his beloved daughter Lucrezia, who had now blossomed into a strikingly attractive sixteen-year-old with the long tresses of curly golden hair she had inherited from her mother. Lucrezia had made no secret of her dissatisfaction with provincial life in the small backwater of Pesaro, ruled by her husband, and was glad to be back amidst the splendours of Rome, where she could attend the lavish banquets thrown by her father and her brother Cesare. She resided, along with her husband Giovanni Sforza, in the Palazzo Santa Maria in Portico, where she had grown up under the care of her aunt Adriana de Milà, in the company of her father's young mistress Giulia Farnese.

Next to return to Rome was Jofrè Borgia, who travelled from Naples in May, accompanied by his wife Sancia of Aragon. Jofrè and his train arrived at the southern gate of San Giovanni in Laterano, followed by over two dozen mules bearing his possessions, each case emblazoned with his royal coat of arms as Prince of Squillace. Alexander VI had laid on a grand ceremonial reception for his fourteen-year-old son. Jofrè was greeted by the commander of the Vatican guard with 200 soldiers, as well as the ambassadors of Spain, Venice and Milan, along with a line up of

Roman dignitaries. Also present was his sister Lucrezia, 'accompanied by some twenty ladies and preceded by two pages on horseback wearing capes'. After the ceremonial greeting, Jofrè and the procession made their way across Rome, past the Colosseum and his former home, the grandiose Borgia palazzo now occupied by Cardinal Ascanio Sforza of Milan, until finally he crossed the bridge of Castel Sant'Angelo into Trastevere. 'Jofrè and Sancia rode to the Vatican, where Alexander peeped down at their approach through a half-closed shutter before going down with Cesare to greet them.'

The gossips of Rome had heard much about the tempestuous temptress Sancia of Aragon, but when they saw her in person they were not wholly impressed. The ever-present Mantuan envoy Gian Carlo Scalona recorded of Sancia:

> In truth she did not appear as beautiful as she had been made out to be. Indeed the lady of Pesaro [Lucrezia Borgia] surpassed her. However that may be, by her gestures and aspect the sheep will put herself easily at the disposal of the wolf. She has also some ladies of hers who are in no way inferior to their mistress, thus they say publicly it will be a fine flock . . . She is more than twenty-two years old,* naturally dark, with glancing eyes, and aquiline nose and very well made up, and will in my opinion not give the lie to my predictions.

Scalona was unimpressed by the fourteen-year-old Jofrè, describing him as 'dark in complexion and otherwise lascivious-looking, with long hair with a reddish tinge'.

The Mantuan ambassador's predictions concerning Sancia would prove correct. Within months gossip was spreading around Rome concerning how 'the sheep had put herself at the disposal of the wolf'. Later, Scalona would write back to Mantua: 'Jofrè, younger than his wife, had not consummated the marriage; he is not a man and, I understand, for many months past the lady Sancia has given herself to the Cardinal of Valencia [Cesare Borgia].'

---

* She was, in fact, just eighteen.

The Borgia reputation for sexual misconduct was already well-estab-
lished by the behaviour of Alexander VI during his days as cardinal and
vice-chancellor. Even so, his behaviour does not appear to have been as
bad as many of his colleagues, or his predecessors in the highest office. In
all fairness, Alexander VI's conduct had been in essence uxorious – albeit
with three successive 'wives'. And admittedly, his third 'bride', Giulia
Farnese, had been of a similar age to his daughter Lucrezia, with whom
she had become friends when they lived together at the Palazzo Santa
Maria. And, of course, there remained the business of the scandalous
'party' in the gardens at Siena. Cardinal Rodrigo Borgia may have been
forgiven by his friend Pius II, on the grounds that the reports had been
exaggerated by his enemies, but most still held firm to the belief that in
this instance there had been no smoke without fire.

Thus, up to this stage, the Borgia family reputation, largely formed by
Alexander VI, had not been markedly more tarnished than that of several
families occupying the upper echelons of the Church. His consummate,
if devious, political expertise, developed over his unprecedented thirty-six
years as vice-chancellor, had certainly earned him powerful enemies, such
as the della Rovere family. On the other hand, many admired his skills,
especially his attempts to strengthen the papacy. As we shall see, at this
stage such plans were merely in their infancy. It is only now that the
Borgia family reputation for depravity would begin to unfold. And it is
no accident that this development took place as his favoured children
– Juan, Cesare, Lucrezia and Jofrè (all his children born to Vanozza de'
Cattanei) – began coming of age.

However, from now on it becomes increasingly difficult to separate
any truth concerning depravity from the exaggerations of rumour and
gossip. Such exaggerations were, of course, encouraged by the Borgia
family's many enemies. Yet it will also be increasingly difficult to deny
that the florid and overblown rumours had their origin in certain seeds of
fact. Especially now that Cardinal Cesare Borgia comes into his own. By
contrast, at this stage Lucrezia Borgia appears to have retained a remarkable element of innocence. As one Borgia biographer put it: 'Lucrezia
was deeply attached to her brother Cesare, who loved her perhaps more

devotedly than he could bring himself to love anyone else.' And she loved him. The evidence suggests that Lucrezia had no idea that her doting brother was having an affair with Sancia. Lucrezia and Sancia were both living in the Palazzo Santa Maria and soon became close friends. Indeed, the two teenagers appear to have brought out a childish aspect in each other's character, often behaving like unruly schoolgirls. On one occasion they attended Mass together at St Peter's, where a Spanish priest delivered a sermon, described by Burchard as being 'too long and boring, which displeased the Pope'. However, as the priest droned on, Burchard was shocked to observe Lucrezia and Sancia leave their seats and slip up the stairs to the choir reserved for the canons, where they began chattering and giggling together.

In August the last of Alexander VI's favoured children, the wayward Juan, 2nd Duke of Gandia, arrived back in Rome, summoned from Spain by his father. He too was accorded a grand reception, despite having left his pregnant wife Maria Enriquez and their son behind in the ducal castle at Gandia. The twenty-year-old Juan revelled in the occasion. Sporting a scarlet cap hung with pearls, and a Turkish cape of gold brocade thrown over his brown-velvet doublet adorned with jewels, he rode into the city on his bay horse with gold fringes and tinkling silver bells. Behind him rode his six squires, who included a dark-skinned Moor dressed in crimson velvet, as well as a gaggle of dwarfs and jesters. He was welcomed with heartfelt joy by his devoted father, who appeared to have forgiven him his earlier misdemeanours. Though, if anything, Juan's character seems to have deteriorated during his time in Spain, where a contemporary chronicler referred to him as being 'a spoilt boy. [He was] a very mean young man, full of ideas of grandeur . . . haughty, cruel and unreasonable.' The inner circle of the Borgia family was now complete.

It was not long before the Mantuan ambassador was reporting a predictable division in the family. The conceited and less intellectually gifted Juan may have been away for three years in Spain, but Alexander VI held him in high regard, a fact greatly resented by Juan's talented older brother Cesare. Just a month after Juan's arrival, the Mantuan ambassador was writing: 'every effort is made to conceal that these sons of the

Pope are consumed with envy of each other.' Both felt they had cause for complaint. It was evident that Cesare had now become his father's closest adviser, whereas Juan seemed to remain his father's favourite. The situation was further exacerbated when Alexander VI revealed his plans to turn the tables on the rebellious Orsini family.

Guidobaldo da Montefeltro, Duke of Urbino and son of the great condottiere Federigo da Montefeltro, was hired as Captain-General of the Papal Forces. He was instructed to lead a campaign against the Orsini, driving them from the papal territories which they had occupied to the north and south of Rome. Assisting the duke as second-in-command, Alexander VI appointed his son Juan. On 26 October the Pope duly presented the Duke of Urbino and the Duke of Gandia with their banners of office in a ceremony at St Peter's, bestowing his papal blessing on their campaign. The two young dukes, resplendent in their shining armour, then led their forces out into the countryside of the Roman Campagna. Guidobaldo da Montefeltro had inherited his father's mercenary army, but had little of his military ability. Juan Borgia had obtained some military experience with the Aragonese army during his time in Spain, but had never taken command of troops in action. Despite their commanders' limited expertise, within two months the papal troops had captured no less than ten Orsini-held castles. However, they proved unable to dislodge the Orsini from their stronghold at Bracciano, and began to lay siege to the massive medieval fortress. Guidobaldo da Montefeltro had been wounded in the initial attack and retired to his tent, leaving Juan Borgia in sole command.

The Orsini defenders of Bracciano were seasoned soldiers and had nothing but contempt for Juan Borgia. In a gesture of mockery they despatched a donkey towards the papal camp. This had a placard placed around its neck proclaiming, 'I am the ambassador of the Duke of Gandia.' An insulting letter addressed to Juan Borgia was inscribed on a scroll which had been inserted in the donkey's anus. News now reached Juan Borgia that a force under the command of Carlo Orsini was on its way to relieve the besieged castle. Impulsively, Juan Borgia decided to lift his siege and march out to confront Carlo Orsini. The two armies met in open countryside some twenty miles south of Bracciano at Soriano on 24 January 1497. In the words of Burchard, the papal army was

> heavily defeated in great dishonour . . . The Duke of Urbino was captured [and] some five hundred of our soldiers were killed and many more wounded, while the Orsini captured all our cannon and utterly scattered our forces.

Juan Borgia was lucky to escape with only a wound to his face, managing to flee as his troops scattered in disarray around him. News of developments had been reaching Rome at regular intervals during the preceding weeks. This had caused Alexander VI to become so sick with worry concerning the fate of the campaign and the safety of his son that he had been unable to attend Mass in St Peter's on Christmas Day. His joy at the safe return of Juan contrasted with the barely concealed scorn of Cardinal Cesare Borgia.

The campaign had resulted in utter failure. As part of the ensuing peace agreement Alexander VI had to consent to surrender all ten captured castles to Orsini control, in return for which the Orsini were to pay an indemnity of 50,000 gold ducats for an assurance of peace. The Orsini were expecting to raise this 50,000 ducats as a ransom for Guidobaldo da Montefeltro; but Alexander VI – ever the wily negotiator – refused to pay a ransom for Montefeltro. Consequently, the Orsini were forced to pay the indemnity, much of which Alexander VI passed on to Juan, as a 'reward'. On top of this, the Pope refused to surrender a couple of the Orsini castles. Even so, the Orsini had extracted the promise of peace, and remained a thorn in the Pope's side.

As if this was not bad enough, Alexander VI now determined to despatch Juan Borgia once more into the field. Although the Pope had been forced to make peace with the Orsini, he was still free to attack the backers upon whom they depended – namely the French, who continued to hold Ostia. Alexander VI called upon the Duke of Gandia's Spanish overlords King Ferdinand and Queen Isabella of Spain, who duly despatched their most battle-hardened commander, Gonsalvo de Córdoba, to lead a force of seasoned Spanish troops from Naples. This new papal force arrived in Rome at the end of February. Whereupon, Alexander VI appointed his son Juan as second-in-command, and ordered Gonsalvo and Juan to march on Ostia, which was now the last remaining French stronghold in Italy. By early March the French had surrendered, although

> the French commander Ménaut Aguerre was later to accuse the Pope of using devilish weapons against the fortress, including some form of poison gas produced by throwing chemicals on to bonfires to the windward of the walls.

This time Juan Borgia had been on the winning side, but on his return to Rome his behaviour would outrage Gonsalvo de Córdoba. Juan would claim to his father that he shared equal responsibility for this victory, in which the artillery he commanded had merely played a minor supporting role.

At Easter some sensational news began spreading through Rome. Giovanni Sforza had suddenly fled the city in secret, riding back to his Adriatic castle at Pesaro, abandoning his wife Lucrezia. This gave rise to all manner of speculation. Some said that he had fled in fear of his life. According to the Mantuan ambassador, Sforza had suspected that he would be poisoned. In the words of Lucrezia Borgia's biographer: 'It may be that hints had been dropped, probably by Cesare, that a husband for Lucrezia was surplus to requirements.' Cesare Borgia's possessiveness with regard to his sister, and his antipathy towards her partners, was to become an increasing trait. Such feelings also seem to have been echoed in her father's feelings towards his daughter. On the other hand, the Milanese ambassador suspected a different reason for Giovanni Sforza's flight: 'I suspect that something concerning the reputation of his wife might have led him into a serious quarrel and then to make a departure in this manner.' Hints that something was wrong with Lucrezia's marriage had been noted for some time.

The rumour-mongers, and all enemies of the Borgia family, had a field day. However, the main reason for Giovanni Sforza's flight may well have been political. It was becoming evident to all that Alexander VI was intent upon forming strong links with Spain and the Kingdom of Naples, where the weak King Ferrantino had been replaced by his uncle Federigo, who still blamed the Sforzas of Milan for inviting the French into Italy. Alexander VI no longer wished to be tied to Milan; he now saw a strong alliance with Naples as the best guarantee of papal independence. In a gesture of papal solidarity Alexander VI decided that he would send a papal legate to the coronation of King Federigo, thus conferring his blessing upon the kingdom which still theoretically remained under the suzerainty of the Pope.

Such a legate would normally have been chosen from amongst the most senior members of the College of Cardinals, but Alexander VI decided to break with precedent by nominating the young Cardinal Cesare Borgia as his legate. This may have made him further enemies amongst the cardinals, but it confirmed the strength of the Pope's bond with Naples. However, in a further familial gesture intended to confirm his links with Naples, Alexander VI decided to reward his favourite son Juan by making him Duke of Benevento, ruler of an enclave of Papal Territory which lay within the borders of the Kingdom of Naples.

Although Cardinal Cesare Borgia was proud to represent his father at the coronation in Naples, this was but a passing honour. Juan, already Duke of Gandia, now held even more titles and land. The undeserving son was becoming ever more powerful, and his arrogance knew no restraint. Now the older brother, Cardinal Cesare Borgia, had even more reason to be jealous.

On the afternoon of 14 June 1497 Vanozza de' Cattanei held a party at her country villa in a vineyard near San Martino ai Monti, on the outskirts of Rome. This was intended as a farewell party in honour of her son Cesare, who was due to depart next day for Naples as papal legate. It was just a week since Juan had been created Duke of Benevento, and he too attended the party. Afterwards, as dusk was falling, Cesare and Juan, along with their servants, set off to ride back into Rome. When they reached the bridge of Castel Sant'Angelo, leading across the river to the Vatican, Juan announced to the company that he had decided to go off alone into the city. Cesare and the others did their best to dissuade him. The streets of Rome were dangerous at night. Juan insisted, but made one concession. He despatched his groom to get his light 'night armour', telling the servant to meet up with him at a nearby piazza. Cesare and the servants reluctantly watched Juan ride off into the night. They assumed he was off to spend the night with some young woman, as he often did. Next day, when Juan did not return, the Pope became increasingly anxious. He summoned Cesare to demand what had happened the previous night. According to the Mantuan ambassador, after Alexander VI had heard Cesare's explanation, he said 'that if he was dead, he knew the origin and the cause'. According to Burchard, the Pope was then 'seized with mortal terror'. He immediately ordered his Spanish guards to search the city. As the soldiers spread through the streets with drawn swords 'the city was in an uproar; many citizens fearing wholesale vendetta closed their shops and barricaded their doors'. The following day Juan Borgia's body was dragged from the Tiber: it had been stabbed repeatedly.

In the words of Burchard:

> When the Pope heard that the Duke [Juan Borgia] was dead and thrown into the river like dung, he fell into a paroxysm of grief, and such was the anguish and bitterness in his heart that he locked himself away in his room and wailed with abandon.

The suspects for this murder were legion. Juan Borgia had incurred widespread hatred by his arrogance alone. Add to this his vendetta against anyone to do with the Orsini, especially after his return from his unsuccessful campaign. To say nothing of the insults he had received on the campaign, which had caused mirth even amongst his own soldiers. Then there was his penchant for seducing the wives of important Roman figures. This seems to have been his reason for venturing into Rome alone that night. Soon all manner of rumours were sweeping through the city. However, the favourite suspect amongst the gossips was, of course, Juan's older brother Cardinal Cesare. It appears that Juan Borgia had even had the temerity to move in on Cesare Borgia's affair with young Jofrè Borgia's wife Sancia.

Despite all such suspicions, circumstantial evidence points against the culprit being Juan's older brother. And Alexander VI himself did not suspect Cesare. The depth of his feelings for his favourite son Juan can be seen in the sheer scale of his grief:

> The Pope neither ate nor drank anything from Wednesday evening until the following Saturday, not from the morning of Thursday to the following Sunday did he know a moment's peace.

On Monday, 19 June Alexander VI was finally in a fit state to hold a consistory, during the course of which he spoke to his cardinals concerning his own suspects, which extended the net even further. Amongst these he included Giovanni Sforza, whom he blamed for anger regarding his wife Lucrezia. He also suspected Guidobaldo da Montefeltro, for resentment over the Pope's unwillingness to pay his ransom. It is indicative that both of these were thought to be trying to get at Alexander VI, rather than Juan. So blind was Alexander VI to Juan's faults that he was even inclined to blame himself for his murder.

In the event, the widespread search throughout Rome for a suspect was called off as suddenly as it had been launched. It seems that a week after the murder, Alexander VI learned the 'truth'. This putative truth remains unknown. Though in time independent reports by, amongst others, the Venetian and Ferrarese ambassadors, Juan's widow Maria Enriquez, as well as Queen Isabella of Spain, all pointed to the same figure. Rightly or wrongly, they were all convinced that the culprit was Cardinal Cesare Borgia. But as we shall see, it is certain that Alexander VI did not suspect him.

One of the many persistent rumours which swept Rome during this period concerned incest in the Borgia family. Some suspected Alexander VI of more than familial love for his daughter Lucrezia. There is no doubting their closeness, to say nothing of the unusual pastimes he chose to share with Lucrezia. The Borgias seem to have enjoyed sex as a spectator sport, which appeared to act as a form of bonding. For the moment, one incident will suffice. On an autumn day, Alexander VI and his daughter happened to be looking out of a Vatican window together when they noticed two mares with winter logs strapped to their backs being led by a peasant. As the mares reached St Peter's Square, the Vatican guards were ordered to cut their straps, throw off the wood and

> lead the mares into the courtyard immediately inside the palace gate. Four stallions were then freed from . . . the palace stables. They immediately ran to the mares, over whom they proceeded to fight furiously and noisily amongst themselves, biting and kicking in their efforts to mount them and seriously wounding them with their hoofs. The Pope and Donna Lucrezia, laughing with evident satisfaction, watched all that was happening from a window above the palace gate.

Lucrezia hardly appears as a high-spirited young innocent in this instance. And, as we shall see, such lack of shame will be confirmed in the months following her husband's flight from Rome.

Similar insinuations of inappropriate closeness with Lucrezia would also emerge where Cesare Borgia was concerned. As we know, Cesare seems to have felt particularly possessive towards his sister. However, Alexander VI's idea of entertainment for his young daughter looks like harmless amusement compared with the way Cesare chose to entertain her. Although the following incidents in fact took place at a later date, they would appear indicative, not to say instructive, with regard to Cesare's harboured feelings. On one occasion Cesare led his sister on to a balcony overlooking a courtyard of felons who had been condemned to death. He then proceeded to raise his crossbow and use the men below as target practice. And on an occasion when a Roman satirist alluded to Cesare's depraved behaviour, he had his tongue cut out and nailed to his severed hand. A man who was willing to demonstrate his feelings in such a fashion, who was also known to be touchy with regard to the men in Lucrezia's life, would soon find occasion to give even more direct vent to these feelings. In the months preceding the flight of Lucrezia's husband Giovanni Sforza from Rome 'in fear of his life', Cesare had evidently not felt constrained from revealing his deep antipathy towards his sister's husband. However, Lucrezia now found herself bereft of a husband and alone. It appears that during this period she consoled herself with a certain Pedro Calderon, known by the nickname 'Perotto', who happened to be her father's chamberlain and a man of whom the Pope was particularly fond. Lucrezia's dalliance evidently came to light, whereupon the Pope was outraged at his daughter's behaviour. According to a letter written by a contemporary: 'Donna Lucrezia has left the palace, where she was no longer welcome, and gone to a convent known as San Sisto . . . Some say she will turn nun, while others say many other things which one cannot entrust to a letter.'

Some months later, Burchard would record: 'Last Thursday Perotto fell, not of his own accord, into the Tiber, and was fished out today. With regard to this matter there are all kinds of rumours circulating in Rome.' According to some reports, Perotto's bound and stabbed body was discovered along with that of Pantasilea, Lucrezia's close attendant. Two reasons have been put forward for this. First, to suggest that Perotto was in fact having an affair with Pantasilea. Second, to silence the one woman who had been a witness to Lucrezia's affair. Later, the Venetian diarist Sanuto would record 'more lurid reports of the death of Calderon clinging to the robes of the Pope while Cesare stabbed him'. Alexander VI could have had a hand in the murder of Calderon, but most sources agree that Cesare Borgia was almost certainly responsible for both of these deaths.

CHAPTER 8

A CRUCIAL REALIGNMENT

FOLLOWING THE MURDER OF Juan Borgia, Alexander VI was prompted
to reassess his strategy with regard to his family. He certainly
discussed with Cardinal Cesare Borgia the possibility of him resigning
his cardinalate and marrying, thus securing the Borgia heritage. (Jofrè's
attempts on this score were rightly discounted.) As we shall see, there is
good evidence for the early date of this discussion between Alexander VI
and Cardinal Cesare Borgia, in the form of a letter that King Federigo of
Naples would write to the Pope.

Juan Borgia's death, and its traumatic effect on Alexander VI, caused
Cardinal Cesare Borgia to postpone his departure for Naples, and it was
some weeks before he set out as papal legate. He was accompanied by
a large train, including some 700 horses, retainers, prelates and various
courtiers. On 6 August Cardinal Cesare Borgia officially crowned King
Federigo at a ceremony held in the ancient cathedral city of Capua, just
fifteen miles north of Naples itself. When King Federigo returned to
Naples, Cardinal Cesare Borgia evidently spoke in private with him.
Cardinal Cesare came up with the startling proposal that he should marry
the king's daughter, an idea suggested by Alexander VI. The Pope had

already succeeded in marrying his illegitimate son Jofrè to the illegitimate Sancia of Aragon, and now he wished to go one step further. However, King Federigo seemed to think that marrying his legitimate seven-teen-year-old daughter Carlotta to Cardinal Cesare Borgia was another matter altogether, even though Cesare had in fact been officially legiti-mized by Sixtus IV. By taking the hand of Carlotta in marriage, Cardinal Cesare Borgia would be putting himself in line to inherit the throne – as Alexander VI well understood.

King Federigo had no wish to give offence to his powerful new friend Alexander VI, so he wrote the previously mentioned letter to the Pope, stating:

> It seems to me that the son of the Pope, who is also a cardinal, is not the ideal person to marry my daughter. If the Pope can make it possible for a cardinal to marry and keep his hat, I'll think about giving him my daughter.

King Federigo was not only prevaricating, he was also wilfully misun-derstanding Alexander VI's proposal. It would have caused outrage throughout Christendom for a cardinal publicly to take a wife and retain his cardinal's hat – even Alexander VI would not have been able to overcome such a difficulty. On the other hand, for a cardinal to resign may have been almost unheard of, but Alexander VI was confident that he could manage this matter. However, for the moment it looked as if Alexander VI's ambitions for his son to inherit the throne of Naples were on hold.

In fact, King Federigo also had other reasons for balking at the marriage of his daughter Carlotta to Cardinal Cesare Borgia. She herself may have been just seventeen, but she certainly had a mind (and a heart) of her own. Her father had sent her to be brought up at court in France, where she had fallen in love with the powerful Breton nobleman Guy XVI de Laval, Count of Laval; as such she made it plain to her father that she had no wish to marry 'a priest who is the son of a priest'. Cesare Borgia remained an outstandingly handsome young man, with his long, lean, well-chiselled face and striking red beard, and was not used to rejection by any woman. Even so, this hardly excused his behaviour during his weeks in Naples, where he lavished the enormous sum of 20,000 ducats on the daughter of the Count d'Aliffe. Such extravagance was becoming an increasing feature of his character, which along with his magnetic charm usually overcame all amorous barriers. Indeed, he does not seem to have restricted his favours to the daughter of the Count d'Aliffe. According to a Roman informant of the Marquesa of Mantua: 'Monsignor Valencia [Cesare Borgia] has returned from Naples after crowning King Federigo and he is now sick with the French disease,' i.e. syphilis. Cesare's Spanish physician Gaspar Torella quickly became an expert in treating this disease, and would even write one of the earliest medical treatises on the subject, in which he outlined his treatment of a patient to whom he gave the pseudonym 'Niccolo the Young'.

However, when Cardinal Borgia returned from Naples he did bring good news regarding Lucrezia's marriage prospects. King Federigo had suggested that he was prepared to let her marry Alfonso, Duke of Bisceglie, the illegitimate son of Alfonso II, son of King Ferrante, whose brief reign had ended in his flight from Naples at the approach of Charles VIII and the French army. Lucrezia's marriage would certainly cement the bond between Naples and the papacy. Yet there remained the small matter that Lucrezia was in fact still married to the absent Giovanni Sforza.

Alexander VI could simply have annulled his daughter's marriage by papal decree, but he did not wish to appear arbitrary in this matter. He knew that any important future partner would have to be completely satisfied that Lucrezia was suitable marriage material. With this in mind, he set up a commission of cardinals, who were expected to declare Lucrezia's marriage null and void. Alexander VI's suggested reason for reaching this decision was that her marriage to Giovanni Sforza was invalid, as her previous betrothal to the Spanish grandee Don Gaspar de Procida had never officially been revoked. Unfortunately, the usually reliable Cardinal Pallavicini, who also happened to be a Sforza, chose to object to such an annulment on canonical grounds. This led Alexander VI to fall back on his most outrageous and ingenious proposal. He claimed that Giovanni Sforza's marriage to his daughter had in fact never been consummated – on account of the bridegroom's impotence. Lucrezia was thus *virgo intacta*.

This suggestion was indignantly denied by Giovanni Sforza, who had made his previous wife pregnant – before she died in childbirth. Besides, admitting to such a suggestion would have made him a laughing stock throughout Italy. According to the Ferrarese ambassador, Giovanni Sforza had claimed to him 'that he had known his wife an infinity of times, but that the Pope had taken her from him for no other purpose than to sleep with her himself'. The gossips throughout Italy had another field day. As we have seen, there may well have been a hint of metaphorical (or at least psychological) truth in Giovanni Sforza's suggestion. And he certainly seems to have believed the rumours. Somewhat reserved by nature, he was not a man given to public displays of affection. The contrary was true amongst the Spanish Borgias, and such affectionate fondlings were easily misconstrued.

Still determined to press ahead with his plan, Alexander VI now turned to his vice-chancellor Cardinal Ascanio Sforza. Cardinal Ascanio Sforza then had a word with his brother Ludovico Sforza, the Duke of Milan. Both of these Sforzas were keen that Milan should remain on good terms with the Pope, despite the fact that Alexander VI was quite evidently trying to withdraw from his alliance with Milan. But the pressure applied by the Duke of Milan and Cardinal Ascanio Sforza eventually prevailed. Giovanni Sforza protested: 'If His Holiness wishes to create his own kind of justice, there is nothing I can do about it; let the Pope do what he likes, but God watches over all things.' In November 1497 Giovanni Sforza finally signed the document of non-consummation. Whereupon the Pope's commission declared that Lucrezia Borgia remained *virgo intacta*, due to the impotence of Giovanni Sforza. On top of this, Giovanni Sforza was even ordered to return the 31,000 ducats which he had received as Lucrezia Borgia's dowry. Such actions may defy credulity, but they do confirm Alexander VI's determination. He was willing to go to any lengths to get his way.

Throughout all this Lucrezia Borgia remained in seclusion at San Sisto. Another reason, apart from the Pope's anger, has been suggested for this long period out of the public eye at such a time. According to a contemporary report, sent from Rome to Bologna, the real reason Perotto had been murdered was 'for having got His Holiness's daughter, Lucrezia, with child'. According to this version of events, which is supported by reports from the Ferrarese ambassador, Lucrezia gave birth to a child, which was either stillborn or died within days of being born. Such an event would necessarily have been shrouded in secrecy – especially during attempts to establish Lucrezia's virginity – which is why there is little supporting evidence for it, apart from contemporary gossip. On the other hand, this matter is complicated by the mysterious appearance amongst the Borgia family of another child, who was known as the *Infans Romanus*. This child certainly existed, and would go on to be named Giovanni Borgia. At the time of Giovanni's birth, Alexander VI issued a bull legitimizing this infant, declaring him to be the offspring of Cardinal Cesare Borgia and an unmarried woman. Later, the Pope would issue a secret bull naming himself as the father of Giovanni. It was generally supposed that the sixty-eight-year-old pope had fathered this child with his mistress the twenty-four-year-old Giulia Farnese.

Under such circumstances it comes as little surprise that Lucrezia Borgia had few regrets concerning her long separation from Giovanni Sforza, and the consequent negotiations which resulted in the procla-mation of her virginity. A ceremony marking the public promulgation of her divorce was held in the Vatican on 17 December 1497. During the course of this she delivered a brief speech of thanks in Latin, which was of such eloquence that the Milanese ambassador declared sycophan-tically: 'If she had been Cicero himself, she could not have spoken with more grace.' Meanwhile, a more trenchant Perugian chronicler described the declaration of Lucrezia's virginity to be so ludicrous that it 'set all Italy laughing [as it was] common knowledge that she had been and still was the greatest whore there had ever been in Rome'. The gossip surrounding the Borgias may sometimes have been exaggerated, but there was no doubting that many now regarded the Pope and his entire family as a disgrace. Regardless, Alexander VI pushed ahead with Lucrezia's marriage to Alfonso, Duke of Bisceglie, the half-brother of Sancia of Aragon, the young Jofrè Borgia's wife.

The marriage between the two seventeen-year-olds, Lucrezia and Alfonso, would take place in Rome some months later. A grateful Alexander VI produced a 40,000-ducat dowry for the bride, who appeared radiantly happy to be marrying the handsome and charming Prince Alfonso, such a contrast to the condottiere Giovanni Sforza, a widower who had been twelve years her senior. The celebrations, with Cesare Borgia as master of ceremonies, lasted over several says of feasting and revels, during which the cardinal frequently led the dancing with his sister or Sancia of Aragon, and sometimes both. The days of revelry were only marred by a fight which broke out at the wedding breakfast between the attendants of Cesare Borgia and those of Sancia of Aragon, preventing the servants from bringing in the traditional sweetmeats and sugared almonds. One can only speculate on the insult which provoked this brawl, and the ensuing melee, during which two bishops were seen to be engaged in fisticuffs.

In the light of the scandalous stories emanating from Rome, it comes as no surprise that in Florence Savonarola was moved to emerge from the seclusion of his cell in San Marco. In defiance of Alexander VI's ban, he now resumed his fiery sermons in Florence Cathedral. Outraged at this disobedience, Alexander VI despatched an ultimatum to the city's ruling Signoria. Savonarola was to be arrested at once and despatched to Rome. Should the Signoria fail to comply with these instructions the entire city of Florence would once again be excommunicated, a threat which he knew would cause great heartache amongst Savonarola's fervently religious followers. And in order to reinforce this threat on a secular level, Alexander VI promised that disobedience of his orders would result in the ruin of the trade upon which the city so relied. All Florentine merchants trading in the city of Rome would be arrested and marched off to the dungeons of the Castel Sant'Angelo, and their stocks of merchandise would be seized from their storage rooms. This edict against Florentine trade, he warned, could also be

RIGHT: Innocent VIII, the ineffectual pope who preceded the Borgia pope Alexander VI.

BELOW: A portrait of Rodrigo Borgia as Alexander VI, which hints at his personal power and depravity.

LEFT: Alexander VI in a more orthodox pose.

BELOW: The notorious King Ferrante I of Naples.

Lorenzo the Magnificent, the ugly but charismatic Medici ruler of Florence.

Giuliano della Rovere, a bitter enemy of the Borgias, who would eventually become Pope Julius II.

Pope Callixtus III, the first Borgia pope, investing Aeneas Piccolomini with his cardinal's red hat. Piccolomini would eventually become Pope Pius II.

A portrait of King Ferdinand II of Aragon and Queen Isabella of Castile, whose marriage would pave the way to a unified Spain.

ABOVE: A woodcut of Rome in 1493, the year after Alexander VI became pope. The turreted fortress to the right is the Castel Sant' Angelo. The pillared building behind it is the old St Peter's Basilica.

RIGHT: The condottiere Federigo da Montefeltro, ruler of Urbino. His portrait was painted in profile after the right side of his face was disfigured in a jousting tournament.

Pope Pius II being carried into Ancona, where he planned to lead his crusade against the Ottomans.

A portrait of Cesare Borgia *c.* 1500 after he had been made Duke of Valentinois by the French King Louis XII.

Three drawings by Leonardo da Vinci believed to be of Cesare Borgia during his third Romagna campaign, suggesting how his features coarsened during his later years.

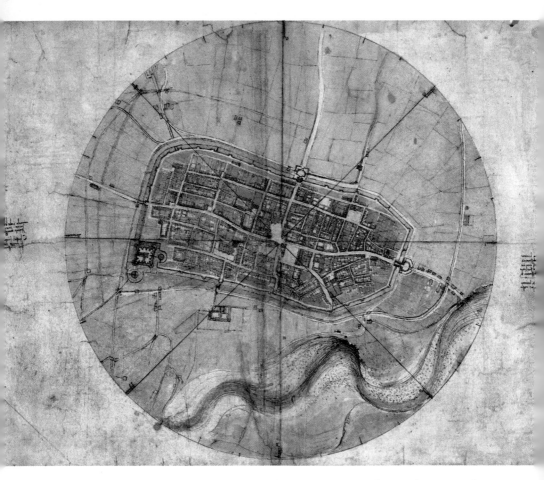

Leonardo da Vinci's map of Imola, which succeeds in combining beauty and great exactitude.

extended by papal order to other cities. Florence would be rendered spiritually and financially bankrupt.

Such a threat appeared irresistible. Florence's new republican government, and the fundamentalist Christian tenor of its society, had caused deep disquiet throughout Italy. Others would certainly heed the Pope's order. Rulers throughout the land feared that their own people might well be inspired to rise up by Florence's republican example, while Church authorities and their congregations were worried by such fundamentalist manifestations as Savonarola's 'Bonfire of the Vanities'. The Renaissance era was a time of increasing prosperity throughout society; none wished to see their valued possessions, however few, publicly burned in the main piazza.

But it was now that Savonarola played his masterstroke. He well knew that leaders throughout Europe were deeply disturbed by the reports of Alexander VI's personal behaviour, to say nothing of his devious political machinations. Consequently, Savonarola decided to write a circular letter to be sent to the leaders of the European powers, calling for a Council of the Church, which could depose Alexander VI and put in his place a more fitting candidate for St Peter's throne. Savonarola intended to send his letter to the Holy Roman Emperor Maximilian I, as well as the kings of England, France, Hungary and Spain, proclaiming:

> Alexander is no pope, nor can he be regarded as one. Aside from the mortal sin of simony by means of which he purchased the Papal Throne, and daily sells Church benefices to the highest bidder, as well as ignoring all the other vices which he so publicly flaunts – I declare that he is not a Christian, and does not believe in the existence of God, and thus far exceeds the limits of infidelity.

According to Savonarola's biographer Pasquale Villari: 'Savonarola then proceeded to invite all the princes of Christendom to summon a council as soon as possible, designating a location which is both appropriate and free from outside influence.' Savonarola also appended an individual message addressed to each of the rulers. For instance, he informed the Holy Roman Emperor that if he did not act and rescue the Church from its present disgrace, then he risked losing all dignity. And, alluding to his prophecy of the death of Charles VIII, he addressed his most personal plea to the French king. Charles VIII's infant son had recently died, causing him deep grief, and Savonarola warned the superstitious young king: 'Be mindful that God has already given you the first sign of his wrath.'

Word soon reached Rome of Savonarola's letter and his intentions. Alexander VI realized that this constituted a serious threat to his authority, let alone his position as pope. At all costs he had to prevent a Council of the Church from being called. Alexander VI was well aware that there were clerics in Florence, most notably the Augustinians, who were deeply opposed to Savonarola, and he ordered them to act. They should see that spies were posted at all the gates of Florence, from their opening at dawn until their closing at dusk. If they saw any friar of the Dominican order attempting to leave the city, they were to detain him. Savonarola was prior of the Dominicans at the city's monastery of San Marco, and Alexander VI rightly suspected that he might try to send his letters through some of his friars.

Now another ally came to Alexander VI's rescue. Besides the Augustinians, the Franciscans also opposed Savonarola, especially for his claim to privileged access to the word of God, as well as for his prophecies, which had taken on the stature of miracles in the eyes of many. A Franciscan monk called Francisco da Puglia challenged Savonarola to an *esperimento del fuoco* ('ordeal by fire'). The one who managed to walk barefoot along a path of red-hot coals and emerge unscathed would be declared the winner – this being a sign from God that he was the true one.

Savonarola regarded such medieval practices as barbaric, and declined to acknowledge the challenge. But one of his more zealous followers decided to take it up on his behalf. On the appointed day a huge crowd gathered in the large main piazza of Florence. From the outset there were various objections on both sides, which held up the proceedings, meanwhile the crowd became increasingly impatient. Then the heavens opened and a heavy rainstorm put out the fire. The situation descended into farce and the disappointed crowd dispersed amidst much discontent.

Feelings were turning against Savonarola, and next day a mob stormed his monastery San Marco. Savonarola was eventually taken prisoner and incarcerated by the authorities. As was common practice at the time, the accused was subjected to torture to try and discover the truth. With surprising speed, Savonarola confessed to heresy. As a priest, Savonarola could be tried only by an ecclesiastical court. To this end, Alexander VI appointed two papal commissioners, who were despatched to Florence. As one of these later admitted, 'They arrived in Florence with their verdict in their bosom.' This time Alexander VI had taken every precaution. Savonarola was duly condemned, and on 23 May was burned at the stake, his ashes being cast into the River Arno so that no monument or shrine could be erected in his memory.

Alexander VI had been ruthless in his defence of his papacy. At the same time, he would now show that he could be equally determined in manipulating the political scene to his advantage.

In late April the news came through that Charles VIII of France had died in a freak accident. He had cracked open his skull on a low stone lintel whilst entering a doorway. Some months prior to his unexpected death, Charles VIII had surprised Europe by signing a peace treaty with King Ferdinand of Spain. In reality, this treaty had little to do with good will. The fact was, both kingdoms had all but exhausted their large treasuries 'after years of conflict with numerous adversaries, including each other'.

As Charles VIII's son and heir had recently died, his throne was inherited by his cousin, the thirty-two-year-old, dashing but astute Louis of Orléans, who had earlier led a French army into Italy in an attempt to rescue Charles VIII on his return from Naples. Louis of Orléans took the name Louis XII, and immediately found himself faced with a serious difficulty. Should anyone choose to marry Charles VIII's widow, Anne of Brittany, they could lay claim to this valuable province, thus splitting it from France. So in order to secure his kingdom Louis XII immediately, and with little reluctance, started proceedings to divorce the wife he had been forced to marry, namely his 'hunchbacked and barren' cousin Joan of France, who happened to be the older sister of the oddly shaped Charles VIII.* Louis XII's intention was to marry Anne of Brittany as soon as possible, before any of the several foreign suitors after her hand could make good their claim. However, in order to do this he would require the assent of the Pope. Alexander VI's position in this matter was further strengthened when he heard from Louis XII that he would deem it a great favour if the Pope would also award a cardinal's hat to his influential chief counsellor Georges d'Amboise, the Archbishop of Rouen.

Alexander VI relished the prospect, and immediately set out his terms to Louis XII. From now on, he would require French support in his political endeavours (which remained as yet undisclosed). And as a mark of this support he would require a gift of French finance in order to pay for the stationing of French troops in Rome, for his defence, and also to be placed at his disposal for any military ventures. Louis XII was only too willing to agree to such requests, for it soon became clear that he had other reasons for wishing to form a strong alliance with the papacy. Louis XII had never forgiven Ludovico Sforza, Duke of Milan, for switching sides after Charles VIII's invasion of Naples. Sforza's act of betrayal in joining the Holy League had left the then Louis of Orléans and his army in a vulnerable position prior to the Battle of Fornovo, contributing considerably to the lack of French mastery of this encounter. Now that he was King of France, Louis XII was determined to wreak his revenge. Louis XII had in fact a distant, but legal, claim to the Duchy of Milan, being descended from a female member of the Visconti family. The Viscontis had ruled Milan prior to the duchy being taken over by the Sforza family almost fifty years previously. Under the circumstances, it took little persuasion for Alexander VI quietly to forget his already tenuous links with Milan. Covertly, Alexander VI gave his blessing to Louis XII's claim.

Simultaneous to these moves, Alexander VI was also privately hatching further plans of his own. With Juan murdered, these now focused on his

---

* After her divorce, Joan of France would go on to found an enclosed religious order of nuns, and would be canonized as St Joan in 1950 by Pope Pius XII.

son Cesare. However, despite all the discussions between father and son, there remained the awkward fact that Cesare was still a cardinal, and thus not yet in a position to fulfil any of the dynastic and military plans which Alexander had in mind for him. According to Burchard, by August 1498 the time had come for Cardinal Cesare Borgia to 'put off the purple . . . with the least possible scandal . . . and with the most decorous pretext'. Such an unprecedented decision needed to be ratified by the College of Cardinals at consistory. Yet the cardinals had no wish to create this kind of precedent: if the Pope could allow his son to cease being a cardinal, he might in time cause others to cease being cardinals.

The cardinals decided to decamp post-haste from the heat of Rome for their country retreats, pleading the recent prevalence of plague in the city. Alexander VI immediately despatched letters ordering their return. A consistory was held, presided over by Alexander VI, 'So the dissident cardinals yielded, and Cardinal Cesare could now take off his [cardinal's] hat and make himself a soldier and get himself a wife.' Coincidentally, an envoy now arrived from Louis XII bestowing upon Cesare Borgia the French title Duke of Valentinois. From this time on the Pope's son would increasingly be known by the Italian version of this title – namely 'il Valentino'.

Never one for clerical activity at the best of times, Cesare Borgia, the new Duke of Valentinois, immediately began celebrating his new status. On the day after setting aside his cardinal's hat he enjoyed himself with a display of bullfighting on horseback, a popular sport in Spain and Cesare Borgia's favourite pastime – though in Italy it was despised as a Spanish custom. According to the Mantuan ambassador:

> In these days [Cesare Borgia], armed as a janissary,* with another fourteen men, gave many blows and proofs of strength in killing eight bulls in the presence of Don Alfonso, Donna Lucretia, and 'his Princess' [Sancia], in Monsignor Ascanio's park, where he had taken them remote from the crowd for greater privacy.

---

* The janissaries were the elite soldiers who formed the Ottoman sultan's personal guard, and as such were a byword for military valour.

Cesare Borgia may have enjoyed showing off to his two favourite women, but such athletic exploits did not always go quite according to plan. Some ten days later Cesare Borgia was exercising in the grounds of the Belvedere just above the Vatican, doing some gymnastics. At the time, what is now known as a 'vaulting horse' was not a piece of wooden apparatus, it was in fact the real thing, i.e. an actual horse or a mule. On this occasion Cesare Borgia

> tried to leap in that manner on to a somewhat taller mule and when he was in the air, the mule took fright and gave him a couple of kicks . . . one on the right shoulder, and the other on the back of his head. He was unconscious for more than half an hour.

There was a reason for Cesare Borgia's strenuous exercise regime. His father Alexander VI had arranged for him to travel to France to meet his new bride, and he was determined to look his best. Going behind the back of King Federigo of Naples, the Pope had contacted his new ally and friend Louis XII, explaining his wish that his son Cesare should marry King Federigo's daughter Carlotta. Alexander VI informed Louis XII that this had been his original plan, and with the young Carlotta resident at the French court the king would surely be able to use his influence in this matter. Louis XII had been only too willing to oblige, and had extended a formal invitation to Cesare Borgia, Duke of Valentinois, to attend his court in France for the marriage ceremony.

By now Louis XII and Alexander VI were both intent upon forming a close alliance between France and the papacy. Alexander VI was only too pleased to accept the backing, and protection, of powerful France; and Louis XII was keen to win the Pope's backing for his plan to take over Milan. Alexander VI's diplomatic bargaining in this matter had resulted in several important promises from the French king. These would result in a new direction for Italian politics which would affect the entire peninsula over the decades to come, as well as aiding Alexander VI in his covert territorial ambitions. Louis XII undertook to fulfil the following commitments.

First and foremost, Cesare Borgia, Duke of Valentinois, would receive an annual income of 20,000 gold francs. Foreign exchange rates could fluctuate during this period, but as this sum was negotiated by Alexander VI we can be sure that it more than compensated for the 35,000 ducats income which Cardinal Cesare Borgia had received from his benefices. On top of this promised French income, the new Duke of Valentinois was also guaranteed by Louis XII a similar annual sum from his ducal estates.[*]

Cesare Borgia was intent upon following his murdered brother Juan into a military career, one for which he had always felt that he would be much more suited than his arrogant and incompetent sibling. Louis XII had understood this too – and was keen to give Cesare a chance to show his mettle. The French king decided to appoint the Pope's son as the commander of a corps of 300 mounted French lancers, which would be maintained in Italy at the king's expense. This in practice may well have amounted to an armed force of up to a thousand men – for each 'lancer' (a commissioned rank) was frequently accompanied by several mounted, and armed, bearers. These attendant soldiers were under the lancer's direct orders, bearing his arms and baggage, and seeing to his general needs. They also fought alongside him in battle. At the same time, it was agreed that Cesare Borgia would accompany Louis XII and the French army on their invasion of Milan. This was not only a great honour, but would give Cesare Borgia some much-needed military experience. It also meant that he was a hostage to fortune should the Pope be inclined to change his mind. This was no idle worry on Louis XII's behalf. Alexander VI had long since proved that he was hardly the most trustworthy of allies, and it was more than likely that either Milan, still in name at least his ally, or Venice, a more than interested party, or indeed both, would call

---

[*] In the late medieval period the Venetian gold ducat contained 3.15 grams of gold. At the same time, the French gold franc contained 4.15 grams. According to such figures, the new Duke of Valentinois had renounced his cardinal's income of 35,000 ducats for a total secular income equivalent to over 52,000 Venetian ducats. France was the richest nation in Europe, and Alexander VI was a very determined negotiator.

upon the Pope's aid to oppose this further invasion of Italy by France. As all knew, there was no telling what the powerful French army might do, once it had crossed the Alps. But this time Alexander VI was determined that these unpredictable invaders would be on his side. The Pope's new alliance represented a significant shift in the balance of power in Italy. This was a considerable gamble, but the Pope was determined to put it to good use. He might have agreed to the stationing of a French force under his son in Italy, but he already had plans for these warriors.

On 1 October 1498 the twenty-three-year-old Cesare Borgia set out from Rome to travel to the court of Louis XII. He was accompanied by an entourage which included over a hundred retainers, all decked out in silk tunics emblazoned with the scarlet and yellow Spanish colours of the Borgia livery. These were followed by fifty baggage mules and strings of laden carts. Cesare Borgia's immediate attendants were all riding horses shod with silver horseshoes, and wearing silver harnesses with tinkling silver bells, echoing the entourage of his brother Juan. Cesare's horse was similarly clad, while he himself was attired in a white brocade tunic, a short black velvet cloak slung over his shoulder.

Cesare Borgia was departing Rome as a suitor to royalty, no less – on his way to marry Carlotta of Naples, the daughter of King Federigo of Naples. Louis XII had overridden her father's objections to her marrying Cesare Borgia. Carlotta was descended from the French royal family on her mother's side, and had grown up at the French court. By now she had come to regard Louis XII as a father figure. Under the circumstances, her genuine father King Federigo, living in distant Naples, and now married to a new wife, had little say in the matter.

There is no doubt that the young Cesare Borgia was out to make an impression. Besides his white tunic, he also wore a black velvet cap sewn with rubies, whilst his boots were sewn with gold brocade and pearls, and his horse was caparisoned in the colours of the French royal house, of which he could now claim membership as Duke of Valentinois. The braggadocio of this occasion as Cesare Borgia rode his prancing stallion at the head of his procession through the streets of Rome is unmistakable. Yet it is not difficult to recognize that his somewhat over-ostentatious display masked a certain inner lack of confidence. This was no mission as a papal legate to the King of Naples, backed by all the authority of the Church. On this occasion he was on his own, venturing outside Italy for the first time, to visit the most powerful court in Europe. The impression he made personally would be germane to his entire future standing. And there was another reason for his lack of confidence. The Mantuan ambassador, who watched Cesare Borgia leave Rome, commented: 'He is well enough in countenance at present, although he has his face blotched beneath the skin as is usual with the great pox.' Despite the ministrations of Cesare's skilled physician Gaspar Torella, who would accompany him to France, the syphilis he had caught in Naples was taking its gradual but inevitable course.

To assist Cesare Borgia in his mission to gain the favour of Louis XII, Alexander VI had arranged for his son to take with him the vast sum of 200,000 ducats. This was to be spent on his way through France and at the French court. Casual extravagance on such a scale was intended to demonstrate to Louis XII that the Pope, and his son, were quite the match for European royalty when it came to wealth. In fact, Alexander VI had found himself in some difficulty when it came to raising this sum; and as we shall see, he would resort to characteristically egregious methods to attain it.

During the reign of Alexander VI's predecessors, when he had played an integral role in the handling of papal finances, the papacy had too often lacked any real influence on the larger Italian stage, to say nothing of the wider European stage, over which it retained little more than theological jurisdiction. Both political and military power had been sorely lacking. This had usually been the result of papal weakness, self-indulgence, financial mismanagement or 'heritage' (the erecting of monuments or buildings, such as the Sistine Chapel, would bestow immortality on their benefactor). There had been little emphasis on building up any real power, apart from more or less unsuccessful attempts to create a Holy League against the Ottomans. Indicatively, a Holy League with real power had only come into being under Alexander VI, when instead of the potential threat of full-scale Ottoman invasion, the Italian peninsula had suffered the very real ravages of Charles VIII's invasion. But Alexander VI had learned from his long vice-chancellorship, as well as from more recent humiliating events during his own papacy. Such mistakes were not to be repeated. The only way for the papacy to gain any real power was for it to form a reliable and lasting alliance with the most commanding European monarchy. And to appear to do so on more or less equal terms. This could be achieved by marriage, but it would also have to be reinforced by a suitable show of affluence. Money served to demonstrate power – even if, in this particular case, such power remained questionable.

Where money was concerned Alexander VI's behaviour had seldom shown any constraints. From his earliest years as vice-chancellor to his present time on the papal throne, the acquisition of wealth had been an integral part of his policy. Benefices were bought and sold, upgraded where necessary, or simply acquired – all in the name of income. Money could not only demonstrate power, it could also buy it. Money was the vital factor. The present case involving his son Cesare's visit to France to marry into royalty was to be no exception. For Cesare to demonstrate sufficient extravagance and largesse, at least 200,000 ducats would have to be raised immediately. Yet this was no easy task, especially when the annual papal income of 300,000 ducats had almost all been spent already. The building and decorating of the Torre Borgia was proving a large drain. On top of this there had been Juan's inept campaign against the Orsini. Little wonder that Alexander VI had taken the unprecedented step of not paying for Guidobaldo da Montefeltro's ransom, regardless of the fact that he had been in papal employ at the time. In Alexander VI's opinion, the Montefeltro family had sufficient funds of their own to organize this matter themselves. And with Cesare now setting off for France, the papal coffers were all but empty. What was he to do? Somehow drastic fundraising measures would have to be put into practice – in the quickest possible time, causing the least possible disruption or antagonism. There was just one target which fitted these requirements. Namely, the Jews.

CHAPTER 9

A ROYAL CONNECTION

D
URING THE CENTURIES WHILE the Moors were gradually being driven from the Spanish mainland, the Jews had fallen under suspicion for their cooperation with Moors. Many Jews had been forced to convert to Christianity, and these were known as *conversos*. In the years following Innocent VIII's confirmation of the sadistic Torquemada as Grand Inquisitor of the Spanish Inquisition in 1487, a reign of terror had ensued.* Any suspected of deviating from the strictest Christian orthodoxy were tortured on the rack. Many *conversos* had been suspected of secretly maintaining the customs and rituals of the Judaic religion, whilst posing as Christians. These had become known as Marranos. During the final expulsion of the Moors from the Spanish mainland in 1492, a large number of Jews, including many *conversos* and Marranos, had fled the country, particularly to Italy. Sources estimate that as many as 9,000 arrived at the borders of the Papal States. Alexander VI initially welcomed these new arrivals, decreeing that they were to be 'permitted

---

* Ironically, it is now known that Torquemada himself was descended from *converso* ancestors. It is possible that this inner conflict gave an edge to his pathological cruelty.

to lead their life, free from interference from Christians, to continue in their own rites, to gain wealth, and to enjoy many other privileges'. Large numbers of these new immigrants were skilled as merchants, as well as in such fields as currency exchange, money-lending, and medicine. In a city such as Rome, which relied so heavily upon the seasonal pilgrimage trade, currency exchange and money-lending proved a boon to local businesses.

Even so, the influx of so many immigrants inevitably began to lead to difficulties with the populace at large. The new population of non-Christians in the Holy City not only looked different, but even the ones who professed to be converted Christians had 'foreign' (i.e. Spanish) cultural habits. The result was increasing friction between the immigrants and the local inhabitants who had not benefitted from the skills of these new arrivals. And while the common populace remained as poor as ever, the immigrants began making money by exchanging currency for pilgrims, engaging in trade and earning fees as physicians.

Consequently, by the time Alexander VI decided upon his opportunistic strike against the Jews, this was seen as a popular move. In order to raise the 200,000 ducats for Cesare's visit to France, Alexander VI ordered that all the goods and property owned by Jews in Rome should be confiscated. But even this did not raise sufficient funds. So Alexander VI found himself casting about for further victims. And it was now that his eye alighted on Pedro Aranda, his Spanish major-domo, who as a reward for his services had been created Bishop of Calahorra, a Spanish appointment which provided lucrative benefices. Pedro Aranda had been born a Jew, but had converted to Christianity during the persecution in Spain some years previously. It was thus comparatively easy for Alexander VI to have him accused of being a Marrano and of carrying out heretical practices within the Vatican. Pedro Aranda was immediately stripped of his bishopric, along with all his possessions and benefices, and confined to the dungeons of the Castel Sant'Angelo. Yet Alexander VI's setback to the Jewish community and its trade would soon be felt amongst the larger populace. Besides being greedy and perfidious, his action was also commercially short-sighted.

On the other hand, there was no denying that Alexander VI had his own far-sighted agenda here. In the early days of the Borja arrival in Italy, when the new Cardinal Alonso de Borja (the future Callixtus III) had taken up residence in Rome, there had been whisperings that the family were in fact Marranos. Such whisperings had over the years grown into common gossip and thence transmogrified into 'the truth'. Alexander VI's initial welcoming of the exiled Jews to Rome, and granting them rights, had only served to revive and confirm the widespread conviction of the Borgias' Jewish ancestry. This 'truth' had long been confirmed by many of the Borgia's Spanish cultural habits, which they had retained, making little attempt to acclimatize themselves to the mores of their adopted country. Most evident was the family habit of conversing amongst themselves in Catalan. Such familiarity confirmed the closeness of the family, as well as its secretiveness – at the same time excluding all those who could not speak this tongue. Spanish and Italian had suffi-cient similarities for an Italian to understand the gist of a conversa-tion being carried out in classical (Castilian) Spanish. But Catalan was another matter altogether. This was not even a dialect of Spanish, it was a separate language exclusive to north-eastern Spain, which derived from the dog Latin used by the Ancient Roman soldiery who had occupied this region, and came from all over the Empire. It was this which led to one of the major misconceptions concerning the Borgias. From cardinals to courtiers, many who heard the Borgia conversing amongst themselves imagined that they were speaking Hebrew.

Hence Alexander VI's confiscation of all Jewish property, followed by his imprisonment of the 'Marrano' Pedro Aranda, Bishop of Calahorra, in the Castel Sant'Angelo, went some way, at least in some quarters, towards allaying anti-Semitic suspicions concerning the Borgia ancestry. Though by now so many had heard tell of the Borgias' devious and outra-geous behaviour that it was difficult to allay any suspicions concerning the family, regardless of race. If Alexander VI could have his daughter Lucrezia Borgia publicly declared to be a virgin, then it was perhaps inevitable that all manner of exaggerated rumours should proliferate. It is this which makes for such difficulties where describing the Borgias is concerned. All one can state – dispassionately – is that they were often better than they appeared. And, as we have seen (and shall certainly see), on occasion they could be far worse.

Many may have been rightly suspicious of Alexander VI and his family, but the Pope for his part had every reason to be equally suspicious of those who encouraged him to trust them. Sending his favourite son Cesare Borgia abroad to marry into the French royal family was just such an occasion. It was only four years since Charles VIII had taken the then Cardinal Cesare Borgia, along with a mule train of papal treasures, as a hostage on his march towards Naples. Borgia père et fils may have managed to outwit the gullible Charles VIII on that occasion, but such a feat was unlikely to be repeated – especially in French territory. If instead of allowing Cesare Borgia to marry his royal cousin Carlotta, Louis XII decided instead to detain him in France as a hostage, this would give the king a profound influence over papal policy. Alexander VI knew the risks he was taking, as did his flamboyant but secretly uncertain son.

Despite such covert worries, Cesare Borgia had been very much his characteristic self when he got wind of his father's plans to subsidize his trip. According to Burchard, he immediately began ordering

> jewels, stuffs, cloth-of-gold and cloth-of-silver, silks and other luxurious goods, much of them imported at considerable expense from Venice.

He also ordered a bespoke commode to take with him; this consisted of a chamber 'covered with gold brocade outside and scarlet inside, with silver tassels within the silver urinals'.

Alexander VI well understood that if Louis XII decided to hold his son hostage, no one would be able to dissuade him from this project. However, a newly created Cardinal d'Amboise might prove a useful ally in case of other difficulties. Alexander VI was becoming increasingly aware of his son's erratic conduct, and he had warned Cesare that there should be no repeat of the diplomatic blunder in Naples involving the Count d'Aliffe's daughter. This time the prospective bridegroom was to be on his best behaviour. Also secreted amongst Cesare Borgia's luggage was the Pope's signed and sealed dispensation for Louis XII to marry Charles VIII's former wife Anne of Brittany. Unfortunately, Alexander VI had not yet been able to persuade the consistory to grant an official annulment of Louis XII's marriage to Joan of France. Such a royal divorce was considered a very serious matter by the College of Cardinals, who insisted upon adhering to the strictures of canon law – which, of course, forbad divorce, even amongst royalty. What was more, Louis XII's prior attempt to divorce his malformed but intelligent wife had already proved more than inept, resulting in 'one of the seamiest lawsuits of the age'. Louis XII had been married to Joan when he was just fourteen, and on the morning after the ceremony the proud adolescent had boasted of 'mounting his wife three or four times during the night'. However, during the divorce suit he had claimed that throughout his marriage 'his sexual prowess had been inhibited by witchcraft'. Whereupon, Joan had demanded how he had managed to make love to her so many times on their marriage night, as he had naively boasted in front of any witness who would listen. All this had inevitably come to the attention of the consistory, leading Alexander VI to conclude that if he was to satisfy Louis XII's wishes for a divorce he would have to try a less orthodox approach. He thus decided to remove consideration of this matter from the jurisdiction of the consistory, and place it in the hands of a specially convened Papal Divorce Committee. So that it could devote closer attention to the matter at hand, this would be convened in France with a number of specially selected local cardinals. Even so, he realized that all this was going to take time.

Temporarily setting aside such worries, the Pope had watched with beaming, paternal pride from the balcony of the Vatican as his son Cesare rode in splendour out across the piazza below, his glorious procession trailing behind him between the lines of awed spectators. In Alexander VI's letter of recommendation to the French King, he had described his son in the most glowing terms: 'We send Your Majesty our heart, that is to say our beloved son, Duke Valentino, who to us is the dearest of all.' There was no doubting this heartfelt paternal emotion, yet at the same time Alexander VI remained well aware of what he was doing. He had already used his beloved daughter Lucrezia to further his political aims. Indeed, he had initially made the mistake of sacrificing her to the wrong cause. Now he was taking the calculated risk of sacrificing his son and heir. On the other hand, if Cesare's mission proved to be a success, the foundations of Alexander VI's ambitious future scheme were laid. It is probable that even Cesare Borgia was only aware of the first half of this scheme; the Pope alone knew the full enormity of what he had in mind.

From Rome Cesare Borgia travelled west to the port of Civitavecchia, where he and his procession boarded a flotilla of French galleys. They sailed the 500 miles to Marseille, where they arrived at the end of October, greeted by a celebratory cannonade, followed by a week of festivities and banquets. Louis XII's court was at the time in residence at Chinon, another 500 miles north-east in the Loire Valley. This journey required Cesare to travel north through Avignon. In an unsettling déjà vu, Cesare's host in Avignon was Cardinal Giuliano della Rovere. Alexander VI's bitter rival was obliged to give Cesare the warmest of welcomes. Cardinal della Rovere could ill afford to deny hospitality in France to a guest of Louis XII. The Pope had also decided that amicable overtures were in order. In fact, Cardinal della Rovere and Alexander VI both required each other's assistance at this particular point. Alexander VI was more than eager that Cardinal della Rovere should use his influence with Louis XII to smooth Cesare's reception at the French royal court. In return, Alexander VI had granted Cardinal della Rovere the honour of being Papal Legate to the French court, where he would preside over the ceremony of bestowing upon Georges d'Amboise his cardinal's hat. The Pope had also assured Cardinal della Rovere that he would be welcome to return to Italy, where his castle at Ostia, his residence in Rome and his estates outside the city would all be returned to him. On top of this, his arrival back in Italy meant he would be able to attend consistories.

As Cesare approached Avignon, Cardinal della Rovere rode out to greet him personally, and accompanied the Duke of Valentinois into the city. An eyewitness recorded: 'Avignon never witnessed such an enthusiastic welcome. Nor in the city had there ever been a more splendid procession.' A festival was held where fountains flowed with wine, and the visitor was

> fêted by ladies and beautiful girls in whom the said Cesare takes much pleasure, knowing well how to dance and entertain them, the dances being morrisses, mummeries and other frivolities.

Yet not all was quite as it seemed – either for the twenty-three-year-old Cesare Borgia or for the fifty-five-year-old Cardinal della Rovere. Both men had syphilis and suffered from the recurrent symptoms of this disease. In the words of a secret informant working for Ludovico Sforza, Duke of Milan, who simply signed his reports 'B':

> Della Rovere has fallen sick of that disease of his: now the flowers are beginning to bloom again [the syphilitic rash]. If God does not help him he will never be quite healthy. They say publicly of Cesare that he has the malady of San Lazzaro on his face, and moreover he is not in a contented frame of mind.

In fact, syphilis was such a novel phenomenon that not even an expert such as Cesare Borgia's personal physician Gaspar Torella would yet have understood the precise manifestations of the disease or the course it would take. By this stage Cesare Borgia would have been suffering from the secondary effects, which manifest themselves in the form of rashes and 'flowering' of dry skin, visible on the face. This was what the Marquesa of Mantua's informant had noted when Borgia had returned from Naples. However, such symptoms usually clear up of their own accord after a few weeks, when the disease enters a lengthy period of latency. This accounts for why the spy 'B' only reports 'they say . . . he has the malady of San Lazzaro'. By this stage Cesare Borgia probably exhibited no syphilitic symptoms and was in the latency period. On top of this, 'the malady of San Lazzaro' usually referred to leprosy, a disease with which Cesare Borgia was certainly not infected.

As Cesare's procession continued north across France, passing through Valence, the capital city of the dukedom of Valentinois, he began to experience an increasing inner feeling of his own inadequacy. Quite simply, the young man who had been a cardinal in a Rome ruled by his father felt out of his depth. He was used to behaving as he pleased, his status – as a cardinal, as the Pope's son – guaranteed without question. Yet in France it was different. He could not avoid sensing that the elitist French nobility regarded him as nothing more than a young upstart: a bastard, devoid of royal, let alone noble blood. While his imposing stature and striking good looks meant that he was frequently misunderstood. On occasions when he felt cowed by his reception, his hesitant reserve was mistaken for aloof superiority; yet when he attempted to assert himself, he was made to feel arrogant and gauche. During a reception held in his honour at Valence, Louis XII's royal representative approached him bearing the elaborate gold collar of the Order of St Michael, the highest chivalric award the French king could bestow. Cesare flared up. He pushed aside the king's representative as he was about to place the gold collar around his neck. Cesare was adamant that it was for the king personally to bestow such an honour: he refused to accept this from a mere underling.

Meanwhile, Cardinal della Rovere pressed on ahead, preparing the way, arranging matters of diplomatic concern. And in this he proved particularly successful. On Tuesday 17 December, the very day before Cesare Borgia was due to arrive at Chinon, della Rovere received the official verdict of the Papal Divorce Committee, presided over by the Cardinal of Luxembourg. Louis XII had been granted an annulment of his marriage to Joan of France. He was now free to marry Anne of Brittany and preserve the unity of his kingdom.

Cesare Borgia's entry into Chinon next day proved a momentous affair. The royal chateau, surrounded by high walls, stood on a hill overlooking the River Vienne (a tributary of the Loire). The chateau was approached by a long ramp leading up to the main gate. Alexander VI and his son had spent much time and trouble choreographing Cesare's arrival at the chateau. Cesare's entrance was intended to be as spectacular as possible, with the aim of impressing both Louis XII and his court of nobles. The procession through the streets of Chinon and up the ramp towards the chateau was led by several dozen liveried attendants. These were followed by no less than seventy mules laden with boxes and chests containing all manner of gifts and treasures. Then came sixteen chargers led by grooms bedecked in the Borgia colours of red and yellow. Last of all came Cesare himself, mounted on a high charger covered with red and yellow satin. According to an eyewitness:

> In his cap were two double rows of five or six rubies, as large as a big bean, which gave out a great light. On the brim of his cap there were also a great quantity of jewels.

Added to this, Cesare wore a collar studded with diamonds said to have been worth 30,000 ducats; and he was accompanied on foot by 'four musicians with trumpets and clarions of silver, richly dressed, playing their instruments without ceasing'. The welcoming crowd of citizens lining the route were awestruck.

On the other hand, the court of Louis XII and his assembled nobles were somewhat less impressed. Fashion had changed in France: mere brash display had given way to a more subtle and civilized restraint. Unlike in Italy, parading such a blatant spectacle of one's wealth was considered tasteless vulgarity. Cesare, whose lavish display was intended to impress upon the French the full might of Italy's wealth and power, had only made himself into a covert laughing stock.

Yet despite the subtle mockery of the French nobility and their courtiers, Cesare was to make an impression upon the one person who mattered – namely, Louis XII. The thirty-six-year-old French monarch graciously did his best to put the bold but awkward young Cesare at his ease. And soon a confident Cesare was exhibiting the legendary Borgia charm. He quickly established a personal rapport with the king, exhibiting to the full his exceptional intellect, responding to the king with impressive wit and aplomb. D'Amboise, Louis XII's closest adviser and friend, was equally impressed.

After enjoying the pleasures of Chinon, the French court and Cesare's entourage moved on. It was customary for the French king to change residences on a regular basis, moving from one magnificent castle to another along the Loire Valley. Cesare Borgia would doubtless have been impressed by these superb chateaux, which remain to this day the finest examples of secular French medieval architecture. Though he would have been of sufficient intellect and taste to appreciate that Italy was already beginning to progress beyond such achievements, its architecture, art and culture by now embodying the unmistakable advances of the Renaissance. Such was the irony of that era. France was indisputably the more powerful country, its riches far exceeding that of any Italian city state. Yet it was the squabbling insecurity of a divided Italy which was giving birth to the modern age.

The French nobility may have been sniggering down their long medieval sleeves at the vulgar excesses of Cesare Borgia's entourage, yet it was their more rigid culture which was receding into abeyance. The tasteless display of Cesare's procession was if anything an aberration: the 'art' of the parade has to this day advanced very little since the pre-classical era. Apropos such matters, it is worth noting that during these very years Leonardo da Vinci was in the employ of Ludovico Sforza, Duke of Milan. Here, besides working sporadically on his Last Supper and attempting to construct unsuccessful flying machines, a large part of his time was devoted to creating fantastical ice sculptures, spectacular stage mechanisms, fantastic costumes and procession floats for the duke's festivals. And as we shall see, ironically it would be Cesare Borgia himself who would rescue Leonardo from such ephemeral pursuits.

Meanwhile, through the early winter months of 1499 Cesare Borgia would accompany Louis XII, Cardinal d'Amboise and the French court as it moved from chateau to chateau along the Loire Valley. For entertainment, the king and his party would set off into the wooded countryside with horns calling through the morning mist as they hunted their prey. This was the falconry season, and instead of gruesome displays of Spanish bullfighting Cesare learned the more delicate art of hunting with the finest trained birds of prey. On returning home to their current chateau, the royal party would dine on game and the finest local French wine.*

There was but one snag, though this would unfortunately skew the entire purpose of Cesare Borgia's visit. Carlotta of Naples, daughter of King Federigo of Naples, still remained in love with Guy, Count of Laval. Louis XII, and even the persuasive Cardinal d'Amboise, proved unable to induce the wilful nineteen-year-old to change her mind. Louis XII felt a genuine fatherly affection for Carlotta, and had no intention of forcing her into marriage against her will, no matter the political importance of such a union between France and the papacy. This left Cesare Borgia in considerable embarrassment. Having set off for France with such extravagant ceremony and intentions, his fruitless return to Italy would, however unjustly, have cast aspersions on his manhood and left him open to public ridicule.

The news of Cesare's failed project also gave Alexander VI considerable cause for thought back in Rome. The Pope's position now looked increasingly precarious. Both Milan and Naples were more than apprehensive over Alexander VI's detente with France. Indeed, in their own separate ways they both felt threatened. Likewise, Spain was becoming increasingly suspicious of the Pope's devious political manoeuvring. On hearing news of the new alliance between France and the papacy, the Spanish ambassador had departed from Rome in a fury. In his view, the papal office was becoming little more than the chaplaincy to the king of France, and if Alexander VI wasn't sufficiently careful he, too, might soon find himself taking refuge in Spain. Suddenly, with the failure of his plan to marry his son Cesare into the French royal family, Alexander VI found himself surrounded by hostility on all sides.

Once again, history was conforming to what Machiavelli would harshly characterize as 'Virtù e Fortuna'. Alexander VI had placed all his ambitions on the Virtù (strength and quality) of his diplomatic

---

* The red wine of Chinon, whose praises would be sung by Rabelais, was at the time widely regarded as the finest wine in France. The vineyards of both Burgundy and Bordeaux had yet to recover fully from the ravages of the Hundred Years War with England, which had ended just decades previously.

manoeuvres. Now Fortuna (luck) had turned against him. March and April passed with the sixty-eight-year-old pope isolated in Rome – worried, afraid and increasingly conscious of his age. Then, once again, history repeated itself. Lucrezia's husband Alfonso, Duke of Bisceglie, suddenly fled Rome in fear of his life – first taking refuge with the Colonna family, now more than ever enemies of the Borgias, and eventually fleeing back to Naples. This time the nineteen-year-old Lucrezia was distraught. She was six months pregnant and the husband she so loved had not even warned her of his imminent departure, for fear of word reaching her father. At the sight of his daughter, wailing in tears, Alexander VI too was stricken with remorse at the turn events had taken. But this was to be no isolated family event. A few weeks later Sancia of Aragon, young Jofrè Borgia's wayward wife, also took flight back home to Naples. This time Alexander VI was less upset. His seventeen-year-old son Jofrè's behaviour was becoming a source of increasing scandal. To such an extent that the Pope had recently taken the extreme step of confining him to the precincts of the Castel Sant'Angelo after he had been involved in yet another drunken brawl, during which a member of the city constabulary had been seriously wounded.

For their own protection, Alexander VI now despatched Lucrezia and Jofrè to Spoletto, in the papal territories some eighty miles north of Rome. At the same time, he wrote to the authorities in Spoletto:

> We trust you will receive Duchess Lucretia [sic], as is your duty, with all due honour as your regent, and show her submission in all things . . . collectively and severally, in so far as law and custom dictate in the government of the city, and whatever she may think proper to exact of you, even as you would obey Ourselves, and to execute her commands with all diligence and promptness.

Indicatively, Alexander VI was appointing the young and pregnant Lucrezia as Governor of Spoleto, rather than Jofrè. It was highly unusual for a young woman to be appointed to such a post (especially in prefer-ence to her male sibling). It also ensured her independence, sweeping powers and her own income – in case of need, or in case political events took a turn for the worse and her father was cut off in Rome. Alexander VI's fortune was now at its lowest ebb and he was all too aware of his vulnerability. Cesare was away in France, his mission come to nothing. There was not a single major city state in Italy that he could trust. He had, by now, betrayed each one of them in his own way by his devious politicking. Meanwhile, he was no longer safe even in Rome, having made enemies of the Colonna, the Caetani and the majority of the aristocratic families of the holy city. Even his cardinals could no longer be trusted.

Then, out of the blue, Fortuna came to Alexander VI's rescue. Back in France, Louis XII had remained so enamoured of his new friend Cesare that he had determined to find for him a French royal bride. Since Carlotta was out of the question, he secured for Cesare the attractive nineteen-year-old Charlotte d'Albret, whose mother was related to Louis XII's new queen, Anne of Brittany. As chance would have it, Charlotte d'Albret was also the younger sister of King John III of Navarre, whose north-eastern Spanish kingdom occupied the Basque region straddling the territory either side of the Pyrenees. Cesare Borgia and Charlotte d'Albret were married in the queen's chamber at the grand chateau of Blois on 12 May 1499. Days later Louis XII wrote delightedly informing Alexander VI that his son Cesare had 'broken his lance' no less than eight times during his wedding night, confessing that this was double the amount he had managed on his own first night with Anne of Brittany. Indeed, Alexander VI was so overjoyed at this news of his son's virile prowess that he insisted Louis XII's letter be read out to the assembled cardinals at his next consistory.

The news that the papacy was now indissolubly linked with the fortunes of France came as more than a relief to Alexander VI. Even though it meant the final extinction of Cesare's remote chance of inheriting the throne of Naples, it had the advantage of reopening papal ties with Spain. More heartening still, news now came through that Louis XII had despatched the first of his forces south towards the Alps. At last he was determined to stake his claim to the duchy of Milan. The leading French forces were commanded by Gian Giacomo Trivulzio, the skilled condottiere who had served Milan under Ludovico Sforza, until Sforza had given command of the army to his rival. Trivulzio had then defected, offering his services to France, determined to wreak revenge on his untrustworthy former master.

Following Trivulzio, the slower-moving main force of the French army began making its way south under Louis XII, accompanied by Cardinal d'Amboise and Cesare Borgia. The Duke of Valentinois had been permitted little time to celebrate his honeymoon at Blois. Though he did find occasion to inform his father that he 'was the most contented man in the world'. The nineteen-year-old Charlotte was showered with gifts: 'brocades, silks and jewels worth 20,000 ducats . . . [a] great long emerald', as well as all manner of silverware, gowns and bejewelled couture. Presumably these had all been recently tailored to fit their new owner, as they had in fact originally been purchased in Rome for Carlotta of Naples. Meanwhile in Paris, according to the Milanese ambassador, the students of the Sorbonne had celebrated Cesare's marriage by staging 'a farce which tended to the great ignominy of the pontiff'. When the king had ordered the authorities to suppress this, 'there had been a great riot'.

By July Louis XII and the bulk of his army had assembled at Lyons in preparation for their march across the Alps into Italy. The king had been particularly impressed by the way in which Cesare Borgia had used the last of his fortune to hire a mercenary army to support the French. Owing to Cesare's extravagance at the French court, there had not been a sufficient amount left from his original funds, so he had been obliged to write home to his father, who had immediately transferred a further generous sum for his son's use. Louis XII had marked his gratitude by granting Cesare Borgia the right to add the armorial bearings of the French royal house to his coat of arms. From now on, the shield of the Duke of Valentinois would bear the coat of arms of the red Borgia bull, quartered with the three golden fleurs-de-lis of France.

Ever the opportunist, Alexander VI had gone so far as to suggest to Louis XII that once France had conquered Milan, Cesare Borgia should be allowed to lead his mercenary soldiers, along with an even larger force than the 1,000 men which Louis XII had already promised, back to Rome. However, instead of marching directly to Rome, Alexander VI proposed that his son Cesare be allowed to lead his forces on a campaign through the north-eastern territories known as the Romagna and the Marches, which bordered the Adriatic. This remote, hilly littoral was officially part of the Papal Territories, but most of its small cities had fallen under the rule of various independent petty tyrants. Whilst for the most part paying little more than nominal dues to their papal overlord, many of these tyrants had imposed notorious regimes similar to that of the 'humanist tyrant' Sigismondo Pandolfo Malatesta, Lord of Rimini, who had publicly sodomized the papal emissary sent by Pius II. Alexander VI saw the subjugation of these territories as the first step in his larger strategy of establishing his own state in central Italy.

With the prospect of action, Louis XII had placed Cesare Borgia in direct command of a squadron of heavy cavalry, so that he might gain some experience in battle. Back in Rome there was another disappearance. Cardinal Ascanio Sforza, setting out on one of his regular hunting trips, unexpectedly slipped away, first seeking the protection of the Colonna family, before fleeing to join his brother Ludovico Sforza in Milan. Within weeks, Trivulzio's leading French forces were approaching the city. On 1 September Cardinal Ascanio Sforza and his brother Ludovico, the Duke of Milan, deserted the city, fleeing north to the Tyrol, where they sought sanctuary with Maximilian I, the Holy Roman Emperor. Milan offered little resistance, and soon the entire territory was under French control.

On 6 October Louis XII entered the city in triumphal procession, escorted by Cesare Borgia and Cardinal Giuliano della Rovere. The occupying French troops were hardly welcomed by the Milanese. Ludovico, Duke of Milan, may not have been particularly popular, but the invaders did little to endear themselves to the local population. The cultured Milanese regarded the French invaders as barbarians. A Venetian report spoke of how: 'The French captains spit on the floors of the rooms, while their soldiers outrage the women in the streets.' Yet not all of the invaders displayed such uncouth behaviour. Ludovico, Duke of Milan, had employed a number of artists, chief of which was, of course, Leonardo da Vinci. Cesare Borgia shared with Louis XII an appreciation of the arts, and the two of them travelled together to the outskirts of Milan, to the monastery of Santa Marie delle Grazie, where Leonardo had painted *The Last Supper*. Louis XII was so overwhelmed by this painting that he 'wanted to remove it to his kingdom . . . but as the painting was done on a wall his majesty failed to have his way'.

Some days afterwards Cesare Borgia paid a visit to Leonardo in his studio at the Corte Vecchio, the abandoned former palace of the city's rulers, whose large, tall-ceilinged rooms and empty courtyards provided the artist with ideal working space. Here Cesare Borgia saw Leonardo's enormous clay model for the Gran Cavallo, the 'Great Horse'. This was intended as a mount for the statue of Francesco Sforza, the powerful condottiere who had been the first of the family to rule Milan after the ousting of the Visconti. The prototype statue was a model of considerable artistic and engineering skill, in preparation for what was intended to be the largest bronze equestrian statue ever cast. Days after Cesare Borgia's visit, French soldiers broke into the Corte Vecchio and began using Leonardo's clay horse for target practice, reducing the model for the finest and largest equine statue yet contemplated to a pile of rubble.

Leonardo had already been planning to leave Milan and was becoming disillusioned with art in general. His errors of judgement over the experimental materials used in the painting of *The Last Supper* meant that, although it had only recently been completed, this masterpiece was already starting to peel from the wall. Leonardo had long wished to try his prowess as a military engineer. He already had pages of elaborate sketches of civil and military engineering projects – as well as blueprints for all manner of advanced weaponry, including tanks, flailing machines and mortars. Following the defeat of the Sforzas, Leonardo was planning to return to his native Florence, but it seems that Borgia made him an enticing offer. He explained to Leonardo in the strictest confidence that he was intending to set out on a campaign to conquer the Romagna and the Marches, with the aim of establishing this territory as a powerful new

Italian state. If Leonardo chose to join him, he would be charged with reinforcing castles, bolstering military defences and the like. But there was the prospect of so much more than just military engineering. The new state would require a complete overhaul of the backward Romagna. New roads, pioneering canals, the building of dams – Leonardo would be entrusted with all of these. He would be building a new state, as well as ensuring its permanence. Leonardo was determined to get back to his native Florence, but it seems he gave Borgia a loose assurance that he might join him some time during the ensuing year.

Unknown to Borgia, Leonardo had already received a similar offer from Naples, to which he was also partially committed. But Borgia's new offer sounded much more interesting. Leonardo must have been more than impressed by the charm and intellectual grasp of this strikingly handsome young man. Here was a combination of learning, aesthetic appreciation and interest in military matters which all but matched his own. Leonardo was undeniably a Renaissance man in the creative sense. Cesare Borgia must certainly have come across as a Renaissance man in the practical sense, in his ambition to apply these new ideas. Leonardo was not to know that Borgia's admirable knowledge of the new humanist ideas may not quite have squared with his actual political practices and their undeniably ruthless application. Here, in Leonardo's view, was undoubtedly a man with a future, and indeed a man who was willing to involve him in this future. Borgia was evidently more than just another capricious patron.

What is also interesting here is how advanced Cesare Borgia's plans were for his new territory. There is no doubt that before setting out for France he had spent long hours discussing these matters in secret with his father. Alexander VI may have understood that his son was capable of hot-headed and impulsive action, but he also recognized Cesare's undoubted capabilities. If the Pope was to succeed in his ambitious plans, and their unprecedented conclusions (the full extent of which even Cesare remained as yet unaware), he would have to rely upon his son. Now that Juan was gone, Cesare was the only reliable family ally he had left: Cesare alone could enable his father to implement his plan. And now that this impulsive young man – often so ruthless and beyond his control – was closely allied to the French king there was hope that he would begin to calm down, to mature, perhaps. Cesare and Louis XII had undoubtedly developed a close friendship, and Cesare had even been admitted into the French royal family. Now that Cesare was well married it was likely that the thoughtlessness of youth would become a thing of the past, allowing his many talents to come to fruition. Alexander VI was proud of his son, seeing so much of his younger self in his difficult offspring. He had no doubt that Cesare would in time become a true Borgia. His cultural learning evolving into wisdom, his impulsiveness evolving into the tactical deviousness required of a true ruler. An heir, no less.

While Cesare Borgia was meeting with Leonardo da Vinci in Milan, Alexander VI was doing his best to sort out some rather more personal matters in Rome. To understand these fully, we must go back a year to the time when Alexander VI stood in his greatest peril. As we have seen, during the previous year Giulia Farnese appears to have given birth to the *Infans Romanus*, who had by now been accepted by the Pope as his son and been named Giovanni Borgia. This would have been Alexander VI's sixth son, and his eighth child.* Shortly after Giovanni's birth, his sixty-eight-year-old father and his twenty-four-year-old mother evidently had a falling out. At any rate, Giulia Farnese certainly moved out of the Vatican. This had wounded Alexander VI deeply; all the indications are that he still doted on '*Guilia la bella*'. Just when his papacy risked falling into turmoil, he had been abandoned by the person who had given him

---

* This includes the three children to the mistress who preceded Vanozza de' Cattanei. As we have seen, the oldest of these, Pedro Luis, had died, passing on his title 1st Duke of Gandia, as well as his royally connected Spanish fiancée Maria Enriquez, to the ill-fated Juan Borgia, Cesare's younger brother. Pedro Luis's younger sister had married well and had produced the child who would many decades later become Pope Innocent X, but for the time being would play no part in Alexander VI's dynastic schemes. The third child of Alexander VI's earlier liaison had died at the age of twenty-four, nine years before his father became pope. This meant that by now Alexander VI's hopes rested on the shoulders of his favourites Cesare and Lucrezia, while Jofrè had become a liability and Giovanni was still an infant.

such solace. This was also the period when he had been dealing with the recalcitrant Savonarola, who kept calling for a Council of the Church, with powers to adjudicate on the Pope's fitness to remain as pontiff. At the same time, Cesare was preparing to depart on his all-important trip to France – the greatest gamble of Alexander VI's career, in the face of opposition from all the major city states in Italy. Either Alexander VI would emerge from this gamble with a cast-iron alliance with France, or his son and heir would be held hostage to curtail his papal powers, bringing all his plans to an abrupt halt. His only solace had been the joyous marriage of Lucrezia to Alfonso, Duke of Bisceglie – until this, too, had been cast asunder with Alfonso's flight back home to Naples.

Yet now, just a year later, Alexander VI was filled with happiness. Not only were his plans for Cesare coming to fruition, but in August his beloved 'Giulia la bella' responded to his pleas and returned to live with him at the Vatican. There ensued an act which may or may not have been connected with this happy event. Burchard reported that a handsome young groom attached to the household of Cardinal Juan Borgia* was found dead in the Tiber, his body grotesquely mutilated. The Pope was a jealous man, especially where Giulia was concerned, and it seems that the young groom had fallen foul of Alexander VI on account of some exaggerated rumour concerning him and Giulia.

In the following month, after constant diplomatic pressure, King Federigo of Naples agreed to send back his son Alfonso, Duke of Bisceglie, who had fled Rome in fear of his life. With the political situation such as it was, and a large French army back on Italian soil, King Federigo could ill afford to upset the Pope. Alexander VI was only too pleased to empha-size his new friendship with the French king, giving the impression that he alone was capable of restraining Louis XII and any thoughts he might have entertained of marching south to pursue the French claim to the throne of Naples.

Alfonso, Duke of Bisceglie, duly departed from Naples. Cautiously, he decided against returning directly to Rome. Instead, skirting the Holy

---

* The Pope's great-nephew.

City, he travelled directly to Spoletto, where he was reunited with his heavily pregnant wife Lucrezia, who was overjoyed at this miraculous reunion organized for her by her father. Not to be outdone, Alexander VI himself travelled north for a brief visit to receive the ecstatic gratitude of his daughter and the wary thanks of her husband Alfonso. But there was more than just pleasure to this visit.

Previously, Lucrezia had always been integral to his plans, but mainly as an asset on the marriage market, useful for forging relations with major powers. However, there must have been something in her strength of character which caused him to entrust her, at least for the time being while Cesare was away, with a more prominent and powerful role. And this, despite her pregnant state and the fact that she would be dealing with male officials in the habit of wielding extensive power on their own behalf.

Alexander VI had recently appointed Lucrezia as governor of Spoletto, though this had appeared to many as little more than placing her there as a proxy for himself. Now, during the course of his short visit north to meet her and her reunited husband, he appointed her to the command of the fortress at Nepi. This was a classic, twelfth-century, high-walled castle, with four large circular defensive towers, one at each corner, garrisoned with a permanent force of papal soldiers. Despite such apparent invulnerability, Alexander VI was determined to fortify Nepi even further, so that it would become impregnable. This was to be his ultimate bolt-hole, where in time of trouble he could hold out until his allies came to his rescue. It had recently been occupied by Cardinal Ascanio Sforza, until he abandoned it to flee north and join his brother Ludovico, Duke of Milan.

Just twenty miles north of Rome, Nepi formed a link with Spoletto in the Papal Territories, adding considerably to Lucrezia's governorship. Alexander VI was consolidating his papal presence north of Rome at the expense of his enemies. Certain estates of the Caetani and the Colonna were also 'absorbed' during the absence of their previous owners who had fled. Alexander VI's appropriations went unopposed, owing to a 'reconciliation' which he had recently engineered with the Orsini family, who now had much more need of the Pope's friendship than his enmity if they wished to retain their possessions and influence in Rome.

Alexander VI also continued to strengthen his position in Rome. Just three years previously he had promoted his great-nephew Juan to the College of Cardinals. Now it was the turn of his fifty-eight-year-old great-nephew Francesco Borgia, who had recently been appointed to the important financial post of treasury general. In fact, he had almost certainly taken over many of the duties of the absent vice-chancellor Cardinal Ascanio Sforza. On 3 November the incumbent Bishop of Cosenza (a city in southern Italy) was staying in Viterbo, north of Rome, when, according to Burchard, he suddenly 'died of the plague', having seemed to be in perfect health the previous day. Three days later, Francesco Borgia was appointed to this lucrative see. (The following year he would become a cardinal, and in his later years he would act as tutor to Alexander VI's youngest son Giovanni.) Having overcome any external vulnerability through his alliance to the French, Alexander VI was determined to consolidate his position in Rome before making his next move.

As Lucrezia Borgia's time drew near, Alexander VI was determined that his daughter should return to Rome, where the best possible medical services were available. The long and difficult journey was made with Lucrezia carried on a litter, while her husband rode beside her. In early November Lucrezia Borgia finally gave birth in Rome to a son, who was named Rodrigo after his grandfather. The Pope was overcome with joy at the birth of his first (acknowledged) grandchild, who would be christened in a grand ceremony at St Peter's. This was attended by all the ambassadors in Rome, as well as the members of the College of Cardinals present in the city. The infant was baptized in an ostentatious silver bowl in the shape of a shell, and the ceremony was performed by the new Bishop of Cosenza. At the ensuing banquet, Lucrezia received 'two silver sweetmeat dishes from the College of Cardinals, laden with 200 ducats which were disguised as bonbons'. Even the infant's father Alfonso, Duke of Bisceglie, now felt safe in Rome as an honoured guest under the protection of his father-in-law the Pope.

The christening of the Pope's grandson in St Peter's, with the College of Cardinals in attendance, was an unprecedented event. And the attendance of all the ambassadors meant that there was no attempt to keep this event a secret. As news of the unique occurrence spread, it was accepted by the long-suffering citizens of Rome as yet a further example of 'Spanish custom'. Others, throughout Italy, were not always quite so tolerant. Beyond Italy, it was another matter altogether. As the rumours spread throughout Christendom, the story was considered too implausible to be given credence. This was yet another slander against the Pope, disseminated by enemies of the Holy Church. Ironically, the reign of Alexander VI was increasingly being viewed as a boost to the Church in some quarters. Here was a strong pope, capable of suppressing a heretic such as Savonarola. Likewise, he was willing to make a bold alliance with France – to the benefit of both nations, to say nothing of bringing a semblance of lasting peace to Italy.

However, scandalous incidents involving the Borgia family were rapidly approaching a tipping point. From now on, the behaviour of the Borgias – in particular Cesare – would begin to evoke an altogether different reaction.

CHAPTER 10

IL VALENTINO'S CAMPAIGN

AFTER LOUIS XII'S TRIUMPHAL entry into Milan in 1499, all the Italian states made sure that their ambassadors were in attendance at the grand banquet which celebrated his conquest. Now France had established a seemingly permanent foothold in the Italian peninsula. What would come next? The neighbouring states of Venice, Florence and Genoa were all in varying degrees wary, while Naples noted that Louis XII had as yet made no move to renounce any French claim to the kingdom. The ambassadors picked up no verifiable gossip concerning his next move. The only thing that struck them was the exceptional favour he seemed to show to his new favourite Cesare Borgia, the Duke of Valentinois, now known throughout Italy as 'Il Valentino'.

In fact, the next political move in the Italian peninsula was all too predictable for those who had concentrated on anything but their own interests. Within days of the fall of Milan, according to Burchard, Alexander VI pronounced that:

> the vicars [i.e. de facto rulers] of Rimini, Pesaro, Imola, Forli, Camerino and Faenza, as well as the Duke of Urbino, feudatories

of the Church in Rome, have failed to pay their annual census to the Apostolic Chamber, and so [the Pope] has removed their titles and declared them forfeit.

Burchard added that the French government in Milan had loaned 45,000 ducats to the Pope, so that he could assemble an army to retake these 'feudatories', and that 'The Duke of Valence, captain of these troops, has received this sum in the name of the Church.'

The above-named cities were all in the Romagna, mostly small towns ruling over a stretch of surrounding countryside. The Romagna itself stretched some 150 miles or so along the north-western Adriatic Coast, extending some 20 to 30 miles inland. This region of remote valleys and woodlands would famously be described by Machiavelli, who came to know it well. His words, as ever, are filled with political acumen, characterizing it as

a breeding ground for all the worst crimes, the slightest incident liable to give rise to outbreaks of widespread murder and rape. This arose because of the wickedness of the ruling lords, and not, as was commonly held, on account of the brutal nature of their subjects. For because these lords were poor, but chose to live as if they were rich, they had to resort to innumerable cruelties, which were inflicted in all manner of ways . . . These people were impoverished, but were subject to no consistent application of law, so they would seek to redress their injuries on others even worse off than themselves.

In fact, such was the prevalent lawlessness that this region had become renowned for providing soldiers to mercenary armies all over Italy. Little wonder that Federigo da Montefeltro, the previous ruler of Urbino,* had been able to raise such an effective force that his services were in constant demand. This had earned him and his comparatively

---

* Technically, Urbino is in the Marche region, just south of the Romagna.

insignificant mountain city a small fortune. The riches of Renaissance Urbino, which remain to this day, stand as his testament; as does its most famous son, Raphael, whose father had been court painter to the Montefeltro family.

Just as Machiavelli so wisely perceived, the unruliness of the region was largely the fault of its more notorious rulers, rather than its indigenous people or its rough terrain. In fact, many parts of the region contained fertile land, large tracts of which could have been amenable to agricultural exploitation, had it not been for the anarchic conditions inspired by its inept, cruel and divisive political rule. The region was also well-protected. Between its powerful northern neighbour Venice lay the buffer states of Ferrara and Bologna. The Apennine Mountains stood before its larger western neighbour Florence. And to the south lay the Papal States north of Rome, a large number of which remained under the Pope's rule. As Alexander VI had already surmised: if such a region became united, and was returned to the fold of the Papal States, it would command the whole of central Italy.

In mid-November Cesare Borgia made a secret dash from Milan to Rome, arriving in the Holy City on the 18th and entering inconspicuously through one of the minor gates at dusk. He had come to consult with his father, whom he had not seen in person since his departure for France almost precisely a year previously. Three days later, Cesare Borgia rode back north in command of some 1,500 soldiers of the Papal Army, all uniformed in the Borgia colours. This force joined up with the French mercenaries whom the Borgias had hired from Louis XII. The French contingent consisted of a formidable force of 4,000 battle-hardened Swiss and Gascon infantry under the control of the Bailly de Dijon, plus 800 cavalry under Yves d'Alègre. Although Cesare Borgia was to be the commander-in-chief, these two experienced commanders would be on hand to guide and advise him in military tactics. Significantly, this force was also accompanied by a number of large horse-drawn cannons. These new French weapons had caused terror throughout Italy when first seen in the invading army of Charles VIII. In battle, they were highly effective against infantry and cavalry alike. But most of all they proved devastating to the walls of any city under siege. These were the weapons which would change the face of war from this time on.

Filled with pride at his new assignment, it was now that Cesare Borgia proclaimed his personal Latin motto: *Aut Caesar aut nihil* ('Either Caesar or nothing'). This hinted at the extent of his ambitions. He was identifying himself with the greatest general of ancient Rome, and would go to any lengths to achieve his aim: death or glory. Late in November, Italy's new Caesar launched a rapid invasion of the Romagna, following the one serviceable road which crossed the heart of the region. This was the ancient Roman Via Emelia, which in traditional Roman fashion travelled in a straight line from Piacenza (in the heart of Milanese terri-tory) directly south-east to the coast at Rimini. Most of the major cities of the Romagna had sprung up at intervals along this trading route.

Just prior to Cesare's invasion of the Romagna, Alexander VI had despatched his trusted young great-nephew Cardinal Juan Borgia on an important diplomatic mission to Venice. This was intended to reassure any Venetian suspicions concerning Cesare Borgia's campaign. The Pope wished to make it clear that he had absolutely no aggressive intent with regard to Venice. Cesare Borgia's invasion was only directed at the Romagna, and although the buffer state of Bologna lay on the Via Emelia, Alexander VI gave his assurance that Cesare's troops would not attack the city or do anything but march peaceably through its territory. The military phase of the campaign would not begin until Cesare Borgia's troops had crossed the Bolognese border and passed into the Romagna. The Venetians accepted the Pope's word, but nonetheless remained suspi-cious. They would keep a close eye on these military proceedings taking place some twenty miles south of their territory. Such a distance was just a day's march and within audible distance of Borgia's cannons.

By 17 November Cesare Borgia had reached the small city of Imola, which surrendered after putting up a perfunctory resistance. He then marched fifteen miles down the Via Emelia to Forli, where the outer city itself quickly capitulated, whereupon the French and Swiss mercenaries began plundering and raping the inhabitants. Cesare Borgia was hardly pleased at this behaviour, which his French commanders did nothing to halt. He excused himself by claiming that he could not control the soldiers, because they answered only to the French king. He did, however, promise that when he himself became Lord of the Romagna no such atrocities would be permitted and that all civil rights would be restored to the people. This was the first public indication that he intended to take over the Romagna as his personal fiefdom and that he already had in mind an idea of how he intended to rule his new territory.

However, although the city of Forli itself and its 10,000 or so inhabitants had been subdued, its ruler had not. This was the formidable Countess Caterina Sforza, the only female ruler in Italy at the time, who had quickly retreated with her soldiers to the safety of the city's fortress. The towering geographical location, flooded moats and spectacularly strong walls of this fortress, which even contained a further walled inner citadel, made it appear all but impregnable.

Caterina Sforza had been born thirty-seven years previously, the illegitimate child of an earlier ruler of Milan. She had demonstrated both remarkable intelligence and wilfulness during her upbringing at the Renaissance court. Her first husband had been Girolamo Riario, who was related to the della Rovere family. The lordship of Imola had been granted to her husband by Pope Sixtus IV. Riario had subsequently been cut down by the invading Orsi family, rulers of nearby Forli. Amidst the mayhem, Caterina had managed to escape to the fortress, abandoning her children as hostages. When her Orsi enemies led her children below the walls and threatened to kill them in front of her, she stood defiantly on the battlements and contemptuously raised her skirts, exposing her nakedness. Boldly, she taunted the Orsi: 'Take a good look, I've still got what it takes to make more children.'

With the aid of Ludovico, Duke of Milan, she had eventually driven off the Orsi. Since then she had ruled Forli through a long troubled period of some twenty years. During this time she had taken several lovers, and inbetweentimes a second and a third husband, neither of whom had survived. When she discovered who had murdered her second husband, she had killed the murderers and all their immediate families, including their wives and children. Her third husband had died just two years previously. Such was her character that she became popularly known as 'the virago' – a title which conveyed both the admiration and the fear in which she was held by her subjects, and indeed throughout the region. None dared to challenge her rule.

Thus was the woman whom Cesare Borgia rode into Forli to meet during a violent December rainstorm. He and Caterina had arranged a parley at the fortress, with the mounted Cesare Borgia shouting up to the flame-haired Countess of Forli on her battlements. Cesare Borgia promised her that if she agreed to surrender, he – in the name of His Holiness Pope Alexander VI – would guarantee her safe passage, as well as compensating her for the loss of her ancestral territory. The tall, powerful Caterina shouted down to him defiantly that she trusted neither him nor his father, and would remain inside her fortress no matter what. The twenty-four-year-old Cesare Borgia had not yet fully grasped the art of negotiation – Italian-style – despite the consummate example of his father. Although her position was apparently impossible, Caterina had already taken steps to outwit the naive Cesare Borgia. She was well aware that according to notions of chivalry, Borgia's French soldiers would consider it a stain on their honour if they went into battle against a woman. And she knew that it was likely to take some time and effort before Borgia managed to persuade them that it was in their best mercenary interests to act otherwise.

Caterina Sforza was in fact playing for time, as the previous day she had secretly despatched a trusted local messenger to ride post-haste to Alexander VI in Rome, bearing a message that she was willing to surrender on any terms. Yet this message was not quite what it seemed. The parchments containing the message were rolled up inside a cane tube, which also contained cloth that had recently been used to wrap the cadaver of a victim who had died of the plague. According to Burchard: 'If the Pope had opened them he would have been poisoned and would have been dead a few hours or days later.' Unfortunately, Caterina's trusted Forli messenger, a musician from her court, had encountered one of his fellow citizens working as a servant in the Vatican. In a loose moment the musician had revealed the secret of his message, which was then betrayed. Both men were slowly tortured to death in order to extract the last vestiges of information in their possession.

Once again, it seems, Cesare Borgia undertook a fast, secret journey back to Rome to consult with his father. Some sources have conflated this journey with his earlier meeting, but there are indications that Cesare Borgia was still, at this early stage, communicating closely in person with his father. The vulnerability of written messages has already been demonstrated. And, as we shall see, however strained the relations became between wily father and headstrong son, their personal contacts would remain as frequent as circumstances allowed. At this stage, Cesare still had a lot to learn from his father, and both understood this.

Cesare Borgia returned to Forli, and on 26 December rode to the edge of the moat for a further parley with Caterina. This time Caterina presented a different face: she lowered the drawbridge and invited Cesare into her castle, so that they could speak in private. Cesare Borgia responded positively, but decided to ride in wearing full armour just in case. As soon as Cesare rode on to the drawbridge Caterina ordered it to be raised, but Cesare managed to escape unhurt. Had he been dislodged from his horse into the moat, he would have drowned.

In reality, Caterina was once again playing for time. She had received intelligence that Ludovico Sforza, Duke of Milan, was on the point of leading an army into northern Italy to retake Milan from the French. When this happened, the French governor of Milan would certainly order the return of the mercenaries under Borgia's command, so that they could assist in the defence of Milan. This would leave Cesare Borgia's forces severely depleted, and in no position to continue his attempt to take Forli. Yet despite such rumours nothing materialized, and Cesare's forces remained undiminished.

Following the incident when Caterina had tried to drown Cesare Borgia in the moat, he realized that this would be a fight to the bitter end. And this time it was Cesare Borgia who had a trick up his sleeve. The chivalric French may have had misgivings about setting up cannon to blast through the walls of a fortress held by a woman, but one of Cesare's closest lieutenants, Dionigi da Naldo, had no such qualms. Caterina was holding his wife and children as hostage inside the fortress. He was determined to get them back, dead or alive – and the same applied to taking their captor, Caterina Sforza. The cannon were lined up along the outer banks of the moat and, not to be outdone, the French soon followed suit. The fortress held the city's treasures and if there was to be any looting they wanted to be a part of this.

After a ceaseless bombardment which went on night and day for ten days, directed by Cesare Borgia himself, the walls were finally breached. The Swiss and Gascon mercenaries poured into the city, hacking and piking their way through the 2,000 defenders. In a last-ditch move, Caterina ordered the magazine of the inner keep of the citadel to be torched, resulting in a massive explosion. But this had the opposite effect to her intention. It sent panic through the ranks of her own troops, rather than the attackers. By nightfall Cesare Borgia and Yves d'Alègre were riding through the main gate into the citadel. Within the hour, they were dragging the bedraggled Caterina Sforza out through the waters surrounding the keep to the large house which Cesare Borgia had commandeered as his residence. Here Caterina was locked in his bedroom, with armed guards posted at the door.

Cesare Borgia now led his mercenary army further down the Via Emelia towards Pesaro, on the coast. This would be a particularly telling prize, since the ruler of Pesaro was Giovanni Sforza, who just two years previously had suffered his humiliating divorce from Lucrezia. During the course of these proceedings he had made a number of insulting slurs on the Borgias, not least of which was that Lucrezia had incestuous relations with her father and her brother Cesare. As we have seen, Cesare was excessively sensitive concerning his close relationship with Lucrezia and his strong feelings for her. These certainly had an incestuous element, which may or may not have remained subconscious. The rumour-mongers of Rome had no doubt that Cesare's relationship did stretch well beyond the borders of normal fraternal love; however, judged from this distance in time such suggestions would appear to have been exaggerations. Either way, Cesare Borgia certainly had a score to settle with Giovanni Sforza, who well realized that his life was in danger. Whether he fled from Pesaro at this point is not clear. What is clear is that Cesare Borgia was cheated out of his revenge by a sudden change in the political situation.

On 26 January 1500 news came through that Ludovico Sforza had launched an attempt to retake Milan, crossing the border into northern Italy at the head of a mercenary army consisting of 9,000 of the best Swiss mercenaries. Yves d'Alègre at once summoned all the troops under his command and marched north to assist in the French defence of Milan. Cesare Borgia was left with little more than a skeleton force, consisting largely of Papal Troops. There was now no question of attempting to take Pesaro; he would have to return to Rome to consult with his father. Before departing, Cesare decided to retain possession of the cities he had overrun, leaving them under the command of Ramiro de Lorqua, his trusted Spanish deputy. Lorqua was ordered to post garrisons at Forli, Imola and other small towns along the Via Emelia which had been taken. Cesare Borgia then set off south across the mountains towards Rome. With him he took a small force of Papal Troops, as well as his prized prisoner Caterina Sforza.

What precisely took place between the charismatic young Cesare Borgia and the strong-willed Caterina Sforza during the weeks they were together – following the fall of Forli, the advance towards Pessaro and the ensuing long march across the Apennines back to Rome – remains a matter of speculation. The usually well-informed contemporary Venetian diarist Sanuto wrote how Cesare Borgia, 'as I hear, was keeping the said lady, who is a most beautiful woman . . . day and night in his room; with whom, in the opinion of all, he is taking his pleasure'. Andrea Bernardi, 'the barber chronicler from Forli', wrote 'of the injuries [committed] on the body of our poor and unfortunate lady Caterina Sforza, who was possessed of great physical beauty', strongly suggesting that Cesare raped his female captive. Cesare Borgia's biographer Sarah Bradford concurs that such rumours may well have been true. 'He was sensual, also had a streak of cruelty in him, and the piquancy of having his beautiful enemy in his power would have appealed to his cruelty as well as his senses.' On the other hand, the thirty-six-year-old Caterina was notorious for taking handsome young lovers, and the charismatically attractive young Cesare would certainly have fallen into this category. Bradford even goes so far as to suggest that 'Caterina's sexual record suggests that she may not have been an unwilling victim.'

Either way, on 26 February 1500 Cesare Borgia finally reached Rome, entering in triumph through the northern Porta del Popolo, proceeding down the main Corso towards the centre of the city. Alexander VI had arranged for his son's grand procession to be led by the College of Cardinals, the foreign ambassadors and the authorities of Rome, decked out in all their finery. This was in the midst of Carnival, the traditional time of revelry, and the city was filled with boisterous visitors, who lined the streets hoping for a glimpse of the conquering hero 'Il Valentino'. Cesare Borgia did not disappoint his audience, riding at the head of his liveried troops in what would become his habitual ceremonial dress: a black velvet tunic and black robe, parted to reveal the single gold collar of the exclusive Order of St Michael, presented to him by Louis XII. Gone were the peacock outfits donned by the immature Cardinal Cesare Borgia, designed to shock, impress and outshine his companions with whom he set out on his hunting trips. His time at the sophisticated French court, in the company of his avuncular friend Louis XII, had instilled in him a new confidence. From now on, at ceremonial occasions, he would stand out from the crowd dressed all in black, 'a colour which with its outward connotations of drama, its inward feeling of narcissism and introversion, was a reflection of his own personality'. Even so, certain symbols of his former braggadocio remained: he was accompanied by his personal guard of 100 men, each with the word 'César'* emblazoned in silver across his chest. And behind him rode Caterina Sforza herself. According to some reports, she too was dressed in black velvet. Make of this what one will.

As the procession turned towards the Ponte Sant'Angelo to cross the Tiber into Trastevere, Cesare Borgia would have seen the new high tower of the Castel, recently constructed by his father, bedecked with fluttering flags. The ramparts of the Castel were lined with heralds sounding clarions of welcome, whilst in the background cannons sounded

---

* The Spanish version of his first name.

salvoes in his honour as he made his way towards St Peter's. His father was waiting to welcome him inside the Vatican, bursting with pride at his son's magnificent achievement (magnified beyond all measure in the eyes of his doting father). Alexander VI received Cesare in the reception chamber abutting the Borgia apartments. This grand hall, reserved for receiving honoured guests such as foreign ambassadors or rulers of state, as well as the occasional 'secret consistory', was known as the Sala del Pappagallo ('Parrot's Room').* When Cesare Borgia entered the papal presence he greeted his father in their familial tongue (i.e. Catalan) and Alexander VI replied using the same language. Then Cesare kneeled to kiss the Pope's foot in the traditional manner. Unable to restrain himself, Alexander VI clasped his son to his bosom, kissing him, overcome with both laughter and tears of joy.

Only when seen in the context of what was to come does this excessive welcome for Cesare Borgia not seem quite so out of proportion. Cesare Borgia's campaign had taken but a modest sliver of territory: a little less than forty miles along the Via Emelia, together with the cities in this stretch, which of course included the agricultural hinterland on either side. It had then been halted in its tracks by the recall of the French mercenaries to defend Milan, thus indicating to all who was the real power behind the campaign. Yet in the mind of Alexander VI, and to a certain extent Cesare Borgia (as far as he knew of his father's ambitious plans), this was but the first step in a far greater endeavour. It simply laid the foundation. Indications of this can be seen in the express orders that Cesare Borgia had given to the Spanish and Italian commanders whom he had left behind in the Romagna, along with their mixed Spanish and Italian garrisons. The brutality and excesses of the conquering French troops were not under any circumstances to be repeated. Cesare's

---

* This received its unusual name because in the early medieval era it contained a live parrot in a cage. According to one of many legends, a parrot (*pappagallo*) was said to indicate that the Pope (*il Papa*) was in residence. It is claimed that this custom is said to have followed the popes into exile during the Avignon papacy, and returned to Rome with them. A wall of the present-day chamber is decorated with a fresco which contains two parrots.

commanders were to treat the local authorities with respect, in order to seek a more equitable and inclusive form of government. The citizens of the Romagna would soon get over any regret they might have had concerning the overthrow of their rulers. Even the respected, though ruthless, Caterina Sforza would not be missed for long in Forlì.

Within three weeks of Cesare Borgia's arrival in Rome the Pope officially declared his son to be 'his temporal Vicar of San Mauro, Imola and Forlì'. Indicatively, this appointment took place before Alexander VI appointed Cesare Borgia as Captain-General of the Papal Forces. Cesare had taken these possessions in the name of Borgia, rather than reoccupying them as Papal Territories. And the administration he was setting up was one loyal to himself, rather than the papacy. The intention is clear. In the event of Alexander VI's death, these Romagna territories were to remain a Borgia possession, rather than pass on to any future pope.

Not until 29 March 1500, well over a month after Cesare's triumphal entry into Rome, would Alexander VI duly invest his son Cesare with the official title of Captain-General of the Papal Forces (*Gonfaloniere e Capito Generale della Chiesa Romana*). As was customary, this ceremony took place in St Peter's Basilica, where the Pope officially presented

> the duke of Valentinois with the mantle and cap of the standard-bearer [Gonfaloniere] of the Roman Church; and after Cesare had taken the customary oath . . . he handed him two blessed banners and the baton of office.

At last, Cesare had now officially taken on the title that he had so envied when it had been held by the incompetent braggart Juan Borgia, his younger brother, prior to his mysterious murder. Alexander VI may or may not at some stage have suspected Cesare of having a hand in that vicious deed, but he had long since dismissed all thought of this from his mind. No, surprisingly, Alexander VI may well have chosen to withhold this appointment from Cesare for reasons other than the nicety of the Romagna being conquered by a Borgia rather than the papal commander.

Throughout his life, Alexander VI had shown scant evidence of piety, leading more than a few to suspect that indeed he had little more than a purely ceremonial belief in the deity. On the other hand, he had always retained a deep faith in another aspect of the supernatural, which many ascribed to his Spanish origins. Alexander VI was a deeply superstitious man. He had appointed his favourite son Juan as Captain-General, only for him to be murdered. A superstitious man may not have wished to tempt fate by appointing his next favourite son to the same post. Alexander VI's excessive joy at Cesare's return from his campaign in the Romagna could well have been prompted by previous superstitious fears. But the ghost had now been laid to rest: Cesare had returned alive after commanding the Papal Troops – he could appoint him regardless. Any such surmise is, of course, no more than speculation, based upon mere clues. I have included them only as possible indications of Alexander VI's character, and the Borgia ethos. Meanwhile, there is, of course, one undeniable fact. As we shall see, Cesare Borgia's appointment to the post of Captain-General was central to Alexander VI's future ambitions for the Borgia family. But such plans remained for the moment covert. What was plain for all to see was merely the first step. As Cesare Borgia's biographer observes: 'The Pope's nomination of his son as official commander of the papal armies implied nothing less than a total Borgia takeover of the Church.'

Yet what was to become of Caterina Sforza? Upon her arrival in Rome, Alexander VI allowed her to reside in the Villa Belvedere, amidst the gardens overlooking the Vatican. Despite the comfort of her surroundings, this was unmistakably house arrest. Alexander VI wished her to sign away her rights as Countess of Forli. This was, at least in part, a formality, for her title was not recognized by the papal authorities. But Alexander VI wished for a cast-iron legal foundation to the Borgia ownership of these newly acquired territories. True to form, Caterina refused to sign any such document. For the moment she placed her hopes in her uncle Ludovico Sforza retaking Milan. And surprisingly, in February 1500, he succeeded in ousting the French from much of Milanese territory. It was probably this which encouraged Caterina to attempt a daring escape. This was organized by a Milanese friar called Lauro Bossi, who was in contact with Ludovico Sforza; but the plot was soon betrayed, and Caterina Sforza was transferred to a grim dungeon in the Castel Sant'Angelo. By April, Milan was once more in the hands of the French, with Caterina's uncle Duke Ludovico being led off to France in chains. It looked as if all hope for Caterina was lost.

A slight restoration of her fortunes would come from an unexpected source. When Yves d'Alègre heard of Caterina's plight he used his influence through Louis XII for her to be treated according to the rules of chivalry. After some time, Alexander VI was pressurized into reluctantly releasing Caterina:

> On 30 June 1501 Caterina emerged from the dungeon. The horrors and sufferings of the months spent in the darkness of her cell had taken their toll. Of her beauty and her bold affirmation of life only traces remained.

Caterina's celebrated red hair had turned white, and she appeared a broken woman. Alexander VI now insisted that she publicly sign away her rights to Forli, and this time she relented. She was then permitted to take refuge in Florence. Her third husband had been a minor member of the ruling Medici family, who placed a villa at her disposal. She would eventually die eight years later, aged forty-six, in the convent of La Murate in Florence.* To her dying day, Caterina would never reveal what took place between her and Cesare Borgia during her time in his captivity. However, in her last days she would confess to a Dominican friar: 'If I could write anything, I would stupefy the world.'

But back to Rome in the months after Cesare Borgia's triumphal entry into the city. This was now 1500, the long-awaited Jubilee Year celebrating one and a half millennia since the birth of Christ. It was

---

* Caterina's son Giovanni, by her third husband, Giovanni de' Medici, would go on to become one of the most successful condottieri of his time, under the name Giovanni dalle Bande Nere. His son, Cosimo de' Medici, would in 1569 become the first Duke of Florence, and later be accorded the title Grand Duke of Tuscany.

(rightly) expected that Rome would be flooded with pilgrims, who soon overcrowded all the inns and taverns, as well as the many makeshift hostelries that opened up. Even the cheapest accommodation of all – the basic hospices maintained by every Christian nation for its visiting citizens who could not afford lodgings – were soon packed to overflowing. The people of Rome would be simply astounded at the numbers who arrived from the faraway nations of northern Europe, most of them making the treck on foot across the Alpine passes.*

At Easter the Holy Year was duly proclaimed by Alexander VI, welcoming all who wished to make the pilgrimage to Rome. However, for those who were unable to make this arduous voyage, he offered special indulgences, which could be paid by such as could afford them. Alexander VI would also make use of the Jubilee Year to gather further funds from those of sufficient clerical position and wealth who wished to be appointed cardinals. In all, during the course of the year he would appoint no less than twelve new cardinals. Of these, a quarter would be Borgias, or related to the family (such as Cardinal Amanieu d'Albret, Cesare's brother-in-law), whilst several more would be Spanish. The appointment of these cardinals was, in fact, as much a financial transaction as a friendly gesture. Costs for these red hats would range from 25,000 ducats (for the wealthy Archbishop of Seville) down to around 5,000 ducats (for Bishop Podocatharo, the loyal papal secretary, who also acted as the Pope's trusted physician). The total amount raised was in the region of 160,000 ducats. As we shall see, this was just the beginning.

The Jubilee Year meant that Rome was soon thriving as never before in recent centuries. Alexander VI ensured that much of the added papal income was used to improve the city. In preparation for the Easter celebrations, Alexander VI had ordered the clearing of the medieval alleyways and slums which bordered the route from the Ponte Sant'Angelo to St Peter's. This enabled the building of a much expanded Via Alessandria:

---

* Several sources ascribe this large northern influx to the many millennial cults which particularly thrived across northern Europe. Large followings were attracted to hellfire preachers claiming that the Holy Year would see the 'end of time' and the 'resurrection of the dead', as prophesied in the Book of Revelation 20: 1–6.

a new, suitably grand approach to the Vatican.* Such drastic demolition would prove more than necessary. It is estimated that on Easter Sunday, 19 April 1500, as many as 200,000 pilgrims were crammed into St Peter's Square and the nearby streets for the Pope to give his traditional blessing.† The clearing of these Trastevere slums was but the beginning of a widespread reconstruction programme which Alexander VI instigated throughout the city. Where previous popes had mainly been preoccupied with building churches and artworks intended as memorials to their own greatness, Alexander VI actually concentrated much of his energies on the city's infrastructure. The myriad of medieval alleyways in the city itself, for so long the haunt of thieves, cutpurses and murderers, now gradually began to give way to more modern thoroughfares worthy of the Holy City of Christendom. Despite Alexander VI financing such extensive improvements for the benefit of his flock, this should in no way be mistaken for evidence of him becoming a reformed character. Alexander VI continued to take a close interest in *all* aspects of his flock. According to Burchard, he even went so far as to violate the sanctity of the confession box. For his titillation and entertainment he induced a penitentiary priest to pass on to him choice titbits of any 'varied and often strange' sins that had been confessed.

Prior to Alexander VI Rome had undeniably acquired a measure of Renaissance adornment, but it was only now that it began to emerge fully as a Renaissance city, or as much of one as could be expected amidst the great ruins of its classical heyday. Florence would always remain the epicentre of Renaissance culture, yet it had not emerged as a political power. Venice continued to enter the new age in its own unique fashion, as a centre of printing, art and commerce – yet its buildings retained elements of eastern Mediterranean influence from its empire. Milan, too, was modernizing, retaining a Renaissance-style court such as the one originally installed by Ludovico Sforza, as well as elements such as Leonardo's plans for the commercial exploitation of its canals. Though its

---

* Later known as Borgo Nuovo.

† This is a larger gathering than for most present-day Easter blessings by the Pope.

crowning cathedral remained essentially a masterpiece of Gothic architecture. Meanwhile, Naples continued its own sporadic awakening to the
new age. The whole of Italy was undergoing a profound change. And
now that the French appeared to be permanently ensconced in Milan,
Louis XII was turning his eye on Naples – as, too, was Spain. In pursuit
of his diplomatic agenda, Alexander VI had established strong links with
both these nations. He foresaw this as his opportunity to establish Rome
as the powerhouse of the new Italy.

CHAPTER 11

BIDING TIME

N OT LONG AFTER CESARE Borgia's triumphant entry into Rome
in February 1500 he learned that Charlotte, the wife he had
left behind in France, was pregnant with his child. Alexander VI was
overjoyed: the Borgia succession was now ensured. The Pope immediately promised several thousand ducats to France to pay for Charlotte's
safe journey to Rome. However, Charlotte replied that she was unwilling
to undertake such a journey on account of her pregnancy. Finally, the
news came through in May that she had given birth to a daughter. This
child would be named Louise, after Louis XII. Charlotte's powerful
father Alain d'Albret immediately sent a message to Rome inviting
Cesare Borgia to visit his wife and new child. According to the Venetian
ambassador, Cesare Borgia courteously replied that 'he cares little for
returning to France'.

It soon became clear to both Cesare Borgia and the Pope that Louis
XII had no intention of permitting Charlotte and her child to leave
France, even if she wished to do so. Louis XII still did not fully trust
the Borgias, especially Alexander VI, and wished to retain Cesare's wife
and heir as hostages to ensure the loyalty of the Pope and his son. At the

same time, there were a variety of reasons for Cesare Borgia not wishing to leave Italy. With the retaking of Milan by the French in April, this meant that Louis XII's mercenary troops would once again be available for Cesare Borgia to launch a further campaign in the Romagna. In pursuit of this aim, Alexander VI immediately began making the necessary diplomatic arrangements to guarantee that the new campaign would take place unimpeded by outside interference. The main difficulties on this front came from Venice and France. The Venetians had to be reassured that Cesare Borgia's conquests in the Romagna posed no threat to their territory to the north, or to the main Venetian trade route down the Adriatic to the ports and islands of its eastern Mediterranean empire (which, although under severe threat from the Ottomans, still included such sizeable possessions as Cyprus and Crete). In order to secure freedom of passage in the Adriatic, Venice had already guaranteed the 'protection' of the coastal city of Rimini and the strategic city state of Faenza on the Via Emelia some twenty miles inland. However, at this stage Venice's military resources were at full stretch. Venice was in reality under severe threat from the Ottoman forces advancing through the northern Balkans. Alexander VI offered to strike a deal with Venice. As Pope he would summon an international crusade against the Ottoman Turks, as long as Venice agreed to withdraw its protection from Faenza and Rimini.

This was a rash promise and Alexander VI knew it. The time, diplomatic effort, and funds required for such an undertaking would be considerable. Alexander VI was soon organizing the financial side. This aspect of the coming crusade could certainly be turned to his advantage. Given sufficient accounting expertise, such as he had gained during his long years as vice-chancellor, it would surely be possible to siphon off sufficient funds to finance Cesare's next planned Romagna campaign. According to Pastor, after despatching envoys to solicit funds from the crowned heads of Europe, Alexander VI turned his attention to lesser fry: 'For his own part, he had imposed a tithe upon all the inhabitants of the Papal States and on the clergy throughout the world.' Then came the cardinals. Now it was time for the new appointees to show their gratitude towards the man responsible for their recent elevation. And such gratitude would not be limited to recent appointees. A list was drawn up of all forty-one cardinals, along with their incomes. Each was to contribute 10 per cent of his income to the crusade fund. There would be no exceptions. Alexander VI was even willing to risk antagonizing his erstwhile rival Cardinal Giuliano della Rovere with a demand for 2,000 ducats. The full roll call, as listed by Pastor, reveals but one exception: the Venetian Cardinal Marco Cornero, whom Alexander VI had appointed so recently that he had yet to receive any income at all. Against his name was listed 'no income' and 'to pay: nil'. He had after all only just paid the full 10,000 ducats for his red hat.

With regard to France and its attitude towards Cesare's coming campaign in the Romagna, Alexander VI decided that his best course was to make what appeared to be further concessions. If Louis XII was willing to continue his support for the campaign, Alexander VI would be willing to appoint the king's close friend and adviser, Cardinal Georges d'Amboise, as Papal Legate for France. Alexander VI was well aware that Cardinal d'Amboise had been angling for this important and highly influential role for some time. As Papal Legate for France, Cardinal d'Amboise would be the Pope's permanent representative in Roman Catholicism's second country. Ever since the Avignon papacy, France had continued to regard itself as second only to Rome. Cardinal d'Amboise's role would thus be more than a merely honorary one. Though Alexander VI was determined to ensure that his papal powers were not seriously usurped.

As a further sweetener, Alexander VI instructed his envoys to the French court to inform Louis XII that he promised to support the French king's claim to the throne of Naples. Like the appointment of Cardinal d'Amboise, this was little more than endorsing the inevitable: Louis XII had made no secret of the fact that he intended to pursue this policy. Although his predecessor Charles VIII may have had a quasi-legitimate claim to the Neapolitan throne, the strength of Louis XII's claim was a little more tenuous. He was not a direct descendant of Charles VIII, merely his cousin. However, it now suited Alexander VI to add his support to Louis XII's claim. Anything to avoid another debacle like Charles VIII marching his troops through Rome.

Cesare Borgia played virtually no part in these negotiations on his behalf and was left kicking his heels in Rome, impatient to lead another campaign into the Romagna. Unable to visit – or even receive a visit from – his French wife Charlotte and their new daughter Louise, the handsome Cesare Borgia was not long in exercising his charismatic sexual charms elsewhere. For the entertainment of cardinals and members of such aristo-cratic families as could afford their expensive charms, there were in Rome a number of discreet, high-class *cortigiani honeste* – so-called 'honest cour-tesans'. These were a class apart from the numerous prostitutes who flocked to the streets and taverns of Rome for the entertainment of the pilgrims and the locals, especially the deprived youths.* As we have seen from Cesare Borgia's mother Vanozza de' Cattanei, such courtesans were often strikingly beautiful, independent women of some distinction, who made sufficient funds from their lovers' 'gifts' to retire as rich women. Such wealthy single women would normally have been vulnerable, but usually had sufficient protection by the mere fact of the power and influence of their former lovers. Witness the fate of the Swiss soldiers who had had the temerity to ransack the property of Cesare's mother and steal her fortune.

During the summer of 1500 the most renowned courtesan in Rome was a certain Fiammetta de' Michaelis. Her legendary beauty and sophistication had already made her a rich woman. Like the dozen or so discreetly well-favoured courtesans living in Rome during this period she lived in some luxury. One of her colleagues was described by the Sienese writer Pietro Fortini as 'resembling a glittering sun with her splendid and rich clothes, her jewels and her gold chains'. The walls of her apartment were hung with fine art, while her bedroom contained 'a bed with superb curtains, a royal bedspread, and above all sheets so fine and white that they in truth seemed as thin, as fine, as the membrane of an egg'. Upon visiting one of these ladies, the Spanish ambassador even went so far as

---

* These were a particular problem in the Italy of this period, where young men were not usually in a position to get married until at least their late twenties, whilst most girls were married off in their teens and were required to be virgins.

to declare that he preferred to spit in the face of a servant rather than defile one of the carpets. Such courtesans were renowned for keeping exotic Moorish servants, as well as dwarfs and monkeys to entertain them and their wealthy gentleman callers. Fiammetta already owned a luxuriously furnished house in Rome, as well as two other properties in the city. On top of this she possessed a fine summer villa with its own vineyard in the nearby countryside. Little is known of Fiammetta's background, apart from the fact that she was born in Florence. Assuming that by this time she was in her late twenties and had spent her childhood in Florence, she would have grown up during the time when Savonarola held sway in the city: an independent but puritan republic. Despite this, Fiammetta certainly acquired an exceptional education, which included classical Latin authors such as Ovid, as well as more modern poets such as Petrarch, both of whom she could recite – or on occasion sing – from memory. Such intellectual accomplishments may well have appealed to Cesare Borgia almost as much as her beauty and her sensual charms. Fiametta also loved dancing, an accomplishment in which Cesare was particularly proud of his skills.

Fiammetta de' Michaelis's affair with Cesare Borgia flourished in Rome during the long hot summer of 1500. Despite his increasing reputation as an ogre, Cesare was still capable of great charm. In this aspect, as in many others, he was very much his father's son. Cesare certainly won Fiammetta's heart – to such an extent that their relationship would remain (at least in her eyes) the most profound in her life. She may have taken important cardinals and scions of aristocratic families as her lovers, both before and after her affair with Cesare Borgia, but she would remain forever attached to her fond memories of him. When she died, twelve years later, she would describe her will as: 'the Testament of la Fiammetta of il Valentino'.*

Cesare Borgia may have been discreet when it came to his nighttime activities, but the opposite was true of his daytime pursuits. He

---

* The Piazza Fiammetta, a wide street near the Piazza Navona, is named after her. This was the site of her main residence, which Cesare Borgia was frequently observed entering, and slipping out of, at night.

was determined to remain at the peak of physical condition in readiness
for his second campaign in the Romagna, and regularly entertained the
populace with his training exercises. As well as his usual daily regime
of vaulting horses (and the occasional reluctant mule), he also went on
regular hunting trips in the environs of Rome. However, most popular
of all were the bullfights, which he staged in the piazza in front of St
Peter's – the uniquely Spanish tradition which had been instigated by
his father on his accession to the papal throne. Alexander VI continued
to enjoy this pastime and would regularly watch Cesare's exploits from
the balcony of St Peter's. At one of Cesare's bullfights, held on 24 June,
according to the Venetian ambassador he

> killed seven wild bulls, fighting on horseback in the Spanish style,
> and he cut off the head of one with his first stroke, a thing which
> seemed great to all Rome.

Cesare Borgia was evidently establishing himself as a star entertainer
with the crowds. These audiences were, of course, swelled by the teeming
hordes of Jubilee pilgrims – who had probably not travelled all the way to
St Peter's in the expectation of observing the Pope watching his twenty-
four-year-old son bullfighting. Cesare's daring exploits in the bullring
provide yet another example of Machiavelli's 'Virtù' in its most powerful
and manly sense. Fighting a wild bull, whether on foot in the modern
more choreographed fashion, or on horseback in the more rough and
ready ancient style, was always a dangerous, sometimes fatal, business for
the fighter.[*]

Yet as always, wherever there was Virtù there was also Fortuna,
which could strike at any moment, and in the most unexpected fashion.
Not long after Cesare's daring feat in the Vatican bullring, Fortuna

---

[*] In Spain, during this period, bullfighting was reserved for the nobility, in much
the same way as jousting was restricted in other parts of Europe. The contest was
between one man on horseback armed with a pike, and a bull with long, sharp
horns. Fighting on foot, and the practice of blunting the horns, were not established until over 200 years later.

manifested itself in what for Alexander VI was a most telling manner. Whilst the Pope was sitting on the balcony of St Peter's watching his son bullfighting, an iron lantern fell from the bell tower above and crashed on to the balcony at the Pope's feet. The superstitious Alexander VI regarded this as an omen, and decided that from this time on he would forgo his afternoon pleasure of watching his son bullfighting. Though, hardly had he done this than Fortuna struck again. The following afternoon, instead of watching his son, the Pope was engaged in a meeting inside the Vatican. Seated beneath the canopy of the papal throne on its raised dais he was discussing political matters with the Spanish Cardinal Bernardino Lopez, who acted as ambassador for Ferdinand and Isabella of Spain. Also present was the papal 'secret chamberlain' Gaspare Poto, who was in all probability taking down the details of the meeting, whose subject matter, as we shall see, almost certainly involved deeply sensitive political negotiations. As sometimes happens during the long Roman summers, the stiflingly hot afternoon was unexpectedly transformed by a sudden ferocious thunderstorm, complete with gusts of high wind and hailstones. Such was the power of the storm that a chimney was dislodged from the Vatican roof and crashed through the ceiling of the room above where Alexander VI was conducting his meeting, in the process killing three people. This crash was so violent that it then caused the floor to collapse into the papal chamber below. At this very moment, Cardinal Lopez and Secretary Poto were rushing to close the windows against the torrent of wind and rain.

The throne where the Pope was seated was engulfed in a heap of tumbling masonry. Cardinal Lopez and Secretary Poto looked on aghast. The Pope had been crushed to death before their eyes. In a panic they shouted to the guards outside the door that the Pope had been killed. The guards burst into the room and at once began pulling at the large heap of fallen stonework. To their astonishment they found the Pope still sitting on his throne, obscured by a thick cloud of dust. A heavy roof beam had fallen across the canopy of the papal throne and Alexander VI had been knocked unconscious. His head was bleeding, his body battered, his arms and hands grazed – but he was alive!

The story of this accident immediately swept through the city and beyond – soon to be followed by rumours that Alexander VI was in fact dead. Such news, spreading from Rome as speedily as it did, could have had serious repercussions. In order to set the record straight, as soon as Alexander VI was sufficiently recovered he summoned the Venetian ambassador. If news of the Pope's death reached Venice, the ruling Signoria would immediately understand the serious implications of this fatal accident. Alexander VI's crusade would be put on hold, maybe even postponed indefinitely. And there would be no reason to trust any invasion Cesare Borgia might launch into the Romagna. The Venetian ambassador Paolo Capello arrived to find Alexander VI sitting up in his bed 'devotedly nursed by Lucrezia and her ladies, one of whom he describes as "his favourite"'. The sixty-nine-year-old Pope was undeniably alive and in full possession of his faculties.

This time Alexander VI's superstition worked the other way. What had just happened was no warning: this was a sign that he was destined by Fortuna to be saved. All his plans would go ahead: his mission would be realized. Cesare would be despatched to the Romagna as soon as his army was gathered; meanwhile, the widespread raising of funds for the crusade would continue. Likewise, the delicate matter that he had been discussing with Cardinal Lopez at the time of the accident would also proceed. Spain had raised serious objections to Louis XII's intention to take over Naples. The Kingdom of Naples had long been close to – and indeed often a possession of – Spain itself. Alexander VI had been in the midst of reassuring the ambassador for Ferdinand and Isabella of Spain that he would persuade Louis XII to share Naples between Spain and France. This would certainly be a difficult task, but the Pope felt sure that, given sufficient diplomatic manoeuvring, it could be achieved.

At the same time Cesare Borgia was assembling his trusted military commanders in Rome, working out in secret the tactics he had in mind for his forthcoming second Romagna campaign. Alexander VI had engineered a form of rapprochement with the Orsini family, who wished to protect their ancestral estates north of Rome, which were technically part of the Papal Territories. The senior member of the family in Rome was Cardinal Giambattista Orsini, who remained wary of Alexander VI, but nonetheless supported him at the consistories, and was regarded as his ally by the other members of the College of Cardinals. Cardinal Giambattista's relations included the brothers Giulio and Paolo Orsini, who were both talented condottieri. They, too, wished to protect their lands outside Rome, and also to aid Cesare Borgia in the expectation of gaining positions of power in the new, Borgia-held Romagna territories. Cesare Borgia had hinted that when the tyrants were deposed from their Romagna cities he would need loyal lords to take their place and run his new administration. Also informed of Borgia's plans were a number of other condottieri and seasoned commanders, mostly unsavoury characters whose loyalty he felt he could rely upon as it was in their interests to support him. Vitelli Vitellozzo was an Italian commander who had served with Cesare Borgia on his first Romagna campaign; his ancestral mountain stronghold of Città di Castello lay vulnerably squeezed between the border of Florentine Tuscany and the Papal Territories. And Gian Paolo Baglioni of Perugia found himself in a similar situation. All of these were keen to ally themselves with Cesare Borgia, being in desperate need of cash to maintain their mercenary armies, which formed the only protection for their minor territories. Joining forces with Cesare Borgia was to be their saving grace, and they listened attentively as the new Captain-General of the Papal Army outlined his proposed tactics. Needless to say, not all of Borgia's secrets were revealed, and the fact that such secrets as he had confided in them did not leak out gave him confidence in the loyalty of his new commanders. Meanwhile, his closest and most trusted commanders remained his compatriots and long-term friends, the Spaniards Don Miguel da Corella and Ramiro de Lorqua. The latter remained at his post as governor of Forlì in the Romagna, but was doubtless kept fully informed of Borgia's intended tactics. Likewise, he held no secrets from Miguel da Corella, who was to all intents and purposes his second-in-command, and was seen constantly at his side during this period.

As previously indicated, Cesare Borgia's feelings towards any man who became close to his sister Lucrezia were always distinctly touchy, to say the least. Now that Cesare found himself living back in Rome he had to put up with the company of Alfonso, Duke of Bisceglie, his sister's much-loved husband and father of her child. Initially, Cesare had done his best to overcome what, in modern parlance, might best be described as his unconscious incestuous possessiveness towards his sister. But as the summer months dragged by, Cesare's daily relationship with Alfonso of Bisceglie soon began to deteriorate. And then, as the summer wore on and Alexander VI's diplomatic intrigues unfolded, it soon became clear that any friendship towards Naples was increasingly alien to Borgia strategy. Worse still, having Lucrezia married to a member of the Neapolitan royal family (even if illegitimate) was more than an embarrassment. Indeed, Alfonso now presented a direct impediment to Alexander VI's negotiations with France and Spain over the division of Naples. How could the rulers of any of these nations trust a man whose favourite daughter was married to a son of the King of Naples?

Bearing in mind the Borgia reputation for ruthlessness, especially where their own interests were at stake, it comes as little surprise that on 15 July Alfonso of Bisceglie should become involved in 'the beginning of another of the darkest Borgia mysteries'. That evening, as Alfonso was mounting the steps from the piazza towards St Peter's, he was suddenly set upon by four men in masks wielding knives. In the words of Burchard: 'He was gravely wounded in his head, right arm and leg, whilst his assailants escaped down the steps.' Somehow Alfonso had managed to beat off his attackers and staggered into the Vatican. He was immediately carried to his bedchamber. As soon as news of this attack reached Alexander VI, he appeared deeply shocked and at once ordered Alfonso to be attended by the chief papal physician. When Lucrezia stumbled upon the scene she was so overcome that she collapsed to the floor unconscious.

The following day, Alfonso's close friend, the Florentine Raphael Brandolinus Lippi, wrote in a letter:

Whose was the hand behind the assassins is still unknown. I will not, however, repeat which names are being voiced, because it is grave and perilous to entrust it to a letter.

Once again, gossip quickly began spreading through Rome. All were convinced that this was the doing of the Borgias. But which one? Alfonso de Bisceglie was a severe impediment to the political plans of Alexander VI. The Pope may have been constantly concerned for the happiness of his daughter, yet at the same time we have seen that he was perfectly willing to use her to further his political aims. Or, on the other hand, allow her marriage to thwart them, as had been the case with her previous husband. For his part, Cesare Borgia had both political and psychological reasons for wanting to be rid of Lucrezia's Neapolitan husband. When questioned about the attack on Alfonso, he replied enigmatically: 'I did not wound the duke, but if I had it would have been no more than he deserved.'

For several days Alfonso lay at death's door. Lucrezia was distraught and remained at her husband's bedside day and night, nursing him, wiping his fevered brow, in constant fear of him slipping away from her into death. The reactions of Alexander VI and Cesare Borgia showed similar concern, if in somewhat contradictory fashion. The Pope ordered that two armed members of the papal guard should remain posted outside Alfonso's bedchamber at all times. Cesare Borgia, by contrast, gave the strictest orders that no one was to bear arms of any kind within the precincts of the Vatican.

Over the next month or so Alfonso began making a gradual recovery, nursed back to life by the loving Lucrezia, her friend Sancia (who was, of course, Alfonso's sister) and their female attendants. Over the long hot days of August, Alfonso started to recover his strength and was soon able to walk unsteadily about his bedchamber, pausing to look out at the sunlit garden below the Borgia apartments. On one occasion, Alfonso is said to have asked Lucrezia for his crossbow, to see if he was strong enough to use it. He fired a bolt down from the window. At that very moment Cesare Borgia happened to be walking across the garden. The bolt missed Cesare. An 'accident' had been averted.

Some days later, during the afternoon of 18 August, Alfonso and Lucrezia's maids, along with Alfonso's uncle, the Neapolitan ambassador, could all be heard laughing together in Alfonso's bedchamber. They were being entertained by the comic antics of Lucrezia's favourite jester, her hunchback dwarf. Suddenly the door was smashed open and Miguel da Corella, the commander of Cesare Borgia's personal guard, burst into the room accompanied by a group of armed men. The Neapolitan ambassador and the maids, along with the dwarf and two physicians, were all chased out of the room. Alfonso's Florentine friend Raphael Lippi described how Lucrezia, 'stupefied by the suddenness and violence of the act, shrieked at [Miguel da Corella], demanding to know how he dared commit such an offence before their eyes and in the presence of Alfonso'. For a moment, da Corella hesitated, overwhelmed by the sheer ferocity of Lucrezia's reaction. He protested that he was simply following 'the orders of another, but that they, if they wished, might go to the Pope, and it would be easy to obtain the release of the wanted man'.

Lucrezia and Sancia immediately ran down the corridor to find Alexander VI. According to Lippi: 'The women returned from the Pope to find the door to Alfonso's chamber barred by armed men.' They were informed that Alfonso was dead. (It subsequently emerged that he had been strangled by Miguel da Corella.) 'The women were terrified when they heard what had happened. Consumed with fear and grief, they shrieked and wailed, their cries resonating through the palace as one called on her husband and the other upon her brother.' Burchard described how: 'Immediately afterwards the dead man's two physicians and his hunchback were arrested and taken to the Castel Sant'Angelo. But they were soon to be set free, owing to their innocence, *a fact which was perfectly well known by those who had ordered their arrest.*'

This time it appears transparently obvious who was ultimately responsible for the deed. Yet certain niggling questions remain. Why would Cesare Borgia have ordered Alfonso to be murdered so publicly? Especially when such a sensational act was liable to upset all his father's delicate diplomacy? One answer lies in the writings of Machiavelli, who would come to understand Cesare Borgia as well as any. When Machiavelli later came to discuss statecraft and leadership, he stressed that to be a successful prince, his subjects as well as his enemies should

---

* Italics in the original.

fear him. Such an act by Cesare Borgia would certainly have instilled fear in the hearts of all those who had dealings with him – friend and foe alike. It seems likely that this was not the first time he had resorted to such drastic measures (e.g. the disposal of his younger brother Juan, Duke of Gandia). And, as we shall see, it would certainly not be the last time he would be suspected of such a deed. Confirmation of Machiavelli's intuition comes from no less than the Venetian ambassador, who wrote home: 'All Rome trembles at this duke, that he may not have them killed.' This is further supported by a coded letter despatched by the Florentine ambassador to his city's ruling Signoria: 'I pray your lordships to take this for your own information, and not to show it to others, for these [Borgias] are men to be watched, otherwise they have done a thousand villainies, and have spies everywhere.'

On the other hand, there remains the awkward question of Cesare's close relationship with Lucrezia. Despite Cesare's hand in the flight from Rome of her first husband Giovanni Sforza, and the blatant nature of his apparent guilt in the murder of her second husband, there is no denying that Lucrezia remained as close to Cesare as ever after these events had taken place. How could this have been so? As Meyer puts it: 'If we could find the answer to that, it would take us to the heart of a connection that bound brother tightly to sister as long as both remained alive.' Meyer also makes the clinching point that: 'The intensity of that connection was obvious to all who observed the two of them together.'

Even so, how could Lucrezia possibly have forgiven Cesare for the murder of Alfonso, whom she evidently loved so deeply? And how could she have suspected anyone else of being responsible for this, when Cesare's henchman Miguel da Corella was indisputably guilty of the murder? Another anomaly is presented by the behaviour of Lucrezia's beloved father, Alexander VI himself. According to Lucrezia's biographer Maria Bellonci: 'Her tears soon got on the Pope's nerves, for he was congenitally incapable of understanding why anybody who was twenty years old and had all her future before her could be so upset.' In the end, he despatched Lucrezia and her retinue north to her castle at Nepi, presumably in the vain hope that her duties as governor of Spoleto might take her mind off things.

But what does the murder of Alfonso, Duke of Biceglie, indicate of the relationship between Alexander VI and Cesare Borgia? Understandably, all manner of exaggerated rumours swept Rome after the murder and hurried burial of Alfonso 'at dead of night . . . with scant ceremony in the chapel of Callixtus III in S. Peter's'. According to one commentator: 'Cesare murdered his brother, slept with his sister, spent the treasure of the Church, and was the terror of his father Alexander.' This is the legend that has come down to us, and it is difficult to deny that there is much to support most of this lurid portrait. The Venetian ambassador reported home: 'The Pope loves and fears his son, who is twenty-seven,* physically most beautiful, he is tall and well-made . . . he is munificent, even prodigal, and this displeases the Pope.' The ageing Alexander VI depended upon his son Cesare for the fulfilment of his plans, just as Cesare needed the Pope's backing. Alexander VI was the strategist and Cesare the agent who acted upon his instructions. But it was becoming clear that Alexander VI was increasingly losing control over his impulsive son. Cesare was evidently aware of much of his father's subtle, long-term strategy, but on occasion lacked sufficient discipline to adhere to his father's more immediate instructions.

---

* Cesare Borgia was, of course, still just twenty-four at the time of Alfonso's murder.

CHAPTER 12

THE SECOND ROMAGNA CAMPAIGN

O N 2 OCTOBER 1500 Cesare Borgia led his army of 7,700 out of Rome up the Ancient Roman Via Flaminia, which led north across the Apennines towards the Adriatic Coast. His army consisted of a mixed group of Swiss, Italian and Spanish soldiers, led by their assorted commanders, which included the Italians Vitellozzo, Paolo and Giulio Orsini, and Gian Paolo Baglioni of Perugia, as well as the notorious Miguel da Corella. Despite the need to lead his force at speed across the mountains, Cesare unexpectedly decided to stop off at Nepi en route. Here he paused his entire campaign while he paid a visit to his sister Lucrezia. Details of this encounter remain unknown. Prior to it, Lucrezia had remained inconsolable on account of the murder of her husband Alfonso, signing all her letters *la infelicissima* ('the most unhappy woman'). To reinforce this, after signing her name she would emphatically cross out her title 'Princess of Salerno' (besides being Duke of Bisceglie, Alfonso had also been Prince of Salerno). Yet Cesare's visit appears to have been a consolation to her, heralding her recovery no less. Within months, Lucrezia would happily return to Rome and live in the Vatican, as before, with her father. And relations with her father appear to have been as close and happy as ever. Though she does not seem to have been aware that Alexander VI was already scheming for her to make yet another strategic marriage.

After leaving Nepi, Cesare Borgia returned to his mercenary troops, who had been reinforced by 2,200 French soldiers sent by Louis XII. This now made up a considerable force, which, according to no less a source than Machiavelli, contained 'nearly all the professional soldiers in Italy'. Heavy winter rain in the Apennine passes made for slow progress, with artillery and heavy cannon constantly getting stuck in mud. Even so, it was clear to all that Borgia was by now in command of an army which could strike anywhere in Italy. By this stage every state in the peninsula had intelligence of his movements, yet his ultimate destination still remained unclear. This was precisely what Cesare Borgia intended (though it is far from certain that this was also part of his father's plan). Where would Borgia's army strike first? Was he taking a roundabout route, before suddenly turning west to take Florence? Or would he press north to take Bologna? Or would he continue along the Via Flaminia to the Adriatic Coast? When it became clear that he was taking the last of these three options, Giovanni Sforza, Lord of Pesaro and Lucrezia's first husband, immediately fled for his life. He had no wish to suffer the same fate as her second husband, which would certainly have resulted if he had been captured. On 27 October, amidst pouring rain, Cesare Borgia rode triumphantly into Pesaro, at the head of his retinue of 150 men-at-arms, all decked out in his personal red and yellow livery. Here he took up residence at the former Lord of Pesaro's palazzo, insisting upon occupying the very bedchamber where Giovanni Sforza and his sister had slept during the time of their marriage.

Within days, various foreign envoys began arriving – most notably Pandolfo Collenuccio, who had been sent as an envoy by the Duke of Ferrara. All wished to obtain an audience with Cesare Borgia, in order to learn of his future plans. As early as 18 October the Venetian Signoria had agreed to grant Cesare Borgia the title *Gentiluomo di Venezia* ('Honorary Citizen of Venice') in the hope that this would dissuade him from leading his army into Venetian territory. But what about nearby Ferrara? Initially,

Borgia had refused to meet the Ferrarese envoy Collenuccio, who was informed that Il Valentino was suffering from an 'ulcer'. According to other sources, he was in fact suffering from 'a sore in the groin'. Evidently symptoms of Cesare Borgia's syphilis had begun to recur. When Collenuccio was at last granted an audience with Borgia he was unable to extract any cast-iron guarantees with regard to Ferrara. This uncertainty persisted, despite several further meetings.

Prior to entering the service of the Duke of Ferrara, Collenuccio had already established a reputation as a humanist philosopher and poet; consequently, his reports back to Ferrara at this time are certainly of interest. He paints a vivid and incisive picture of Cesare Borgia:

> He is a brave and powerful character, capable of largesse of spirit, who prefers to deal with plain-speaking men . . . He is filled with aspiration and has a longing for greatness and renown.

But Collenuccio could not avoid noticing a darker side to Cesare, referring to him as being 'ruthless when it came to revenge'. Collenuccio does, however, appear to have misjudged one aspect of Cesare Borgia's character, commenting that 'he appears to be much more interested in defeating states, with little interest in possessing them or organizing their governance'. This, as we have seen, was not the case with his first campaign in the Romagna, and would certainly not be the case with his second. Collenuccio was also fascinated by Cesare Borgia's habits and apparently eccentric daily routine:

> He lives his daily routine as follows. He does not go to bed until between 3 o'clock in the morning and 5 o'clock in the morning.*

---

* I have used modern clock times. In fact, Collenuccio recorded the times as they were measured during this period. Loosely (with adjustments, according to the seasons) the end of the day came with the 6 p.m. ringing of the Angelus bell – though in some cities it ended with sunset or even the closing of the city gates. (This meant that the next day *began* at 6 p.m.) Thus, Collenuccio in fact described Borgia as going to bed at 'the eighth, ninth or tenth hour of the night', i.e. from 3 a.m. to 5 a.m. our time.

This means that he does not get up until around 2 in the afternoon. As soon as he is dressed he sits down at the table, and it is here that he attends to the business of the day.

Despite Collenuccio's evidence, this was not Borgia's permanent regime. For instance, it would have been impossible for him to conduct his military campaign adhering to such hours. On the other hand, Borgia was renowned for keeping to a nocturnal routine when he could. Two reasons may account for this. Firstly, it is possible that the syphilitic 'blooms' had begun to reappear on his face. These would have been far less discernible by candlelight. Also, suitably positioned candles in the darkness of his chamber lent a dramatic effect to his presence, which he often used to intimidate his audience – in particular foreign envoys, or on occasion even his commanders.

Imola and Forli had fallen to Cesare Borgia on his first Romagna campaign, and he now sought to form a territorial link between these two cities and his most recent conquests. Having taken Pesaro on the Adriatic, he marched north up the coast to Rimini, stronghold of the notorious Malatesta family. The outrageous yet 'humanist' condottiere Sigismondo Malatesta had long since died, and the city was now ruled by his grandson Pandolfo Malatesta, who lacked even an iota of his ancestor's civilizing culture or military skills. In fact, he was no more than an odious thug, and like many such characters he fled at the first sign of any real danger. Consequently, Cesare Borgia was welcomed into Rimini by its citizenry.

From here Borgia led his troops north-west up the ancient Roman Via Emelia, where only Cesena and Faenza lay between him and his captured territory at Imola and Forli, which had been left under the rule of his Spanish governor Ramiro de Lorqua. Cesena, which had also previously been under Malatesta rule, simply surrendered, but Faenza chose to resist. The ruling Manfredi family were popular, and even though the present ruler Astorre III Manfredi was just fifteen years old, the population rallied around him. The citizens locked the gates and manned the battlements, preparing to face Borgia's forces, which duly arrived on

17 November. Two days later a surprise attack by Borgia's troops was repulsed with heavy loss of life, and Borgia prudently decided it would be better to lay siege to the city and starve it into submission. But this proved no simple matter. According to the contemporary local chronicler Bernardino Zambotti, writing some weeks later in December:

> Duke Cesare's troops who were camped around Faenza have moved because of the heavy snow and severe frosts, and also because more than 800 of them have been killed in the fighting. The men of Faenza are defending vigorously and there are 2,000 brave soldiers in the city . . . The duke has retired to the castle at Forli for his safety and his men have set up their winter camp around Imola.

Meanwhile, serious divisions were becoming evident amongst Borgia's forces. Two months earlier, as his army had passed through the territory of his commander Baglioni on its way towards the Romagna, the uncouth behaviour of the Spanish soldiers had outraged the local Italian inhabitants. The contemporary Perugian chronicler Francesco Matarazzo recorded what took place when they passed through the city of Perugia and the surrounding Umbrian countryside:

> The Spaniards washed the feet of their horses in wine, and what they could not drink or consume they spilled on the earth. And when they went away . . . they threw in excrement into all the casks of muscat wine [and] shat on the floor under all the tables at which they ate . . . All the jars of confections . . . they emptied and then filled with excrement . . . and where they had been none could go for the stench.

Such behaviour quickly led to the Italian soldiers developing a deep hatred for the Spanish contingents – hard men, who themselves held the Italian soldiers in contempt for their manners and more civilized habits. As a result, Borgia was forced to take great pains to ensure these groups were kept apart. When it came to setting up winter quarters, the Italian and the Spanish contingents were forced to camp outside different cities. Borgia also issued orders to his Spanish commanders that far stricter discipline was to be maintained amongst their troops. Such outrages as they had perpetrated in Perugia and Umbrian territory were not to be tolerated in the Romagna. Soldiers found guilty of wanton rape and pillage were to be publicly hanged before the populace, and all troops were to pay the locals for provisions. Borgia remained determined to ensure that his rule was welcomed by the people of the Romagna.

The winter break would last for some months, and during this time Borgia decided that Cesena, with its strategic position on the Via Emilia, and access to the sea ten miles away at Porto Cesenatico, was to be the capital of the new Borgia state. Here he celebrated Christmas in style, inviting all the local dignitaries to his residence, the former Palazzo Malatesta, for a Christmas Eve banquet. Christmas Day saw a series of competitive games in the main square, which were much enjoyed by the citizenry. During the following days Cesare Borgia and a group of his friends took to riding out to the country villages, taking part in running races and feats of strength with the local peasants. A contemporary chronicler recorded how Borgia himself

> ran as swiftly as a horse, and many times ran races with the youths, to whom he gave a start and passed them nonetheless. With his bare hands he could break a horseshoe and any thick cord.

All this would inspire a lasting loyalty amongst the tough peasants of the Romagna, who were used to cruel tyranny. They had never before been ruled by such a charismatic lord, let alone played games with him.

Borgia now travelled on to Forli, where he remained for three weeks – though few, even amongst his own soldiers, knew that he was in the city. Borgia had returned to his nocturnal regime, and word he had received from Alexander VI had suddenly made him wary of traitors. He also took this time to prepare the next surprise moves in his campaign, which he had been instructed to carry out by his father.

Back in Rome, Alexander VI continued with his diplomatic attempts to persuade European states to contribute to the Venetian-led crusade against the Ottoman Turks. As early as October he had despatched papal legates to Spain, Portugal, France, the German states, as well as Denmark and Sweden. Fundraising for the crusade had begun in earnest, and all would be required to despatch significant sums to the papal exchequer. Military contributions would also be expected. The renowned Spanish military leader Gonsalvo de Córdoba soon arrived in Venice with a fleet of fifty-six ships. The crusader fleet was now ready to set sail, led by the powerful Venetian navy. It was at least partly in gratitude to Alexander VI for this reinforcement that the Venetian Signoria had awarded his son Cesare the title *Gentiluomo di Venezia*.

By December 1500 the combined Venetian–Spanish fleet had driven the Ottomans from the strategic Ionian island of Kefalonia at the mouth of the Adriatic. For this, and his ensuing part in turning back the Ottoman tide, Gonsalvo de Córdoba would become known as '*El Gran Capitan*'. Alexander VI had now learned that after the proposed French and Spanish takeover of Naples, and its partition between these two powers, the Spanish were intending to appoint Gonsalvo as the military commander of their portion of Naples. Gonsalvo was a man to be wary of: a headstrong general who might easily renege on any agreement and try to implement a Spanish takeover of the entire kingdom. Alexander VI was well aware that the joint takeover of Naples was bound to involve difficulties, but conflict between Spain and France was to be avoided at all costs.

Alexander VI was also deeply concerned that Cesare Borgia should stick to the plans they had agreed for the Romagna. Alexander VI wished his son to secure this territory with the minimum possible aggression towards any of the bordering states. Florence certainly felt threatened, now that Cesare Borgia had occupied the territory which lay between the eastern border of its Tuscan hinterland and the Adriatic Coast, formerly an important commercial route linking Florence to ports which enabled it to trade valuable commodities with the eastern Mediterranean. Siena, south of Florence, had now allied itself with Alexander VI, adding further to Florentine fears. The republican leaders of Florence were well aware that Alexander VI favoured a restoration of the former Medici rulers. A republican government, which could be voted in or out of office by the will of the people in genuine elections, set an uncomfortable precedent. Not only for the Pope, but for many rulers in the Italian peninsula. However, the Florentine Signoria was reassured by the existence of its firm alliance with France – ironically, a hangover from the time of Savonarola and his lasting impression on Charles VIII that he was the 'instrument of God'. When Louis XII succeeded Charles VIII he had reassured Florence of his continued support. The city of Florence, and indeed all the province of Tuscany which remained within its control, would remain under French protection.

Despite Alexander VI's strenuous diplomatic activities on behalf of the crusade and Venice, as well as his continuing attempt to mastermind his son Cesare's campaign in the Romagna, the seventy-year-old Alexander VI seemed in remarkably good health. According to the Venetian ambassador, he

> looks younger every day. He never lets his worries keep him from
> sleep, is continually cheerful, and never does anything unless he
> wants to: his children are his main concern: other matters do not
> trouble him.

Alexander VI well knew that the future of his ambitions lay in the hands of Cesare and Lucrezia.

Back in the Romagna, with winter coming to an end, Cesare Borgia was reassembling his troops. On 28 February 1501 he entertained his Spanish contingent to a bullfight in Imola. During the following month 2,000 new French troops arrived and the siege of Faenza resumed in earnest. Despite being heavily outnumbered and outgunned, the citizens of this small city put up a spirited defence. They were inspired to hold out by their popular and strikingly handsome teenage ruler Astorre III Manfredi, aided by his half-brother Giovanni. Even so, by mid-April the continuous bombardment from the heavy French cannon had begun to take its terrible toll on the all but starving inhabitants. On 25 April Astorre III finally surrendered. Cesare Borgia, in his effort to win the hearts of the Romagna people, decided to be magnanimous. He declared his admiration for Astorre III Manfredi and his brother, offering them gifts and assuring them that they would be welcome to enrol in his army.

As early as the evening of 26 April 1501 news reached Rome that Faenza had surrendered to Cesare Borgia. The event was celebrated the next day with a great feast and public rejoicing, the roar of cannon sounded from the ramparts of the Castel Sant Angelo and peals of church bells rang out over the city, as bonfires blazed into the night. At the following consistory Alexander VI awarded his son the title Duke of Romagna. This marked a considerable promotion: not until 1532 would Florence be elevated to a dukedom. And furthermore, Alexander VI declared that Cesare Borgia would hold the dukedom 'in his own name'. This qualification is of deep significance. It reinforced the fact that Cesare Borgia was not retaking the Papal Territories in the name of the Pope; he was openly and incontrovertibly establishing a hereditary Borgia dukedom.

Following the surrender of Faenza, the two Manfredi half-brothers would be given an honourable escort back to Rome to meet Alexander VI. Cesare Borgia's part in what followed is difficult to discern, but on balance one would expect that he knew their fate full well. On the arrival in Rome of Astorre III and Giovanni, Alexander VI ordered them to be flung into the dungeons of the Castel Sant'Angelo, where they were entrusted to the care of the sadistic gaolers. Here, according to several mostly reliable sources, including Guicciardini, the handsome young teenage boys underwent a series of grotesque humiliations. A year later they would both be put to death. According to the contemporary chronicler Sigismondo of Foligno: 'Cesare de Borgia gave the order to strangle them and cast their bodies into the Tiber.' Burchard also records how the two brothers 'were found in the Tiber, choked and dead, the lord of Faenza, with a stone around his neck'. Pointedly, Burchard does not ascribe this crime to Cesare Borgia. Either way, it was evident that no one would be permitted to interfere with Cesare Borgia's aim of becoming the popularly acclaimed ruler of the Romagna.

Having taken Faenza, Cesare Borgia marched his troops up the Via Emelia towards Bologna. He was aware that he could not actually attack the city of Bologna, as it was under the protection of his sponsor Louis XII. However, just as Borgia had hoped, the Bolognese felt intimidated by Borgia's reputation for ruthlessness and unpredictability. Faced with Borgia's approaching troops, Bologna's ruler Giovanni Bentivoglio hastily surrendered Castel Bolognese, the city's advanced defensive outpost on the Via Emelia, which was in fact already surrounded by territory taken by Borgia. A peace treaty was immediately negotiated between Borgia and Bentivoglio, in which Borgia knew that he had the upper hand. He thus permanently sealed their agreement by insisting upon a marriage between Bentivoglio's son Ermes and a daughter of his own commander Giulio Orsini. On top of this, Bentivoglio was coerced into providing 100 men-at-arms,* paid out of the city's exchequer, who would join Borgia's forces for the defence of the northern border of his Romagna dukedom. Such a move effectively forestalled any possible Venetian aggression against Borgia. This was a wise precaution, presumably part of Alexander VI's secret strategy, as the Venetians now found themselves hedged in by their traditional enemy Milan, which appeared to have fallen permanently into French hands, as well as Cesare Borgia and his expanding Romagna. Alexander VI may have helped Venice in its vital crusade to keep the Ottomans at bay, but the city knew well enough not to trust him entirely.

In characteristic form, Cesare Borgia now made a totally unexpected move. He turned his attentions south, towards Florence. This city, too, was of course under the protection of Louis XII, but once again Borgia did not feel himself restrained by this alliance with his French backer. Borgia sent a series of threatening messages to Florence's ruling Signoria, demanding that they take him on as their condottiere. Should they refuse this 'request', Borgia warned them, they might well find that he had been

---

* This was not quite such a small token unit as it might at first appear. It effectively meant a fighting force of several hundred men. Much like a lancer (see above), a man-at-arms was a mounted knight, who was usually attended by his own group of one or more armed retainers.

hired as a condottiere by one of their enemies. The Florentines knew that if they agreed to take on Borgia as their condottiere, this would have given him freedom to move his army at will across Florentine territory, claiming that he was engaged in 'protective' manoeuvres. The threatening presence of such an army would have given Borgia a controlling influence over the Florentine republican government, allowing him to bully them into reinstating the former Medici rulers. To back up his threats, Borgia reminded Florence that his father the Pope was now allied to their southern neighbour and enemy Siena. Without giving the Signoria time to reply, Borgia decided to give a demonstration of his power by despatching his commander Oliverotto da Fermo with 200 cavalry through Siena and across Florentine territory to bolster the forces in Pisa, Florence's second city, which had recently rebelled against its Florentine overlords.

The Florentine Signoria found itself in disarray. Its exchequer was already bankrupt, having emptied its savings to pay off Louis XII for his protection. The city, therefore, had no money or means of hiring the services of any condottiere and his mercenary army to defend it – even if this condottiere was Borgia himself. While the Signoria dithered, Borgia made his move, launching his entire army across the Apennines into the heart of Florentine territory, marching directly towards the city itself. Only when he reached Campi, less than ten miles short of the city walls, did he halt his advance. The Florentine diarist Biagio Buonaccorsi recorded:

> At this time the city found itself in the greatest disorder and with practically no men under arms. Many of the citizens were overcome with fear and fled ... the place was in the grip of apprehension and mayhem.

On 14 May Borgia issued a list of demands to the city of Florence, insisting that the ruling Signoria agree to take him on as the city's condottiere, at the same time demanding an immediate down payment of 36,000 ducats for his services. The Signoria sent back their agreement next day, but no money (because they simply didn't have any). For three agonizing days the city awaited its fate. Then suddenly, without warning, Borgia's army decamped and marched swiftly towards the coast. In what would become a familiar tactic of Cesare Borgia, his bullying demands had in fact been a bluff. By now he had received an urgent message from Alexander VI warning him that Louis XII was furious at Borgia's behaviour and had ordered immediate action from his military commander in Milan, d'Aubigny.* An army of over 3,000 French soldiers had immediately been despatched south to drive Borgia from Florentine territory.

But Cesare Borgia was not to be completely undone. Marching his troops post-haste to the coast, he launched an attack on the independent port city of Piombino, with the intention of toppling its hated tyrant Jacopo IV Appiano and placing himself as ruler. After seizing the nearby offshore islands of Elba and Pianosa, Borgia began to lay siege to Piombino. But he was then interrupted by an urgent message from Alexander VI summoning him to Rome. Consequently, he left Vitellozzo and Baglioni in charge, and they soon finished off the job.

Florence may not have fallen, yet it was now all but encircled by Borgia allies. Also, Cesare Borgia had learned an important lesson about the Florentine leadership. It was susceptible to bullying, and its republican Signoria appeared to be incapable of decisive action. This was largely due to the fact that the ruling Signoria was a committee, consisting of eight elected men, led by a Gonfaloniere who only held office for two months. ('Gonfaloniere' literally means 'flag-bearer', but in practice meant 'head'

---

* Despite his name, d'Aubigny was in fact a Scotsman named Bernard Stewart. The Scots had maintained their 'Auld Alliance' with France, and the French army contained a considerable number of '*Scottese*'. Likewise, many Scots served as mercenaries in Italy during this period. When Cesare Borgia led his army in triumph into Rome after his first Romagna campaign, the spectators had been delighted at the sight of a contingent of bearded warriors in kilts marching behind a man playing the bagpipes. Many sources describe this Scottish contribution. See, for instance: Philippe Contamine, 'Entre France et Écosse: Bérault Stuart, seigneur d'Aubigny (vers 1452–1508), chef de guerre, diplomate, écrivain militaire', in James Laidlaw (ed.), *The Auld Alliance: France and Scotland over 700 years* (Edinburgh University Press, Edinburgh, 1999).

or 'leader' – as can be seen from the fact that Cesare Borgia's official title was 'Gonfaloniere of the Papal Forces'.) The Florentine Gonfaloniere's short rule had originally been intended to eliminate the possibility of a Gonfaloniere becoming a tyrant. However, during the course of the previous century the entire democratic apparatus of Florence had been undermined by the rich and powerful Medici family, who corrupted the democratic voting procedure. This ensured that their own chosen candidates occupied all positions of power, especially the Signoria – as well as the leading Gonfaloniere, who became little more than a puppet. But now the Medici had been ousted from power and a democratically elected, uncorrupt Signoria and Gonfaloniere were in place. Even so, this still made for a cumbersome and ineffective method of rule, and in the following year, the able, respected Piero Soderini would be elected Gonfaloniere for life. Borgia's invasion and ultimatum had demonstrated to the Florentines the deep flaw in their form of government.

The question now arises as to how much of a role Cesare Borgia himself played in the surprise moves taken at the end of his second Romagna campaign. Alexander VI appears to have been completely cognizant with Borgia's moves against Bologna, willing to take the risk of upsetting both his Venetian and his French allies. Likewise he may well have suggested that Cesare Borgia should communicate to the Florentine Signoria the vulnerability of their position, along with the threatening suggestion that they hire Cesare Borgia as their condottiere. However, Cesare Borgia's rash and rapid advance across Florentine territory almost to the gates of Florence itself appears to have taken the Pope completely by surprise (almost as much as it did Louis XII). Cesare Borgia would put forward an ingenious excuse for this aggressive action – which had almost put paid to all of Alexander VI's lengthy political machinations. According to Borgia, his Italian commanders – the Orsini brothers and Vitellozzo – were determined to take revenge for the many wrongs and transgressions which the Florentines had over the years perpetrated on their small neighbouring territories. If Borgia had not led them himself, they may well have broken ranks and invaded Florence of their own accord, bringing all manner of chaos to the region. Even Machiavelli, who was a member of the Florentine delegation sent to meet up with Borgia at Campi, appears to have believed this excuse. How much truth Alexander VI himself saw in it is another matter. Was his impulsive son now completely beyond his control? Or was he perhaps more reliant upon the wishes of his mercenary commanders than he appeared? As we shall see, these questions – Alexander VI's central worries – would produce some totally unexpected answers.

CHAPTER 13

THE BORGIAS *IN EXCELSIS*

Soon after Cesare Borgia arrived in Rome, his father Alexander VI began putting into place the final details before the French invasion of Naples. King Federigo had refused to join Alexander VI's Venetian-led crusade against the Ottomans. Worse still, when he learned that France and Spain were secretly intent upon conquering Naples and dividing his territory between them, he turned as a last resort to Sultan Bayezid II and signed a treaty with the Ottomans. In a characteristic display of hypocrisy, Alexander VI used this as an excuse to issue a bull excommunicating King Federigo, at the same time insisting that by allying himself with the Ottomans he had forfeited all right to his throne. This lent a veneer of spurious legitimacy to Alexander VI's scheme for the conquest of Naples.

Throughout the early summer of 1501 the French army began assembling at Ponte Milvio, the ancient Roman bridge across the Tiber a couple of miles north of Rome's city walls. Here d'Aubigny's force was joined by the forces of his experienced military colleague Yves d'Alègre. Alexander VI was determined that the French army should remain beyond the precincts of the city: there was to be no repeat of the humiliating circumstances during Charles VIII's march south to Naples in 1494. As a show of good will, Alexander VI ordered regular provisions be shipped out to the French army, along with sixteen Roman prostitutes for the entertainment of the French soldiery.

As soon as Vitellozzi and the Orsini brothers returned from their successful conquest of Piombino, Cesare Borgia led his combined troops to join the French. Borgia's Papal Army was further reinforced by a contingent of mercenaries from his newly conquered territory of the Romagna. Having proved his military competence during the campaigns in the Romagna, Cesare Borgia and his troops were allowed to march in the vanguard of the force which proceeded south towards Naples. This was also intended to reinforce the legitimacy of the invasion: Borgia was the Gonfaloniere of the Papal Forces, and Naples remained, in theory at least, subject to the Pope's overlordship. However, there was no doubting the actuality of what was taking place, and the driving force behind it. Whereas Cesare Borgia's army numbered over a thousand men, the battle-hardened French force backing him consisted of more than ten times this amount. To this was added some 200 cavalry and more than two dozen artillery pieces, including several of the largest cannon yet seen in Italy. Borgia was here gaining further military experience, at the head of the largest assembled active force in Europe at the time, with France's two most experienced generals at his side.

The first obstacle they encountered within Neapolitan territory was the ancient Etruscan city of Capua, which was defended by King Federigo's condottiere Fabrizio Colonna. On 24 June a combined Papal and French force under Cesare Borgia led the assault on the city, which was soon overrun. In the aftermath of victory the troops under Borgia's command, which included a large contingent of French soldiers

killed around 3,000 soldiers and 200 cavalrymen. As well as this, they slaughtered without mercy all priests and nuns they could find in churches and monasteries, as well as the women. Many young girls were viciously raped. The total dead eventually numbered over 6,000.

According to the contemporary historian Guicciardini, Cesare Borgia had the women of the city locked in a tower and chose forty of the most beautiful for himself. This latter is certainly untrue, though it is typical of the dark legends that had by now begun to accrue around the Borgia name. Even so, the atrocity at Capua is remembered in the city to this day. In mitigation of Borgia, it has been claimed that the slaughter may well have been encouraged by the Orsini brothers, whose family were now mortal enemies of their aristocratic Roman rivals, the Colonna family. When the Orsini brothers personally captured Fabrizio Colonna, Cesare Borgia offered to pay them if they handed over Colonna or put him to the sword. But the Orsini brothers had now begun to harbour suspicions about the Borgia family and their ultimate motives, so they allowed Fabrizio Colonna to pay a large ransom for his freedom and kept the money for themselves. Whereupon Fabrizio Colonna rode post-haste south to Naples, where he joined his cousin Prospero Colonna, who was in charge of defending the city from the invaders.

The French army now continued south through Neapolitan territory, laying waste all in its path. In Naples itself King Federigo adopted a similar policy to that of his brother King Alfonso II when he had faced the army of Charles VIII seven years previously. He decided that his overwhelming priority was not to defend his kingdom and its subjects (most of whom had grown to despise him), but instead to save his own skin by whatever means possible. To gain time, he sent a peace mission to negotiate terms with d'Aubigny. Suspecting that little would come of this, he was pleasantly surprised when the French commander offered him generous peace terms. In return for renouncing all claims to the throne of Naples, King Federigo would be permitted to flee to the offshore island of Ischia. Here he would surrender to the French, whereupon he would be put aboard a French ship and transported to France. Louis XII promised to grant him the title Duke of Anjou, along with an annuity of 30,000 livres (approximately equivalent to 36,000 ducats), enabling him to live out his retirement in a chateau by the Loire.

King Federigo agreed with alacrity to this plan and within two days he abandoned his subjects, sailing for Ischia. Meanwhile, the Spanish commander Gonsalvo de Córdoba took possession of the southern region of the kingdom, where Federigo's thirteen-year-old son Ferdinand, Duke of Calabria, bravely held out for another six months at Taranto, before surrendering. He was immediately shipped to Spain, lest he should at a later date press his own claim to the throne of Naples. After three years of comparative comfort, his father King Federigo would die at Tours. On the other hand, the brave young Ferdinand of Calabria is said to have spent some years in a Spanish dungeon before the King of Aragon took pity on him, ordered his release and arranged for him to marry one of his relatives.

Louis XII was pleased by the rapid outcome of the expedition against Naples, and handsomely rewarded Cesare Borgia for his role in this victory, granting him 40,000 ducats. Half of this came from Louis XII's new income from the Kingdom of Naples, with the other half coming from the sequestered income of the captured Ferdinand of Calabria. Alexander VI was determined that the papacy too should benefit from this victory, and negotiated with the fallen King Federigo to obtain his defeated army's all-but-intact artillery for a bargain price. As ever, the former long-term vice-chancellor to the papacy was constantly concerned with accruing as much wealth and power as possible to the Holy See. In part, this was certainly intended to further his future ambitions, yet there was no denying the element of instinctive greed. The latter had certainly been in evidence earlier that summer when the extremely wealthy Venetian Cardinal Giovanni Zeno had died at his residence in Padua. As observed by the modern historian Kenneth Setton: 'Often living beyond their means (and falling into debt) to maintain their exalted social position, few cardinals resident at the Curia left estates as large as that of Zeno.' Giovanni Zeno had been created a cardinal over thirty years previously by his Venetian uncle Pope Paul II, and since that time had steadily accumulated an exceptional number of lucrative benefices – all duly noted by the ever-watchful eye of the Pope's (and the ensuing popes') indispensable vice-chancellor. When Cardinal Zeno died in early May 1501, his will revealed his fortune to be in excess of 250,000 ducats. According to his will, a tenth of this was to be donated to charity, with the larger part being bequeathed to the city of Venice, in order to aid its war against the Ottoman Turks. According to no less than Johann Burchard, who had himself now been papal master of ceremonies for almost twenty years, Alexander VI peremptorily declared that '[Cardinal Zeno's] will was null and void, with all the goods left by the deceased belonging to His Holiness'.

Alexander VI was now over seventy years old, and despite remaining physically robust, he was beginning to feel his age. Unable to bear the intense summer heat of Rome, on 27 July he departed the city for the cooler climes of Sermoneta, a picturesque hilltop town some twenty miles south of the city. Here he took up residence in the fortress overlooking the surrounding plain. Cesare was away, playing his part in the French invasion of Naples, so Alexander VI took the unprecedented step of leaving in charge of papal affairs in Rome the one person he felt he could trust – namely, his twenty-one-year-old daughter Lucrezia. This act speaks volumes: not only about his trust in his daughter, but also about his belief in her administrative capabilities, as well as her ability to hold her own in a totally male world. This was no rash, isolated decision, swayed by his doting love for his young daughter. It will be remembered that during Alexander VI's low period in 1498, with Cesare Borgia away in France and the Pope left alone in Rome surrounded by his enemies, he had ordered Lucrezia to retire to Spoleto for her own safety. Yet at the same time, he had appointed her governor of Spoleto and entrusted her with a letter calling upon the local authorities to obey her commands. Although pregnant, Lucrezia had evidently exercised her powers with some accomplishment, despite the fact that she was only eighteen years old. Yet this had involved the administration of a mere province. Now, just three years later, she was being entrusted with handling the papacy itself. According to Burchard:

> The Pope gave her the authority to open all his letters, and told her that if she encountered any problems she was to seek out the advice of Cardinal Jorge da Costa and the other cardinals whom she had the power to assemble if necessary.

From this, it seems clear that Lucrezia was even granted the power to summon and preside over a consistory. It is worth stressing that this was the formal meeting of the College of Cardinals, which took – or ratified, for the Pope – the most important decisions affecting the Curia, the papal government itself. This was an immense responsibility. Lucrezia Borgia in effect held all the powers of the Pope, to say nothing of the daily running of his office. Fortunately, she was lucky to have the trusted advice of Cardinal da Costa, a remarkable man of immense experience and wisdom. Astonishingly, the Portuguese Cardinal da Costa was by now ninety-four years old,* but remained a sympathetic and understanding figure in full possession of his faculties, as can be seen from the following anecdote retailed by Burchard:

> I do not know the precise nature of the problem, but Lucrezia felt it necessary to seek out Cardinal da Costa, informing him of the advice given her by the Pope, and explaining to him the difficulty on which she needed his advice. Cardinal da Costa was of the opinion that the problem was not serious, and told her, 'when the Pope discusses an issue in consistory, the vice chancellor, or in his absence the cardinal who has been appointed in his place, takes down the minutes of the meeting and records the way the cardinals present voted. All we really need is for someone to make a note of our conversation.' Lucrezia informed da Costa that she was quite capable of writing, whereupon the cardinal enquired of her: 'So where is your pen?' [In Italian the word *penne* not only means 'pen', but is also vernacular for 'penis'.] Lucrezia well understood da Costa's pun and smiled.

On such evidence, Lucrezia was more than capable of looking after herself in a man's world. All this would suggest that she was not only emotionally close to her father, but was also aware of his plans, at least in so far

---

* Cardinal da Costa would not die until 1508, when he was 102 years old, making him the oldest cardinal ever in the history of the Catholic Church.

as he was willing to reveal these. Indeed, Lucrezia may well have been consulted upon such matters to a greater extent than the frequently absent and increasingly headstrong Cesare. The innocent adolescent Lucrezia, who had slipped away during boring sermons to the choir loft with her young sister-in-law Sancia to tell stories and giggle together, had now become a woman. Despite the trauma of her two broken marriages and the tragic affair with her father's manservant, she had developed into an adult of considerable intelligence and assurance – a maturity well beyond her years. Furthermore, judging from the paintings in which she appears, with her falling tresses of curled, golden hair, she had become a striking beauty.

After a month in the country Alexander VI returned to Rome fully revitalized and set back to work with a vengeance. There were several matters to be dealt with, the two most important of which concerned Lucrezia. For a start, there remained the problem of the *Infans Romanus*, the three-year-old Giovanni Borgia, who had now become fully integrated into the Borgia family. As we have seen, the Pope had previously issued a public bull specifying that Cesare Borgia was the father of this child (whilst he was still a cardinal). It was only now that Alexander VI made public the secret bull legitimizing the *Infans Romanus* as his own son. But it was also becoming clear that Giulia Farnese had not been the mother of this child, as her relationship with Alexander VI seems to have ended some time before his birth. Indeed, it now emerged that Lucrezia was almost certainly the mother. It had previously been thought that the child born to Lucrezia in seclusion at San Sisto had been stillborn or had died in infancy, but it now became evident that this was not the case. Lucrezia was most likely the mother of the mysterious *Infans Romanus*, with the father having been Perotto, the Pope's manservant who had been murdered by Cesare, along with Lucrezia's maid. Little wonder that Alexander VI had ordered Lucrezia to be confined in the convent of San Sisto. Here she had been able to give birth under circumstances of some secrecy, whereupon the 'stillborn' child had been whisked away. However, Alexander VI's secret bull naming himself as the father of the *Infans Romanus*, along with the growing rumours that Lucrezia was the mother, would inevitably confirm in the minds of some that Alexander VI and Lucrezia had been involved in an incestuous affair. As far as we can tell, this was certainly not the case, despite their evident closeness. Their habit of affectionately caressing each other in public, after the Spanish fashion, as well as incidents such as the two of them enjoying the sexually charged sight of horses fighting to mount a mare, hardly staunched such rumours. There is no doubting the fact that the Borgias themselves contributed heavily to the scandalous exaggerations which swirled around them, and revelations in Alexander VI's formerly secret bull can have done nothing but stoke such rumours. On the other hand, much of their actual known behaviour, especially in the case of Cesare, falls little short of the legend already beginning to form around their name.

We now come to the second matter concerning Alexander VI and Lucrezia. This most clearly of all illustrates the ambiguity of the Pope's feelings for his daughter. Having let her take charge of the papacy, albeit briefly, he now returned to using her as a mere pawn to further his own aims. For some time Alexander VI had been intent upon securing Cesare's Romagna state against any possible threat from its powerful northern neighbour Venice. This he now sought to achieve on a more perman- ent basis by securing a new husband for Lucrezia in the form of Alfonso d'Este, the twenty-four-year-old heir to the Duchy of Ferrara. Despite his age, Alfonso was already a widower, having previously been married to Anna Sforza, the direct descendant of a former duke of Milan. She had died in childbirth four years previously, her timely death breaking the tie between Milan and Ferrara prior to the ousting of the Sforzas and the French takeover of Milan. For several months now Alexander VI had been negotiating with Ercole I d'Este, Duke of Ferrara, in an attempt to secure the duke's agreement to a marriage between his son and Lucrezia. Ercole I had been firmly against such a match: the illegit- imate (and two times married) daughter of the Pope was hardly the kind of wife he had in mind for his son and heir – whose pedigree through the aristocratic d'Este family linked him to the ruling families of Naples, Spain and formerly Milan. Besides, he had no wish for the d'Este family to form some transient link with the papacy, especially in the form of the notorious Borgia family, whose power and importance would vanish as soon as the seventy-year-old Alexander VI died. Ercole I had plans of his own for his son. Marriage into the French royal family would secure his dukedom against both the power of neighbouring Venice, as well as the rapacious new Duke of Romagna, Cesare Borgia. Louis XII himself appeared to be favourable to a marriage between Alfonso and the aristocratic Mademoiselle de Foix, who was descended from French royalty.

However, Ercole I soon found himself outwitted by the master tactician Alexander VI. The Pope had already made contact with one of Louis XII's senior advisors, Cardinal de Rohan, who owed his red hat to Alexander VI. Within no time, Cardinal de Rohan set about persuading Louis XII of the desirability of Lucrezia Borgia as a bride for the young Alfonso. As a result, Louis XII decided to withhold his blessing on any engagement to Mademoiselle de Foix, and instead married her off to the King of Hungary. He suggested to Ercole I that if he was really so set against his son marrying Lucrezia Borgia, he should perhaps demand of the Pope that she bring with her an exorbitant dowry. When Ercole I received the news that Louis XII appeared no longer interested in allowing the d'Estes to marry into French royalty, he is said to have flown into 'paroxysms of rage'. But he knew that he could not afford to risk upsetting Louis XII by making his real feelings plain.

Despite this setback, Ercole I was determined to rebuff Alexander VI's designs upon his son, and chose to follow Louis XII's advice to the best of his ability. Even Alexander VI was taken aback by the enormity of Ercole I's demands for Lucrezia's dowry, commenting that the aristocratic duke 'bargained like a tradesman'. Whereupon Ercole I was forced to defend himself against the accusation that he was making 'importunate demands' upon the Pope. Alexander VI refused to be put off and eventually a dowry was agreed. This consisted of '100,000 ducats in cash, plus . . . an annual income amounting to some 3,000 ducats'. On top of this the Pope would reduce the tax which was paid to the Pope by the Duchy of Ferrara (this territory being nominally part of the ancient Papal States) from an annual 4,500 ducats to a nominal 100 ducats. Alexander VI accepted these inflated terms. Even so, Ercole I insisted that it was only his wish to remain on good terms with Louis XII, as well as the Pope and his dangerous son Cesare Borgia, that made him 'condescend to such an unequal relationship'. Cesare certainly played a significant role in these negotiations, not least by providing the go-between who conveyed the messages back and forth between Rome and Ferrara. The messenger concerned was the Spanish hardman Ramiro de Lorqua, Cesare's most trusted commander, who had been given the task of governing Cesare's Romagna territory during his absence.

These horse-trading negotiations dragged on throughout the early months of 1501. They would not come to a peak until August of that year, the very time when Alexander VI was out of Rome and had given Lucrezia 'authority to open all his letters'. This time there can be no doubt that Lucrezia, far from being a mere instrument in the foreign policy of her father and her brother Cesare, took an active role in deciding her own fate.

The accomplished and level-headed Lucrezia saw this as her opportunity. Maybe at last she could put behind her the wreckage of her personal life of broken teenage engagements, disastrous love affairs* and her two previous marriages. On top of all this, her one close female friend, her sister-in-law the adventurous Sancia of Aragon, had now become politically and personally non grata in the Vatican. Following her lover Cesare's marriage to the French Charlotte d'Albret, and Alexander VI's reversal of his policy towards Naples, the Pope had ordered Sancia's confinement in the Castel Sant'Angelo. No, Lucrezia realized, if she were to marry Alfonso d'Este she could perhaps make a life of her own in Ferrara, far from the overbearing influence of her father and her possessive brother. According to all reports, Alfonso d'Este was not a particularly prepossessing catch – but it seemed he was also not a strong-willed man and appeared to have little interest in anything other than pursuing his own pleasures. The challenge of creating a life of her own under such circumstances, with the prospect of eventually becoming Duchess of Ferrara, appealed to the new Lucrezia,

---

* There have been suggestions that her 'indiscretion' with the ill-fated Perotto may not have been her first such affair.

who had by now learned enough from the example set by her father and her elder brother to be confident of achieving whatever she set her mind upon. Though unlike them, she was of course a woman and would have to employ her charm, and disguise her determination, in order to achieve whatever schemes she had in mind. She was, by now, undoubtedly a Borgia.

As the negotiations over Lucrezia's dowry gradually edged towards a successful conclusion, her behaviour underwent a distinct change. She now set aside her mourning for her husband Alfonso, Duke of Biseglie, whose murder had taken place a year previously, and in August the Mantuan ambassador reported:

> Up to now Donna Lucretia, according to the Spanish usage has eaten from earthenware and maiolica. Now she has begun to eat from silver as she is almost no longer a widow.

Lucrezia Borgia's betrothal to Alfonso d'Este was announced on Saturday, 4 September 1501 'around the time of Vespers' (i.e. late afternoon). This was celebrated by the firing of cannon salvoes from the high walls of Castel Sant'Angelo 'without ceasing from Vespers to nightfall'. However, the future bride and groom remained in their separate cities, not expected to meet until the time of the actual wedding ceremony, which, in accordance with contemporary practice, would be held in the bridegroom's home city. Next day, Lucrezia Borgia rode in procession, accompanied by four bishops and a detachment of some thirty horsemen, while the great bell of the Capitol was rung, and many fires and beacons were lit on the Castel Sant'Angelo and all over the city. This was probably more a reflection of the Pope's exuberant happiness, than that of his daughter – who was nonetheless pleased, after her own fashion.

On 25 September Cesare Borgia arrived back in Rome from the successful French war against Naples. He was said to be exhausted after the campaign and at once retired to bed. There were conflicting reports: the Ferrarese ambassador wrote, 'I thought he was ill, but yesterday evening he danced without intermission and will do so again tonight at

the Pope's palace where the illustrious Duchess [Lucrezia] is going to
supper.' An entry from Burchard's *Journal* is more illuminating:

> The Duke [Cesare] has recently been ill again with his old
> complaint, which returned upon him after the conquest of Naples
> and has, some of his physicians think, affected his mind as well
> as his body. Although forcing himself to take part in dances and
> entertainments, it is seen and reported by his servants that they
> discover him exhausted and sometimes in pain upon his bed.

On 25 September Alexander VI and Cesare Borgia travelled north of
Rome to Civita Castellana for a week-long inspection of the fortresses
in this region, which they had 'acquired', along with the estates formerly
belonging to the aristocratic Caetani family. As before, Lucrezia would
be left in charge in Rome. The same would happen when the Pope and
his son left Rome on 17 October for another week-long inspection of
the fortresses they had seized from the Savelli and Colonna families,
some of which were being significantly reinforced. It had also been
decided by Alexander VI that the Orsini family should be rewarded with
a number of these estates for their loyalty to the Borgia family, especially
to Cesare on his previous campaigns in the Romagna. The Pope and his
son were ensuring that all territory surrounding Rome remained firmly
under their control. There was to be no repeat of the insubordination
shown to the Pope by his autocratic enemies after Charles VIII had
returned to France – when the Colonna had occupied Ostia and the
castles outside Rome owned by the aristocratic families had continued
to fly the French flag. Admittedly, the powerful Orsini had played a
leading role in these affronts to papal authority. But now that they had
demonstrated their loyalty, at least for the time being, it was only right
(and strategically useful) that they should be rewarded for this. With the
long-established aristocratic families thus divided, they could no longer
use their combined powers to curb the influence of the papacy, as had
previously been the case. At the same time, Alexander VI's possession
of the territory and castles north of Rome meant that the direct route

through the Apennines to the Romagna remained firmly under the control of the Papal Forces.

As was customary, all military activity had halted for the winter. There were good practical reasons for this. The Apennines, in particular, were rendered impassable to large contingents of soldiers, cavalry and artillery when the passes were clogged with mud and snow. Even so, Cesare Borgia was already making plans to launch a third campaign in the Romagna with the intention of securing the entire territory for himself. All Italy was aware of this. But the question remained as to whether the territorial ambitions harboured by himself and his father would remain limited to the Romagna.

In preparation for Lucrezia Borgia's wedding, Ercole I of Ferrara despatched a request to Rome for a copy of the Borgia family tree, so that this could be exhibited in his palace and added to his own tree of distinguished ancestors. The d'Este family had considerable pretensions in this field. They were related to both Neapolitan and Spanish royalty (Aragon branch), as well as the Dukes of Milan (Sforzas) and the Gonzaga dynasty (rulers of nearby Mantua). Such were the pretentions of Ercole I that he even went so far as to imitate the Roman emperors on his Ferrarese coinage, having himself styled as *divus* ('deified one'). As we have seen, Alexander VI was also interested in forming links with distinguished rulers, but only in the present, and for present gain. The past was now of little interest, and the dubious Borja claim to be descended from royalty, in the form of Ramiro I, appears to have been overlooked on this occasion. In reply to Ercole I's request for a Borgia family tree, a spurious genealogy was quickly concocted showing the Borgias as descendants of Don Pedro of Atares, the feudal lord of Borja and pretender to the throne of Aragon. Whereas the Borgia claim to be descended from King Ramiro I of Aragon was dubious, their claim to be descended from Don Pedro was patently false, as this particular scion of the House of Aragon had died without producing any offspring.

What Ercole I and his court genealogist made of this bogus claim is not recorded. On the other hand, the reports from the Ferrarese ambassador to Rome were scrutinized with great interest. Ercole I was determined that the behaviour of his son's future wife should be seen to bear no relation to the notorious rumours circulating throughout Italy concerning both herself and her brother. An envoy despatched by Ercole I to Rome expressly for this purpose reported:

> I hope that Your Excellency will be well satisfied with the most Illustrious Madonna [Lucrezia], for she is endowed with so much graciousness and goodness that she continually thinks of nothing else, save how to serve you.

By now, Ercole I had no less than four envoys reporting back to him from Rome. However, the despatches concerning Cesare's behaviour were less reassuring. According to one, even the Pope himself

> lamented that [his son Cesare] turned night into day and day into night, comporting himself in such a manner that it left room for doubt that if his father died he would be able to keep what he had conquered. [The Pope] commended the Duchess Lucrezia as the opposite for her prudence and willingness to receive [people] benevolently, praising the way in which she had governed Spoleto, and the way in which she could capture the heart of the pontiff in every matter she dealt with him.

From this despatch it can be seen that the Romagna was now regarded throughout Italy as Cesare Borgia's personal fiefdom, even if it was felt that he would need to defend this claim after the death of his father.

Inevitably, one of the Ferrarese envoys eventually managed to gain a more realistic idea of Lucrezia's personal life: 'Whenever she is at the Pope's palace, the entire night, until two or three in the morning, is spent dancing and at play, which fatigues her greatly.' All this is as nothing compared to one particularly outrageous party, news of which appears to have eluded all four Ferrarese envoys – though it was to be recorded in lurid detail by master-of-ceremonies Burchard:

On Sunday evening, 31 October, Don Cesare Borgia gave a supper in his apartment in the apostolic palace, with fifty decent prostitutes or courtesans in attendance, who after the meal danced with the servants and others, fully dressed and then naked . . . chestnuts were strewn about, which the prostitutes, naked and on their hands and knees, had to pick up [with their vaginas] . . . The Pope, Don Cesare and Donna Lucrezia were all present to watch. Finally prizes were offered to those men who fucked these prostitutes the greatest number of times.

The Perugian chronicler Francesco Matarazzo even went so far as to report that the Pope 'had the lights put out, the men and women left their clothes and had diversion'. Despite the possibility of exaggeration in these reports, some of the details have a compelling particularity. If nothing else, the Borgias certainly seemed to be living up to their reputation.

The question now inevitably arises as to the spiritual beliefs of these three central figures. With regard to Alexander VI, could his behaviour be reconciled with a belief in the divine? Did the Pope believe in God? During the thirty-six years prior to his papacy, when Cardinal Rodrigo Borgia had been vice-chancellor to no less than five popes, this had involved him in regular attendance at daily services and a host of other religious observances. However, his licentious behaviour is certainly at variance with profound Christian belief – which involved an afterlife in Hell, Purgatory or Paradise. His character hardly encouraged hope of redemption. Even so, his deeply superstitious nature would seem to indicate a more than perfunctory belief in supernatural forces and a metaphysical world. And as more than one commentator indicates, after he became Alexander VI, 'the Pope was scrupulous in the outward obser-vances of his religious duties and had an apparently sincere devotion to the cult of the Virgin Mary'. Such contradictions make it difficult to discern the precise nature of Alexander VI's belief, if indeed it existed.

As for his daughter Lucrezia: despite her behaviour up to this stage in her life, it would seem that her closeness to her father inspired an unostentatious but deeply held belief in God. Any psychological damage

she might have incurred – during her father's erratic use of her as a political pawn, and her brother's murderous intentions towards her partners
– does not appear to have dented her faith. So far, religion may have
played little demonstrative role in her life; yet as we shall see, an element
of steadfast faith would emerge more clearly in her later years.

With Cesare Borgia we come to a different spiritual status altogether.
From his student years Cesare had made plain his lack of belief in any
form of conventional deity. Indeed, his 'arrogant atheism' had been
the cause of deep irritation, and often anger, in his father. (Ironically,
this would seem to reinforce a spiritual aspect, not always evident, in
Alexander VI.) Cesare Borgia's behaviour had invariably echoed his lack
of Christian belief. During his intellectually dazzling youth, when he
had been 'the handsomest man in Italy' and his charm had matched his
brilliance, he had shown no evidence of any spiritual inclination. Even
after his appointment as cardinal at the exceptional age of eighteen, he
had continued as before. Admittedly, his indulgent behaviour had not
been particularly unusual. By this time, cardinals had become a byword
for excessive wealth and worldliness. What makes Cesare Borgia stand
out is his psychological make-up. Long before he contracted syphilis, his
character had begun exhibiting elements of dangerous instability. The
extravagant peacock who delighted in hunting with his friends, charming
all who came into contact with him, would on occasion disappear without
warning for days on end, prostrate in his bed in a darkened chamber.
From the outset there appears to have been a persistent and crippling
depressive element in his personality. On top of this was his peculiar
sensitivity. Beneath all the swagger and wilfulness lay a deep vulnerability.
He seldom forgave even the most minor slight and was liable to wreak
drastic revenge. The previously mentioned Roman satirist who had his
tongue cut out and nailed to his severed hand was not an isolated victim
of Cesare Borgia's sadistic retribution. Tales of other similar incidents
soon spread. Those who insulted the Pope's son were liable to end up
floating in the Tiber, their corpses hideously disfigured. Likewise, his
preternatural closeness to his sister had inspired at least two murders –
her beloved husband Alfonso had followed her lover Perotto into the

Tiber. And her first husband Giovanni had only eluded Cesare by fleeing for his life. As we have seen, these murders were far from being the only ones in which he had been directly involved. The ruthless elimination of his arrogant and inept younger brother Juan, his unfortunate predecessor as Captain-General of the Papal Forces, was perhaps his most sensational outrage. By this later stage in his military career, when he had proved his powers as a military commander in the conquest of his own territory, his increasingly impulsive unpredictability had demonstrated that he remained but loosely under his father's charge. And this, despite the fact that the strategy and diplomacy which paved the way for these achievements was almost entirely his father's doing. No, with Cesare Borgia we seem to have a mind characterized by a total absence of spirituality, allied with flashes of brilliance and instability.

CHAPTER 14

CESARE STRIKES OUT

A ccording to Roman gossip, during the autumn of 1501 Cesare Borgia continued with his sapping regime of almost nightly parties in his apartments at the Vatican. Only occasionally was he seen on the streets of Rome during the hours of daylight. Yet such occasions were witness to a dramatic development. Not only did Cesare Borgia dress from head to toe in his customary black velvet tunic and black robe, but he also wore a black mask. According to the contemporary physician Paolo Giovio, this was to cover the syphilis 'blooms' that had once again erupted, disfiguring his face, which Giovio described as 'swarthy and deformed by blotches'. However, Giovio was not resident in Rome during this period and may well have been recounting gossip. No other source mentions Cesare having any facial disfigurement at this time. Furthermore, modern knowledge of syphilis suggests that after the appearance of the rashes marking the secondary stage of this disease, such as appeared on his face after his return from Naples in 1498, no further disfigurement was likely to appear for several years – until the appearance of the hideous, and often fatal, tertiary stage of this disease. However, with treatment – even such basic medication as provided by his personal physician Gaspar Torella – the tertiary stage frequently did not appear. Thus, it seems highly unlikely that Cesare Borgia was suffering from conspicuous facial 'blooms' during this period. More likely, he adopted the wearing of a black mask for other reasons. Dramatic effect may well have been one of them. It has also been suggested that this black mask could have acted as a disguise when he rode through the streets of Rome accompanied by his attendant guards. Any political or vengeful assassin could not have been certain that this man in the black mask was in fact the actual Cesare Borgia – or merely a body double, intended to draw out anyone intent on taking his life.

Likewise, the reports of Cesare Borgia having almost nightly parties would also seem to have been an exaggeration, especially as the autumn turned to winter. In line with previous occasions, Cesare Borgia would have been preparing himself physically for the rigours of his third campaign in the Romagna. His mind was also concentrated on the coming campaign, whose strategy he had already begun to plan.

Reports by the Ferrarese envoys must have allayed any fears on behalf of Ercole I concerning the worthiness of Lucrezia Borgia becoming his daughter-in-law. He now agreed to allow her proxy marriage to take place in Rome. This was celebrated with due pomp and ceremony on 30 December. Lucrezia Borgia is described as arriving in the piazza before St Peter's 'dressed in a robe of gold brocade, designed in the Spanish style, with a long train behind, which was carried by a young girl. She was escorted by the brother of her husband.' There followed a service in the Vatican, during which a sermon was delivered by Niccolò Maria d'Este, Bishop of Adria (an illegitimate nephew of Ercole I). Evidently, the bishop had not consulted with Alexander VI prior to delivering his sermon, or he would have known of the Pope's inability to tolerate any but the shortest of homilies from the pulpit. Consequently, the bishop was interrupted by the Pope 'on several occasions', calling on him to terminate his sermon. Despite this, Lucrezia's proxy wedding ceremony was successfully completed.

It happened to coincide with the opening of the Carnival horse races, which appear to have monopolized the attention of her brother Cesare.

The races took place over a course which ran through the streets of Rome from the Campo dei Fiori to St Peter's, a distance of around a mile. As we have seen, Cesare Borgia took such horse races extremely seriously – as did his chief rival in this field, Francesco Gonzaga, Marquis of Mantua. This was the Gonzaga who had fallen out with Cesare when his horse had cheated in the vain attempt to win the Palio at Siena in 1493. Gonzaga was described as 'short, pop-eyed, snub-nosed and extremely brave, and was regarded as the finest knight in Italy'. It was he who had somewhat ineptly commanded the forces of the Holy League at the decisive Battle of Fornovo against the army of Charles VIII. Gonzaga regarded Borgia with contempt: an upstart bastard devoid of breeding or honour, and was determined to teach him a lesson, at least on the racing field.

During the 30 December Carnival races, there were three main races. The first, between Barbary horses (close relatives of the Arab horse); the next between genets (small Spanish horses); and the third between mares. The traditional prize in each case was a bolt of fine cloth. But between Cesare Borgia and Francesco Gonzaga much more was at stake. According to Burchard, during each of the three races

> There was much violence and cheating. The Barbary belonging to Francesco Gonzaga, Marquis of Mantua, came first, but did not receive the bolt of cloth because the horse lost its rider, who had fallen off at the start of the race, so the prize went to the Barbary belonging to Duke Cesare. The prize for winning the genets' race was given to Duke Cesare's household, though his horse did not begin with the others at Campo dei Fiori but was seen leaving the vice-chancellor's palace [formerly the Borgia residence] before the pack arrived, which was how he managed to come first. During the mares' race one of Duke Cesare's grooms crossed the course on the Ponte Sant'Angelo, causing the leading mare to lose her jockey.

This time Gonzaga had been roundly vanquished. Cesare Borgia would not allow himself to be defeated on his own ground; any more than his father, the Pope, would tolerate being subjected to a lengthy lecture on morality during a sermon in his own church. These two incidents serve as exemplary illustrations of how the Borgia now regarded themselves; and, by implication, how they had come to be regarded throughout aristo-cratic Italy. They also indicate one salient fact: the Borgia were now in charge, ruling on their own terms.

Lucrezia's proxy wedding in Rome was followed by a round of ex-travagant celebrations, including bullfights in St Peter's Square and further races of all kinds. Indeed, the celebrations were said by some to have been on a scale not seen in the city since ancient times. Alexander VI was deter-mined that his daughter should lack nothing. And her father-in-law in distant Ferrara, Ercole I, seemed to feel a similar soft spot for the woman who was soon to be united with his son and heir. Ercole I had despatched to Rome a delegation of no less than 1,500 people – including all the top citizens and nobles of Ferrara. Amongst the many wedding gifts which accompanied this delegation was a piece of jewellery valued at no less than 70,000 ducats. Ercole I well knew the extravagance of which Alexander VI was capable, and was determined that the d'Este family should not be seen to be outdone during the wedding celebrations in the Holy City.

Finally, the time came for Lucrezia to depart for her married life in Ferrara. On 6 January 1502, as snow fell over the rooftops of Rome, Lucrezia rode out at the head of a large procession. She was wearing a protective cloak made of cloth of gold, lined with ermine, and the mule on which she rode 'was harnessed very richly with beaten gold and a long wide cloth of mulberry velvet'. Her father was observed moving hurriedly from window to window of the Vatican, eager to catch glimpses of her as she rode away. It was as if he knew that he would never see her again.

Lucrezia's two young children were not permitted to make the journey with their mother. According to the dictates of contemporary protocol, the new bride was expected to arrive in Ferrara alone, as if she were a virgin. She also divested herself of all her titles and estates – many of them linked to former Colonna and Savelli properties given to her by her father. These would be passed on to her children. Thus Rodrigo, her two-year-old son by her murdered second husband Alfonso, Duke of Bisceglie, became Duke of Sermoneta, while the elder, illegitimate Giovanni (the *Infans Romanus*) inherited the duchy of Nepi. This would seem to be a further indication that Giovanni was her son – though it does not confirm this.

On leaving Rome, Lucrezia and her procession made their way north towards the Apennines. For the first few miles beyond the city walls she was accompanied by Cesare, but after ensuring that the soldiers of the Papal Guard were sufficiently briefed to protect her on her journey, he took his farewell of his sister and rode back to Rome. His feelings at this point can only be surmised; he, too, appeared to be losing the person he held most dear.

Lucrezia and her long procession now continued up the Via Flaminia and over the mountains. This was no simple procession. Lucrezia's baggage train alone consisted of forty-two mules, draped in her own personal colours of yellow and mulberry; and it carried a trousseau worth well over 200,000 ducats. Lucrezia was also accompanied by her husband Alfonso d'Este's two brothers, Ferrante and Sigismund, who carried with them the 100,000-ducat dowry given by Alexander VI. Indeed, the Pope had drained the papal coffers with his generosity towards his daughter, whose trousseau was accompanied by a small fortune in expensive jewellery. After all the expenses of the dowry, the marriage and the entertainments, Alexander VI found that he simply had no money left to provide for all the transport involved in his daughter's procession to Ferrara. As a result, he issued an order to all the cardinals resident in Rome that they were each required to provide two horses or two mules for the journey. (As Burchard later recorded in his diary: 'None of these animals was returned.') Lucrezia's procession was also joined by several hundred of the Ferrarese delegation that had been despatched to Rome by Ercole I, and inevitably such a travelling party required a numerous armed guard. According to the contemporary Venetian diarist Marino Sanuto the younger, Lucrezia Borgia's procession consisted in all of '753 people, 426 horses and 234 mules'.

The procession would take almost a month to cover the winding 300-mile journey to Ferrara. (The direct journey would normally be covered by a fast courier in around four days.) As if travelling across the snowy mountain passes and along muddy highways in midwinter was not tiring enough, at every place where Lucrezia stayed on her journey she would expect to endure whole days of celebrations. These were not always willingly provided, but each city knew that all of Italy was watching, and lavish entertainments were a requirement if it was to maintain any reputation. After passing through Perugia, the next main stop was at Urbino, home of the Duke Guidobaldo da Montefeltro and his wife Elizabetta, a member of the Gonzaga family. Guidobaldo da Montefeltro had never forgiven Alexander VI for not paying his ransom after he had been taken prisoner while fighting for the papal forces alongside the Pope's son Juan Borgia. Guidobaldo's wife Isabella, both as a Gonzaga and an avid gossipmonger, also had strong reasons to despise Lucrezia. Nevertheless, lavish hospitality was laid on by the hosts day and night, whilst a façade of gracious hospitality was maintained.

From Urbino, Lucrezia proceeded to the coast, along the route mapped out for her by her brother. Here she was obliged to stay at Pesaro, a city resonant for her of the most painful memories. It was here that she had lived with her first husband, the hapless Giovanni Sforza. By now Lucrezia was exhausted. Forsaking all hospitality and protocol, she simply absented herself. According to one of the Ferrarese envoys: 'She kept always to her room, to wash her hair but also because she is rather solitary and remote by nature.' From now on, Lucrezia's stays at the small cities along her route were more often to be punctuated by days 'to wash her hair'. She may have been increasingly tired, but she was determined to look her best when she finally, for the first time, encountered her husband Alfonso d'Este.

Upon reaching her brother's new territory in the Romagna, Lucrezia was greeted by Ramiro de Lorqua, Cesare's Spanish governor. Ramiro de Lorqua would have made an intimidating figure at the best of times, but more so for Lucrezia, who was well aware that he was the crony of her brother's other close commander, Miguel da Corella, the man who had strangled her second husband Alfonso. For the most part, Lucrezia's hosts were impressed by her beauty, culture and courtly demeanour. This was far from the depraved figure of legend which had been spread by the gossips of Rome, exaggerated by correspondents throughout Italy.

Meanwhile in Ferrara, Lucrezia's husband Alfonso d'Este was overcome with curiosity concerning his new bride, a feeling which was further inspired by the incoming reports of her grace and beauty. Any previous misgivings he might have had about his future wife, and her scandalous reputation, vanished. He decided at once that he must see her for himself. Disregarding all protocol, he made a dramatic gesture, riding full tilt out to see her at Bentivoglio, a small town across the border in Bolognese territory, even before her ceremonial entry into the state of Ferrara. According to Zambotti: 'This act pleased everyone, and especially the bride and her ladies, that his lordship wished to see her.'

Alfonso d'Este was a curious mixture of aristocrat and coarse soldier. Four years older than the twenty-one-year-old Lucrezia, he had a physically powerful presence. But his romantic gesture was in fact out of character. More of a man's man, his rough and ready attitude and manners made him a good leader of men and soldier. On the other hand, where women were concerned he preferred the prostitutes in the town's more boisterous taverns. Despite this, he was not devoid of intellect or skill. He knew the humanist poets, yet preferred working with his metalworkers, designing new cannon. While Lucrezia was warily touched at his sudden appearance, Alfonso was much more impressed. Boldly he proposed that he and Lucrezia should consecrate their marriage without delay, a suggestion to which Lucrezia courteously demurred. Whereupon, he wished her a bluff farewell and rode off back home, leaving Lucrezia and her retinue to board the barge which was to take them downriver to Ferrara. Here she duly arrived on 30 January, some twenty-four days after setting out from Rome.

Before the gates of Ferrara Lucrezia was graciously received by her seventy-year-old father-in-law Duke Ercole I d'Este. Lucrezia was acclaimed with a rapturous welcome as she rode through the streets. The balconies of the houses on either side were draped with tapestries; cannon boomed from the ramparts of the Castel Tedaldo; and fanfares of trumpets rang out at her approach. The central piazza of Ferrara was so packed with its citizens that, according to one onlooker, 'if a grain of millet had fallen from the sky it would not have reached the ground'.

Over the coming days Lucrezia was described as 'full of life and gaiety'. On the actual wedding night it was reported that Alfonso had 'broken his lance three times'. News of this was duly relayed to a delighted Alexander VI. Alfonso would spend every night with his new bride, but rose early. During the daylight hours he resumed his old habits in the foundry and the taverns. Alexander VI was not bothered by reports of this, merely commenting: 'Being young, it does him good.' Meanwhile, Lucrezia lay in bed late through the mornings. Despite all the many novelties of the charming new city in which she found herself, Lucrezia had already begun to feel pangs of homesickness for Rome and her family.

Back in Rome Alexander VI, accompanied by a large papal entourage including seven cardinals, seven bishops and a hundred or so attendants, travelled to Civitavecchia, where they planned to take ship to the newly acquired papal possession of Piombino, further up the coast. According to Burchard:

> Three boats were prepared for the Pope's journey ... and oarsmen were needed. They used all those prisoners in jail for petty crimes, and they also found many men in the inns of Rome, or on the piazzas, who were persuaded by violence or deception, whatever was necessary.

The precise details of the Borgia plans were not yet clear, but it was evident that Piombino was a key strategic possession with regard to Florence. Not only did it establish an important base to the south of the city's territory, but its location as a port was particularly significant in view of Florence's continuing war with its western port of Pisa. As this war continued throughout the spring, the ever-increasing tax bill to pay for the war had led to a wave of unrest sweeping the republic. Both Alexander VI and Cesare Borgia were mindful of the fact that Florence remained under the protection of Louis XII. But they were also aware that if the collapse of the republican government could be engineered, with the people calling for a restoration of Medici rule, then Florence might well become little more than a puppet protectorate of the Pope, or at least a close ally extending papal influence throughout the central territory of Italy.

When Alexander VI and Cesare Borgia returned to Rome, they heard that the unrest in Florentine territory had spread, with an uprising in the southern city of Arezzo. In preparation for Borgia's third campaign in the Romagna, his commander Vitellozzo had assembled a force of 3,500 men at his headquarters in nearby Città di Castello. Taking advantage of the situation, Vitellozzo immediately marched towards Arezzo, where the city gates were flung open and his troops welcomed as saviours. Next thing, news reached Rome that Piero de' Medici was in Arezzo, accompanied by Borgia's commander Baglioni; meanwhile, Vitellozzo had begun to march his troops north along the Val di Chiana in the direction of Florence. These developments took Alexander VI and Cesare Borgia completely by surprise. They had no intention of invading Florence, especially following Louis XII's warning to Cesare Borgia after his impulsive 'invasion' of Florentine territory during his previous campaign. No, they had other plans to achieve their aims where Florence was concerned, and these moves were sabotaging their entire secret strategy.

Cesare Borgia had purposely been keeping the whole of Italy in suspense as to when he would launch his next campaign into the Romagna. This was part of the policy he had agreed with Alexander VI. Though now he had no alternative but to launch his campaign at once, at the same time sending word to Vitellozzo and Baglioni ordering them to join him. On 10 June Cesare Borgia left Rome, marching post-haste along the Via Flaminia towards the Romagna. He was accompanied by his commanders Paolo and Giulio Orsini, and Oliverotto da Fermo, at the head of 7,000 men. Under summer conditions, they were able to march speedily up the Via Flaminia and into the mountains. Their evident target was Camerino, before moving on to the coast to take the port of Sinigalia. Indeed, Alexander VI had already paved the way for this by excommunicating Giulio da Varano, the ruler of Camerino, on a charge of fratricide. (This, along with parricide, were time-honoured methods by which the petty tyrants of the Campagna achieved power.)

In order to reach Camerino and the coast, Cesare Borgia had to march his troops across a southern stretch of Urbino territory. As a courtesy he sent ahead to Guidobaldo da Montefeltro (theoretically a papal ally, despite the earlier difficulty over his ransom) for permission, which was quickly granted. No sooner had this happened than Cesare Borgia, in a masterstroke of treachery, swept his troops north in a rapid advance to attack the city of Urbino itself. Cesare Borgia had previously requested Guidobaldo da Montefeltro to send his troops to aid Vitellozzo in the Val di Chiana, thus leaving Urbino defenceless. Guidobaldo da Montefeltro fled for his life, only just managing to elude Borgia's pursuers by zigzagging through the Apennine passes, before finally making it to the safety of Mantua, which was ruled by his wife's family, the Gonzagas. Urbino was not only the cornerstone protecting the south-western edges of the Romagna, but it also posed a further threat to Florence, which found itself gradually being encircled by Borgia's forces. Gonfaloniere Piero Soderini and the republican government of the city had been taken completely by surprise by recent developments. As the Florentine diarist Luca Landucci put it: 'The Florentines had been caught with their breeches down and their arse in a bucket, while all around were laughing at them.'

Piero Soderini immediately delegated two of his most trusted colleagues – his brother Francesco Soderini, Bishop of Volterra, and the experienced emissary Niccolò Machiavelli – to ride post-haste to meet Cesare Borgia. Soderini knew that they could not trust Cesare Borgia, but he insisted that they at least try to gauge his intentions. It looked as if Borgia no longer cared that Florence was under French protection. After two days' hard riding across the mountains, Machiavelli and the Bishop of Volterra arrived exhausted at Urbino, where they were immediately marched under armed guard to the main hall of the palace. Here they found Borgia waiting for them

> by the light of a single flickering candle, which showed only dimly the tall figure clad in black from head to foot without jewel or ornament, the still, white features as regular as a Greek statue and as immobile.

Before they could even begin to put Soderini's question to Borgia, he launched into a tirade, castigating the two Florentines: 'I am not pleased with your government. How can I trust you? How can I be sure you will not attack me? You must change your government and pledge to support me – for I have no intention of letting this state of affairs continue.' He concluded, ominously: 'If you do not want me as a friend, you will find me your enemy.'

Machiavelli had a suspicion that this bullying was a bluff. Yet for all his diplomatic experience, he could not be sure. He well knew of Borgia's reputation for recklessness: it looked as if he was liable to do anything. He also sensed that this reaction was just what Borgia intended.

In fact, Borgia was intent on cowing Gonfaloniere Soderini into signing an agreement to hire him as Florence's condottiere. Should he succeed, he would all but control Florence, yet without upsetting Louis XII. At the moment the French king was preoccupied over a quarrel with Spain concerning their joint division of Naples, but Borgia realized it would not be long before he despatched French troops south from Milan to drive Vitellozzo and Baglioni from Florentine territory. Although Vitellozzo and Baglioni were acting on their own initiative, Borgia knew that an agreement with Florence would be seen as in all their interests, and he would soon be able to reassert his control over his wayward commanders. However, despite Borgia sending Machiavelli speeding back to meet with his master, Gonfaloniere Soderini refused to give a direct answer. This was no show of strength; in fact, Soderini found himself overwhelmed by the situation. But to buy time he decided to give in to one of Borgia's lesser demands, i.e. that Florence should loan him the services of its most famous military engineer, Leonardo da Vinci. As we have seen, Cesare Borgia had met Leonardo some three years previously when he had arrived in Milan with the conquering forces of Louis XII, and he had gone to view Leonardo's *Last Supper*. Indeed, Cesare Borgia may well have come to some loose arrangement that Leonardo should one day work for him. Leonardo had found himself disillusioned with painting at this stage in his life, and had been keen to devote his creative talents to civil and military engineering.

Borgia's meeting with Leonardo in Milan, along with the request (demand) to Soderini, confirms one salient fact. Borgia was intent upon reinforcing the defences and the infrastructure of his new state in the Romagna. Improvements to castles, novel military equipment, canals and hydraulic schemes – Leonardo's notebooks are littered with drawings of such projects. These date from the previous years during his employment by Ludovico Sforza and his movement to Florence after the French occupation of Milan. Hiring Leonardo indicates the seriousness of Cesare Borgia's plans for his new dukedom. The wild hinterland of the Romagna was to be transformed into a powerful and impressive new state – taking its place as a major player on the Italian political scene.

Within a month Leonardo da Vinci had taken up residence in Cesare Borgia's camp. It was some time during this period that Leonardo made three sketches of Borgia. These show that the fine features of 'the handsomest man in Italy' had now hardened. At just twenty-seven years old Borgia was already beginning to show the first signs of middle age. The years of hard living, hard campaigning, and the driving quest for power had turned Borgia into the formidable figure who had so frightened Machiavelli and the Bishop of Volterra in the palace at Urbino.

After taking Urbino, Cesare painstakingly organized the wholesale ransacking of the city. Under Guidobaldo da Montelfeltro's father, the formidable Federigo, the city and its palace had accumulated a superb collection of Renaissance art.* This was transported lock, stock and barrel by mule and cart over the road forty miles north to Cesena, which Borgia intended to make the capital of his new state. Leonardo recorded in his notebook: 'mules carrying rich loads of gold and silver, many treasures and great wealth'. A local chronicler claimed that as many as 180 mules a day were required to transport all the rare books, tapestries and paintings. Cesena itself was some nine miles from the sea, and it must have been around this time that Borgia discussed with Leonardo the building of a canal from the coast at Cesenatico to link his capital with the Adriatic.

---

* Not for nothing was this the small, out-of-the-way city which had produced Raphael, who had learned his art here, before leaving just a year or so prior to Borgia's invasion.

During July Borgia also continued to direct his military operations from Urbino. The Orsini brothers and their forces had been ordered to continue on to Camerino, following the apparent original target of Borgia's campaign. Here they laid siege to the ancient but well-fortified hill town and its seventy-year-old ruler Giulio Varano. On orders from Borgia, the Orsini brothers struck a deal with Varano: if he surrendered the city to Borgia's forces, he and his family would be allowed safe passage to neutral territory. Varano agreed – whereupon he was seized and flung in the castle dungeons, with his sons being put to the sword. Borgia would have no truck with such 'negotiations'. Machiavelli, who was still travelling regularly back and forth, carrying messages between Florence and Borgia in Urbino, duly took note of Borgia's latest conquest, discretely recording the news of his treachery in his latest despatch to his master Soderini back in Florence. Then suddenly Cesare Borgia vanished.

Even the normally imperturbable Leonardo exclaimed in his notebook: 'Where is Valentino?'* Leonardo's notebooks are for the most part devoted to his scientific and artistic investigations. Indeed, this is the only mention he makes of Borgia in any of his notebooks – an indication of the confusion felt by him, and all those around him, on being so unexpectedly abandoned by their employer.

Borgia had, in fact, fled from his camp outside Urbino under cover of darkness. Disguised as a Knight of St John, he had ridden off into the night, accompanied by just three of his most trusted personal guards. But why had he fled? And where was he going? Borgia's intelligence, reinforced by secret messages from his father in Rome, had revealed a series of dramatic events. Louis XII had set up his court at Asti, in Milanese territory. Here, he had soon been informed of Borgia's treacheries in the taking of Urbino and Camerino, the taking of Arezzo by his commander Vitellozzo, and Baglioni's continued advance up the Val di Chiana towards Florence. Louis XII had been angered by what he saw as another betrayal by Borgia, namely of his trust, and had despatched a large contingent of French soldiers south to guard Florence and repel any invaders of Florentine territory. At the same time he had sent a

* i.e. Borgia.

firmly worded message to Borgia, ordering the immediate removal of all
Baglioni's forces from the Val di Chiana and the withdrawal of Vitellozzo's
troops from Arezzo. The trouble was, Borgia knew that there was little
chance of either Baglioni or Vitellozzo heeding his commands. He had
recently discovered that both Baglioni and Vitellozzo, and probably the
Orsini brothers too, were plotting against him. All of them owned castles
and territories along the south-western flank of the Romagna, and had
realized that Borgia's next logical move would be to overrun these territories and absorb them into his new dukedom.

Yet this was not all. Cesare Borgia's treacherous behaviour had
provoked alarm throughout the region. All those who held grudges
against the Borgia family, as well as those who felt under threat from
Cesare's continuing seizure of territory, had travelled to Milan to put
their grievances before the French king. These included the dispos-
sessed Guidobaldo da Montefeltro, as well as a son of Giulio Varano
of Camerino who had managed to escape the massacre of his brothers.
Also present were Bentivoglio of Bologna, whose territory was clearly
vulnerable, as well as Francesco Gonzaga of Mantua, who felt similarly
under threat. Inevitably, the old Borgia enemy Cardinal Giuliano della
Rovere was also at the king's side. And more ominously still, Alexander
VI's friend Cardinal Giambattista Orsini had slipped away from Rome
to add his voice to those advising Louis XII to put an end to the Borgia
family's misuse of power. The only heartening news for Cesare Borgia had
been that Vitellozzo and Baglioni appeared to have heeded his orders and
withdrawn from Florentine territory. However, this news was tempered
by the fact that he now knew these two commanders were plotting against
him and had joined forces with the Orsini brothers.

Impulsive as ever, Cesare Borgia had decided to take matters into his
own hands. He would abandon his camp and ride north to meet Louis
XII. Here he would confront his enemies and persuade Louis XII of his
loyalty. When Alexander VI learned what was happening, he was angered
beyond measure at Cesare's rash gesture, which was liable to upset all
his well-laid plans. Yet at the same time he could not help but express
his admiration at Cesare's bravery. In a way, he too suspected that there

might perhaps be no other means of saving the day. Everything depended on how Cesare handled his meeting with Louis XII.

Given the importance, to say nothing of the danger, of Cesare Borgia's courageous dash for Milan, his next move came completely out of the blue. Having reached Imola, he suddenly decided to make a detour off the Via Emelia which led directly to Milan. Without warning, he turned north and headed for Ferrara. At the time of his greatest peril, when the very fortunes of the Borgias hung in the balance, he had decided to pay a visit to his sister Lucrezia.

CHAPTER 15

CHANGING FORTUNES

Lucrezia Borgia, now gifted by marriage with the aristocratic name of d'Este, and at last independent of her dominating father and possessive brother, had been determined from the outset to make a success of her new life in Ferrara. This had not proved easy, despite the welcome accorded her by her new father-in-law Duke Ercole I. Her husband Alfonso d'Este had also shown his warm feelings for his new wife, after his own fashion. He enjoyed her company at night, but his daytime pursuits remained unaltered: smelting cannon in the armoury, and roistering away his leisure hours with his fellow soldiers in the taverns. This left Lucrezia largely to her own devices. As part of the marriage agreement, Alexander VI had insisted that Ercole I provide his daughter with a generous annual allowance of 12,000 ducats. Ercole I was a man of parsimonious tastes, who had in his earlier years avidly read the works of Savonarola, a native of Ferrara before he travelled to make his name in Florence. Lucrezia, by contrast, was accustomed to living, and dining, in style with her father and her brother, and continued her somewhat extravagant ways in Ferrara, sharing her table with her large retinue of mainly Spanish attendants. During Lent, when meat was forbidden, Ercole I fed his retinue on the most stringent diet. On the other hand Lucrezia, aware that fish was permitted, chose to dine on 'dishes from oysters and scampi to sturgeon, crayfish and caviar'.*

Ercole I was convinced that Lucrezia could easily manage on 8,000 ducats a year, but the Pope refused to countenance any such austerity for his daughter. However, Ercole I did retaliate by insisting that Lucrezia should replace her numerous Spanish attendants with a more modest retinue of local women. Lucrezia accepted this with equanimity, determined to remain on good terms with her father-in-law. She soon charmed her new attendants, who much preferred the livelier atmosphere of Lucrezia's apartments and style of life.

However, amongst these attendants were a number of spies, briefed to report on her behaviour. These had been recruited by her sister-in-law Isabella d'Este, who was married to Francesco Gonzaga, Marquis of Mantua. Isabella, Marquesa of Mantua, was six years older than Lucrezia and a formidable personality. Lucrezia's new sister-in-law was renowned for her humanist culture and learning, her aristocratic connections throughout Italy, and her snobbishness.† In Isabella's eyes, the illegitimate Spanish Lucrezia was a parvenu. Worse still, when Lucrezia's husband succeeded to the dukedom of Ferrara, Lucrezia would become a duchess and socially outrank her.

From the outset, Lucrezia started at something of a disadvantage in Ferrara. Its citizens would always compare her – unfavourably – to Ercole I's wife, Isabella's mother Eleanora of Naples, the formidable Duchess of Ferrara who had died nine years previously. Eleanora had ruled Ferrara when her husband was away serving as a soldier, and during

---

* During the sixteenth century, Beluga sturgeon were fished from the River Po, and their roe was used for making caviar.
† Isabella d'Este was used to getting her own way. When Leonardo da Vinci passed through Mantua after leaving Milan, she had insisted he paint her portrait. Leonardo had drawn an initial sketch, before continuing on his journey. For years afterwards she pestered Leonardo, his patrons, as well as her powerful friends, insisting that they induce him to complete the task she had imposed upon him. Leonardo, who could be equally obdurate when he chose, managed to elude her wishes, becoming increasingly irritated at her persistent letters.

the consequent period when he was sick. She had proved a popular and able ruler, and Lucrezia's role as the future duchess meant that she lived in Eleanora's shadow. The citizens of Ferrara, to say nothing of Isabella d'Este, remained ignorant of the fact that Lucrezia had not only proved an able ruler of Spoletto, but had on occasion even taken over her father's duties as pope.

Lucrezia's situation in Ferrara was hardly helped by the news of her brother Cesare's third campaign in the Romagna. His treachery in the taking of Urbino and Camerino made him even more despised throughout Italy than he had been beforehand. And despite the fact that Lucrezia's position in Ferrara guaranteed its continued safety from Cesare, she remained unpopular amongst its citizens. Meanwhile, Isabella d'Este became terrified of Cesare Borgia, especially after her brother-in-law Guidobaldo da Montefeltro had sought refuge from Borgia at her court. Mantua now stood in even more danger from Cesare Borgia, despite Louis XII's guarantee of protection, which she rightly suspected was hardly of great concern to the French king. Little wonder that Isabella's husband Francesco Gonzaga, Marquis of Mantua, had rushed to join Borgia's enemies gathering in Milan at the court of Louis XII.

By now Lucrezia had already become pregnant. This news had been greeted with enthusiastic joy by Alexander VI in Rome. According to Burchard: 'His Holiness has taken on a new lease of life in consequence of the news from Ferrara.' This 'new lease of life' took the form of an extreme rejuvenation in the seventy-one-year-old Pope: 'Every night he is commanding into his presence young women chosen from the best Roman brothels.' And this reinvigoration certainly extended beyond the mere voyeurism that Burchard's words might suggest. According to one account, the Pope summoned his unfortunate son Jofrè, along with his irrepressible wife Sancia and her current lover, to his apartments. After a while, he left the room, accompanied by Sancia. Later, when he returned, he informed Jofrè and her lover that Sancia was 'still worth the serious attention of a young man'.*

---

* This suggestive story, circulated by Burchard and others, may have the appearance of exaggeration. On the other hand, there is no denying that it is characteristic.

Meanwhile in Ferrara, as Lucrezia's pregnancy progressed she became increasingly ill. Initially, she had retired to the countryside, resting in Ercole I's villa at Belriguardo, some five miles south-west of the city in the Po valley. However, this had only brought about a temporary respite, and on her return to Ferrara she had collapsed and taken to her bed. Alexander VI wrote furiously from Rome, berating Ercole I, claiming that her illness was due to her suffering because he had limited her allowance. During the stifling heat of summer, Lucrezia's health deteriorated still further. Alexander VI grew even more concerned. In his opinion, his daughter had been poisoned. (Such a suspicion was hardly surprising, in the light of his own not infrequent resort to this method.) But it soon became clear that Lucrezia was merely suffering from an extreme form of an unknown malady which had spread through the entire court.* Even her normally thoughtless husband Alfonso became worried and soon began spending each night sleeping in an antechamber to her room. At the same time the Pope despatched his personal physician to Ferrara; and Cesare, too, ordered his Spanish pox-doctor Gaspar Torella to attend his sister. By mid-July Lucrezia was suffering from paroxysms and periods of delirium: she appeared to be on her deathbed. Little wonder that her loving brother Cesare, even in his greatest hour of need, felt impelled to divert from his frantic dash to the court of Louis XII in Milan, and make for Ferrara.

On the evening of 28 July Cesare Borgia galloped into Ferrara. Here he found that Lucrezia had rallied somewhat, so that she was able to sit up in bed and receive her brother. According to Lucrezia Borgia's Italian biographer Maria Bellonci, Cesare and Lucrezia 'spent the whole night conversing in the incomprehensible dialect of Valencia'. It seems they were both concerned that she might die. Cesare is said to have promised her that he would make the mysterious *Infans Romanus* his heir as Duke

---

* Such maladies were a regular occurrence all over this region, probably stemming from the high summer humidity of the Po Valley and its susceptibility to malaria and other purely local ailments. Lucrezia, fresh from Rome, would not have developed any immunity to such local diseases, although Rome too regularly suffered from its own malarial outbreaks during the summer months.

of Romagna. Does this confirm that Giovanni Borgia was the son of Lucrezia, or perhaps Cesare? Or, more sensationally (and improbably), both? The rumour-mongers certainly favoured the latter. Either way, it does seem a curious matter for Cesare to be discussing with Lucrezia on what was assumed to be her deathbed.

After Cesare Borgia rode from Ferrara at dawn, Lucrezia suffered a serious relapse. But she did not die, and she did not lose her child. Cesare and his two attendants continued their hectic gallop to Milan. When forced by exhaustion to spend the night at Modena, Cesare sent an express messenger ahead to Milan to inform Louis XII of his imminent arrival. By now Louis XII was growing tired of being pestered by so many of Cesare's enemies who had arrived at his court, and was pleasantly surprised at this unexpected news of his visit. According to the contemporary chronicler Bernardi, Louis XII confided to the governor of Milan: 'I have a piece of information to give you, which no one else is yet aware of. His Excellency, Cesare Borgia, is . . . at this moment on his way hither.' This news was conveyed by Louis XII in a stage whisper, so that all in attendance – including Borgia's enemies – overheard him and were thrown into consternation. Worse was to follow. According to an eyewitness, Louis XII personally greeted Cesare Borgia on his arrival:

> His Most Christian Majesty welcomed and embraced him with great joy and led him to the castle where he had him lodge in the chamber nearest his own, and he himself ordered the supper, choosing diverse dishes.

Indeed, the French king even went so far as to give Borgia his own 'shirts, tunic and robes', as he could see that Cesare had ridden with no baggage of his own. Cesare's enemies were thrown into disarray by Louis XII's references to Cesare as 'my cousin and my kinsman'. The fact is, Louis XII had formed a genuine affection for Cesare Borgia during their time together in Chinon, when Cesare had married into his family. And despite all the vexation he had caused Louis XII on his previous campaign – his menacing of Bologna, his blatant invasion of Florentine territory, even his treacherous behaviour on his present campaign – Cesare remained in the king's eyes like a prodigal son. In his time of need, he had turned to Louis XII, regardless of personal danger. Unbeknown to Cesare's enemies at the French court, Louis XII also had very real diplomatic reasons for favouring Borgia. French relations with Spain had broken down over the division of conquered Naples, and Louis XII was pleased to feel he could rely upon the support of Cesare and his papal army. Consequently, Louis XII decided to reward his wayward young ally even further. Discreetly, he gave Borgia permission to take Bologna, which continued to believe itself under French protection. Furthermore, Louis XII decided that Cesare Borgia's infant daughter Louise, by his distant and long-suffering wife Charlotte d'Albret, should be married to the equally young Federigo Gonzaga, heir to the Marquis of Mantua.*

These moves would ensure that the entire northern border of Borgia's Romagna possessions would be protected by allied states. Louis XII was all in favour of Borgia's Romagna dukedom, which also served to protect much of the eastern flank of Milanese territory, apart from the northern stretch, which bordered on Venetian territory. At the time, Venice remained preoccupied with defending the remnants of its eastern Mediterranean empire from the predations of the Ottoman Turks, and thus provided little threat to the territory of its traditional enemy, Milan. Yet should it ever turn its attentions once more to Milan, Borgia's Romagna and its allied states would prove a more than useful ally.

Meanwhile in Rome Alexander VI was aghast at recent developments. The Venetian ambassador to Rome wrote:

> The Pope is not content with this recent journey of his [son], and is deeply troubled, because from an unimpeachable source I hear that the Duke went without any consultation nor informing His Holiness.

---

* Federigo also happened to be the son of Isabella d'Este, who would do everything in her power to prevent this match.

Here was yet another example of Cesare Borgia's reckless behaviour. Quite contrary to all Alexander VI's strategy, Cesare Borgia had placed himself at the mercy of Louis XII. Alexander VI remained deeply suspicious of the French king's intentions and felt sure that Louis XII would keep Cesare Borgia hostage in order to restrain the Pope's natural sympathies for the Spanish in Naples. However, when Alexander VI learned of the full extent of Louis XII's generosity towards Cesare and his territorial ambitions, and how he had dismissed the Borgia enemies from his court, the Pope's outlook shifted somewhat.

> He praised the prudence of the Duke, that with the ability of his mind he had made the king so friendly towards him, when at first he seemed to regard him as a rebel.

At the next consistory, Alexander VI regaled the assembled cardinals with a eulogy on his son's bravery. Even Machiavelli would write: 'The Duke is not to be measured like other lords, who have only their titles, in respect to his state; but one must think of him as a new power in Italy.' This would be the beginning of Machiavelli's understanding of the profound and disturbing principles of political reality. Here was the man who would eventually feature as the exemplary, yet necessarily amoral, ruler in *The Prince*. Such was the master of 'Virtù e Fortuna'.

The only Borgia enemy who remained at the court of Louis XII was Francesco Gonzaga, Marquis of Mantua, whom the king had specifically invited to remain. Prior to Cesare Borgia's arrival, Francesco Gonzaga had informed the Venetian ambassador that if Borgia ever dared show his face in Milan, he would challenge 'that bastard son of a priest' to a duel and in doing so rid Italy of the Spanish cur. Yet, just days after this, Louis XII had managed to persuade Gonzaga that it was in his best interests to betrothe his young son and heir to Borgia's infant daughter. How on earth had he managed this? Louis XII needed as many troops as possible to combat the Spanish in Naples. He had already covertly withdrawn his protection from Bologna, and he could just as easily abandon Mantua to its fate. Borgia would certainly have seized the opportunity to add

Mantua to his Romagna state. If Francesco Gonzaga wished to remain the ruler of Mantua, he was forced to come to terms with Borgia. Worse still, Borgia drove a hard bargain. If he was to trust Mantua, Francesco Gonzaga would have to expel the fugitive Guidobaldo da Montefeltro, former ruler of Urbino, from his court. Borgia well realized that Guidobaldo da Montefeltro represented a threat to his rule: he could easily prove a rallying point for those opposed to him. At the same time, Cesare Borgia decided to play a trick on Guidobaldo da Montefeltro and discredit him. Borgia contacted his father and Alexander VI offered Montefeltro a cardinal's red hat. This would normally have been seen as a great honour; however, Montefeltro was already married. Borgia had ascertained some valuable gossip concerning Montefeltro. Although he had been married for fourteen years, he had no children; and the reason for this was because he was sexually impotent. This meant that he was certainly in a position to accept a cardinalate, and the offer of a red hat signalled that his secret was now out. Although Guidobaldo's wife loyally and angrily declared her intention to stand by him, Borgia knew that this leaked gossip would certainly put an end to any chance of Montefeltro heading the opposition to his rule. Such was the Italian obsession with 'manhood' that no army would have accepted him as a leader.

As Alexander VI wisely realized, Cesare Borgia's bold journey to Milan had achieved a political coup. And one of even more significance that even Louis XII himself understood. It was the prescient Machiavelli, still attached to Borgia's camp in the Romagna, who perceived the full implications of what had taken place. With his wide knowledge of diplomatic policy throughout the Italian peninsula, Machiavelli had come to the conclusion 'that the French knew nothing of politics'. Blinkered by his own military might, Louis XII had made two fatal diplomatic blunders. Firstly, he had invited yet another foreign power into the peninsula: namely, Spain. And secondly, he had relied upon the power of people he could not trust: namely, the Borgias. The consequences of these mistakes would only gradually become apparent.

After a month at Louis XII's court, which had by now moved to Genoa, Cesare Borgia took his leave of his royal mentor on 2 September.

His parting words were fulsome with gratitude: 'Sacred Majesty, I render infinite thanks for the great benefit I have received from you ... When the time comes I will present myself to you at the head of ten thousand men.' The latter refers to Borgia's promise to aid Louis XII in his war against the Spanish in Naples 'when the time comes'.

On his way back to the Romagna, Cesare Borgia once again broke off his journey to visit Lucrezia in Ferrara, arriving on the night of 7 September. Here he found that his sister's situation had deteriorated disastrously. The beginning of September had marked the seventh month of her pregnancy, but her ill-health and weakness had been such that her physicians had despaired for her life. Just two days prior to Cesare's arrival, she had given birth to a stillborn child, and remained too ill to receive her brother when he arrived. The following morning, Cesare browbeat the physicians into allowing him to see her. Whereupon her temperature rose alarmingly and the assembled physicians concurred that she should be bled, this being the only remedy which could save her. As one of the physicians would later report to her father-in-law Ercole I:

Today at the twentieth hour [i.e. around two in the afternoon] we bled Madonna [Lucrezia] on the right foot. It was exceedingly difficult to accomplish it, and we could not have done it but for the Duke of Romagna, who held her foot. Her Majesty spent two hours with the Duke, who made her laugh and cheered her greatly.

The following evening she suffered a further relapse and a priest was called so that she might be given the last rites. Unexpectedly, this led her to rally. Despite the situation, her brother Cesare decided that he could no longer afford to linger in Ferrara and rode off into the night. He would never again set eyes on his sister; though she, for her part, would in time do her utmost to assist Cesare, and even on occasion protect his life.

Cesare Borgia's apparently callous flight from Ferrara was in fact no such thing. Despite his success at the French court, Borgia knew that he, too, was now fighting for his life. Rumours that several of his senior

commanders were continuing to plot against him continued to circulate.
Borgia decided to set up his court in Imola, and began implementing a
comprehensive plan for the governance of his new dukedom. In many of
the larger towns he appointed talented local administrators who had not
been tainted by corruption or links to their previous tyrants. For the most
part, these figures were only too pleased to take part in the new administration, and willingly swore their allegiance to the new duke. Where
insufficient talent or expertise was available, educated young priests were
recruited from the local monasteries, mainly to occupy clerical posts.
Although Borgia maintained garrisons at the major towns and cities,
these initially met with little opposition from the citizenry. The people of
the Romagna appeared hardly concerned with the treacherous methods
Borgia had used to gain his territory, they were simply pleased that the
days of tyranny and lawlessness seemed to be over.

Meanwhile, Leonardo da Vinci was despatched on a tour of the local
fortresses, sketching their fortifications and suggesting improvements.
As already mentioned, his duties were not confined to military matters.
Judging from the sketches of the region which appear in Leonardo's
notebooks, his plans for the improvement of the region's infrastructure
were ambitious indeed. During his previous stay in Milan, working for
the now deposed Sforzas, he had undertaken a number of projects for the
utilization of canals throughout the region. Now, it appears, he planned
similar water-driven irrigation and transport projects for the Romagna.
The ten-mile-long canal from Cesena to the sea at Cesenatico was but one
of many similar projects he had in mind. However, apart from the hints
and sketches extant in Leonardo's remaining notebooks no comprehensive
description of these schemes has come down to us. It is known that Borgia
drew up a list of projects and undertakings, but this has been lost.

Even so, the importance that Borgia attached to Leonardo's role can
be seen in the wording of the 'pass' which he personally issued to his
resident master of all trades. This specifically states:

All will allow [the bearer of this signed document] free passage . . .
will welcome him in a friendly fashion and allow him to inspect,

measure and examine anything he wishes . . . You will provide him with any men he requires and give him any help, assistance and favours he asks. It is our wish that for any work to be carried out within our states, beforehand each engineer be required to consult with him and conform to his judgement.

This virtual carte blanche ends with the chilling words: 'Let no man presume to act otherwise, unless he wishes to incur our wrath.'

In a surprise move, on 14 August 1502 Borgia dismissed his tough and trusted Spanish commander Ramiro de Lorqua, whom he had previously left to administer the Romagna during his absence. Lorqua was downgraded from being governor of the Romagna territories, and instead appointed military governor of Rimini. This was a significant step. Lorqua was a stout, fifty-year-old Spaniard renowned for his arrogance and cruelty. Borgia had appointed him because he knew that under Lorqua there would be no question of any uprising amongst the turbulent people of the Romagna against their new rule. But things had changed. From now on, Borgia had no desire for the Romagna to be regarded as a conquered territory. By this stage he felt that he could trust his new subjects and wished them to regard themselves as citizens of an independent, self-administered state – though with himself as ultimate ruler. In place of the heavy-handed Lorqua, Borgia appointed the renowned humanist scholar Antonio di Monte Sansovino as governor. This was a popular choice throughout the region. Sansovino had been born nearby in eastern Tuscany, and was described by Machiavelli as 'a most learned man of highest repute'. Sansovino, now named as 'President of the Romagna', was tasked with implementing a new justice system for the entire region, as well as selecting suitable magistrates to administer this new system. Guicciardini, in his contemporary history of Italy, would go so far as to record that Borgia 'had placed in the government of those peoples, men who had governed them with so great justice and integrity, that he was greatly loved by them'.

As we shall see, consequent evidence will tend to confirm this view. The local people had resented being governed by Borgia's Spanish commanders, a bunch of uncouth hardmen who knew little of justice. For such military men, rule and civil order equated with the harsh realities of how to retain the loyalty of their own unruly soldiery, i.e. the likes of those who had shat in the wine barrels at Perugia. Yet despite Borgia's efforts, the ever-perceptive Machiavelli noted how even Borgia tended to turn a blind eye to the unruly and lawless behaviour of the Spanish and French garrisons stationed at the main centres of population. Borgia relied upon these troops to defend his new Romagna dukedom. There still remained the threat from Borgia's Italian commanders, who were strongly rumoured to be planning a coup against him. For the most part, the latter remained at home in their nearby territories – Vitellozzo at Città di Castello, Bentivoglio at Bologna, the Orsini brothers in their castles outside Rome, and so forth. All were ostensibly waiting on Borgia's orders.

Cesare Borgia now received an urgent secret message from Alexander VI. The Pope's intention was to discuss further strategy with his wayward son. The two of them arranged to hold a clandestine meeting at Camerino. It was easy enough for Cesare Borgia to leave Imola, giving as an excuse his wish to make a round of inspection of his new domains. Meanwhile, Alexander VI slipped away from Rome on the pretext that he needed to take some rest at one of the papal estates in the countryside. The recently conquered city of Camerino provided an ideal meeting place. If it somehow got out that they were meeting here, they had a good excuse. It had been decided that Giovanni Borgia, the four-year-old *Infans Romanus*, should be appointed as Lord of Camerino – the initial step in bringing him up to be Cesare Borgia's heir to the dukedom of the Romagna.

In early September Alexander VI and Cesare Borgia held a series of covert consultations at Camerino. Sequestered alone in a private room at the castle, their conversation was conducted exclusively in Catalan, so that not even an eavesdropper could understand the gist of what they were saying. First of all it was necessary for the Pope and his son to patch up the differences that had emerged between them during the pursuance of their supposedly common policy. All his life, Alexander VI had believed in the pursuance of patiently executed, covert schemes: this was how he had managed to remain vice-chancellor to no less than five popes through thirty-five years. This was how he had learned to understand and manipulate the intricate workings of papal power. The Pope was now growing visibly older and his dissipations had left him tired. Now was not the time to change the slow but steady habits of a lifetime: years of patience and effort, murder and marriages, to establish his ultimate power base in Rome. Only now were his schemes finally approaching fruition. Only now was the full enormity of his ambitions becoming clear. Alexander VI was aware that he would soon die, and he intended nothing less than to pass on the papacy to his son.

As Captain-General of the Papal Forces (by this time considerably reinforced with Spanish soldiers and French backing) Cesare Borgia ruled over much of the Papal Territories of the Romagna and the Marches. When Alexander VI died, his son would be in an unassailable position to take charge of Rome. He could then decide that owing to the seriousness of the unresolved position in Naples, it would not be possible to hold a conclave immediately. In the ensuing power vacuum, he would be obliged to take on the powers of the Pope on a 'temporary' basis. Having thus established himself, it would be all but impossible to dislodge him. He would receive the backing of the French king for supporting Louis XII's claim to Naples. The papacy would then become a Borgia inheritance.*

Alexander VI had spent years piecing together his strategy for a Borgia inheritance. Though in his early years as pope this had all but fallen apart, owing to the blundering invasion of Charles VIII. But now the French were his allies, and with sufficient guile this alliance could be manipulated to become an equal partnership. Alexander VI needed to stress this with the utmost urgency to his son. Cesare Borgia's tendency

---

* As indicated in the prologue to this work, the next steps would be the unification of Italy, followed by the establishment of a new Roman Empire. The politics of realizing such a dream would have been long, complex and fraught with difficulties. However, as Machiavelli makes plain many times in *The Prince*, the longing for a united Italy and the re-establishment of a great Roman Empire was a growing dream during this period. Indeed, it was arguably the main idea behind Machiavelli's notorious masterpiece.

to precipitate action – such as placing himself at the mercy of Louis XII – was liable to be the undoing of Alexander VI's patiently developed strategy, which would only succeed if it was advanced step by step. Any rash move was liable to be the undoing of Alexander VI's life's work.

In order to reinforce this point, Alexander VI decided to give his son a lesson in statecraft. For Cesare Borgia to defeat his enemies he needed to outwit them. Only cunning would enable him to overcome his untrustworthy Italian commanders. Alexander VI informed his son that when he returned to Rome he intended to send a despatch to Paolo and Giulio Orsini, ordering them as commanders in the Papal Army to report to their Captain-General. They were to join Borgia on a campaign to take Bologna. This would seek out their loyalties. Despite their treacherous machinations, the Orsini brothers remained unaware of precisely how much Cesare Borgia knew about or suspected their lack of loyalty. Bologna was the territory of Bentivoglio, one of the conspirators, and their reaction to the Pope's orders would bring matters out into the open.

Cesare Borgia attempted in vain to dissuade Alexander VI from taking this provocative action. For once, his strategy was ahead of his father's: Borgia was by now a highly skilled military commander. Unbeknown to his father, Cesare's apparent hesitation in taking Bologna had been for a good reason. Even if the Orsini brothers, along with Vitellozzo and Baglioni, had all joined him on the march to Bologna, Borgia knew that this would leave the southern Romagna exposed to an attack by forces that Vitellozzo and the others would leave behind to guard their territories and their castles, which remained exposed along the Florentine border.

Despite the Pope's planned action, Cesare Borgia decided to return to Imola and then wait to see what transpired. The longer he did nothing, the sooner the French troops promised to him by Louis XII would arrive to strengthen his own limited forces. At present he had just 5,000 men scattered in garrisons guarding the cities throughout the Romagna. Louis XII had promised him 3,500 mixed infantry and cavalry. Although these would be tough French troops, he knew they would be no match for the combined forces of the Orsini brothers, Vitellozzo, Baglioni and the others. In Borgia's estimation these commanders could muster at least 9,000 foot soldiers and 1,000 cavalry.

Despite Cesare Borgia's decision to sit things out, it was Alexander VI's despatch to the Orsini brothers from Rome that set things in motion. In a way, it was the combination of apparently contradictory strategies adopted by the Pope and his son which would bring things to a head. Prompted by the urgency of their situation, the Orsini brothers turned to the senior member of their family for advice. This was Cardinal Giambattista Orsini. Earlier, when he had been a close friend of Alexander VI, their dinner parties together had become notorious, on occasion featuring scenes reminiscent of Ancient Rome. However, Cardinal Orsini was more than just another louche, aristocratic senior member of the Church. He was in fact a man of considerable, if devious, intellectual capacity, who was characterized by Machiavelli as 'a man of a thousand tricks'. In response to Alexander VI's summons to the Orsini brothers, Cardinal Giambattista Orsini decided to call a clandestine meeting of all the conspirators at the Orsini stronghold of La Magione. This was a fortress on the eastern shore of Lake Trasimeno, some 100 miles north of Rome and within easy distance of the territory belonging to most of the conspirators. Those who attended were an unsavoury bunch of petty tyrants and condottieri. Paolo Orsini, the more prominent of the two brothers, was in fact illegitimate and known to be 'vain, weak, credulous and mentally unstable'. The Orsini brothers' close friend Vitellozzo arrived on a stretcher, suffering from such a painful bout of syphilis that he could do little but groan. Oliverotto, Lord of Fermo and a typical small-city tyrant, was notorious for his 'infinite treacheries and cruelties'. He had gained his title by inviting all his relatives to a banquet and slaughtering them, including the kindly old uncle who had adopted him after his parents had died. Baglioni, who ruled the nearby city of Perugia, was if anything even worse, being described by Machiavelli as 'a man of vicious heart . . . and great cowardice [notorious throughout Italy] for having committed incest with his sister, and killing his cousins and nephews in order to become ruler of Perugia'. Also attending this meeting was Ermes, son of Bentivoglio of Bologna, now married to an Orsini; as well as Guidobaldo, the ousted young Duke of Urbino.

During the course of the conspirators' discussions, a leader emerged in the form of the fifty-year-old Pandolfo Petrucci, the treacherous and vicious ruler of Siena, who had married into the influential Borghese family and would later assassinate his father-in-law in order to retain power. Petrucci had latterly come to realize the vulnerability of his state, now that Florence was under the protection of Louis XII, and Borgia's Romagna was expanding to the east of his territory. While the other conspirators presided over small city states, Petrucci ruled a republic whose territory was almost comparable to that of its northern neighbour Florence. It was he who suggested to the conspirators that they should make secret approaches to both Venice and Florence, the two major states who had good reason to be suspicious of Borgia's expansive policies in the Romagna. At the same time, Baglioni warned that his fellow conspirators must present a united front, for if not they 'would be devoured one by one by the dragon'. All present at La Magione solemnly swore to trust one another, despite previous family differences.

For once, it looked as if the Borgias were faced with a treacherous alliance capable of putting an end to all their territorial ambitions in central Italy. Inevitably, both Cesare Borgia and the Pope separately had their informants at La Magione. Just as they had both suspected, it soon became clear that the treacherous conspirators barely trusted one another and soon began splitting into factions, hatching their own plots against each other. Cesare Borgia seized on this opportunity and immediately sent a secret message to the man he considered to be the weakest character amongst the plotters: the unstable Paolo Orsini. Borgia offered Paolo Orsini generous terms: no loss of his properties, which would remain under the protection of the Pope, if he returned to fight at Borgia's side. Inevitably, word of Borgia's offer to Paolo Orsini soon spread amongst the other conspirators. Some even began to conclude that the best chance of retaining their territories, and their lives, lay in returning to Borgia and accepting the Pope's protection. Baglioni of Perugia remonstrated against these appeasers, telling them that they could never trust the Borgias.

Widely thought to be a portrait of Lucrezia Borgia at her most glamorous.

LEFT: The only verified portrait of Lucrezia Borgia, which appears on a mural in the Borgia Apartments.

A highly flattering portrait of the ugly and misshapen French King Charles VIII, who would invade Italy shortly after Alexander VI became pope.

King Louis XII of France, who succeeded after the death of Charles VIII, and whose backing of Cesare Borgia would prove decisive.

RIGHT: The spirited Sancia of Aragon, the illegitimate grand-daughter of King Ferrante I of Naples, who would be married to the unfortunate Jofrè Borgia.

BELOW: Cardinal Georges d'Amboise, who would become a powerful figure in the French court of King Louis XII.

le Cardinal damboise
archeuesq. de Rouen

The formidable Caterina Sforza, ruler of Imola, who would attempt to defy Cesare Borgia.

The fabulously wealthy Cardinal Guillaume d'Estouteville, who would become a friend of Carinal Rodrigo Borgia.

Guidobaldo da Montefeltro, who would succeed his father Federigo as Duke of Urbino with disastrous consequences.

One of the magnificent halls in the Borgia Apartments, with its distinctive Spanish floor tiling.

Niccolò Machiavelli, who would act as Florentine envoy to the court of Cesare Borgia during his third Romagna campaign.

RIGHT: The fundamentalist friar Girolamo Savonarola, who took over Florence and defied Alexander VI.

BELOW: The fortress at Nepi, one of the Borgia strongholds outside Rome.

Alfonso d'Este, the heir to the dukedom of Ferrara, who became Lucrezia Borgia's third and final husband.

Back in Rome, Alexander VI had begun to suspect that the conspirators held the upper hand, sensing that all his long-term plans for a Borgia heritage might yet come to nothing. News now reached the Holy City that on 7 October there had been a spontaneous uprising at San Leo, some twenty miles north of Urbino. The strategic hilltop town and fortress had declared itself independent of Borgia rule. This news threw Alexander VI into a paroxysm of anger, and the Venetian ambassador Giustinian described him as 'raging like a bear' and cursing the treachery of the Orsini family, whom he suspected had been behind this revolt.

Meanwhile, Cesare Borgia quietly ordered some of his Spanish commanders to assemble their troops and march to join him at Imola. Then in the second week of October news reached Borgia that Guidobaldo da Montefeltro, aided by Vitellozzo and Orisini, was marching on Urbino. Two of Borgia's most trusted hardmen – Ugo de Moncada and the notorious strangler Miguel da Corella – were commanding the city's garrison, but Borgia ordered them and their troops to make a tactical withdrawal. Consequently Duke Guidobaldo da Montefeltro entered the city unopposed, where he was received 'with the love all the people had for the said duke, who was their ancient and rightful lord'. Cesare Borgia had decided against having his troops drawn into conflict where they were unwelcome. He felt sure that, given time, he would be able to turn the population of Urbino against the weak and indecisive Guidobaldo, who had previously abandoned them at the first sign of trouble. Borgia's intention remained to make the whole of the Romagna into a united dukedom of loyal subjects.

Yet when news that Urbino had thrown off the Borgia yoke began spreading through the countryside, it encouraged the citizens of Fossombrone, just ten miles to the east, to rise up of their own accord. This was a provocation which Moncada and Corella, whose troops happened to be passing nearby, felt unable to ignore. Expressly contravening Borgia's orders, Moncada and Corella marched on Fossombrone, where the citizens had taken refuge in their local fortress. Moncada soon discovered a secret tunnel beneath the outer walls, and during the ensuing battle the citizens of Fossombrone – mainly peasants wielding sticks and farming implements – were put to the sword. Cesare Borgia was furious, and ordered Moncada and Corella to march post-haste to join him at Imola. In Urbino, Vitellozzo soon received word of this. Emboldened by his recent 'victory', he marched across country and succeeded in ambushing Moncada and Corella outside the village of Calmazzo a few miles south-east of Urbino. Vitellozzo routed the heavily outnumbered Spanish troops: Moncada was taken prisoner, and Corella just managed to escape with his life, heading with the few remaining Spanish troops to take refuge in Fano on the coast.

By this time, Bentivoglio of Bologna, together with his son Ermes, had marched south-east down the Via Emelia with 2,200 troops. They soon overran Castel San Pietro, just seven miles up the road from Borgia's headquarters in Imola. Borgia still remained in communication with Lorqua, commander of Rimini, over two days' forced march away, but he realized that to all intents and purposes he was under siege. His situation was rapidly deteriorating. The conspirators were aware that the Venetians were studying the unfolding events closely. There was no doubt that Venice wished to see an end to Borgia's territorial ambitions. The only thing holding them back was the risk of coming into conflict with Louis XII. In an attempt to bring about a final resolution, the conspirators again sent word to Florence, pleading with Gonfaloniere Soderini to join them. This was their chance, once and for all, to put an end to the scourge of Cesare Borgia. Alexander VI could only look on in horror from Rome. The entire edifice of all his ambitions appeared on the brink of collapse. It looked as if the days of his son Cesare were numbered: just one move by his enemies and all was lost.

CHAPTER 16

CESARE SURVIVES

MACHIAVELLI WAS THE FLORENTINE envoy with Borgia's court in Imola during this period. As such, he was in close contact with Borgia and able to study him closely. Machiavelli's conclusions were far from being as pessimistic as the circumstances seemed to warrant. Shrewdly, he took account of what he considered to be the two most salient facts: the character of Borgia himself and the implications of the wider political picture. On 23 October he wrote to Soderini in Florence:

> The territory of this lord [Cesare Borgia] has been governed largely by his good fortune; the main factor here being the general opinion that the King of France will support him with troops and the Pope will send the money to pay for them. And another factor is the delay of his enemies in launching a final attack on him. In my opinion it is far too late now to do him any harm, because he has sent soldiers to protect all his important cities and made sure that they are fully provisioned to withstand a siege.

Machiavelli may have overestimated Borgia's control of his defences, but he had certainly not overestimated the man. Admittedly, the French forces of Louis XII remained a week's march away in Milan, but there were still opportunities at hand. It was now that Borgia reaped the rewards of his policy towards the citizens of his new dukedom. As already mentioned, the general lawlessness and consequent uncultivated countryside that had prevailed in the Romagna for centuries meant that few men could support themselves and their families by farming the land. Hence a large portion of the male citizenry were used to hiring themselves out as mercenaries. So when Borgia despatched Corella on a recruiting drive, he was quickly able to hire 1,000 infantry, all keen to fight for their new duke. Similarly, Borgia himself managed to raise 800 infantry from the Val da Lamone, just south of Imola: a region that was famous for the calibre of its fighting men. At the same time, he sent urgent despatches to the French at Milan, requesting to hire 500 Gascons (generally reckoned as the finest soldiers in the French army) and some 1,500 men from the famed Swiss infantry.

By now Alexander VI had begun raising funds so that his son could pay for all these measures. The Pope's methods were characteristic. One example will suffice. Fortunately for Alexander VI, the wealthy Bishop of Cortona had recently died. Regardless of the Bishop's will, Alexander VI 'seized all the bishop's goods, even selling the wheat that was found in Cortona; he also sold the diocese to a Florentine for 2,000 ducats'. By such means, the Pope had soon raised 18,000 ducats, which were immediately despatched to Cesare Borgia at Imola. So great was the Pope's relief at the miraculous resolution of his son's predicament that he even promised there would soon be more funds to follow.

Yet the situation in the Romagna was not Alexander VI's only pressing problem at this juncture. The Pope found himself becoming ever more embroiled in the threatening clash between the French and the Spanish over the partition of Naples. With his usual diplomatic deviousness, Alexander VI appealed to Venice for support: 'it would be bad for both of us if Spain took over Naples, but still worse if it fell totally into the hands of the French'. Alexander VI wished to appear as a strong ally of the Venetians, in order to prevent them from interfering with his son's campaigns in the Romagna. His concern regarding the French and the Spanish in Naples was genuine enough: he was determined to ally himself with whoever might emerge as the victor. But which one was it to be? On the other hand, he wished to appear to the Venetians as being more generally concerned for the good of the entire Italian peninsula. Indeed, such is the complexity of his diplomatic machinations at this point that it is difficult to discern precisely what he was doing. He wanted the French to support Cesare Borgia in the Romagna, but was against them in the matter of Naples. Similarly, his natural inclination towards the Spanish in Naples was tempered by his wish to see them return to Spain. At the same time, his mixed feelings towards Venice were evident. The Pope was an impressive tactician, and his policies were such that none could be sure precisely where his preferences lay. All that counted was that the Borgias came out on top. And he was undeniably capable of the subtle machinations necessary to make such an outcome possible. On the other hand, the necessary power to realize this outcome lay in the hands of the ever-unpredictable Cesare Borgia.

Back in Imola, Cesare Borgia continued with his own version of subtle diplomacy towards the conspirators, who still posed a threat to the Romagna. Paolo Orsini had predictably been tempted by Borgia's letter promising protection of the Orsini lands and a reconciliation for his family with the Pope. On 24 October Machiavelli's latest despatch from Imola to his master in Florence reported: 'Paolo Orsini is in Cesena this evening, and is expected here tomorrow morning to speak to the duke [Borgia].' When finally they met, Borgia 'used every device of diplomacy to reassure Paolo Orsini, giving him gifts of money, clothes and horses'.

Orsini was quickly won over; so much so that he agreed to return and deliver a message from Borgia to his fellow conspirators, offering them, too, the prospect of reconciliation. By now Borgia was well aware that the conspirators were not only divided amongst themselves, but also to an extent individually incapacitated or incapable of taking to the field against him. Vitellozzo, for instance, was once again laid low with syphilis; while Guidobaldo da Montefeltro had been stricken with gout in Urbino.

By now the mild weather of October had given way to the rain and mud of November, rendering any concerted military action on either side out of the question. Despite this, French soldiers now began arriving at Imola from Milan, marching down the Via Emelia, which, owing to its Ancient Roman foundations, was less liable than the country roads and passes to descend into an impassable bog of mud. Back in Rome Alexander VI reinforced his son's peacemaking policy by staging a generous reconciliation with his old friend Cardinal Giambattista Orsini. Alexander VI and Cardinal Orsini had similar characters and had long enjoyed banqueting together. They soon reverted to their 'customary diversions', which involved feasts lasting long into the night, where they were entertained by courtesans, for, in the opinion of the Pope, 'without them there was no feast worth having'. Alexander VI may have been seventy-two years old, but he was quite capable of keeping up with his younger boon companion, who was himself well into his fifties. Such entertainments frequently lasted until after dawn. Alexander VI and Cardinal Orsini also came to a private agreement. According to Burchard, Alexander VI 'had told the Cardinal that he would resign the papacy in his favour, on condition that he undertook to protect and defend the Duke [Cesare Borgia]'.

Vitellozzo had been the next of the conspirators to cave in, conveying via Paolo Orsini that he, too, was willing to sign an agreement with Borgia, so that they could resume their alliance. In return, Borgia agreed to resume his payments to his two condottieri, so that they could pay their mercenaries. When Duke Guidobaldo in Urbino heard that his two friends had deserted the cause, he at once took fright and fled the city in fear of his life. Despite his crippling gout, he travelled on a mule, disguised as a monk. But such was his physical and mental condition that he had only travelled seven miles down the road before he suffered a nervous collapse. Fortunately for him, he was taken in by a loyal subject, who sheltered him secretly in his home.

Cesare Borgia was well aware that Guidobaldo da Montefeltro remained a popular figure amongst the citizens of Urbino, and equally conscious that these same citizens no longer trusted him after his treacherous lightning coup against the city the previous June. Consequently on 6 December Borgia sent to Urbino his new ally Paolo Orsini, accompanied by the wise and popular Antonio di Monte Sansovino, the new governor of the Romagna. These two were warily welcomed by the population, who were won over when Orsini read out a proclamation granting pardon to all citizens who had recently defied the authority of the Duke of Romagna. Later Sansovino proclaimed the civil rights of all the people of Urbino. On top of this, any of Borgia's soldiers occupying the city who transgressed against the rights of the citizens were to be reported to the civil authorities, who would punish the offenders with a public execution. These civic proclamations were guaranteed by Cesare Borgia himself.

Cesare Borgia made sure that this news quickly spread throughout his Romagna territories. Gradually, even the most obdurate of Borgia's new citizens were being won over by their new ruler. They were beginning to trust him. An era, unprecedented since Roman times, was coming into being in the Romagna. Further evidence of this can be seen in a work which was painstakingly created by the Duke's chief engineer. During this period, whilst Borgia's court was in Imola, Leonardo da Vinci drew a highly detailed map of the city. This was not only a work of precise cartography, but also a work of art. The map was from the bird's-eye perspective common to all modern maps. This was a novelty during the period. Larger territorial maps from this period may have been commonplace, but smaller-scale maps, especially of such exactitude, were not. Each dwelling, from hovels to mansions to the larger fortress, as well as each street and alleyway within the city walls, were all meticulously detailed. How could he have achieved such a feat? Especially without the aid of a tower or mountain or nearby elevation? It is now known that Leonardo invented his own hodometer, resembling a barrowless wheelbarrow, whose studded vertical wheel clicked off its circuits on a horizontal wheel mounted above it. Together with this, and the aid of focal points to ensure interrelated accuracies of direction, he and his team of assistants completed their bird's-eye picture of the city to an exactitude which even matches the most modern maps of the contemporary city's old quarter.

This was almost certainly the forerunner of a larger scheme which Borgia intended for each of the cities in his Romagna territory. As a project it can be compared to the Domesday Book which William the Conqueror drew up to cover all of England. But where the Domesday Book consisted of lists and inventories, the project begun by Leonardo would have been a more visually oriented representation. Its obvious purpose would have been for taxation, and the mapping of houses and property. However, it also speaks of a much more sophisticated – and perhaps even enlightened – attitude towards civil government. Leonardo was helping Borgia to lay the foundations for the most modern state in Italy. Cesare Borgia may have been an impetuous, even murderous and certainly devious character; but when it came to his new state he was as obsessively protective of it as he was of his own close family.

In an unexpected move, the hiding Guidolbaldo da Montefeltro was now offered asylum by Vitellozzo at his home in Città di Castello. This was unmistakably Borgia's doing, but Guidobaldo decide to accept the offer nonetheless, if only to preserve his life. The price Borgia extracted for this act of clemency was that Guidobaldo da Montefeltro formally renounce his rights to the city and territories of Urbino. Whether or not Guidobaldo did in fact accept this last condition, a proclamation to that effect was now issued by Borgia. This ensured that the citizens of Urbino cooperated wholeheartedly with Sansovino without feeling that they were betraying any allegiance to their former ruler – whom they knew to be a weak character at the best of times. More and more people all over the Romagna were being won over by Borgia's rule, though some, with longer memories, still feared that he might yet revert to his older ways, placing them under the rule of his brutal and detested Spanish commander Ramiro de Lorqua.

By now all but one of the conspirators had come to separate agreements with Borgia. Finally, Bentivoglio of Bologna despatched an ingratiating letter to Borgia. Overjoyed that the northern border of his territory was now completely protected, Borgia replied generously, forgiving Bentivoglio for his 'mistake'. To reinforce their rapprochement, Bentivoglio undertook to supply Borgia during the coming year with 200 men-at-arms and 200 light cavalry. In return, Borgia promised he would supply Bentivoglio with a force half this size if at any time during the next eight years his territory came under threat. In return for this guarantee, Bentivoglio was to pay him a fee of 12,000 ducats a year. In order to cement his alliance with all the other former conspirators, Borgia now suggested that they should meet up, together with their forces, outside the coastal town of Sinigalia at the end of December. Sinigalia was officially an outpost of Urbino territory, which had been given as a fiefdom to the twelve-year-old Francesco della Rovere, whose mother was a sister of Guidobaldo of Urbino. As the della Rovere family remained bitter enemies of the Borgias, and Guidobaldo had 'signed away' his territory, Borgia appeared to relish the prospect of taking this lightly guarded city with his combined forces – which now included the French, his own troops, and would soon include the combined armies of the former conspirators. Alexander VI, who was aware of Cesare's plan to march on Sinigalia, understood that his son would then march his army south, to add Ancona to his territories. Only after this would he join up with the forces of Louis XII for the coming campaign against the Spanish in Naples. The Pope now raised a further 15,000 ducats for Cesare, whose army was by this time costing the vast sum of 2,000 ducats a day to maintain.

Only Machiavelli retained his suspicions about what Borgia had in mind. Earlier, Machiavelli had written a despatch to Soderini in Florence concerning Borgia's attitude towards the conspirators, remarking: 'I fail to understand how such injuries can expect to find forgiveness.' And now Bentivoglio, too, began to have his misgivings, excusing himself from the 'reconciliation' at Sinigalia, choosing instead to remain in Bologna.

As the winter nights drew in, Borgia reverted to his old habits. Machiavelli reported: 'He does not emerge from his chamber until around midnight . . . This lord is very secretive and I do not believe that what he is going to do is known to anybody.' Borgia was seldom seen during daylight hours, and conducted all his business under cover of night. Stories circulated that he had taken once more to wearing a black mask, supposedly to cover the syphilitic 'blooms' which had returned to disfigure his face. Once again, this appears to be part of the legend, at least where the effects of syphilis are concerned. Leonardo da Vinci's sketches of Cesare Borgia, drawn around this time, show no sign of any disfigurement. And even if these were intended as merely loose preliminary sketches for a full-scale portrait – which they may well have been – it is highly unlikely that an artist of Leonardo's visual integrity would not have hinted at such marks. Especially when the three sketches in question cover Borgia's face from three different angles: profile, three-quarter profile and full-face on. However, reports of his erratic conduct were certainly not part of the legend. Borgia's behaviour, seldom predictable at the best of times, now began to exhibit severe mood swings. This aspect of his personality was never far below the surface, but appears now to have become an unmistakable characteristic as the strain of his position continued to mount. Machiavelli's observations seemed more pertinent than ever. No one could even begin to guess what Borgia was up to, or what he might do next. Back in Rome, Alexander VI seems to have been developing his own similar concerns with regard to his son.

Then suddenly, on 10 December, Borgia decided to leave Imola. In the midst of a snowstorm he and his troops began marching south-west down the Via Emelia in the direction of the coast. The general situation at Imola had been deteriorating for some time. As Machiavelli had reported from Imola just days earlier, Borgia's troops had stripped the city bare, 'devouring everything down to the very pebbles'. Meanwhile:

> All the cities in this region of the Romagna are short of victuals and supplies, and when the next expected batch of French soldiers arrives things are liable to get worse, unless this Lord [Borgia] manages to secure supplies from elsewhere. I inform your lordships [i.e. the Florentine Signoria] of this development so that you can take precautions against any cross-border raids into Florentine territory.

Machiavelli was preparing his masters for any eventuality; he knew Borgia only too well.

Two days later, Borgia halted his march and set up camp at Cesena. News of his abrupt exit from Imola, followed by his equally unexpected halt at Cesena, rather than marching on to Sinigalia as planned, soon reached Rome. Alexander VI was driven to despair. Despite the intended secrecy of his son's manoeuvres, he couldn't restrain himself, shouting and raging about his son's behaviour: 'What the devil is he doing? Why is he staying there? We told him to move on at once.' The idea was that he should reach Sinigalia as soon as possible. According to Giustinian's despatch to Venice, the Pope was soon resorting to the most unpapal behaviour, even for Alexander VI, pacing the corridors of the Vatican, screeching in Spanish, repeatedly calling his son: 'Bastard son of a whore!'

On 20 December Cesare Borgia received some devastating news. According to Machiavelli, an informant of his amongst the French officers, Baron de Bierra, confided to him: 'In two days we will be leaving here and will return to the duchy of Milan. Those are the orders we have just received.' Machiavelli's despatch continued: 'This event came completely out of the blue and the entire court is turned upside down . . . No one really knows what is happening and everyone has a different explanation.' Machiavelli understood that Louis XII was summoning his troops, especially his heavy cavalry, in preparation for his march on Naples. But next morning he learned an entirely different story from one of Borgia's officers: 'The Duke no longer has sufficient funds to pay the French.' Yet after asking around, he discovered yet another 'explanation'. Apparently the French commanders were in the habit of following their own orders, and had no respect for Borgia's military expertise. Borgia no longer wanted men he could not rely upon to follow his orders immediately and to the letter, and was sending them home. Within days the entire French contingent of over 3,000 of Borgia's best troops had departed, marching up the Via Emelia for Milan.

When news of the French departure reached Rome, Alexander VI appeared to be genuinely frightened. Giustinian reported back to Venice: 'The suspicions that the Duke can do anything of great moment have ceased.' The Pope and informed opinion in Rome appeared to have given up on Cesare Borgia, while things were now moving so fast that

Machiavelli was often sending more than one despatch a day to his masters in Florence. Even so, Machiavelli's opinion on the spot was no less pessimistic than opinion in Rome: 'It is said that the Duke is due to march south in the direction of Pesaro. On the other hand, he is now down to less than half his forces and two-thirds of his reputation.'

Yet Borgia himself remained as unpredictable as ever. On the very day that the last of his French soldiers departed, he decided it was time to have a ball. Literally. The five leading citizens of Cesena were instructed to mount a grand reception to mark the arrival of their duke in his capital city. The ball duly took place, with Cesare Borgia appearing to be in the best of spirits. A local chronicler recorded how he particularly enjoyed the dancing, with his eye drawn to a young local beauty by the name of Cleofe Marescotti 'with whom he was greatly taken, and it seems that his feelings were returned'. The chronicler does not record the reaction of the beautiful Cleofe's husband, who happened to be one of the hosts.

This particular evening was to prove a classic Borgia occasion. One of the kind which Cesare, his father, and even his sister Lucrezia, seemed to relish. It was of such stuff that the Borgia legend was built. For beneath the glittering occasion of the ball, dark events were taking place – of a wholly unexpected and sensational nature. On leaving Imola, Cesare Borgia had summoned his fearsome and trusted commander Ramiro de Lorqua from Pesaro, and it was the evening of the ball when he arrived. The arrogant, stocky little figure – whose typical pose was to jut out his beard and stick his kid-gloved hands in his belt, before delivering the most terrifying commands – was flabbergasted by his reception. Borgia's oldest and closest compatriot, whose friendship stretched back to the glory days of his time at university in Pisa, was summarily seized, disarmed and flung into the city dungeons. Two days later, on 25 December, Machiavelli reported:

> This morning Lorqua was discovered with his body cut in two
> on the piazza where he still lies and all the people have been able
> to see him. No one is sure of the reason for his death, except it

so pleased the duke, who by doing so demonstrated that he can make and unmake men as he wishes, according to their deserts.

This passage omits some of the macabre details. Lorqua's body was wrapped in his finest brocade cloak, his kid-gloved hands at his sides. His body had been decapitated with his head stuck on a lance beside the blood-spattered axe and wooden execution block. It was also evident that prior to his execution he had undergone days and nights of vicious torture.

Even for Cesare Borgia this would seem to have been an excessive display, and it certainly struck terror into the hearts of the citizens of Cesena, as well as throughout the Romagna as the news rapidly spread. Yet astonishingly, such terror was not Borgia's intention – or, at least, not fully his intention. Machiavelli was undeniably correct in inferring that this was intended as a demonstration of Borgia's power, no matter who was concerned. Yet it was also, bizarrely, intended to mollify his subjects. There would be no more barbarous rule, such as that inflicted by Lorqua. Those days were over – or so he wished to convey.

However, Lorqua's days of gruesome torture – during which Borgia must have been present – appear to have confirmed certain information which had come to Borgia's notice. For some time, Borgia had harboured suspicions that Lorqua had secretly made a pact with Vitellozzo and the other conspirators. They had guaranteed Lorqua that if they took over the Romagna, he would be restored as its efficient military governor. Now Borgia learned even more. Under torture, Lorqua revealed that the conspirators had even gone so far as to hatch a plot to assassinate him. It is possible that Borgia even knew about this assassination plot already.

Yet there was one even more compelling piece of evidence regarding Lorqua that had come to Borgia's attention. Some eleven months earlier, when his sister Lucrezia had travelled from Rome to meet her new husband in Ferrara, Lorqua had been delegated by Borgia to protect her procession during its passage through the Romagna. According to news which had reached Borgia, during this journey an incident had taken place 'affecting the honour of Madonna Lucrezia'. This incident had involved Lorqua. As we have already seen, Cesare was extremely touchy where his sister was concerned, especially with regard to sexual matters – whether these involved legal husbands or less qualified lovers. The lucky ones had managed to flee for their lives. Others had suffered a grisly fate. And it appears that Lorqua was no exception.

Now that Borgia had not only lost his crack French troops and murdered his most able Spanish commander, the question arose as to what course he would follow next. Alexander VI was at a loss and remained particularly agitated. Similarly nonplussed were the former conspirators awaiting their 'reunion' with Borgia at Sinigalia. Did Borgia even have enough troops to thwart any plans they might be harbouring for his assassination? Soderini and the Signoria in Florence were also keen to know of Borgia's intentions, demanding that their envoy inform them precisely what was happening. But even Machiavelli remained at a loss, writing on 26 December how Borgia was:

> A highly secretive man and I am convinced that no one but he alone knows what his next move will be. His chief secretaries have told me that he only reveals something when he orders it to be done. He does not do anything unless he is forced to do it, and only then does he act, never otherwise.

Confirming Machiavelli's assessment, next day Borgia suddenly left Cesena, riding south-east down the Via Emelia. To everyone's surprise he left his meagre forces behind and was only accompanied by his small personal corps of men-at-arms. Some time after he left, his forces followed orders to proceed behind him at a distance, splitting into small groups and fanning out across the countryside. Anyone watching these troop movements would understand that Borgia was trying to make his reduced forces appear a lot larger than they actually were. What they would not have realized was that some way behind these troops, the 800 tough mercenaries from Val da Lamone were beginning to assemble, and the 1,500 crack Swiss mercenaries from Milan were now only a day's march away. Just eight miles south of Cesena, Borgia crossed a small river known as the Rubicone. It seems that this modern Caesar was fully aware of the significance of what he was doing.

Two days later, on 28 December, Borgia reached the coastal town of Pesaro. Here he received a despatch from Oliverotto concerning Sinigalia, whose ruler the twelve-year-old Francesco della Rovere had long since fled. Oliverotto informed Borgia that he had taken the small city, although the castellan of the fortress was holding out, refusing to surrender his keys to anyone but Borgia in person. Oliverotto also informed Borgia that the other former conspirators were waiting to greet him – including the Orsini brothers and Vitellozzo. All except for Baglioni, who, despite their reconciliation, had belatedly decided that he did not trust Borgia and had returned with his troops to Perugia. Was this meeting an attempt to trap Borgia? The following day Borgia sent word to Oliverotto that he would meet him and the others at Sinigalia on 31 December. In preparation for this, all but Oliverotto's troops were to withdraw from the small city to the surrounding countryside, leaving room for Borgia's troops to garrison Sinigalia. It looked to all the world as if Borgia was indeed marching into a well-laid trap.

That evening, Borgia had a meeting with his ever-loyal Spanish commander, Miguel da Corella, 'the strangler' – along with seven of his Spanish, Swiss, Gascon and Italian commanders. Borgia emerged from the meeting in ebullient mood. Even Machiavelli professed himself baffled at what was happening. In the following days, rumours began to spread throughout central Italy. Was Borgia planning to join forces with Oliverotto and his former co-conspirators in order to march on Florence? Or Siena? Or perhaps Perugia? Or even to march into Neapolitan territory and join up with the forces of Louis XII? Or was Borgia unwittingly entering a trap? All manner of rumours began reaching Rome, and it was evident that Alexander VI had lost all control over Cesare – to the point where he feared for his son's life (and perhaps even his own). Finally, on 30 December, Alexander VI underwent a transformation. It was evident that he had received a secret despatch from his son. Overcome with relief at this news – whatever it was – Alexander VI summoned his old friend Cardinal Orsini to join him at a private banquet in the Vatican, to celebrate with another long night of louche entertainment, such as they both enjoyed so much together. Unable to contain himself, the Pope joyfully informed his court: 'We are all awaiting [Borgia's] return for Carnival. No one can celebrate the way he does. He will do a thousand follies and throw away several thousands of ducats.' Carnival was the traditional time of revelry before Lent. Initially a short period, this had now been extended to begin as early as 26 December. It looked as if the Pope was confidently expecting his son to return to Rome at the beginning of the new year.

Meanwhile, on 30 December Cesare Borgia marched his troops further down the coast to Fano, just a short day's march from Sinigalia. He had already sent Miguel da Corella ahead with a message to Vitellozzo and the others that he would be arriving next day. Da Corella had also been ordered to seek out a suitable palazzo for Borgia's residence when he arrived.

CHAPTER 17

BORGIA'S 'RECONCILIATION'

Amidst the misty winter dawn on the last day of 1502, Cesare Borgia and his troops emerged from the small coastal city of Fano and marched down the coast road towards Sinigalia. An observer noted that although Borgia was not riding out into battle, he was wearing chain-mail body armour and a full breastplate, as well as being fully armed. Accompanying him were his personal bodyguards, all fully armed and clad in their colourful red and yellow Borgia livery. As the sun rose, the pikes and polished breastplates of the following Swiss contingent glinted in the early light.

A mile outside Sinigalia, Borgia encountered Vitellozzo and three of the Orsini – Paolo, Francesco and Roberto – who had ridden out to greet him, accompanied by a detachment of cavalry. Unarmed and wrapped in a green cloak against the cold, Vitellozzo rode up to Borgia on his mule and dismounted, cap in hand. He was inevitably apprehensive, but became visibly relieved when Borgia, too, descended his mount and placed his hand on Vitellozzo's outstretched hand, greeting him in the French fashion. They embraced emotionally. Then Borgia moved forward and embraced the three Orsini in similar fashion. As they stood together,

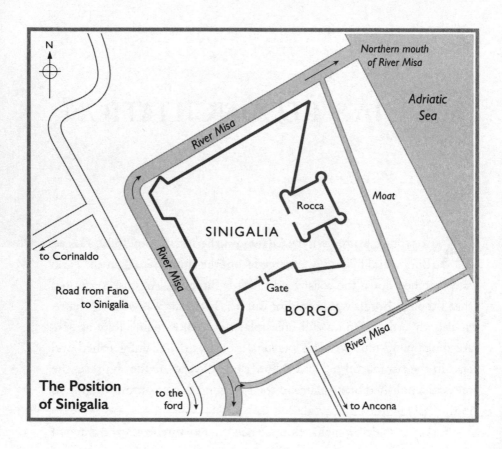

The Position of Sinigalia

Borgia enquired why Oliverotto was not with them. They informed him that Oliverotto had remained behind at the Borgo, the houses outside the city walls, where he was waiting for them with a force of 1,000 infantry and 150 cavalry. Borgia gestured to his henchman Miguel da Corella to go and fetch him. According to Machiavelli, who later spoke to eyewitnesses: 'Borgia winked knowingly at Don Miguel before he set off on his errand.'

Oliverotto soon joined them, and together the six men rode towards Sinigalia. Soon they were talking easily amongst themselves as they had in the old days. The former plotters, and even Borgia himself, all appeared happily relieved at how well things had gone, and within the hour they had reached Sinigalia.

The walled city as well as its Borgo were surrounded by a moat, with a wooden bridge across the moat leading to the one gate in the city walls. Borgia's advanced guard of heavy cavalry clattered across the slats of the bridge, down the street through the Borgo towards the city gate. Executing a skilled, pre-arranged manoeuvre, they separated into two columns, and then wheeled around to face one another – leaving what appeared to be a ceremonial guarded passage towards the open city gate. This effectively sealed off Oliverotto's troops enclosed in the moat-bound Borgo, at the same time cutting them off from Vitellozzo's troops, which were camped in the countryside to the south of the city.

A thousand Swiss and Gascon infantry now marched across the bridge, between the protective lines of cavalry, and through the gate into the walled inner city of Sinigalia itself. Borgia, accompanied by Oliverotto, Vitellozzo and the three Orsini, rode in behind them, accompanied by Oliverotto's armed escort, with Borgia's contingent of liveried men-at-arms bringing up the rear. No sooner had they entered the city gate than it was swung closed behind them. By this stage the former conspirators were becoming increasingly apprehensive at the well-drilled military exercise unfolding around them. Borgia rode ahead down the street, leading them up to the archway before the palazzo which Miguel da Corella had selected for his commander's headquarters. Here the five former conspirators made to take their leave of Borgia, but he would have none of it. Giving them his word that they were quite safe, Borgia bade them dismount and follow him. Now that they were reconciled they needed to sit down together and discuss their future strategy. With some reluctance, all five followed Borgia up a stairway and into the main salon, where Borgia gestured for them to take their seats around a table. According to a contemporary account:

> Having remained a while with them, [Borgia] said that for necessities of nature he must withdraw, but would soon return. Hardly had he left the room than there entered the men deputed for the work, who bound their hands behind their backs and took them prisoner.

Paolo Orsini screamed out for Borgia, forcibly reminding him that he had given them his word. But by this time Borgia was already out in the courtyard. Having mounted his horse, he ordered the officer in charge of Oliverotto's armed escort to withdraw and rejoin their main force outside the city wall in the Borgo. As they followed this order and made their way down a narrow main street of the Borgo, they were immediately confronted and cut down by Borgia's troops, whose columns were still continuing to march across the wooden bridge into the Borgo. By now the rest of Oliverotto's troops in the Borgo found themselves heavily outnumbered and quickly surrendered their arms.

Whilst this was taking place, Borgia himself rode to the fortress (*rocca*) within the city walls, where the castellan hastily presented him with the keys to the fortress gate. The castellan had been watching from the high fortress ramparts as the murderous assault unfolded across in the Borgo. Borgia then interrogated him, telling him to point out from the ramparts whereabouts in the countryside the troops of Vitellozzo and the Orsini were encamped on the hills and further down the coast. Borgia then despatched his heavy cavalry into the countryside to find them. As the troops of Vitellozzo and Orsini were unaware of what had happened, and were mainly encamped in isolated detachments, they were quickly deceived and offered little or no resistance. Borgia's troops then disarmed them.

Meanwhile in the streets and alleyways of the Borgo, things had taken a turn for the worse. Borgia's Spanish and French troops had run amok, slaughtering anyone whom they suspected of being a sympathizer of Oliverotto or the della Rovere family, embarking on an orgy of pillage and rape. By now it was late afternoon. At this stage Machiavelli and Leonardo arrived with Borgia's entourage in the wake of his troops. Each, in his own different way, was deeply traumatized by the slaughter and mayhem they witnessed first-hand, as they were ushered by their accompanying guards towards the gate into the safety of the city. As they entered through the gate, Borgia was riding out, on his way to try and put a stop to the mayhem. He briefly halted his horse, and with an air of triumph shouted across to Machiavelli that he had taken Vitellozzo, Oliverotto and the three Orsini prisoners.

Borgia had already decided on his prisoners' fate. During the early hours of 1 January 1503 Vitellozzo and Oliverotto were despatched in characteristic fashion by Miguel da Corella. His preferred method of strangling was in the so-called 'Spanish style'. This involved a loop of lyre string around the neck, with a lynch pin inserted and then twisted, gradually tightening the string until the victim was throttled. Before their execution, Borgia had managed to extract from his prisoners confessions about their secret alliance with Lorqua, as well as their plan to assassinate him. (Since learning of this from Lorqua, Borgia had worn a chainmetal suit both night and day.) Borgia also learned that they, too, had hatched a plot to take place at Sinigalia, but Borgia's well rehearsed troop movements had outwitted them. In the early hours, Borgia summoned Machiavelli to his presence and informed him of the fate of Vitellozzo and Oliverotto, remarking of the Orsini: 'We are taking them as prisoners to a similar end.'

By 3 January 1503 a secret message from Borgia had reached Alexander VI in Rome, informing him of what had happened at Sinigalia. The Pope's reaction was immediate and typical. That night he sent a joyful message to Cardinal Orsini, with whom he had banqueted just four days previously, though without revealing to his guest on this occasion what he had learned of his son's intentions. Now, the Pope

informed Cardinal Orsini that Cesare Borgia had succeeded in taking
Sinigalia, yet omitting to mention any further details. The following
morning Cardinal Orsini hastened to the Vatican to congratulate his
friend the Pope on his son's great victory. Upon arrival, he was seized
by the guards and marched off to the Castel Sant'Angelo, where he
was cast into a dungeon. Even as this was happening, Alexander VI
ordered the seizure of Cardinal Orsini's palazzo, and the transporta-
tion of all its luxurious contents to the Vatican. The cardinal's mother
and other women of the house were evicted and left to wander the
streets of Rome with nothing but the clothes they stood up in. Other
Roman relatives, or friends, of the conspirators suffered a similar fate.
Giustinian's despatch to Venice on 6 January described how 'the Pope
has become obsessed with seizing all the gold he can find'. He also
added ominously that the Pope had promised him: 'What has happened
so far is nothing compared with what is planned for the future.'

It is worth bearing in mind this last remark. Alexander VI's aston-
ishing ambitions for his son and the future of the papacy had only just
begun. During the coming days and weeks, all Italy would be abuzz over
Cesare Borgia's deeds at Sinigalia. Astonishingly, widespread reaction
was not one of revulsion. Machiavelli, who had himself been so terrified
by what he had witnessed, would write with admiration:

> The Duke's actions are accompanied by a unique good fortune, as
> well as a superhuman daring and confidence that he can achieve
> whatever he wants.*

If Italy was to be great again, this was precisely how its leader should
behave. In a similar vein to Machiavelli, Louis XII himself – with more
perception than he perhaps realized – declared Borgia's feat to be 'an act

---

* Here we can see in embryo Machiavelli's idea concerning 'Virtù e Fortuna',
which he would develop to such notorious effect in *The Prince*. Despite his years
of diplomatic experience, this was the first time he had witnessed first-hand the
workings of raw power in action – and he would never forget it, or its place in
realpolitik.

worthy of a Roman hero'. Even the contemporary historian Paolo Giovio, usually so critical of the Borgias, could not help but admit that Cesare Borgia's feat at Sinigalia was 'a most beautiful deception'. Here perhaps was the strong leader for which all Italy had so long been waiting. Did Alexander VI and Cesare Borgia between them have sufficient power and skill to unite Italy and create a new Roman Empire? There were many who now thought so.

No sooner had Borgia completed his triumph at Sinigalia than he moved on. Leaving the city as early as 1 January 1503 he marched post-haste with his combined troops and cavalry inland for the Via Flaminia, heading south-west into the Apennines. In tow, he brought the three captured Orsini in a caged cart. By now winter had set in with a vengeance and Borgia faced 'the worst possible weather, as unfavourable for war as can be imagined'. But already things were turning his way. The citizens of Fermo, hearing that their detested tyrant Oliverotto had been murdered by Borgia, immediately sent word expressing their wish to become part of Borgia's new Romagna, with its enlightened laws and administration. Next a delegation from Vitelozzo's Città di Castello surrendered their city unconditionally to Borgia.

Such were the appalling conditions that it was 13 January before Cesare Borgia and his troops managed to cover the fifty miles from Sinigalia to Città di Castello. The following day a message finally reached Borgia from Alexander VI in Rome, informing him that Cardinal Giambattista Orsini had been confined in the dungeons of Castel Sant'Angelo.* Whereupon, Borgia ordered Miguel da Corella to dispose of the three caged Orsini 'in the Spanish manner'.

Within days news reached Borgia that Baglioni had fled from nearby Perugia. Hard on the heels of this came a message from the citizens of Perugia, surrendering the keys of the city to Borgia, welcoming him as their new ruler and informing him that Baglioni had taken refuge with Pandolfo Petrucci in Siena. Borgia well knew that Petrucci had been the driving force behind the meeting of the conspirators at La Magione, and

---

* By now Cardinal Orsini was seriously ill, and within a matter of weeks he would be dead, slowly poisoned on orders from Alexander VI.

was determined to track him down – even if this meant marching into Siena. However, he was mindful of the fact that Siena, like its northern neighbour Florence, remained very much under the protection of Louis XII. Thus he sent ahead a message to Louis XII in Milan, assuring the French king that he had no designs on these territories under his protection. His sole concern was to capture all those who had plotted against him.

Louis XII knew his young protégé Cesare Borgia only too well, and refused to believe his assurances. If Borgia marched into Siena, and even Florence, in the middle of winter, it was unlikely that he would retreat until the winter was over, or even then. By which time Louis XII knew that it would be all but impossible to dislodge him – especially when so many of his own French troops were down in Naples contesting the territory with the Spanish. Accordingly, Louis XII despatched the sternest possible message to Alexander VI, ordering him to restrain his son. As Pope he surely had the authority to order the Captain-General of the Papal forces to desist from such action, which went against all their shared interests. Indeed, Alexander VI was more than aware of the consequences of Cesare's latest actions. Worst of all, by marching towards Siena, Borgia was leaving Rome, and even the Pope himself, dangerously exposed to the remnant forces of the Orsini family, who still occupied their strongholds around La Magione to the north of Rome.

Once again, Alexander VI was beside himself with fury. This time he summoned all the ambassadors in Rome to an audience, where he made it plain to them:

We have done everything in our power to make [Borgia] give up the enterprise of Siena . . . nonetheless, he is absolutely resolved to disregard us . . . we promise you that since we have sat in this chair [the papal throne] we have never heard of anything which causes us greater displeasure. And nonetheless we must have patience: he wills it thus, and it seems to him that he can do to us with impunity that which he is doing.

Judging from Alexander VI's last, somewhat cryptic comments, there is a suspicion that he retained a covert sympathy for his son's actions. He would not be disloyal to Cesare. On the other hand, Alexander VI found himself seriously exposed. The Orsini family had 'succeeded in making an alliance with several of the expelled Colonna and Savelli lords, who, although their hereditary enemies, understood that the threatened overthrow of the Orsini was to confirm their own ruin'.

Heedless of Alexander VI's wishes, Cesare Borgia launched into Sienese territory, allowing his Spanish troops a free hand to lay waste anything in their path. According to Burchard, writing in Rome on 23 January:

> By the time they reached San Quirico* all they found were two old men and nine aged women. The Duke's soldiers hung these unfortunates by their arms and lit a fire beneath their feet to make them reveal where the local treasures had been hidden.

The victims knew nothing and 'died hideously'; then the soldiers 'smashed everything . . . and burned it to the ground'. But Borgia was not in fact intent upon taking Siena, only on taking Petrucci himself. Unfortunately for Borgia, Petrucci happened to be a fairly popular ruler. Even so, Borgia issued an ultimatum to the citizens of the city: if within twenty-four hours they had not driven out Petrucci, 'we will proceed to exterminate all the towns, subjects and goods that are yours, and also your city and all its citizens'. However, as Machiavelli had suspected during his initial confrontation with Borgia some six months previously in Urbino, when Borgia appeared at his most fearsome he was often bluffing. Once again, this proved to be the case. Firstly, he dared not provoke Louis XII any further. And secondly, news had now reached him from Rome that the Orsini were preparing to march on his father.

In order to succeed, Borgia's bluff had to convince Petrucci right away. Petrucci immediately replied to Borgia, promising to leave Siena on condition that he was granted safe passage to ride north to the safety of the

---

* A small town some twenty miles south-east of Siena.

northern city state of Lucca, on the other side of Florence. Unexpectedly, Borgia agreed at once. Petrucci fled, but Borgia sent a squadron of cavalry to hunt him down, nonetheless. For his part, Petrucci had never trusted Borgia and chose to make his way to Lucca cross-county, using obscure byways and little-known paths, avoiding all the main thoroughfares.

Borgia's obvious next move was to march south and confront the Orsini. But to his father's horror, Borgia halted short of Orsini territory, taking up quarters with his army in the city of Viterbo, some forty miles north of Rome. By now Alexander VI had become so panicked and exasperated by Cesare's behaviour that he even threatened to excommunicate him. Yet as ever, Cesare's behaviour alternated between impulsiveness and low cunning. This time he knew precisely what he was doing. Borgia opened talks with the Savelli and Colonna families, making it plain to his father (and the Orsini) that he was not willing to waste his time attacking their all but impregnable strongholds at Bracciano and Pitigliano. The reasons he gave Alexander VI were perplexing. Bracciano was the fortress of Giangiordano Orsini, a character of such exasperating unpredictability that even the Orsini themselves had branded him a 'public madman'. What was less well known, to all but Borgia himself, was that Giangiordano had been opposed to the Orsini joining the conspirators at La Magione. However, Borgia's excuse to his father for not attacking Giangiordano was that Louis XII had appointed both of them to the French chivalric Order of St Michael, whose rules decreed that no member should take up arms against a fellow member. Similarly unconvincing (at least to the Pope) was Borgia's reason for not attacking Niccolò Orsini at Pitigliano. Cesare informed his father that Niccolò was a condottiere regularly hired by the Venetians to command their forces, and he had no wish to endanger his new dukedom in the Romagna by antagonizing Venice.

In fact, if Borgia had launched an all-out attack on the Orsini he could well have destroyed them. This would have placed him at risk of irritating both Louis XII and Venice, though he suspected that neither of these powers would have been willing to intervene over such a move. Instead, by negotiating with the Savelli and the Colonna, as well as holding back from attacking the Orsini, Borgia was planning for the future. Alexander VI, who was by now seventy-two, was at last beginning to show his age. As ever, it was Machiavelli who had understood Borgia's strategy. Several months earlier, Machiavelli had written to his masters in Florence: 'When the Pope dies, [Borgia] will still need to have some friends in Rome.' Machiavelli had astutely divined the Borgia family's overweening ambitions: he saw that Borgia was lining himself up to take his father's place. Alexander VI's aim had been nothing less than establishing a hereditary papacy. In which case, Cesare Borgia would be well served if he had made allies of the powerful aristocratic families of Rome. Even so, if he was to achieve this, Borgia knew that he would have to teach the Orsini a lesson. Already the family was split: first he would demonstrate his power, then his magnanimity.

As usual, Cesare Borgia's next move came as a complete surprise – to both Alexander VI and the Orsini family. On 19 February Borgia and his troops swiftly vacated Viterbo, marching thirty miles south to lay siege to the Orsini fortress at Ceri, the stronghold of Giulio Orsini, brother of Cardinal Giambattista Orsini (who now lay at death's door in the dungeons of Castel Sant'Angelo).

Ceri was just twenty miles west of Rome, strategically placed to cut the sole supply line which kept the Holy City alive – namely, the Tiber, which connected Rome to the port of Ostia. Ceri consisted of a thick-walled fortress which lay at the summit of a sheer outcrop of rock and appeared utterly impregnable, both to cannon and to siege. Borgia also knew that Giulio was the one Orsini who would never be persuaded to join him. Thus Cesare Borgia now chose to employ his secret weaponry: the ingenious devices which had been designed for him by Leonardo da Vinci. These included 'mortars capable of firing multiple explosive projectiles, mobile precision artillery and large-scale catapults', as well as a 'huge machine held to be capable of carrying up to 300 men up to the ramparts'.

The assembly of these siege machines proved to be a time-consuming operation. This was initially overseen by Leonardo himself, and would be the last important work he would complete for Cesare Borgia before he was finally permitted to return to his native Florence. (His friend Machiavelli had managed to engineer his own return almost immediately after the events he had witnessed at Sinigalia.) Cesare Borgia was little interested in the details of assembling these 'machines' and decided to return to nearby Rome for the last of the Carnival season. Despite Alexander VI's joy at this prospect just two months previously, the very opposite was the case now. The Pope was outraged that his son had decided to abandon his campaign just to come and enjoy himself in Rome. Relations between Alexander VI and Borgia deteriorated rapidly. At one point Giustinian even sent a despatch to Venice describing how the seventy-two-year-old Pope and his twenty-seven-year-old son had ended up brawling together. Despite this, and doubtless other contretemps, Alexander VI and Cesare Borgia did in fact remain close. They were both pursuing the same aim: the establishment of a Borgia dynasty. In order to achieve this, both these headstrong characters knew that they each needed the other. Indeed, it may well have been this fact, as much as anything, which contributed to the turbulence of their indissoluble family relationship.

For two weeks Cesare Borgia lived it up in Rome, once again reverting to his preferred nocturnal lifestyle. Giustinian comments that during this time he was never seen without a mask. Whether this was due to an efflorescence of his syphilitic symptoms, or because he wished not to be identified – for his own safety, as much as anything else – is not clear.

By March Cesare Borgia was back directing operations at the siege of Ceri. Maintaining Borgia's army, and the siege, was proving as expensive as ever, and Alexander VI was once again hard-pressed to raise funds for the upkeep of his son's continuing campaign. In mid-March Alexander VI issued a bull creating no less than eighty new positions in the Curia. The purchase of these positions, by those who wished to hold them, brought in over 60,000 ducats. But even this was not enough. Early in April the Venetian Cardinal Michiel was suddenly taken ill at his palazzo in Rome. Two days later he was dead. Inevitably, poisoning was suspected, and Alexander VI's consequent actions did little to allay such suspicions. Before dawn, on the very night that Cardinal Michiel had died, Alexander VI ordered the cardinal's palazzo to be stripped of all its valuables, luxury fittings, art and so forth. Giustinian records how several days later he arrived at the Vatican to find Alexander VI personally engaged in counting out the dead cardinal's fortune, exclaiming in exasperation: 'Look at it, there are only 23,382 ducats. Yet word has spread around that I've got hold of 80,000 to 100,000 ducats.'

To make up for this unexpected lack, Alexander VI resorted to his old tactic of appointing new cardinals. Candidates for these posts had to be Spanish, or of proven loyalty to the Borgia cause, as well as being possessed of sufficient financial resources and ostensible spiritual rectitude. By now, such candidates were becoming increasingly scarce. In the end Alexander VI appointed nine new cardinals, each paying up to 20,000 ducats for the privilege of such exalted office. In this way he managed to raise around 130,000 ducats. In the words of Giustinian: 'thus demonstrating to the world that His Holiness was capable of expanding the papal income at will'.

By early April Giulio Orsini had agreed to surrender Ceri on condition he was given free passage to the Orsini fortress at Pitigliano. Borgia agreed; and to the surprise of many, Giulio was permitted to reach safety. This was an astute move on Borgia's part. When the Orsini at the fortresses of Bracciano and Pitigliano saw Borgia's leniency, they too agreed to surrender. All this avoided any further drain on the Pope's resources. At the same time, the all-powerful Louis XII ordered that the Borgia family and the Orsini family should sign a truce.

Later that same month the situation in Italy would undergo a dramatic and unexpected transformation. News arrived from Naples that on 28 April the army of Louis XII had unexpected been defeated by the Spanish general Gonsalvo de Córdoba at Cerignola, just over 100 miles north-east of Naples. Within three weeks the Spanish had taken the city of Naples itself, and the French forces were withdrawing to the port of Gaeta, in the hope of being transported back to France. Alexander VI now found himself in a quandary. He had always secretly favoured the Spanish cause in Naples, but in order to fulfil his strategy he knew that he needed the support of the winning side. Hence his adherence to the cause of Louis XII. In view of the dramatic turn of events, Alexander

VI decided to switch sides. However, to the Pope's exasperation his son Cesare decided to remain loyal to his friend Louis XII, who still held his wife Charlotte and young daughter Louise in France. Then Cesare, too, reckoned that it might be in his best interests if he joined his father in support of Spain. With Louis XII weakened, his guarantee of protection to Florence and Siena looked in doubt. Here was Cesare Borgia's opportunity to enlarge his dukedom to include the whole of central Italy.

Yet there now followed another twist in the plot, which further complicated Alexander VI's position. News reached Rome that in northern Italy the French were assembling an army to march south and relieve their forces, which were under siege at Gaeta, before launching a campaign to drive the Spanish out of Naples altogether. Alexander VI was once more faced with the prospect of having to rethink his policy towards Naples. However, by now Alexander VI was so deeply committed to the Spanish cause that he was allowing the Spanish to recruit mercenary soldiers in Rome itself. But all those years spent dealing, and double-dealing, with papal affairs during his time as vice-chancellor now came into their own. Only the most practised of diplomats would have undertaken the moves now made by Alexander VI, in consultation with his son Cesare, who himself by this stage required little education in the art of deception.

Alexander VI covertly made contact with the French, promising to instruct Cesare Borgia and his Romagna army to join forces with the French on their march south. Borgia's force would be a considerable boost, as he was now so confident of his popularity in the Romagna that he could afford to withdraw almost all of his garrisons from the newly expanded Papal States. In return for this force, Alexander VI proposed that his son Cesare should be allowed to rule Naples. This was not such an outrageous suggestion as it might appear. After all, the Pope indicated, it was surely better to have this troublesome kingdom ruled by a reliable ally, rather than having the French army constantly overstretched in the attempt to maintain French rule in southern Italy.

As if this triple-dealing was not enough, Alexander VI now showed his true colours by opening undercover negotiations with the Venetians. He suggested to his new 'partner' that if the Spanish were driven out of

Naples, this was surely the time for the Papal Army to join forces with Venice and drive the French from Milan. Then, once again, the Italian peninsula would be rid of foreign interference.

It takes little imagination to see that it would be but a short step from here to a united Italy, with the Pope himself as the presiding figure. And this was precisely what Alexander VI had in mind. Step by step the new Roman Empire would come into being.

During the early summer Cesare Borgia began reinforcing his army in Rome. Such was his popularity in the Romagna that many mercenaries from the region soon flocked to join his colours. By mid-summer Borgia had assembled a force of 600 cavalry, 4,000 battle-hardened foot soldiers and the prospect of more to come. In contrast to Borgia's previous forces, this was very much his own army, all swearing allegiance to the Captain-General of the Papal Forces. Its members were outfitted in the Borgia colours of quartered red and yellow, emblazoned with the name 'César'. This was more than just a vainglorious echo of the imperial Roman past. Backed by Alexander VI's extensive papal funds, it could afford to recruit the finest fighting men available in neighbouring European countries: Swiss mercenaries, Spanish soldiers, and even the much-feared Stradiots, Balkan mercenaries who had withstood the Ottomans.

There followed yet another snag. It soon became clear that the French army being assembled in Milan would take some time to arrive. By which stage, the Spanish may well have overrun Gaeta. Having placed himself in a position where he now faced a number of decisive diplomatic options, Alexander VI found it impossible to withdraw from the hot and increasingly hazardous summer climate of Rome. The summer of 1503 would prove even more hot and calamitous than usual in the Holy City. The tolling midday church bells would ring out over the silent, deserted streets of the heat-stunned city. Yet just a few hours later, as the shadows lengthened and the comparative coolness of dusk began, the city would be invaded by malaria-bearing mosquitoes from the Pontine Marshes to the south, as well as those which had colonized the stagnant pools in the all but dry riverbed of the Tiber.

The death toll in the fetid slums of the city always rose during the long stifling summer months, but this year it became exceptionally high. So much so that rumours were soon spreading of an outbreak of bubonic plague in the city. Alexander VI did his best to isolate Trastevere and the Vatican, but still the deaths continued to spread, with all classes being affected. On 1 August news reached Alexander VI that his nephew Cardinal Juan Borgia-Lanjol, one of the first 'nephew-cardinals' he had appointed in the early months of his reign as pope, had died. Rumours that he had been poisoned by enemies of the Borgia soon began to spread, but Alexander VI discounted them. Cardinal Borgia-Lanjol had been notorious for his gluttony, and by time of his demise at fifty-seven years old, he had become massively overweight. Alexander VI, conscious of his own somewhat expanded figure, could not help but remark as he stood at the window in the Vatican, watching his nephew's coffin pass: 'This month is a bad one for fat people.' Now more than ever, the superstitious Alexander VI was conscious of the fact that no less than four of his recent predecessors on the papal throne had died in Rome during the height of summer. As the Pope continued to watch his nephew's funeral procession pass across the piazza below, an owl suddenly flew in through the open window and fell dead at his feet. Whereupon Alexander VI's face paled and he cried out: 'This is an evil, evil omen!' Then he ran from the room.

Yet even during this perilous time of rapidly shifting political fortunes Alexander VI did receive one piece of news which he celebrated with unalloyed joy. Some time around midsummer he learned that he had fathered yet another illegitimate son, by a Roman woman whose identity remains unknown. The infant was christened Rodrigo, after his illustrious father. Meanwhile, his oldest surviving son Cesare continued to behave in his own inimitable fashion. Seemingly unconcerned by the growing diplomatic and other troubles facing his father, Cesare set out at first light each morning, riding into the cool misty countryside to go boar-hunting. Only after several hours hard riding would he return before the heat of the day set in, whereupon he would take to his bed in his apartment.

During the first week of August, Alexander VI and Cesare Borgia were invited by the Venetian Cardinal Adriano da Corneto to a party to celebrate his recent elevation to the rank of cardinal. The party took place during the cooler hours of the late afternoon and was held at the cardinal's sumptuous villa, set amidst hillside vineyards on the northern outskirts of Rome. It was attended by a number of senior clergy. Six days later the normally robust Alexander VI was stricken down by a mysterious illness and spent all that evening vomiting. The following day Cesare Borgia, who was planning to join his troops assembling at Perugia, was also laid low with a similar violent illness. Despite intense precautions, including sealing off the Vatican, news soon leaked out that Alexander VI and Cesare Borgia had both been poisoned.

According to these rumours, the Pope and his son had attended Cardinal da Corneto's party with the intention of poisoning their wealthy host and confiscating his possessions. Such funds were apparently needed to maintain Cesare Borgia's forces, and the poisoning would have echoed the recent poisoning of Cardinal Michiel for similar purposes. A servant had been bribed to administer the poison, which was known as 'cantarella'. This was the Borgia's own favoured poison and came in the form of a white powder with a pleasant, sugary taste. The precise ingredients of this 'eternity powder' remain unknown, but it was almost certainly an arsenic preparation. According to the contemporary historian Paolo Giovio, cantarella was a 'time poison' whose efficacy depended upon the strength of the mixture: 'It did not overwhelm the vital forces in the manner of the active venoms by sudden and energetic action but by insensibly penetrating the veins it slowly worked with mortal effect.'

Seemingly Alexander VI and Cesare Borgia had made the fatal error (or possibly been tricked into the mistake) of drinking the wine intended for Cardinal da Corneto. In the opinion of many, the delayed action of the poison on both the Pope and his son confirmed that it was cantarella. As the rumours of what had taken place spread beyond Rome, it soon became clear that Alexander VI and Cesare Borgia were both on their deathbeds.

CHAPTER 18

LUCREZIA IN FERRARA

IMMEDIATELY THE NEWS OF what had taken place in Rome arrived in Ferrara. It was broken to the twenty-three-year-old Lucrezia Borgia by Cardinal Ippolito d'Este, the younger brother of her husband Alfonso. When the poet Pietro Bembo called to offer his condolences, he found Lucrezia inconsolable, prostrated with grief. He wrote to her two days later:

> As soon as I saw you lying there in that darkened room and in that black gown, so tearful and disconsolate, my feelings overwhelmed me and for a long time I stood there unable to utter a word, not knowing even what to say. Instead of offering sympathy, I felt in need of offering sympathy to myself. I left, fumbling and speechless, overcome with emotion at the sight of your misery.

Despite his deep, empathetic emotions, Bembo could not refrain from adding some level-headed advice: 'This is not the first misfortune which you have had to endure at the hands of your cruel and malign destiny . . . You would do well not to allow anyone to assume, as some might be led to infer in present circumstances, that you bewail not so much your loss but what may betide your present fortunes.'

Should her father and her brother die, Lucrezia would be left without support, her position diminished, at the mercy of the enemies of the Borgia family, as well as the enemies she herself had made at Ferrara and amongst the d'Este family. As we have seen, from the outset Lucrezia was resented by her haughty older sister-in-law Isabella d'Este, the Marchioness of Mantua. For Isabella, the sight of the upstart Lucrezia, illegitimate and Spanish to boot, living in the very apartments once occupied by her beloved mother, the deceased Eleanora, Duchess of Ferrara, was difficult enough.* The thought that Lucrezia would one day assume her mother's title was all but unbearable to her. Although in Lucrezia's presence she went out of her way to appear formally courteous, when Isabella returned to Mantua she received long, almost daily letters from her spy at the Ferrara court, describing in meticulous detail Lucrezia's life. We now know that this spy was Bernardo di Prosperi, who worked in the chancellery and was thus ideally placed to recount all the latest court gossip, which he poured into 'letters, running into thousands'.

Lucrezia remained resentful of her high-minded father-in-law Duke Ercole I for curbing what he saw as her extravagant ways, as well as sending back to Rome so many of her Spanish attendants. Though the court records show that Lucrezia still retained a considerable number of attendants with Spanish-sounding names. Despite this, she continued to feel lonely – away from Rome, married to a barely compatible husband, and living under the constant shadow of the revered dead Duchess Eleanora.

Even so, Ferrara had its consolations for Lucrezia. Under Ercole I, especially during his earlier years when he had been married to the formidable Eleanora, the city of Ferrara had blossomed into a centre of Renaissance culture, a reputation which it still retained when Lucrezia arrived. Ercole I had laid out a planned city of wide paved streets, whose

---

* Ironically, Isabella herself was just as Spanish as Lucrezia, her mother having been Eleanora d'Aragona. However, Lucrezia insisted upon clinging to her Spanish roots and was resented for speaking incomprehensible Catalan with her favourite Spanish attendants.

straight vistas replaced the winding alleyways of the ancient medieval city. And amongst the new palazzi and piazzi he even built the Sala nova delle Commedie, claimed as 'the first purpose-built hall for the performance of plays' since classical times. Consequently, all manner of artists, thinkers, musicians and poets had been drawn to the Ferrarese court.

Lucrezia had always been keen on music and poetry, and soon made friends with Ercole Strozzi, an accomplished poet who was a member of the wealthy Florentine banking family which had been exiled by the Medici. The thirty-year-old Strozzi was clearly attracted by Lucrezia, and when he made the seventy-mile visit to Venice he would invariably return with rolls of her favourite colourful expensive fabrics. Lucrezia quickly had these made up into the latest fashionable garments, in which she delighted to appear at court, along with her similarly attired attendants – as was duly noted by the ever-observant Bernardo di Prosperi. Strozzi would even dedicate one of his finest poems, 'La Caccia' ('The Hunt'), to Lucrezia, in recognition of how much she enjoyed watching the hunts which took place in the large walled hunting park which Ercole I had enclosed beside one of his refurbished ducal palaces. Lucrezia was fond of Strozzi, but not physically attracted to this club-footed figure who was forced to hobble about the city on crutches.

In the summer she took to travelling down the River Po in her brightly painted barge to visit Strozzi in his lagoon-side Renaissance villa at Ostellato, some fifteen miles west of Ferrara. As ever, she was wont to make a characteristically spectacular entrance. Her Italian biographer Maria Bellonci described her:

> She was now twenty-three, remember, and was wearing cloth of gold and emeralds and pearls; her hair was fine and fair, and she was accompanied by her suite of women, girls-in-waiting, clowns and drummers.

It was here at the Strozzi villa that Lucrezia encountered the Venetian Pietro Bembo, who was already gaining renown as a humanist scholar and one of the finest poets of his age. Bembo was ten years older than

Lucrezia, and had long straight dark hair, which encompassed his sensitive, almost effeminate features. The chemistry between them appears to have been immediate and they soon became lovers. Of necessity, this was a highly discreet affair, whose true nature can only be gleaned obliquely from the frequent tender letters between them. Not for nothing have these been called 'The Prettiest Love Letters in the World'. Even so, it is difficult to assess the precise nature of the undeniable love between Lucrezia and her '*Messer Pietro mio*' ('My Master Pietro').

At the time, Bembo was – in the manner of Dante's Beatrice and Petrarch's Laura, during previous centuries – cultivating the notion of an intense platonic love, as distinct from actual physical love. However, there are indications that this might not have been the case with Lucrezia. She may well have been the younger of the two, but she was certainly the most experienced in the realities of love, no matter how perilous the repercussions. Bembo sent her some of his loveliest sonnets:

> Those beautiful tresses the more I love them,
> The much more harm they do to me.
> Unloose the knot that ties them,
> Release the gold of all I crave to see . . .

Lucrezia, who knew that her poetic talent could never match his, chose to copy out for him some lines by the fifteenth-century Aragonese poet Lope de Estúñiga:

> I think that should I die,
> And my desire die with me,
> Such great love would end
> The world would be bereft of love . . .

They exchanged poems and letters, as well as mementoes. The last included a medallion with Lucrezia's profile, and a curly lock of her long golden hair. In this correspondence, perhaps more than anywhere, we hear the true voice of Lucrezia. When Bembo wrote to her, comparing his heart to a crystal ball in which he read his feelings for her, she replied: 'Messer Pietro mio . . . Your, or our joint, crystal as it should be called . . . I cannot think what to say, or imagine, so much is their identity, as great as any through all of time.' She ends by telling him 'from now on, call me f.f'. A nickname? A secret lover's name? A code even? Some of her letters were written in Spanish, apparently 'for reasons of semi-secrecy'. When the affair began, her husband Alfonso was travelling abroad on one of the regular tours he undertook inspecting the fortifications of various cities. These would on occasion take him as far away as Paris, and once even to London, where he met Henry VII. Yet his loyal informants kept him abreast of the latest news and gossip from the court at Ferrara.

In one letter to Lucrezia, Bembo records words they had spoken together 'on the balcony with the moon as witness'. Earlier, during the stifling summer weather, he wrote suggestively, 'Here the heat is unusually intense,' and asked if she felt the same. Inevitably it seems that suspicions were aroused. Bellonci suggests that Alfonso's informants told him of 'too many kisses' – although in his letters Bembo takes care to mention only his burning desire to kiss her hand.

When Alfonso and his retinue unexpectedly arrived at Ostellato, ostensibly for some hunting, Bembo quickly disappeared back to Venice. But he would soon return and make contact with Lucrezia. These comings and goings, dated letters and so forth, are recorded fact. But Bellonci's gloss on the truth would appear to be a little too romantic. Had Alfonso any firm suspicions? If so, Bembo would in all likelihood have disappeared more permanently, to Venice or elsewhere. Such affairs were not taken lightly by cuckolded husbands. Some years later, Ercole Strozzi's amorous exploits in Ferrara would lead to him being discovered early one morning 'with twenty-two stab wounds in his body and his hair pulled out'.

Then in August the news reached Lucrezia of the poisoning of her father and her beloved brother Cesare, which left her prostrated with grief. Some time later it was confirmed that her father had died, but that Cesare remained alive. However, he was so ill that he was not expected to survive.

It soon transpired how right Bembo had been to advise Lucrezia to restrain her grief and look to her own future. Now that the Pope was dead, her link to any central power had also died. And without support from Cesare she was left completely on her own. Indeed, her position was far more precarious than she realized. Her father-in-law Duke Ercole I pointedly did not visit her to console her in her grief. Instead, he wrote to his envoy in Milan, asking him to convey to the French that the Pope's death was 'in no way displeasing to us'. It was not long before Louis XII revealed a similar attitude, with the Ferrarese envoy reporting from the French king's court that Louis XII had personally told him: 'I well know that you were never content with this marriage,' going so far as to say 'that Madonna Lucretia [*sic*] was not the true wife of Alfonso'. This insinuation was based on the fact that Lucrezia's divorce from Giovanni Sforza on grounds of impotence had been a farce. Yet perhaps the most important factor of all which contributed to the insecurity of her position was that she had not yet produced an heir.

However, unbeknown to Lucrezia her position remained secure, at least for the time being, owing to the fact that Ercole I was unwilling (and probably unable) to pay back the colossal dowry her marriage had gifted him.

CHAPTER 19

THE UNFORESEEN

IT HAD TAKEN ALEXANDER VI six days to die: a period of intense illness during which he had been subjected to all manner of increasingly desperate medical remedies. One such grotesque episode took place on 15 August, when the Pope was carried from his bed and placed in a large olive-oil cask filled with ice and water. The shock of this immersion caused the skin to peel from his body, which eventually drove him into a delirium.

On 18 August Alexander VI would finally die, ending a reign of eleven years and seven days: one which to this day many consider to have been the most notorious in papal history. Yet this opinion has not been universally upheld. Over the coming century and a half no less than two popes – and not minor ones either – would rate Alexander VI highly – indeed, very highly. When, later in the century, Sixtus V was asked to name the most illustrious popes, he replied: 'St Peter, Alexander and ourselves.' And when, during the middle of the following century, Urban VIII was asked the same question, he replied: 'St Peter, St Sylvester, Alexander and me.'

According to modern medical opinion, the symptoms exhibited by Alexander VI bear no relation to arsenic poisoning. It now seems evident that as Cardinal da Corneto's party lasted into the evening, the Pope and Cesare Borgia were stung by malaria-bearing mosquitoes. This is reinforced by the fact that Cardinal da Corneto himself also fell ill with the same symptoms, though he would recover.

Despite modern knowledge indicating that Alexander VI, his son, and the Venetian cardinal were all infected with malaria, the news that Alexander VI had died of poison (and the story that he had poisoned himself by mistake) soon spread across Europe. Within four days of his death news had reached Florence; days later it reached Ferrara, then Milan and Venice. Weeks later it had spread across Christendom, even reaching the ears of an earnest nineteen-year-old student at the University of Erfurt in Germany. This was Martin Luther, whose disgust at papal depravity would later split Christendom in two.

And what of Cesare Borgia? He would eventually recover. Years later, he would tell Machiavelli:

> He had thought of what might happen on the death of his father, and had made suitable provision for all eventualities, except for the one possibility that at the time of his father's death he, too, would be at death's door.

Fortuna had deserted Cesare Borgia. In his enfeebled state he could not have seized the papal throne, even if this had been his intention; or, as may have been the case, asserted his position as the all-powerful Captain-General of the Papal Army.

> If he had been healthy at the time of Alexander's death, every-thing would have been easy for him . . . and though he could not dictate who became pope, he could dictate who did not.

Even if the Borgias had not converted the papacy into a hereditary fiefdom, as many suspected them of plotting, with Cesare Borgia as an all-powerful Captain-General of the Papal Army they could just as easily have emerged as the power behind the throne, becoming pope-makers and reducing the Pope himself to a puppet figure. With the emergence of a powerful Roman state, Cesare Borgia might then have fulfilled his father's dreams of a united Italy, even a second Roman empire.

Yet Cesare Borgia was not one to despair so easily. As it was, he decided to take the only action that appeared open to him. Summoning all his strength, he would try his utmost to make the best of his situation, and perhaps survive to fight another day. According to Burchard, who was in the Vatican at the time:

> Borgia, who was sick, sent downstairs Don [Miguel da Corella] with an escort of heavily armed men. These entered the Pope's apartment and secured all the doors behind them. Then one of them unsheathed his dagger and threatened Cardinal Casanova* that he would slit his throat and throw him out of the window if he refused to hand over the keys to the papal treasure. The terrified cardinal handed over the keys. Then Don [Miguel] and his men went, one after the other, into the chamber behind the Pope's bed. They took all the money that was there and two caskets containing around 100,000 ducats.

On top of this, Miguel da Corella and his men are known to have stolen gold plate and jewels worth around 300,000 ducats. Though according to Burchard they missed the locked chamber beside the Pope's bedroom, which contained priceless papal accoutrements (bejewelled mitres, rings and so forth) sufficient to have filled several chests. Da Corella and his men then carted all they found up to Cesare Borgia's apartment. With such money at his disposal, Borgia could now bide his time, watching the course of events, awaiting his opportunity.

Meanwhile, the body of the Pope was laid out in the main hall of the Vatican, the location of many of Alexander VI's most debauched 'entertainments'. Just two candles illuminated his open bier through the darkness of the night. Not a single person stood vigil. The Vatican was

---

* The sixty-eight-year-old Spanish cleric who was papal chamberlain to Alexander VI, and had been appointed a cardinal just over two months previously.

virtually empty: most of the servants and officials had fled, carrying with them any remaining valuables they could lay their hands on.

Next morning, as the chanting monks bearing candles accompanied Alexander VI and his bier out of the hall, a scuffle broke out as the Vatican guards attempted to wrench the gold candlesticks from the hands of the monks. During the ensuing fisticuffs, the Pope's cadaver was tipped off its bier. That afternoon, Burchard found the Pope's body, which had become so bloated and disfigured that it was barely recognizable as human:

> The skin of his face was the colour of black cloth, like that of the most black of Africans, and it was disfigured with purple blotches. His nose had swelled up and his tongue was so enormous that it filled his entire mouth and ballooned out between his wide open lips.

Those who witnessed this sight swore that they had never seen anything so ghastly in their lives. Worse was to come, when the bier carrying the Pope's cadaver reached the graveyard. As all were afraid to touch this hideous object, the body was eventually dragged to its open grave by a rope tied around its foot, and unceremoniously dumped. Burchard continues:

> The six porters whose duty it was to bury him began making blasphemous jokes about the Pope and his grotesque appearance. The carpenters had made the coffin too narrow and too small, so they bent the mitre, wrapped the body in some old cloth and began stuffing it into the coffin anyhow, pummelling at it with their fists to make it fit.

Upon hearing the news confirming the death of Alexander VI, the far-flung cardinals hastened to Rome to join their resident colleagues for the conclave to elect a new pope. Yet such was the gathered cardinals' fear of Cesare Borgia, no matter how ill he might have been, that they decided against holding the conclave in the Vatican. Instead, they congregated at the Church of Santa Maria Sopra Minerva, a mile away across the Tiber in the heart of Rome itself.

This decision was not taken lightly, for the city was in its usual state of ferment between the death of a pope and the election of his successor. This time the turbulence took the form of rival gangs marching through the streets, shouting slogans in favour of the Orsini, the Colonna or the Borgias. The city was on the brink of chaos and the Orsini were determined to seize this opportunity for revenge on the Borgias. But even on his sickbed Cesare Borgia succeeded in outwitting the Orsini. He sent word offering an alliance with the Colonna, promising them back their seized estates and castles in return for their support.

Yet Rome also found itself under serious external threat. The French army, which had been marching south to relieve its garrison under siege by the Spanish at Gaeta, halted some fifty miles north of Rome at Viterbo. Meanwhile, the Spanish had called off their siege of Gaeta and marched north, halting at Marino, just ten miles south of the Holy City. Such were the inauspicious circumstances under which the conclave began. But how would the cardinals vote? Cesare Borgia's reputation, even in his parlous state, looked set to hold the balance of power. The Spanish and French armies may have stood opposed to each other on either side of the Holy City, but both wanted the backing of Borgia and his army. Meanwhile, inside the conclave the Spanish cardinals were expected to follow Borgia's bidding. And whichever side won the papacy would in all likelihood become the major power throughout Italy.

Ironically, despite Cesare Borgia's power in Rome, his dukedom in the Romagna appeared to be crumbling fast. Taking advantage of Borgia's evident incapacity, the Venetians had acted swiftly. During the first week in September they moved troops to take Cesenatico on the coast, and loaned further forces to Guidobaldo da Montefeltro so that he could retake Urbino. Encouraged by the Venetian moves, Baglioni had reoccupied Perugia, Vitellozzo had moved on Città di Castello, Pandolfo Malatesta had moved back into Rimini, and even Lucrezia's ex-husband Giovanni Sforza had taken back Pesaro. But Borgia's capital Cesena, as well as the strategic cities of Imola and Faenza on the Via Emelia, had remained loyal to their duke.

In Rome, events soon began to transform the situation with a similar swiftness and unpredictability. Doubts had been voiced concerning the validity of a conclave which did not take place inside the Vatican. Consequently, with the backing of the College of Cardinals a delegation of ambassadors was despatched to the Vatican, intent upon persuading Cesare Borgia to leave, so that the conclave could take place in the Sistine Chapel. Borgia agreed to allow this, but only under two conditions. Whoever was elected pope must reinstate him as Captain-General of the Papal Forces; and word should be sent to Venice demanding that it cease to interfere in the Romagna. These terms were agreed and Borgia made ready to leave the Vatican. It seemed that he would abandon his stronghold in Rome.

Arrangements were made for Cesare Borgia to meet up with his new ally Prospero Colonna across the Tiber at the Porta del Popolo. Colonna had been fighting alongside the Spanish in Naples and would accompany Borgia south to the safety of the Spanish army. By allying himself with the Colonna, Borgia had allied himself with the Spanish, who could now confidently expect that the Spanish cardinals would ensure that their candidate would become pope.

Borgia left the Vatican with a large armed guard commanded by Miguel da Corella. Borgia himself was so ill that he needed to be carried on a litter, born aloft by eight liveried halberdiers in the Borgia colours. Borgia himself was obscured from public view by closed crimson curtains. The litter was followed by Borgia's favourite black stallion, covered with a black velvet coat adorned with a golden motif depicting his ducal crown. Many of the spectators were struck by the resemblance to a funeral procession. Little did they realize how much deeper this resemblance went. Behind the curtains of Borgia's litter lay a cadaver-like figure. Borgia was a ghost of his former self, his limbs emaciated, his face like a skull, its skin disfigured with syphilitic blooms.

The resemblance to a funeral was reinforced by the family procession following the closed litter. This was led by Cesare's mother Vanozza, accompanied by Borgia's gaggle of illegitimate children; as well as Jofrè Borgia, Cesare's younger brother; and Giovanni Borgia, the *Infans Romanus*. (Lucrezia's acknowledged four-year-old son Rodrigo, by the murdered Alfonso, Duke of Bisceglie, would be transferred to Naples, where he would be looked after by Lucrezia's childhood friend Sancia, who had abandoned her complaisant husband Jofrè Borgia.) Also amongst this 'family' group, the Mantuan ambassador noted the presence of 'women of every kind'. And bringing up the rear was a heavily guarded mule train, bearing the strongboxes which contained Cesare's valuables, including as much of Alexander VI's treasure as he had managed to find and carry off.

Yet even in his weakened state, Cesare Borgia was still capable of a treacherous guile which would have made his father proud. Instead of heading across the Ponte Sant'Angelo into Rome to meet Prospero Colonna at the Porta del Popolo, Miguel da Corella unexpectedly ordered Borgia's procession to turn left, down the way to the Porto Viridaria, a smaller gate in the Vatican walls. Here, the procession was met by an advanced guard from the Papal Army, which escorted Borgia north towards the family stronghold at Nepi, where the French army was camped nearby. Borgia had deceived the Spanish and abandoned their cause in favour of the French. Within three days, Louis XII had issued a proclamation to the Romagna that their duke was 'alive and well and the friend of the King of France'. Any territory wavering in its support for Borgia quickly issued a declaration of loyalty to his cause.

During the following weeks Lucrezia Borgia in Ferrara would prevail upon her husband Alfonso to let her raise troops, which could be sent to the aid of her brother's forces in the Romagna. Alfonso, as well as his father Ercole I, proved unexpectedly favourable towards Lucrezia's wishes. By now the ruler of Ferrara had come to the conclusion that his state stood in peril of the Venetians if they took over the Romagna. Only if this state was ruled by Borgia would Ferrara be assured of an ally against the ever-constant threat of its powerful neighbour Venice. Lucrezia was able to raise 1,000 infantrymen and 150 crossbowmen, which set off under the command of Pedro Ramirez, one of the two Spanish brothers whom Cesare Borgia had left in command of his capital

Cesena. Lucrezia's troops successfully saw off the threat to Cesena, Imola and Borgia's other garrisons holding out along the strategic line of the Via Emelia. For the time being Cesare's hold on the Romagna remained; meanwhile, his health continued to improve as he lay in bed, biding his time within the stronghold of Nepi.

Back in Rome the conclave had by now met to elect a new pope. At the outset it became clear that the conclave was split into two opposing factions, the Spanish and the French, each capable of blocking the other. Between these camps was a minority of Italian cardinals, most of whom had let it be known that their vote was available to the highest bidder. Borgia had issued orders that his exiled enemy Cardinal Giuliano della Rovere should at all costs be prevented from reaching Rome in time to take part in the conclave. However, the wily cardinal had been prepared for this and managed to slip into Rome on the very day after the prostrate Borgia and his heavily armed procession left for Nepi.

Meanwhile, Louis XII now made it plain to Borgia that his own choice for pope was the French Cardinal Georges d'Amboise, the close advisor whom Alexander VI had appointed to the cardinalate at the time of Cesare's marriage in France. The French king clearly expected Borgia to deliver the votes of all the Spanish cardinals to elect his chosen candidate. Here indeed was a witches' brew of conflicting forces, as the cardinals filed in to register their first vote. Out of this the well-prepared Cardinal della Rovere emerged with fifteen votes, while Cardinal d'Amboise commanded just thirteen. And it soon became clear that neither of these two candidates could obtain the necessary two-thirds majority amongst the thirty-seven cardinals present. The only answer favourable to both sides was to elect a compromise candidate of sufficient age and infirmity that a new papal election would soon be required. There was but one candidate who fitted the bill: the ailing sixty-four-year-old Cardinal Francesco Piccolomini, who was duly elected on 22 September. The new pope took on the name Pius III, in recognition of his Piccolomini uncle who had become Pius II some forty-five years previously.

By now Borgia was making an all but miraculous recovery; though for tactical purposes he decided to keep this news to himself. He was intent upon returning to Rome to see Pius III, with the aim of insisting that he keep the promise made by the College of Cardinals that he would be confirmed by the new pope as Captain-General of the Papal Forces. Yet now that Borgia's father was no longer pope he required permission from the new pope to enter the Holy City. According to the Ferrarese envoy, Pius III spoke to him about Borgia: 'They tell me he is very ill [and I] indeed most deeply pity him. He wants to come to Rome to die, so I have given my permission.' Within two weeks of Pius III's election, Borgia returned to Rome, at the head of several hundred of his own liveried soldiers.

Cardinal della Rovere confronted the enfeebled pope, enraged that he had permitted Borgia to re-enter the Holy City. Pius III could only reply that he had been tricked into allowing Borgia back, pleading with Cardinal della Rovere: 'I am neither a saint nor an angel, but only a man and liable to err.' Next it was Borgia's turn to visit the new pope, where the old man was subjected to the full radiance of Cesare's charm. Pius III had discovered that the papal exchequer was empty; worse still the Vatican had been stripped of all its expensive furnishings, while its gates were besieged by debtors, all claiming they had loaned money to the Pope's predecessor. Why, it appeared that Pius III did not even have sufficient funds to pay for his coming coronation, and the accompanying lavish celebrations expected of him. Within days of becoming pope he would be disgraced.

Cesare Borgia generously assured Pius III that he was more than willing to loan His Holiness sufficient funds for his coronation, and the relieved pope confirmed Borgia's reappointment as Captain-General of the Papal Forces. A dismayed Giustinian reported back to Venice: 'Borgia is far from being as ill as all believed. He speaks in his arrogant manner and promises that he will soon be back with all his possessions in the Romagna.'

Two days later Pius III was crowned pope. Borgia and his liveried troops then marched into the Vatican at the head of a convoy bearing Cesare's possessions. This was accompanied by his 'family' – including mother, brother, children and 'assorted women' – who proceeded to take up residence in the Borgia apartments. The Spanish, the Colonna, the Orsini, to say nothing of Cardinal della Rovere, could only look on aghast. Borgia and his troops were now in sole command of the Vatican and the frail figure of Pius III. With the backing of the French, it looked as if Cesare would soon re-establish his complete control of the Romagna, and a grateful Louis XII would in all likelihood allow him to take over Florence. Cesare Borgia was on the point of establishing himself as the power behind the Pope and master over all of central Italy. The strategy of Alexander VI, and the predictions of Machiavelli, were on the verge of becoming reality.

By enacting Machiavelli's Virtù at its most ruthless, Borgia had succeeded. Yet not for nothing is Fortuna often likened to a wheel. Once again the wheel turned and Fortuna would desert Borgia. On 18 October, just twenty-six days after being elected pope, Pius III died, bringing to an end one of the briefest reigns in papal history. For his own safety, Borgia now moved into the Castel Sant'Angelo, along with his 'family'. This included two of his known illegitimate children: an infant son, Girolamo, and an infant daughter, Camilla Lucrezia. Also members of this group were the five-year-old *Infans Romanus* Giovanni, Lord of Camerino (possible son of Alexander VI, but more likely of Lucrezia, fathered by the murdered servant Perotto); and the four-year-old Rodrigo, Duke of Bisceglie (the title he had inherited from his murdered father Alfonso, Lucrezia's second husband). Cesare Borgia had an anointed heir in the form of Giovanni, Duke of Camerino, as well as a good number of spares in case Giovanni proved inadequate. But he would need to maintain his power while this generation came of age.

Once more the Holy City was faced with the prospect of another conclave; and once more it looked as if there would be a stalemate between those who favoured Cardinal d'Amboise and those who favoured Cardinal della Rovere. This situation induced Cardinal della Rovere to resort to some desperate politicking. As the cardinals began arriving in Rome, Cardinal della Rovere promulgated a rumour that if the Frenchman Cardinal d'Amboise was elected he would take the papacy back to Avignon, causing another schism. And no one wanted this. Even so, it soon became clear that Cardinal della Rovere could still not be sure of obtaining the necessary majority. In desperation, he reverted to an extreme plan, which would once again turn the wheel of fortune for Cesare Borgia. On 29 October, just two days prior to the opening of the conclave, Cardinal della Rovere approached his bitter enemy Borgia with a surprising offer. If Borgia could persuade the Spanish cardinals to vote for him, Cardinal della Rovere promised to reappoint Borgia as Captain-General of the Papal Forces, as well as lend his support to Borgia in his effort to retake his lost lands in the Romagna. And to demonstrate the cardinal's good faith, this agreement would be sealed by a marriage between Borgia's legitimate daughter Louise (now aged four, but still living in France) and the cardinal's thirteen-year-old nephew Francesco della Rovere, the former ruler of Sinigalia.

Borgia found himself in a serious quandary. Should he desert the French after all they had done for him? Yet despite Louis XII's promises, French support had done little to turn the tide in his favour in the Romagna. This agreement with Cardinal della Rovere meant that he would retain his military power as Captain-General, and be able to regain his power base in the Romagna. Without these two he would have nothing, now that his father was gone. Borgia signed the agreement, and when the conclave took place Cardinal della Rovere was duly elected by an overwhelming majority on the first vote. At fifty-nine he had at last acceded to the throne he had so long coveted, whereupon he took the papal name Julius II.

Despite all the people's rejoicing at the election of a comparatively young and certainly energetic Italian pope, who looked as if he would reign for some time, Julius II was hardly a popular man. The contemporary Florentine historian Guicciardini records that he

> was known to be very difficult by nature and formidable with everyone. He was notoriously restless . . . and had inevitably offended many people, arousing the hatred and provoking the enmity of many great men . . . He had been a very powerful cardinal for a long time . . . and his cause was greatly promoted by

the immoderate promises which had been made to anyone who might prove useful to him.

This last aspect did not bode well for Borgia. And so it turned out. Despite Julius II's promises, he now seemed reluctant to reappoint Borgia as Captain-General of the Papal Forces. By happenstance, Machiavelli had now arrived in Rome, despatched by Florence to be an observer at the papal elections and the beginning of the new pope's reign. In Machiavelli's opinion, Borgia had been 'deluded and blind to support a man whom his family had so sorely offended'. No such man could be trusted to keep his word. Even so, Machiavelli reported of Borgia that

> according to some of his men he has also sent orders to northern Italy enlisting soldiers there, too. It appears that he is raising these troops so that when he is once more made Captain-General of the Papal troops he will launch a campaign to recover his territories in the Romagna.

Julius II had apparently granted Borgia permission to march his troops to Ostia. Whereupon Borgia informed Machiavelli that 'he is taking action to prevent the Venetians from becoming masters of the Romagna, and the Pope is ready to assist him'. When Borgia reached Ostia, he planned to embark in papal galleys for the journey north to link up with the troops he had enlisted in northern Italy.

Yet to reach the Romagna it would be necessary for Borgia to march his troops across Florentine territory. He sent ahead for permission to do this, but Gonfaloniere Soderini adamantly refused Borgia's request, apparently confident that the French would not abandon their support for Florence. Borgia, too, evidently knew more of French intentions than he had let on, for he seemed to think that this refusal put an end to all his plans. What on earth could he do now? Machiavelli wrote that suddenly Borgia was a changed man: the duplicitous, self-confident braggart he had known had given way to a man 'paralysed with indecision, become suspicious of everyone, and [he] appeared generally unhinged in his behaviour'.

But Machiavelli knew Borgia all too well, and observed that this transformation in his character

> may be due to the natural volatility of his personality. On the other hand, he is used to having the luck of the devil, and this totally unexpected collapse of his fortunes may well have stunned and unnerved him.

Unpredictable as ever, Borgia suddenly left Rome for Ostia. Here he began dividing his troops into separate detachments. His intentions remained obscure. Many thought he had gone mad. Others suspected that he intended to send these troops in separate detachments across Florentine territory to rejoin at Cesena, which along with Imola still remained loyal to him. When news of Borgia's actions reached Rome, Julius II decided that it was time he too took action. On 12 November the new Pope despatched an envoy to Ostia ordering that Borgia surrender Cesena, Imola and any other lands which he still held in the Papal Territories. When Borgia ignored this order, the Pope sent the entire Papal Guard to arrest Borgia. Borgia was still not fully recovered and resting in one of the papal galleys, whose captain betrayed him to the soldiers sent by Julius II. His own soldiers, feeling leaderless after his surprise arrest, chose not to attempt to rescue him. Borgia was then escorted back to Rome.

Eyewitnesses report that on entering Rome Borgia appeared a dejected man, plunged into depression. To the surprise of all, Borgia was not sent to the dungeons of the Castel Sant'Angelo, but housed in the Vatican under heavy armed guard. Julius II was attempting to encourage Borgia to divulge the passwords to the fortresses that remained loyal to him in the Romagna. On 1 December 'news arrived that Don Miguel had been taken prisoner, and his force disarmed by Gian Paolo Baglioni on the border between Florentine territory and Perugia'. Borgia had now lost his closest Spanish commander.

The very next day, Julius II appointed Guidobaldo da Montefeltro as Captain General of the Papal Forces. The Pope had finally broken his promise to Borgia, just as Machiavelli had suspected he would. In fact, he had done no more than Borgia himself would have done. On the other hand, Borgia had found himself with little alternative but to accept the Pope's promise. He was being backed into a corner. Immediately after his appointment, Guidobaldo of Urbino paid a visit to Borgia in the Vatican. A later report of this meeting by Guidobaldo himself describes Borgia as falling on his knees and abjectly begging Guidobaldo to forgive him for taking Urbino and all the wrongs he had perpetrated on him. Borgia may have been a broken man, but this report rings false. It goes against all we know of Borgia. As we have seen, when Borgia was distressed he may have exhibited 'unhinged behaviour' in accord with the 'natural volatility of his character', but he never gave up; he was always scheming how to turn the tables on his enemy. His pride in himself – arrogance even – would not have permitted him to behave in such a fashion, even if only for deceitful purposes. Prostration and begging forgiveness do not appear to have been part of his emotional vocabulary. Indeed, this interpretation of Borgia's character is reinforced when we learn that the account which Guidobaldo gave to Giustinian immediately after his meeting with Borgia makes no mention of such histrionics. Even so, certain things do remain clear: by the end of this meeting, Borgia had agreed to return to Guidobaldo all the treasures which he had looted from Urbino. And, most significant of all, he finally surrendered the passwords to his fortresses in the Romagna. Was this the end?

By no means. Cesare Borgia remained as deceitful as ever. Making covert contact with troops who had remained loyal to him, Borgia initiated two daring exploits. First, a secret convoy of wagons was organized to transport out of Rome all the papal treasures he had looted from Alexander VI's apartment on his death. And second, orders were despatched to Cesena, instructing the commanders of the garrison, the Ramirez brothers, to send a secret mule train carrying all Borgia's treasures out of the Romagana. Both of these convoys were ordered to carry their precious cargoes to Lucrezia Borgia for safe keeping in Ferrara. Unfortunately for Borgia, in both cases spies disclosed the purpose of these convoys. Following frantic searches by Papal Troops in Florentine territory, as well as over the northern Romagna, both convoys were intercepted. A further blow to Borgia's fortunes came when he learned that Miguel da Corella had been transported to the Castel Sant'Angelo, where he was being tortured. Julius II was determined to extract every last piece of information he could about Borgia.

By now heavy snow had begun to fall in the Apennines, all but blocking the mountain passes. Not until 14 December did Julius II's envoy reach Cesena, presenting the commanders of the fortress, Pedro and Diego Ramirez, with the password. But still the Ramirez brothers refused to surrender, insisting that such secrets could have been obtained from Borgia only by means of torture. The Spanish commander who had been sent to accompany the envoy and act as go-between with the Ramirez brothers was seized as a traitor. Whereupon the Ramirez brothers had him tortured to death, his mutilated body left hanging from the walls.

Julius II decided to try a different tack with Borgia, who still remained under house arrest in the Vatican. He would ruin Borgia financially and then put him on trial. Despite the superiority of his position, Julius II hesitated to take the obvious step and have Borgia murdered. (Ironically, Borgia was at the time occupying the very apartment where, on his orders, Lucrezia's beloved second husband Alfonso of Bisceglie had been strangled by Miguel da Corella.) Julius II remained comparatively inexperienced and unsure of himself as pope, and had no wish to create the precedent of murdering his enemy so early in his reign. So he set about accumulating financial claims against Borgia from all those who had been robbed by him. For instance, Guidobaldo of Urbino was persuaded to put in a claim for a colossal 200,000 ducats for his losses. Others, including the families of the rulers deposed from the Romagna cities, were also encouraged to put in claims for financial damage. Likewise, Florence began drawing up a list of compensations it was owed for incursions into its territory by Borgia and his commanders (no matter that many of these had been murdered at Sinigalia). The total claims against Borgia soon exceeded 300,000 ducats. As for bringing a legal case against Borgia, this proved much easier. Julius II implicated Borgia in many of the murders committed by his father Alexander VI – particularly those of Cardinals

Michiel and Orsini, who had also been robbed of all their possessions. By putting Borgia on trial, Julius II wished to avoid alienating the Spanish cardinals, as well as displeasing the powerful Louis XII, who unpredictably still retained his sympathies for Borgia.

Meanwhile, despite the heavy winter, fighting continued in Naples between the French and the Spanish. Then finally on 28 December the Spanish commander Gonsalvo de Córdoba defeated the French army on the banks of the Garigliano River, thus bringing an end to French resistance. Whereupon, the French garrison at Gaeta surrendered. Borgia's ally Louis XII now only had a foothold in Italy, far to the north in Milan. As Machiavelli had previously observed in one of his despatches: 'It looks as if little by little Borgia is sinking into his grave.'

CHAPTER 20

DESPERATE FORTUNE

THERE IS NO DOUBTING that at this point Borgia's fortunes were at a low ebb. Yet, judging from his behaviour, the turning point appears to have come some weeks earlier. It was when he learned that he had been refused permission to cross Florentine territory that he became 'unhinged'. Why should this far-from-major setback have so distressed him? At the time, he still had the backing of Julius II and could thus have marched his troops on the usual route to the Romagna – from Rome up the Via Flaminia and across the Apennines.

It now becomes clear that Borgia's plan to sail his troops from Ostia masked another plan. This would have involved the final secret which Julius II was trying in vain to extract from Miguel da Corella. The Pope had managed to lay his hands on all the treasures which Borgia had ransacked from the papal apartments, as well as those he had stolen from Urbino, but he was convinced that Borgia had access to further funds which had been secreted elsewhere by Alexander VI. And Julius II was correct – indeed, far more correct than he could possibly have realized. Alexander VI, in connivance with his son Cesare, had hidden away a vast fortune. This was deposited with banking houses in Genoa and according to most estimates amounted to a colossal 300,000 ducats. But for Borgia to lay his hands on such funds he would need to travel to Genoa in person. The real reason for Borgia's apparent overreaction on being denied permission to cross Florentine territory now becomes evident. The papal galleys transporting him and his troops from Ostia would have docked at the Florentine port of Pisa. Here, Borgia could have taken a further ship or travelled overland, accompanied by an armed cavalry column, to Genoa to withdraw his funds from the banks. Under guard from the troops he was already assembling in northern Italy he could then have transported the money to Cesena. With such funds at his disposal, he would have been able to recruit soldiers and campaign as he had done in the old days, when he had relied upon Alexander VI to support his army. Little wonder then that the Gonfaloniere Soderini's refusal to let Borgia cross Florentine territory had brought Borgia to the very brink of despair. The clue lay in the secret of the Genoa accounts. A secret which Julius II was determined to uncover by whatever means. A secret which Miguel da Corella loyally refused to divulge . . . Though there remains the possibility that he had no knowledge of the Genoa accounts, which may well have been known only to Cesare Borgia and Alexander VI.

The final stages of Borgia's career read like a fast-moving adventure story. As the wheel of Fortuna continues to turn, the man of Virtù does his utmost to seize his every opportunity. By early 1504 the situation in Rome had reached an impasse. Borgia remained under house arrest in the Vatican, while Julius II continued building his case against him, as well as accumulating the claims with which he intended to ruin him. But the Pope remained mindful of the larger picture. He now had to come to terms with the Spanish, who had taken over Naples. And the Spanish, in the form of the many senior cardinals who had been appointed by Alexander VI, were pressing Julius II to release Borgia. The impasse remained, but by this stage both Julius II and Borgia were convinced, in their own minds, that they were on the point of gaining the upper hand.

At this point it is worth noting that at the end of his life Machiavelli would judge Cesare Borgia and Julius II as the two men who had most impressed him throughout his long diplomatic career. What was taking place during these early weeks of 1504 was nothing less than the old era bargaining with the new, for the highest stakes. Finally, at the end of January, the leader of the Spanish cardinals, Cardinal Vera, managed to broker an agreement between Julius II and Borgia. If Borgia was willing to surrender his fortresses in the Romagna, the Pope would allow him to go free and retain whatever assets he possessed. Julius II was certainly not aware of the enormity of this amount. But could Borgia trust the Pope, who had already broken his promise to appoint him as his Captain-General? On 8 February Giustinian reported: 'Borgia's situation is extremely desperate and no one gives much hope for his life.' Borgia slept with an unsheathed sword at his side, in the very chamber where murder had been committed on his orders. But Julius II was equally desperate. He needed Borgia's fortresses in the Romagna before Venice made another move into the region. Without them, he would be threatened by Venice in the north, as well as Spanish Naples in the south. And with the French still in Milan, he would be surrounded by enemies. Compared with the power wielded by Alexander VI, his papacy would be reduced to the impotence of mere spiritual authority. It was little consolation that this was what the papacy was intended to be. This was not why Julius II had become pope.

In mid-February, under pressure from the Spanish, Julius II permitted Borgia to travel down the Tiber to Ostia, where he would be released if all went according to plan and his Romagna fortresses were surrendered to papal authority. To Borgia's consternation, on his arrival at Ostia he was immediately marched into confinement within the formidable walls of the local fortress. On orders from Julius II, he was being held in the custody of the Spanish Cardinal Carvajal, who had given his solemn word not to release Borgia until news arrived that his last outposts in the Romagna were in papal hands.

On 19 April news reached Ostia that Borgia's Romagna fortresses had surrendered to the Pope. Whereupon, Cardinal Carjaval released Borgia. By chance the news reached Ostia before it had reached Rome.

As it turned out, Julius II had had no intention of releasing Borgia and was furious when he heard that Borgia was free.

At this point Borgia made a fateful decision. He could have sailed north to seek the protection of the French in Milan. Despite Borgia's treacherous behaviour, Louis XII still remained favourably disposed towards him. In fact, Louis XII was expecting him to journey to Milan, where he intended that Borgia should be given a command in the French army. But instead Borgia chose to head south for Naples, where he had already sent his family for safe keeping. He was greeted at Naples by his brother Jofrè, and Sancia (who had become the mistress of the Italian condottiere Prospero Colonna), as well as the Spanish cardinals who had taken up residence in this new Spanish territory.

Naples itself was ruled by Gonsalvo de Córdoba, as viceroy for King Ferdinand of Spain. Despite past differences, Gonsalvo de Córdoba welcomed Borgia, and began assisting him in raising troops and artillery for a coming campaign to take Florence. In fact, Gonsalvo had secretly reached an agreement with Borgia that in the event of Borgia taking Florence, Gonsalvo would be created Lord of Piombino and thus rule his own independent state. Gonsalvo had begun to chafe under the irksome commands of King Ferdinand. But Gonsalvo was also a realist, and when he received an order from Spain that Borgia was to be imprisoned he obeyed at once. Julius II had persuaded King Ferdinand that they should form an alliance against the French, and the price for this arrangement was the imprisonment of Borgia. This hit Borgia like a bolt from the blue, on the very night before he was due to set sail for Pisa and his invasion of Florence. In yet another twist of fate, Borgia was marched off to the Castel Nuovo, where he was imprisoned in the notorious cell know as Il Forno ('The Oven'), which lived up to its name during the stifling heat of the Neapolitan summer. Julius II had requested that Gonsalvo should force Borgia into surrendering his fortress at Forli, which was still holding out in the Romagna, despite earlier reports of its surrender. Gonsalvo assured Borgia that if he ordered the surrender of Forli, he would be set free. After sweating it out in Il Forno for two months, Borgia finally signed the order for the surrender of Forli. On 11 August Borgia's besieged commander Mirafonte swung open the gates of Forli and marched out his troops beneath the Borgia banner, 'all proclaiming their allegiance with loud cries of "César! César!".'

On 20 August Cesare Borgia was 'released' from the Castel Nuovo, only to find himself being marched aboard a galley bound for Spain, under the command of his enemy Prospero Colonna. When Borgia arrived in Spain, King Ferdinand immediately had him dragged off in chains to the mountain fortress of Chinchilla, 700 feet up in the remote hinterland of Valencia. Julius II had informed King Ferdinand that Borgia must never again be allowed to set foot in Italy, and in return King Ferdinand promised to put Borgia on trial for the murder of his own brother Juan, Duke of Gandia (a Spanish dukedom), as well the murder of his brother-in-law Alfonso, Duke of Bisceglie (a Neapolitan dukedom, now under Spanish jurisdiction).

Yet even now, help was at hand for Borgia. Although Alfonso, Duke of Bisceglie, had been the one husband whom Lucrezia Borgia had loved, she had no wish to see Cesare stand trial for his murder. Lucrezia began using all her influence to secure her beloved brother's release. Ercole I had died in June, which meant that Lucrezia had succeeded as Duchess of Ferrara, and she was determined to use her new position to the utmost on Cesare's behalf. She made contact with Juan d'Albret, King of Navarre, who was brother-in-law to both Lucrezia and Cesare through Cesare's marriage to Charlotte d'Albret. Together Lucrezia and Juan petitioned both Julius II and King Ferdinand to grant clemency to Cesare. All this proved to no avail, and Borgia continued to rot in his cell at Chinchilla. Months passed, autumn turned into winter and then into spring 1505. By summer Borgia could bear it no longer. As a privileged prisoner, he was permitted to take the air once a day on the battlements in the company of the prison governor de Guzman. One day, Borgia hurled himself on de Guzman, attempting to throw him off the battlements. But owing to the debilitating effects of his illness and his months of confinement, Borgia was no longer the man he had once been. He was quickly overpowered and dragged back to his cell. Later the following month Borgia was transferred to the more formidable fortress of La Motta, 300 miles from the Mediterranean coast in the garrison town of Medina del Campo.

Then once again Fortuna came to Borgia's rescue. On 26 December 1505 Queen Isabella of Spain died. Queen Isabella had acted as a stabilizing influence on her overly suspicious husband King Ferdinand, who now began to suspect even his most loyal supporters. The first to incur King Ferdinand's suspicions was Gonsalvo de Córdoba, whom the king suspected of plotting to declare himself ruler of Naples. King Ferdinand decided that the only way to rescue this situation was to send Borgia, along with Spanish troops, to depose Gonsalvo. It looked as if Borgia would return to Italy at the head of an army, depose Gonsalvo, and himself become viceroy of Naples. From here it would have been but a short step to recovering the Romagna . . . But sanity prevailed, as King Ferdinand's advisors pointed out the consequences of his plan for Borgia. Ferdinand would outrage Julius II, as well as making an enemy of Louis XII of France, who had finally washed his hands of Borgia and wished for closer ties with Spain.

Surprisingly, conditions at La Motta now improved for Borgia. The commander of the local garrison and prison governor, de Cardenas, had taken a liking to Borgia, admiring him for his previous exploits in Italy and the loyalty he had inspired in his Spanish commanders. De Cardenas had also begun to hear rumours of King Ferdinand's former plans for Borgia, and realized that if the political climate changed there remained a chance that Borgia might yet end up as his commanding officer. Consequently, Borgia soon found himself supplied with man-servants, who brought him meals from de Cardenas's personal kitchens. Either through these servants, or from de Cardenas himself, Borgia also came into possession of a long rope.

During the night of 25 October 1506 Borgia began lowering himself from the high walls of La Motta, where three armed accomplices were waiting with horses at the bottom of the dry moat. The alarm was immediately raised and the sentries on the battlements cut the rope, causing Borgia to fall and injure himself. But the waiting accomplices bundled him on to a horse and all four galloped off into the night. They then headed into the mountains for a castle on de Cardenas's estate. Borgia would hide here for a month, recovering from his injury. Despite armed men scouring the countryside, Borgia then made it north to the Bay of Biscay, where he took ship east along the coast to the refuge of the Kingdom of Navarre. Here he was welcomed in the capital Pamplona* with open arms by the king, his brother-in-law Juan d'Albret. Cesare triumphantly proclaimed his escape by sending a note to Lucrezia in Ferrara, signed 'César, Duke of Romagna'. When news of Borgia's escape from La Motta reached Italy it caused a sensation, and there was much quiet rejoicing in the cities of the Romagna.

Borgia immediately began reviewing his plans to regain the lost territory of his dukedom. The treasury of Navarre was empty, and King Juan was therefore unable to assist him. Meanwhile, Borgia's 300,000 ducats remained in the banks of Genoa. (There had been rumours that he had somehow managed to extract his monies, and that these had been carried to Rome. Yet despite Julius II mounting an exhaustive search of the city nothing was found, and it seems probable that the entire sum remained in Genoa.) Never one to be daunted, Borgia now boldly wrote to Louis XII, suggesting that he should be paid the handsome dowry which he had been promised on his marriage to Charlotte d'Albret. Louis XII was unimpressed with this appeal to his honour by a man who had so many times failed to honour his own promises.

Uncharacteristically, Borgia now chose to repay the loyalty shown to him by King Juan. Navarre was split by a vicious civil war after a revolt by Beaumonte, Count of Lerin, and Borgia volunteered his services to King Juan, who appointed him commander of the royal forces. Finally

---

* Ironically, the bishopric of Pamplona had been one of the earliest benefices obtained for the fifteen-year-old Cesare Borgia by his father, who had then been vice-chancellor to Pope Innocent VIII. Despite this being Cesare's first lucrative source of income, he had never previously shown any interest in the city, let alone visited it.

recovered from his injuries, and no longer beset by illness,* Borgia once again cut an imposing figure before the stocky fighting men of Navarre. A contemporary report described him as 'a big man, strong, handsome and in the full flight of his manhood'.

In January 1507 the newly revitalized Cesare Borgia led 10,000 Navarese troops into the field. He was soon pressing Beaumonte's forces into retreat. On 11 March, as night was falling, Borgia reached Viana, close to the border, some fifty miles south-west of Pamplona. He immediately laid siege to the local fortress, which was held by Luis, the eldest son of Beaumonte. During that night, under cover of a torrential storm, Beaumonte's men managed to penetrate Borgia's lines and get into the city. Borgia woke at dawn to a scene of chaos and confusion. After donning his chainmail and breastplate he mounted his horse and set off with his guards in pursuit of a fleeing column of Beaumonte's men. During the course of this chase Borgia became cut off from his men and rode into a ravine, where he was ambushed by three knights. One knight plunged his lance under Borgia's arm, where his body was unprotected by his armour, dislodging him from his horse. With daggers drawn, the knights then fell upon him, stabbing him to death. Not realizing the identity of their victim, the knights stripped him of his crested helmet and armour, leaving his butchered body as 'bare as a hand' where it had fallen.

Thus did Cesare Borgia, erstwhile Duke of Romagna, succumb to the final twist of Fortuna on an obscure mountainside in northern Spain on 12 March 1507. He was just thirty-one years old.

Borgia had at last been deserted by power and fortune. But he would

---

* Borgia's illness remains something of a mystery. According to Cardinal Carvajal, whilst Borgia was under his charge in Ostia, he 'had been in some pain, and he seemed to me to be suffering from the French disease [syphilis] . . . His face was blotched and disfigured with pustules.' Despite Cardinal Carvajal's description bearing a close resemblance to syphilis, Borgia's subsequent behaviour indicates that he was unlikely to have been suffering from the debilitating effects of tertiary syphilis. Indeed, if it was in fact malaria which had struck down Cesare and his father after the party in Rome, according to modern medical opinion this might well have cured him of his syphilitic ailment.

not be deserted by Machiavelli, who chose to make him the central figure in his masterpiece of political science *The Prince*. Machiavelli would use Borgia as an exemplar,

> for all those who rise through strength and good fortune . . . Had he succeeded, as he was on the point of doing when Alexander VI died, he would have gained such power and reputation that he might then have stood alone, reliant on his own strength and prowess, no longer subject to the power and fortune of others.

The Prince, and its Borgia hero, would embody realpolitik 300 years before the coining of this word, and its direct influence would extend through history to the modern day. A copy of Machiavelli's work would be found in the coach Napoleon abandoned on his retreat from Moscow. Hitler was an avid reader; Mussolini was given to grandiose recitations; and it would become bedside reading for Saddam Hussein.

EPILOGUE

NEWS OF CESARE BORGIA's death would take six weeks to reach his sister Lucrezia in Ferrara. On hearing what had happened, she is said to have cried out: 'The more I turn to God, the more he turns away from me.' Despite this, she is said to have maintained her composure until she reached the sanctuary of her apartment, where she locked herself in. Behind the closed door she could be heard wailing out his name, again and again, in an agony of grief.

Precisely how much Lucrezia had 'turned to God' at this point is another matter. She was now twenty-seven years old and had been Duchess of Ferrara for almost two years. Despite a number of miscarriages she would not produce an heir to the dukedom until the following year. He would be named Ercole, after his grandfather.

Lucrezia's intense affair with the poet Bembo – which may or may not have been physically consummated – would continue in epistolary form after he left Ferrara at the end of 1503. However, despite the continuing fervour of her letters, some time prior to Bembo's departure Lucrezia began a torrid affair with Francesco Gonzaga, Marquis of Mantua. The dashing condottiere was seven years older than Lucrezia and was said to have had an animal magnetism where women were concerned. Unlike the romantic and high-minded Bembo, this was a man more like her father and her brother, and there is no doubting that their relationship was strongly physical, an aspect confirmed by their passionate love letters. An added piquancy for Lucrezia was the fact that Francesco was the husband of her enemy Isabella d'Este.

On Julius II's accession to the papal throne, he had quickly made his intentions clear:

> I will not live in the same rooms as the Borgias lived. He [Alexander VI] desecrated the Holy Church as none before. He usurped the papal power by the devil's aid, and I forbid under the pain of excommunication anyone to speak or think of Borgia again. His name and memory must be forgotten. It must be crossed out of every document and memorial. His reign must be obliterated. All paintings made of the Borgias or for them must be covered over with black crêpe. All the tombs of the Borgias must be opened and their bodies sent back to where they belong – to Spain.

Not for nothing would Julius II go down in history as the 'warrior pope'. He would personally lead the Papal Army into the Romagna. His intention was to return northern Italy to its former state: to restore all the Papal Territories to papal rule, to reinstate the Medici as rulers of Florence, and to conquer Ferrara. The threat to Ferrara, and Lucrezia Borgia, would remain – with Francesco Gonzaga doing his best to mediate with Julius II. Not until 1512 would the Pope be thwarted at the Battle of Ravenna. Here the Papal Forces and the Spanish were defeated by the French and Italian forces, the latter local soldiers being under the command of Lucrezia's husband Alfonso d'Este.

Lucrezia's court would in time become a centre of culture rivalling that of Isabella d'Este at nearby Mantua. Lucrezia's life during this period has led many to concur that she became 'a respectable and accomplished Renaissance duchess, effectively rising above her previous reputation'.

The legends of incest, murder and poisoning – which cling to her name to this day – would become a thing of the past during the last years of her own lifetime. Meanwhile, amidst several miscarriages she would produce four further children, all legitimate offspring of her husband Alfonso. It was the debilitating effects of this frequent childbearing which would fatally weaken her, bringing about her death in 1519 at the age of just thirty-four. Thus passed into history the last of the legendary Borgias: Callixtus III, Alexander VI, Cesare Borgia and Lucrezia Borgia. Of these, it would be the last three who established the Borgia reputation – for better or worse, deserved or undeserved. Other Borgias would go on to become cardinals, archbishops and dukes. A distant descendant would even become a pope (Innocent X). And finally, in the seventeenth century, a Borgia would become a saint: St Francis Borgia. (St Francis, the epitome of all the qualities that Alexander VI had lacked.) Later, more distant descendants would include two young women who became queens of England, marrying Charles II and James II, respectively.

Yet a trio such as Alexander VI, Cesare and Lucrezia, who had achieved infamy in their rise to the very brink of transforming western Christendom into their own family fiefdom, would not appear again. For almost four centuries the Borgia apartments, with their Catalan tiles, luxuriously painted walls, including emblematic bulls and a depiction of Alexander VI at prayer, would remain unoccupied, silent and bereft of furnishings, sealed off from the outside world as if they harboured a contagious bacillus. Now they have been reopened, becoming a tourist attraction, their strange decor and chilling history stirring the imagination of the lines of visitors from all parts of the globe, which over 500 years ago Alexander VI had divided into two by drawing a line.

ACKNOWLEDGEMENTS

All authors rely to a great extent upon the advice and guidance of their colleagues. This was more than ever the case with *The Borgias*. The help I have received from a host of colleagues, friends and informed readers both in Britain and Italy has enabled me to uncover much material which remained new to me, as well as to correct errors and misjudgements which appeared in my work. Any such which remain are entirely my own doing. Where the manuscript is concerned particular mention should be made of my editor at Atlantic, James Nightingale, as well as James Pulford who stood in for him when he was away on paternity leave. The role of Ian Pindar in shaping my final manuscript was expert, exact and imaginative – without him the book would not be what it is. I would also particularly like to mention the indexer Chris Bell, whose eagle-eye proved invaluable in unravelling several knotty problems far beyond her remit.

As ever, I would like to thank my long-term agent Julian Alexander, to whom this work is dedicated. Also his assistant Ben Clark, who remains ever-helpful. I would particularly like to thank the staff at the several libraries and record offices I have consulted both in the UK and abroad, who have provided me with so much helpful information and guidance. As always, without the unfailingly helpful staff at Humanities 2 in the British Library this book would not have been possible.

SOURCES

PROLOGUE: THE CROWNING MOMENT

p. 2 **'the world's first blood transfusion'** See Jacalyn Duffin, *History of Medicine: A Scandalously Short Introduction* (Toronto, 1999), p. 171.

p. 2 **'to take for nourishment . . .'** Gerard Noel, *The Renaissance Popes: Culture, Power and the Making of the Borgia Myth* (London, 2006) p. 70.

p. 2 **'Since the fall . . .'** F. Guicciardini, *Storia d'Italia*, ed. Panigada (Bari, 1929) I, p. 2.

p. 3 **'begat eight boys . . .'** Epigram of the contemporary poet Marullus, cited in Latin in Ludwig Pastor, *History of the Popes*, trans. F. I. Antrobus, 40 vols (London, 1950 edn) Vol. 5, p. 240.

p. 3 **'Rather than the death . . .'** Innocent VIII's words were recorded by the contemporary Roman diarist Stefano Infessura. See, for instance, Christopher Hibbert, *The House of Borgia* (London, 2009) p. 34. (In some later references, I have used the Folio Society (2017) edition of this work.)

p. 3 **'hardly a day passed . . .'** See Pastor, *History of the Popes*, Vol. 5, pp. 318–9.

p. 3 **'the needle of . . .'** From the Italian *ago di balancia*, which literally translates as 'needle of the balancing scales', but the more poetic version referring to a compass has become the popularly accepted English translation. See, for instance, the entry on the Medici family by the renowned Italian Renaissance scholar Pasquale Villari in the celebrated 1911 edition of the *Encyclopædia Britannica*, Vol. 18, p. 33.

p. 4 'a black cross which . . .' et seq.: for the full context and sources of these citations see my *Death in Florence* (London, 2011), pp. 114, 132.

p. 6 'They were twenty-three . . .' See Peter De Roo, *Material for a History of Pope Alexander VI, His Relatives and His Time* (Bruges, 1924), Vol. 2, p. 314. Other sources give differing numbers. Although De Roo is not always reliable, owing to his zeal to defend Alexander VI from his detractors, he does in this case appear to have undertaken more extensive archival research in this matter.

p. 8 'handsome, of a pleasant . . .' Gasparo di Verona, cited Pastor, *History of the Popes*, Vol. 2, p. 451.

p. 8 'possessed singular cunning . . .' et seq., Francesco Guicciardini, *The History of Italy*, trans. S. Alexander (London, 1969), Book 1, p. 10.

p. 8 'numerous abbeys in Italy . . .' et seq., Jacopo da Volterra, cited Sarah Bradford, *Cesare Borgia* (London, 1976), p. 26.

p. 8 'He possesses more . . .' Cited Hibbert, *The House of Borgia*, p. 33.

p. 8 'unbecoming behaviour at . . .' See Pastor, *History of the Popes*, Vol. 2, p. 452, who cites Pius II's letter from 'The Secret Archives of the Vatican'.

p. 9 'squint-eyed and . . .' See various refs, including Maria Bellonci, *Lucrezia Borgia* (Milan, 1952 edn), p. 27; Sarah Bradford, *Lucrezia Borgia* (London, 2004), p. 16; Bradford, *Cesare Borgia*, p. 32.

p. 9 'during that time he . . .' Sigismondo de' Conti, cited ibid., Vol. 5, pp. 386–7.

p. 10 'four mules laden . . .' et seq., see Stefano Infessura, *Diario della città di Roma*, ed. O Tommasini (Rome, 1890), p. 282.

p. 10 'primarily [Borgia's] election . . .' Guicciardini, *The History of Italy* (1969 edn), p. 5.

p. 11 'it was a measure of . . .' Marion Johnson, *The Borgias* (London, 1981) p. 87.

p. 11 'We have for Pope . . .' et seq., cited Hibbert, *The House of Borgia*, p. 30.

p. 11 'Flee, we are . . .' Variations of this remark were widely reported. See, for instance, Michael Mallett, *The Borgias: The Rise and Fall of a Renaissance Dynasty* (London, 1969), p. 120.

p. 12 'as a good and . . .' Cited Johnson, *The Borgias*, p. 89.

p. 13 'Power and Fortune': A reference to Niccolò Machiavelli's prescription for political success: 'Virtù e Fortuna'. Open to several translations. The one I have chosen here is more appropriate in this general context. As we shall see, in the course of this work, other interpretations may appear more relevant in particular instances, such as 'Force and Chance' or 'Guts and Luck'.

CHAPTER 1: ORIGINS OF A DYNASTY

p. 17 'The election to the papacy . . .' Gerard Noel, *The Renaissance Popes* (New York, 2006), p. 23.

p. 18 'Old wood to burn, old wine . . .' et seq. These sayings appear in various forms in a number of works: see, for instance, G. J. Meyer, *The Borgias* (New York, 2013), p. 22.

p. 21 'Cattle grazed in the . . .' See Ferdinand Gregorovius, *History of the City of Rome in the Middle Ages*, trans. Annie Hamilton (London, 1900–2 edn), Vol. 2, p. 276 et seq.

p. 22 'By the time of the conclave . . .' See Hibbert, *The House of Borgia*, p. 12.

p. 22 'by far the most intelligent . . .' John Julius Norwich, *The Popes: A History* (London, 2011), p. 242.

p. 23 'in such poor health that . . .' Hibbert, *The House of Borgia*, p. 12.

p. 24 'the wooden table where . . .' *Giovanni Rucellai ed il suo zibaldone*, ed. A. Perosa, 2 vols (London, 1981), Vol. 1, pp. 70–72.

p. 24 'is seated in a chair of . . .' See Norwich, *The Popes*, pp. 63–4, citing the fifteenth-century Adam of Usk in his *Chronicle* (British Library Add. MS 10104).

p. 25 '*Duos habet et bene* . . .' Fernand Leroy, *Histoire de Naître: d'enfantiment primitif à l'accouchement* (Brussels, 2002), pp. 100–1.

p. 26 'Deeply pious, dry as dust . . .' Norwich, *The Popes*, p. 242.

p. 27 'an appreciation for the arts and sciences . . .' Alexander VI, drawing on material from De Roo.

p. 28 'he built galleys in the . . .' Norwich, *The Popes*, p. 242.

p. 29 'Your majesty should . . .' et seq., cited Meyer, *The Borgias*, p. 45.

p. 30 'I believe . . . the Pope has . . .' et seq., Antonio da Trezzo (14 February 1458) to Francesco Sforza, cited Pastor, *History of the Popes*, Vol. 2, p. 469n.

p. 30 'Jewels, table services, church . . .' et seq., see Noel, *Renaissance Popes*, p. 26.

p. 31 'The Pope shows signs of being pleased . . .' Antonio da Pistoia (4 July 1458) to Francesco Sforza, cited Pastor, *History of the Popes*, Vol. 2, pp. 559–61, doc. 52.

CHAPTER 2: THE YOUNG RODRIGO

p. 34 'when eight years old . . .' De Roo, *Alexander VI*, Vol. 2, p. 10.

p. 34 'Vatican records show Rodrigo . . .' See Meyer, *The Borgias*, p. 58.

p. 35 'the most eminent and . . .' Contemporary citation, see De Roo,

Alexander VI, Vol. 2, p. 29.

p. 35 'the most eminent and judicious . . .' cited De Roo, *Alexander VI*, Vol. 2, p. 29.

p. 35 '[Rodrigo Borgia] is handsome, of a . . .' Gasparo da Verona, cited Pastor, *History of the Popes*, Vol. 2, p. 451.

p. 36 'What he lacked was the . . .' et seq., see Norwich, *The Popes*, pp. 354–5.

p. 36 'he seems to have preferred . . .' see Mary Hollingsworth, *The Borgia Chronicles* (London, 2011), p. 170.

p. 37 'in him were combined rare . . .' cited Pastor, *History of the Popes*, Vol. 2, p. 449.

p. 37 'Rodrigo did not take holy . . .' et seq., see Mallett, *The Borgias*, p. 97.

p. 38 'the other cardinals hoped to deceive . . .' Aeneas Silvius Piccolomini, *The Secret Memoirs of a Renaissance Pope*, eds F. A. Gragg and L. C. Gabel (London, 1988), pp. 66–7.

p. 39 'not only a quantity of mildly pornographic . . .' See Norwich, *The Popes*, pp. 244–5.

p. 40 'kept them in fear of death . . .' et seq., Piccolomini, *The Secret Memoirs of a Renaissance Pope* (London, 1960 edn), pp. 32–4.

p. 41 'There were so many people . . .' et seq., cited Pastor, *History of the Popes*, Vol. 2, pp. 83–4.

p. 42 'That evening in the church . . .' ibid., Vol. 2, pp. 501–2, doc. 5.

p. 42 'his condition is such . . .' ibid., Vol. 2, p. 348n.

p. 43 'You traitorously used our money . . .' Letter from Callixtus III to King Alfonso of Naples, dated 1456. See ibid., Vol. 2, pp. 365–6.

p. 43 'There was a bitter argument in . . .' Piccolomino, *Memoirs*, p. 71.

p. 43 'The pope died today at nightfall . . .' See Pastor, *History of the Popes*, Vol. 2, p. 563, doc. 54.

p. 45 'This meant the loss . . .' Noel, *Renaissance Popes*, p. 29.

p. 45 'It was common talk that . . .' et seq., Aeneas Piccolomini, *Memoirs of a Renaissance Pope* (London, 1960 edn), pp. 79–87. All descriptions of the conclave, with the exception of the two mentioned below, come from these pages.

p. 46 'This may have been Cardinal Calindrini . . .' Noel, *Renaissance Popes*, p. 29.

p. 48 'This shocking scene was . . .' et seq., ibid., p. 31.

p. 48 'the father of several . . .' et seq, including citations, see Hibbert, *The House of Borgia*, pp. 18–19.

p. 49 'The palace is splendidly decorated . . .' Ascanio Sforza, cited Mallett, *The Borgias*, p. 96.

p. 50 'Anyone who used this great . . .' Meyer, *The Borgias*, p. 91.

CHAPTER 3: RODRIGO BORGIA EMERGES IN HIS TRUE COLOURS

p. 53 'trussing up a Papal emissary . . .' Robert Hughes *Spectator* 7 August 2013

p. 54 'We have learned that three days . . .' This letter is cited in varying lengths and translations. See Pastor, *History of the Popes*, Vol. 2, p. 452; Mallett, *The Borgias*, p. 98; Hollingsworth, *Borgias*, p. 85; Meyer, *The Borgias*, p. 102; et al.

p. 55 'the first light thrown . . .' Pastor, *History of the Popes*, Vol. 2, p. 452.

p. 55 'the usual polish of . . .' et seq., see Meyer, *The Borgias*, p. 103.

p. 56 'fell seriously ill . . .' Piccolomini, *Memoirs*, p. 161.

p. 58 'The priesthood is derided by . . .' See Hollingsworth, *Borgias*, p. 84, citing Piccolomini, *Memoirs*.

p. 59 'amateur crusaders from . . .' Meyer, *The Borgias*, p. 112.

p. 60 'The vice-chancellor is sick . . .' See Pastor, *History of the Popes*, Vol. 2, p. 455n.

p. 61 'in high standing' Cited Hollingsworth, *Borgias*, p. 97.

p. 62 'yesterday [Cardinal Rodrigo Borgia] was seen . . .' ibid., p. 100.

p. 63 'his extensive collections of . . .' Noel, *Renaissance Popes*, p. 50.

p. 63 'dark and damp, and . . .' See Hollingsworth, *Borgias*, p. 105.

p. 63 'a monster of cruelty and . . .' See Meyer, *The Borgias*, p. 127.

p. 63 'unworthy of the . . .' See Johann Kirsch, 'Pope Formosus', *Catholic Encyclopedia* (London, 1909 edn).

p. 63 'his two weaknesses . . .' See Norwich, *The Popes*, p. 246.

p. 64 'After the boys' race he . . .' Platina, *Vitae Pontificum*, p. 380, reprint in Vol. 3, Part 1, *Rerum Italicarum Scriptores* (Citta di Castello, 1923–4).

p. 64 'after an immoderate feasting . . .' Noel, *Renaissance Popes*, p. 53.

p. 66 'a monument of medieval cuisine . . .' See 'Bartolomeo Platina' in John Dickie, *Delizia! The Epic History of the Italians and their Food* (London, 2008), p. 67.

p. 67 'No account of how he . . .' See Meyer, *The Borgias*, p. 140.

p. 69 'A fearful storm arose at . . .' De Roo, *Alexander VI*, Vol. 2, p. 204.

p. 71 'the son of a cardinal . . .' Cited Hollingsworth, *Borgias*, p. 130.

CHAPTER 4: THE WAY TO THE TOP

p. 74 'brilliant suite' et seq., Pastor, *History of the Popes*, Vol. 4, p. 279.

p. 74 'The wars in France . . .' ibid., p. 280.

p. 74 'the scarcity of bread . . .' et seq., De Roo, *Alexander VI*, pp. 220–3.

p. 77 'he was content to . . .' Cited in the most illuminating work on the conspiracy: Lauro Martines, *April Blood: Florence and the Plot against the Medici* (London, 2003), p. 158.

p. 77 'pledge of the great love' et seq., cited Bradford, *Cesare Borgia*, p. 23.

p. 79 'There is substantial . . .' Colin Heywood, 'Mehmed II', *Encyclopedia of the Ottoman Empire* (New York, 2009), p. 368.

p. 81 'working hard for support' et seq., cited Hollingsworth, *Borgias*, p. 140.

p. 81 'And so, rivals as they were . . .' Norwich, *The Popes*, p. 251.

p. 82 'He slept almost continuously . . .' See Noel, *Renaissance Popes*, p. 70.

p. 83 'Who would not make sacrifices . . .' Christopher Lascelles, *Pontifex Maximus: A Short History of the Popes* (Horley, 2017), p. 186.

p. 85 'Of the worldly Cardinals . . .' Pastor, *History of the Popes*, Vol. 5, p. 362.

p. 85 'he never missed . . .' Sigismondo de' Conti, cited ibid., pp. 386–7.

CHAPTER 5: A NEW POPE IN A NEW ERA

p. 89 'I am pope! . . .' Hibbert, *The House of Borgia*, p. 30.

p. 90 'The town which gave Law . . .' Pope Alexander VI, *Statua et novae reformations Urbis Romae* (Book IV, folio 1).

p. 90 'Alexander VI . . . rode through Rome . . .' See Tuchman, *March of Folly*, p. 77, drawing on several contemporary sources.

p. 91 'began most admirably' Cited Meyer, *The Borgias*, p. 182.

p. 92 '*Giulia la bella*' et seq., see citations Bradford, *Lucrezia Borgia*, p. 35; Tuchman, *March of Folly*, p. 77; Hibbert, *The House of Borgia*.

p. 92 'the Bride of Christ' et seq., see Will Durant, *The Renaissance* (New York, 1953), pp. 412–3; Hibbert, *The House of Borgia*, p. 27; Bradford, *Lucrezia Borgia*.

p. 92 'We have heard that you . . .' Cited Hibbert, *The House of Borgia*, p. 27.

p. 96 'The great hall, known as the Sala Reale . . .' This description is mainly taken from Johann Burchard, *At The Court Of The Borgia*, ed. and trans. Geoffrey Parker (Bath, 1996 edn), pp. 64–7. For clarity, I have at certain points interwoven other translations and citations, which appear in Hibbert, *The House of Borgia*, pp. 37–9 and Hollingsworth, *Borgias*, pp. 183–5.

p. 96 'As only an ecclesiastic . . .' et seq., Geoffrey Parker's footnote to Burchard, *Court of the Borgias*, p. 65.

p. 96 **'When all the ladies . . .'** et seq., ibid., p. 65 et al, including Johannes
Burchard, *Liber Notarum* (Paris, 2003 edn), pp. 82, 96; as well as
Hollingsworth, *Borgias*, p. 184, and Hibbert, *The House of Borgia*, p. 39,
citing Infessura.

p. 98 **'the rest were candidates for . . .'** Hollingsworth, *Borgias*, p. 187.

p. 99 **'He brought back parrots . . .'** ibid., p. 178.

p. 101 **'impatient, arrogant and spiteful'** Such views were widespread. See in
this instance Christopher Hibbert, *Florence: Biography of a City* (London,
1993), p. 149.

p. 101 **'the Sword of the Lord . . .'** et seq., see Donald Weinstein, *Savonarola
and Florence* (Princeton, 1970), pp. 87–96.

p. 101 **'Besides hunting, which . . .'** et seq., Jacob Burkhardt, *The
Civilization of the Renaissance in Italy*, trans. S. Middlemore (London,
1928 edn), Book 1, Vol. 5, pp. 36–7.

p. 102 **'white marriage'** Cited Meyer, *The Borgias*, p. 205.

p. 103 **'The new pope no longer saw his daughter's . . .'** Bradford, *Lucrezia
Borgia*, p. 24.

p. 103 **'Juan, duke of Gandia . . . had been sent . . .'** et seq., see Meyer, *The
Borgias*, p. 204.

p. 104 **'the handsomest man in Italy'** Cited Michael Mallett, entry on
'Cesare Borgia', *Encyclopædia Britannica* (2002 edn).

p. 104 **'he had gained such profit . . .'** Cited Bradford, *Cesare Borgia*, p. 24.

p. 105 **'Giovanni, legitimate son . . .'** see ibid., p. 24.

p. 105 **'The day before yesterday . . .'** The Ferrarese ambassador, cited ibid.,
pp. 30–1.

CHAPTER 6: 'THE SCOURGE OF GOD'

p. 107 **'Those who professed to tell . . .'** Guicciardini, *Storia d'Italia*, 1.9,
cited Hollingsworth, *Borgias*, p. 195.

p. 108 **'the greatest peace . . .'** See F. Guicciardini, *Storia d'Italia*, ed.
Panigada (Bari, 1929), Vol. 1, p. 2.

p. 108 **'he seemed more like . . .'** Guicciardini, *The History of Italy*, trans.
Sidney Alexander, p. 49.

p. 108 **'His prodigious sexual appetite was . . .'** See Paul Strathern, *Death
in Florence* (London, 2011), p. 169. This and the preceding description
derive from a host of contemporary sources.

p. 110 **'Charles delayed his own . . .'** See Meyer, *The Borgias*, p. 225.

p. 112 **'On 30 January news arrived . . .'** *Le Journal de Jean Burchard*, trans.
Joseph Turmel (Paris, 1932), p. 218. Johann Burchard's *Diarium sine*

rerum urbanarum commentarii (1483–1506) was written in Latin, and a
three-volume version was published by Louis Thuasne in 1883–5. This,
and the Latin translation by Enrico Celani (1907–13), have various
(differing) lacunae. The most reliable and readily available collation of
these is Joseph Turmel's French translation, each of whose entries have a
numbered references to Celani and Thuasne, for those who wish to check
the original Latin sources.

p. 113 **'All these Italians . . .'** Various versions of this remark appear in a
range of sources, including Guicciardini. It is said to have been overheard
by Cardinal Giuliano della Rovere.

p. 113 **'On their way into the city . . .'** et seq., Burchard, *Journal*, cited
Hibbert, *The House of Borgia*, p. 56.

p. 113 **'robbed her of 800 ducats . . .'** Burchard, cited Bradford, *Cesare Borgia*,
p. 49.

p. 115 **'Taking his treasures with him . . .'** De Roo, *Alexander VI*, Vol. 4, p. 183.

p. 115 **'The reputation of the last two . . .'** Guicciardini, *History of Italy*,
cited Hibbert, *The House of Borgia*, p. 62.

p. 116 **'with a white powder'** See *The Memoirs of Philippe de Commynes*, ed. S.
Kinser, trans. I. Cazeau (South Carolina, 1973), Vol. 2, p. 487 n 224.

p. 116 **'The French were stupid, dirty and . . .'** Assembled from cited
passages, see in particular: Bradford, *Cesare Borgia*, p. 50; Hibbert, *The
House of Borgia*, p. 62; also Mallett, Guicciardini et al.

p. 118 **'This illness, which was unknown . . .'** Guicciardini, *Storia d'Italia*
(Rome, 1967 edn), Vol. 2, ch. 13.

p. 118 **'Even in faraway England . . .'** et seq., see Meyer, *The Borgias*, p. 232.

p. 118 **'It took time to establish . . .'** De Roo, *Alexander VI*, Vol. 4, pp. 208–9.

p. 119 **'resolved to place . . .'** See ibid., p. 209 n 121, citing as sources
Gregorovius, *History of the City of Rome in the Middle Ages* and De
Cherrier, *History of Charles VIII*.

p. 119 **'was called the Holy League . . .'** ibid., p. 209.

p. 120 **'Alexander, however, thought . . .'** Meyer, *The Borgias*, p. 233.

CHAPTER 7: THE BEST OF PLANS . . .

p. 124 **'to discourse with you . . .'** See Documento XXIII Pasquale Villari, *La
Storia di Girolamo Savonarola . . .* , Vol. 1 (2 vols, Florence, 1887)

p. 124 **'firstly, because my body . . .'** For full text of this letter see Girolamo
Savonarola, *Le Lettere*, ed. Roberto Ridolfi (Florence, 1933), pp. 55–8.

p. 125 **'By yesterday morning the floods . . .'** See Pastor, *History of the Popes*,
Vol. 5, pp. 479–80.

p. 125 'announced in consistory...' Guicciardini, *Storia* (Rome, 1967 edn),
Vol. 2, ch. 3.

p. 126 'covering walls and ceiling...' et seq., Bradford, *Cesare Borgia*, p. 54.

p. 127 'widely recognized as the most...' Hibbert, *The House of Borgia*, p. 73.

p. 127 'Without Giuliano ....' Bradford, *Cesare Borgia*, p. 53.

p. 128 'accompanied by some twenty...' Burchard, *Journal*, cited Hibbert,
The House of Borgia, p. 74.

p. 128 'Jofrè and Sancia rode...' See Bradford, *Lucrezia Borgia*, p. 54.

p. 128 'In truth she did not appear...' Scalona, cited ibid., p. 54.

p. 128 'Jofrè, younger than his...' et seq., Scalona, cited Bradford, *Cesare
Borgia*, p. 56.

p. 129 'Lucrezia was deeply attached...' Hibbert, *The House of Borgia*, p. 74.

p. 130 'too long and boring...' Burchard, *Journal*, cited ibid., p. 76.

p. 130 'a spoilt boy...' Aragonese chronicler Geronimo Zurita, cited ibid.

p. 130 'every effort is made...' Scalona, cited Bradford, *Cesare Borgia*,
p. 56.

p. 132 'heavily defeated in great...' Burchard, *Journal*, cited Hibbert, *The
House of Borgia*, p. 77.

p. 133 'the French commander Menaut Aguerre...' See Mallett, *The
Borgias*, p. 159, citing original French source: G. Ouy, 'Le pape Alexander
VI a-t-il employé les armies chemique?', *Receuil de traveaux offerts à C.
Brunel* (Paris, 1955) Vol. 2.

p. 133 'It may be that hints...' Bradford, *Lucrezia Borgia*, p. 56.

p. 133 'I suspect that something concerning...' Cited Bradford, *Cesare
Borgia*, p. 60.

p. 135 'that if he was dead...' ibid., p. 61, citing Scalona.

p. 135 'seized with mortal terror' Burchard, *Journal*, cited ibid.

p. 135 'the city was in an uproar...' ibid., p. 61, drawing on contemporary
sources.

p. 135 'When the Pope heard...' et seq., Burchard, *Journal*, trans. Turmel
(Paris, 1933), p. 292.

p. 137 'lead the mares into the courtyard...', ibid., p. 312.

p. 138 'Donna Lucrezia has...' See Gregorovius, *Lucrezia Borgia* (London
2017 edn), p. 125.

p. 138 'Last Thursday Perotto...' ibid.

p. 138 'more lurid reports of the death...' Mallet, *Borgias*, p. 328 n 18,
citing Sanuto, *Diarii*, Vol. 3, cols. 842 ff.

CHAPTER 8: A CRUCIAL REALIGNMENT

p. 140 'It seems to me that the son . . .' et seq., King Federigo of Naples letter to Alexander VI (September 1497), cited Hibbert, *The House of Borgia*, p. 93. The Roman informant to the Marquesa of Mantua was Donato de' Preti.

p. 142 'that he had known his wife . . .' Cited Bradford, *Cesare Borgia*, p. 69.

p. 142 'If His Holiness wishes . . .' Cited ibid., Hibbert, *The House of Borgia*.

p. 143 'for having got His Holiness's daughter . . .' Christoforo Poggio, agent for the Bentivoglio family of Milan, cited Bradford, *Lucrezia Borgia*, p. 68.

p. 143 'If she had been Cicero . . .' See Hibbert, Bradford et al.

p. 145 'Alexander is no pope . . .' et seq., cited Pasquale, *Villari La Storia di Girolamo Savonarola* . . . (2 vols, Florence, 1887), Vol. 2, pp. 132–3.

p. 147 'they arrived in Florence . . .' Several versions of this appear in Savonarola's main biographies. See Ridolfi, Villari et al. In particular, Pacifico Burlamacchi, *La Vita del Beato Girolamo* Savonarola (Florence, 1937).

p. 147 'after years of conflict . . .' See Meyer, *The Borgias*, p. 278.

p. 148 'hunchbacked and barren' See Hibbert, *The House of Borgia*, p. 96, echoing several reliable sources.

p. 149 'put off the purple . . .' et seq., Burchard, cited Hibbert, *The House of Borgia*, pp. 97, 98.

CHAPTER 9: A ROYAL CONNECTION

p. 155 'permitted to lead their life . . .' James Carroll, *Constantine's Sword* (Boston, 2002), pp. 263–4.

p. 158 'jewels, stuffs, cloth-of-gold . . .' Burchard, cited Hibbert, *The House of Borgia*, p. 100.

p. 159 'one of the seamiest lawsuits of . . .' et seq., see J. R. Hale, *Renaissance Europe: Individual and Society 1482–1520* (New York, 1972), pp. 15, 16.

p. 159 'We send Your Majesty our heart . . .' Papal communication, cited Bradford, *Cesare Borgia*, p. 83.

p. 160 'Avignon never witnessed . . .' et seq., contemporary source, cited Hibbert, *The House of Borgia*, pp. 101–2.

p. 161 'Della Rovere has fallen sick . . .' Agent B, working for Ludovico Sforza, Duke of Milan, cited Bradford, *Cesare Borgia*, p. 87.

p. 163 'In his cap were two double rows . . .' et seq., contemporary eyewitness, cited Hibbert, *The House of Borgia*, p. 104.

p. 166 'We trust you will receive Duchess Lucretia . . .' Letter from Alexander VI to Priors of Spoletto, cited Bradford, *Lucrezia Borgia*, p. 80.

p. 168 'was the most contented man . . .' et seq., cited Bradford, *Cesare Borgia*, pp. 100, 101.

p. 169 'The French captains spit on . . .' Venetian report, cited ibid., p. 104.

p. 175 'two silver sweetmeat dishes from . . .' Burchard, cited Hollingsworth, *Borgias*, p. 252.

CHAPTER 10: IL VALENTINO'S CAMPAIGN

p. 177 'the vicars [i.e. de facto rulers] of Rimini . . .' et seq., Burchard, *Diario*, cited Hibbert, *The House of Borgia*, p. 112, et al.

p. 178 'a breeding ground for all the worst crimes . . .' Niccolò Machiavelli, *Discorsi*, Book 3, ch. 29, sec. 1.

p. 181 'Take a good look . . .' Natalie Grazziani et al., *Caterina Sforza* (Milan, 2001), p. 108. Versions of this remark are also supported by Guicciardini and Machiavelli.

p. 182 'If the Pope had opened . . .' Burchard, *Journal*, cited Hibbert, *The House of Borgia*, p. 114.

p. 185 'as I hear, was keeping the said lady . . .' et seq., the citations in the following section come from the named sources, as well as many being cited in Bradford, *Cesare Borgia*, pp. 112–3, 115; Ottavia Niccoli, *Prophecy and People in Renaissance Italy* (Princeton, 1990), p. 136; Ernst Breisach, *Caterina Sforza* (Chicago, 1976), pp. 232–6; Leonie Freida, *The Deadly Sisterhood* (London, 2012), pp. 219–20; and De Roo, *Alexander VI*, Vol. 4, pp. 299–305.

p. 188 'his temporal Vicar of San Mauro . . .' et seq., see de Roo, *Alexander VI*, Vol. 4, p. 306.

p. 188 'the duke of Valentinois with . . .' See de Roo, *Alexander VI*, Vol. 4, p. 307, citing as his source Burchard, *Diario*, Vol. 3, pp. 26–31.

p. 189 'the Pope's nomination of his son . . .' Bradford, *Cesare Borgia*, p. 118.

p. 190 'On June 30, 1501 Caterina . . .' Burchard, *Borgias* (2003 French edn), p. 308.

p. 190 'If I could write . . .' Cited Bradford, *Cesare Borgia*, p. 157.

CHAPTER 11: BIDING TIME

p. 195 'he cares little for returning . . .' Paolo Capello, cited Bradford, *Cesare Borgia*, p. 120.

p. 196 'For his own part, he had imposed . . .' et seq., see Pastor, *History of the Popes*, Vol. 6, pp. 90–1.

p. 198 'resembling a glittering sun with . . .' et seq., Pietro Fortini, cited ibid., p. 122.

p. 199 'the Testament of la Fiametta . . . ' Rome City archives, cited ibid.

p. 200 'killed seven wild bulls . . . ' Paolo Capello, Venetian ambassador, cited Bradford, *Cesare Borgia*, p. 122.

p. 202 'devotedly nursed by Lucrezia and . . . ' Paolo Capello, cited ibid., p. 123.

p. 204 'the beginning of another . . . ' See Meyer, *The Borgias*, p. 303.

p. 204 'He was gravely wounded . . . ' Burchard, *Journal* (Turmel), p. 305.

p. 204 'Whose was the hand behind . . . ' Raphael Brandolinus Lippi, cited Bradford, *Lucrezia Borgia*, p. 89.

p. 205 'I did not wound the duke . . . ' Contemporary source, cited Meyer, *The Borgias*, p. 304.

p. 206 'stupefied by the suddenness . . . ' This description by Lippi, and Burchard's ensuing description, from Burchard, *Journal* (Thuasne), Vol. 3, p. 69, appear in several versions: see, for example, Woodward, *Cesare Borgia*, pp. 180–1 and Maria Bellonci, *Lucrezia Borgia*, pp. 139–40.

p. 207 'Her tears soon got . . . ' Bellonci, *Lucrezia Borgia*, p. 140.

p. 207 'All Rome trembles at this Duke . . . ' Cited Bradford, *Cesare Borgia*, p. 129.

p. 207 'If we could find the answer . . . ' et seq., Meyer, *The Borgias*, p. 305.

p. 207 'I pray your lordships to take this . . . ' Cited Bradford, *Lucrezia Borgia*, p. 93.

p. 208 'at dead of night . . . ' See Woodward, *Cesare Borgia*, p. 181.

p. 208 'Cesare murdered his brother . . . ' Contemporary, cited Bradford, *Cesare Borgia*, p. 129.

p. 208 'The Pope loves and fears . . . ' Venetian ambassador Paolo Capello, cited ibid., p. 130.

CHAPTER 12: THE SECOND ROMAGNA CAMPAIGN

p. 209 '*la infelicissima*' et seq., many sources; see, for instance, Hibbert, Bradford, Bellonci.

p. 210 'nearly all the professional . . . ' Machiavelli, cited Hibbert, *The House of Borgia*, p. 132.

p. 211 'He is a brave and powerful character . . . ' et seq., Pandolfo Collenuccio, *Commentarium*. These citations appear in various forms in a number of sources, e.g. Bradford, Woodward.

p. 213 'Duke Cesare's troops who were . . . ' Bernardino Zambotti, *Diario Ferrarese 1476–1504* (Bologna, 1928), p. 302.

p. 213 'The Spaniards washed the feet of . . . ' Francesco Matarazzo of Perugia, see *Chronicles of the City of Perugia 1492–1503*, trans. E. S.

Morgan (London, 1905), p. 168. I have adapted Morgan's translation to fit the circumstances.

p. 214 'ran as swiftly as . . .' Cited Bradford, *Cesare Borgia*, p. 141.

p. 216 'looks younger every day . . .' See Pastor, *History of the Popes*, Vol. 4, p. 80.

p. 217 'Cesare de Borgia gave the order . . .' et seq., see De Roo, *Alexander VI*, pp. 317–18.

p. 219 'At this time the city . . .' Biagio Buonaccorsi, *Diario 1498–1552* (reprinted Rome 1999), p. 106.

CHAPTER 13: THE BORGIAS *IN EXCELSIS*

p. 224 'killed around 3,000 soldiers and . . .' Burchard, *Liber Notarum* (Paris, 2003 edn), pp. 372–3.

p. 226 'Often living beyond their . . .' See Kenneth M. Setton, *The papacy and the Levant* (Philadelphia, 1978), p. 533 n 107.

p. 227 'will was null and void . . .' Burchard, *Journal*, trans. Turmel (Paris, 1932), p. 278.

p. 227 'The Pope gave her the authority . . .' et seq., Burchard, *Liber Notarium* (Paris, 2003 edn), p. 374.

p. 231 'paroxysms of rage' See Bradford, *Lucrezia Borgia*, p. 104.

p. 231 'bargained like a tradesman' et seq., contemporary sources, cited ibid., pp. 108, 109.

p. 233 'Up to now Donna Lucretia . . . .' Alessandro Luzio, *Isabella d'Este e I Borgia con nuovo documenti* (Milan, 1916 edn), p. 533.

p. 233 'without ceasing from Vespers . . .' et seq., Burchard, *Liber*, p. 375.

p. 233 'I thought he was ill . . .' Ferrarese ambassador, cited Hibbert, *The House of Borgia*, p. 150.

p. 234 'The Duke [Cesare] has recently . . .' Burchard, *Journal*, cited ibid.

p. 236 'I hope that Your Excellency . . .' Letter from Bartolommeo Bresciani, cited Edmund Gardner, *Dukes and Poets in Ferrara, Fifteenth and Sixteenth century* (London, 1904) p. 402 n.

p. 236 'lamented that [his son Cesare] turned . . .' Cited Bradford, *Lucrezia Borgia*, p. 120.

p. 236 'Whenever she is at the Pope's . . .' Ferrarese envoy, cited Hibbert, *The House of Borgia*, p. 150.

p. 237 'On Sunday evening . . .' Burchard, *Journal* (Turmel), p. 310.

p. 237 'had the lights put out . . .' See Francesco Matarazzo, *Chronicles of the City of Perugia 1492–1503*, trans. E. S. Morgan (London, 1905), p. 209.

p. 237 'the Pope was scrupulous ...' et seq., see Hibbert, *The House of Borgia*, p. 152.

CHAPTER 14 CESARE STRIKES OUT

p. 241 'swarthy and deformed ...' Paolo Giovio, paraphrased Bradford, *Cesare Borgia*, p. 131.

p. 242 'dressed in a robe of gold ...' et seq., Burchard, *Liber Notarum* (Paris, 2003 edn), p. 387.

p. 243 'short, pop-eyed, snub-nosed ...' See David Nicolle, *Fornovo 1495* (Oxford, 1996), p. 13.

p. 243 'There was much violence and cheating ...' Burchard, *Liber Notarium* (2003 edn), pp. 386–7.

p. 244 'was harnessed very richly with ...' Letter from Beltrano Constabili to Ercole d'Este (6 January 1502).

p. 245 'None of these animals ...' Burchard, *Diarium* (London, 1963), cited Hibbert, *The House of Borgia*, p. 162.

p. 245 '753 people, 426 horses ...' See Bradford, *Lucrezia Borgia*, p. 137.

p. 246 'She kept always to her room ...' Letter to Ercole d'Este (22 January 1502).

p. 247 'This act pleased everyone ...' et seq., Zambotti, etc., cited Hibbert, *The House of Borgia*, pp. 164–9.

p. 248 'Three boats were prepared for ...' See Burchard, *Liber Notarium* (Paris, 2003 edn), p. 399.

p. 250 'The Florentines had been ...' Luca Landucci, *Diario* (Florence, 1883 edn), p. 245.

p. 250 'by the light of a single flickering ...' See Garret Mattingly, 'Machiavelli' in *The Penguin Book of the Renaissance*, ed. J. H. Plum, p. 64, collated from Machiavelli's writings.

p. 251 'I am not pleased with your government ...' et seq., Machiavelli despatch to Florence (22 June 1502). For this and other despatches, see *Opere di Machiavelli*, ed. Bertelli (vols 6–8, Milan 1968–72), where the despatches are printed in chronological order. My translations.

p. 252 'mules carrying rich loads ...' Leonardo, *Notebook*, L, 91r.

p. 253 'Where is Valentino ...' *Literary Works of Leonardo da Vinci*, ed. Jean Paul Richter (2 vols, New York, 1970), No. 1420.

CHAPTER 15: CHANGING FORTUNES

p. 258 'dishes from oysters and ...' See Hibbert, *The House of Borgia* (Constable, 2009 edn), p. 218.

p. 259 '**Every night he is commanding . . .**' et seq., Burchard, *Journal*, cited Hibbert, *The House of Borgia* (Folio Society, 2017), p. 171.

p. 260 '**spent the whole night . . .**' Maria Bellonci, *Lucrezia Borgia*, trans. B. Wall (London, 2000 edn), p. 204.

p. 261 '**I have a piece of information . . .**' et seq.

p. 261 '**His Most Christian Majesty . . .**' et seq., Niccolò da Corregio, writing from Milan (8 August 1502), cited Bradford, *Cesare Borgia*, p. 187.

p. 261 '**my cousin and . . .**' Andrea Bernardi, *Cronache Forlivese*, ed. G. Mazzatinti (Bologna, 1895), Vol. 2, p. 13.

p. 262 '**The Pope is not content . . .**' Sebastian Giustinian, cited Bradford, *Cesare Borgia*, p. 187.

p. 263 '**He praised the prudence of the Duke . . .**' et seq., cited ibid., p. 188.

p. 264 '**that the French knew . . .**' See Machiavelli, *The Prince*, sec. 17, ch. 3.

p. 265 '**Sacred Majesty, I render . . .**' Bernardi, *Cronache Forlivese*, Vol. 2, p. 14.

p. 265 '**Today at the twentieth hour . . .**' Letter written by one of the attendant physicians to Duke Ercole (8 September 1502), cited Bradford, *Cesare Borgia*, p. 119.

p. 266 '**All will allow . . .**' The original of this document is held in the Archivo Melzi d'Eril at the Villa Melzi on the shore of Lake Como at Bellagio. It is cited in many biographies of Leonardo; see, for instance, Serge Bramley, *Leonardo: the Artist and the Man*, trans. Sian Reynolds (London, 1992), p. 181.

p. 267 '**a most learned man . . .**' Cited Woodward, *Cesare Borgia*, p. 256.

p. 267 '**had placed in the government . . .**' Guicciardini, *Storia d'Italia*, cited Bradford, *Cesare Borgia*, p. 216.

p. 271 '**a man of a thousand . . .**' et seq., Machiavelli, *Decennale primo*, lines 406–8. Machiavelli's quotes re Olivoretto come from *Il Principe*, secs 3, 5, ch. 8; Baglioni, sec. 2, ch. 27; *Discourses*, 1 etc. Other details are repeated in many sources, such as Villari and Ridolfi.

p. 272 '**would be devoured one . . .**' Gianpaulo Baglioni, cited Hibbert, *The House of Borgia*, p. 183.

p. 273 '**with the love all the people . . .**' Zambotti, *Diario*, p. 342.

CHAPTER 16: CESARE SURVIVES

p. 275 '**The territory of this lord . . .**' Machiavelli despatch (24 October 1502), *Opere*, ed. Bertelli (Milan, 1968–72), Vols 6–8.

p. 276 '**seized all the bishop's goods . . .**' Burchard, *Diario*, p. 414.

p. 276 '**it would be bad for . . .**' Cited 2 December 1502, Giustinian, *Dispacci*, Vol. 1, pp. 242–3.

p. 277 'Paolo Orsini is in Cesena...' et seq., Machiavelli despatches 24 et seq. October 1502.

p. 278 'customary diversions' et seq., Burchard, cited Pasquale Villari, *The Life and Times of Machiavelli*, trans. L. Villari (2 vols, London, 1892), Vol. 1, p. 328.

p. 281 'I fail to understand how...' Machiavelli despatch 27 October 1502, et seq., despatches November 1502.

p. 282 'All the cities in this region of...' Machiavelli despatch 16 November 1502.

p. 283 'What the devil is he...' et seq., cited Giustinian, despatch 23 December 1502.

p. 283 'In two days we will be leaving...' et seq., Machiavelli despatch 20 December 1502.

p. 283 'The Duke no longer has sufficient...' Machiavelli despatch 23 December 1502.

p. 283 'The suspicions that...' Giustinian despatch, cited Bradford, *Cesare Borgia*, p. 202.

p. 284 'It is said that the Duke...' Machiavelli despatch 23 December 1502.

p. 284 'with whom he was greatly...' cited Bradford, *Cesare Borgia*, p. 202.

p. 284 'This morning Lorqua was discovered...' Machiavelli despatch 26 December 1502. This despatch was dated 26 December because Machiavelli wrote it that night, i.e. after 6 p.m., which marked the end of 25 December and the beginning of the new day.

p. 285 'affecting the honour of...' See Woodward, *Cesare Borgia*, p. 225 n 2.

p. 286 'A highly secretive man...' Machiavelli despatch 26 December 1502.

p. 288 'We are all awaiting...' Giustinian despatch to Venice 1 January 1503.

CHAPTER 17 BORGIA'S 'RECONCILLIATION'

p. 291 'Borgia winked knowingly...' From Machiavelli, *A Description of the Method used by Duke Valentino [Cesare Borgia] ... Oliverotto da Fermo and Others*, see Machiavelli, *Works* (trans. Gilbert), Vol. 2, p. 167.

p. 292 'Having remained a while...' From 'A Florentine Account', cited Bradford, *Cesare Borgia*, p. 205.

p. 293 'We are taking them as prisoners...' Machiavelli despatch 1 January 1503.

p. 294 'the Pope has become...' et seq., Giustinian despatch 6 January 1503.

p. 294 'The Duke's actions are...' Machiavelli despatch 8 January 1503.

p. 294 'an act worthy...' Cited Woodward *Borgia*, p. 285.

p. 295 **'a most beautiful deception . . .'** Paolo Giovio, cited Bradford, *Cesare Borgia*, p. 207.

p. 295 **'the worst possible weather . . .'** Machiavelli despatch 1 January 1503.

p. 296 **'We have done everything in our . . .'** Alexander VI, cited Bradford, *Cesare Borgia*, p. 209.

p. 297 **'succeeded in making an . . .'** de Roo, *Alexander VI*, Vol. 1, p. 417, citing several sources, including Balan, *Storia d'Italia*, Vol. 5, p. 417.

p. 297 **'By the time they reached San . . .'** Burchard, *Journal* (Turmel), p. 350.

p. 297 **'we will proceed to . . .'** Cited Charles Yriarte, *César Borgia: sa vie, sa captivité, sa mort* (Paris, 1889), Vol. 2, p. 134.

p. 299 **'When the Pope dies . . .'** Machiavelli despatch 8 November 1502.

p. 299 **'mortars capable of firing . . .'** et seq., Yriarte, *Borgia*, Vol. 2, p. 140.

p. 301 **'Look at it . . .'** Giustinian despatch 13 April 1503.

p. 301 **'thus demonstrating to . . .'** ibid., 31 May 1503.

p. 304 **'This month is . . .'** et seq., see Pastor, *History of the Popes*, Vol. 6, pp. 131–2, who had it from the contemporary chronicler Sigismondo dei Conti, though he suggests 'there is some confusion in the dates'.

p. 305 **'It did not overwhelm . . .'** Paolo Giovio, cited Rachel Erlanger, *Lucrezia Borgia* (London, 1979), p. 227.

CHAPTER 18: LUCREZIA IN FERRARA

p. 307 **'As soon as I saw you . . .'** et seq., letter from Bembo to Lucrezia Borgia (22 August 1503). See Letter XV in *The Prettiest Love Letters in the World: Letters between Lucrezia Borgia and Pietro Bembo 1503–1519* (London, 1987), trans. Hugh Shankland.

p. 308 **'letters, running . . .'** See Bradford, *Lucrezia Borgia*, p. 159.

p. 309 **'the first purpose-built . . .'** See Thomas Tuohy *Herculean Ferrara* (Cambridge, 1996)

p. 309 **'She was now twenty-three . . .'** Bellonci, *Lucrezia Borgia*, p. 209.

p. 310 **'The Prettiest Love . . .'** See ibid., esp. p. 23. Shankland attributes this phrase to Byron, when he saw the MS of Lucrezia's letters in the Ambrosiana Library in Milan. Byron was so struck by these letters that he copied them all down, as well as stealing 'one long strand from the lock of [Lucrezia's] hair'.

p. 310 **'Those beautiful tresses the more . . .'** Original Italian, see after Letter I in Shankland, *Letters*.

p. 310 **'I think that should I die . . .'** Original Spanish, see *The Letters*, Part 1 (1503–1505), ibid.

p. 311 **'for reasons of . . .'** ibid., p. 24.

p. 311 **'on the balcony with . . .'** ibid., Letter XVI.

p. 311 **'Here the heat is . . .'** ibid., Letter VIII.

p. 311 **'too many kisses'** Bellonci, *Lucrezia Borgia*, p. 228.

p. 311 **'with twenty-two stab . . .'** See Bradford, *Lucrezia Borgia*, p. 282.

p. 312 **'in no way displeasing . . .'** Ercole I to Ferrarese envoy in Milan (24 August 1503).

p. 312 **'I well know that you . . .'** Ferrarese envoy at Macon to Ercole I (8 September 1503).

CHAPTER 19: THE UNFORESEEN

p. 313 **'St Peter, Alexander . . .'** et seq., cited Mallett, *Borgias*, p. 9.

p. 314 **'He had thought of what . . .'** et seq., Niccolò Machiavelli, *The Prince*, trans. Stephen J. Milner (London, 1995), p. 63.

p. 315 **'Borgia, who was sick . . .'** Burchard, *Journal* (Turmel), p. 355.

p. 316 **'The skin of his face . . .'** et seq., ibid., p. 359.

p. 319 **'women of every . . .'** Mantuan ambassador despatch 2 September 1503.

p. 319 **'alive and well and the . . .'** Cited Bradford, *Cesare Borgia*, p. 202.

p. 321 **'They tell me he . . .'** Despatch from Beltrando Constabili, Ferrarese ambassador to the Papal Court, cited Hibbert, *The House of Borgia*, p. 201.

p. 321 **'I am neither a saint . . .'** et seq., Giustinian despatches 6, 7 October 1503.

p. 323 **'was known to be very . . .'** Giustinian cited Hibbert, *The House of Borgia*, p. 203.

p. 324 **'deluded and blind . . .'** See Mallett, *Borgias*, p. 257, where he is paraphrasing.

p. 324 **'according to some of his men . . .'** Machiavelli despatch 10 November 1503.

p. 324 **'he is taking action . . .'** ibid., 11 November 1503.

p. 324 **'paralysed with . . .'** et seq., ibid 14 November 1503.

p. 325 **'news arrived that Don Miguel . . .'** Machiavelli despatch 1 December 1503.

p. 328 **'It looks as if . . .'** ibid., 3 December 1503.

CHAPTER 20: DESPERATE FORTUNE

p. 333 **'all proclaiming their . . .'** Andrea Bernardi, *Cronache Forlivese 1476–1515*, trans. G. Mazzatinti (Bologna, 1895), pp. 406–7.

p. 335 **'Cesar, Duke of . . .'** See, for instance, Bradford, *Cesare Borgia*, p. 282.

p. 336 **'a big man, strong . . .'** Cited ibid., p. 285.

p. 336 **'had been in some pain . . .'** Reported conversation with Carvajal in Giustinian despatch 26 April 1504.

p. 336 **'bare as a hand'** Cited Erlanger, *Lucrezia Borgia*, p. 272.

p. 337 **'for all those who rise . . .'** See Machiavelli, *The Prince*, ch. 7, paras 13, 14.

EPILOGUE

p. 339 **'The more I turn . . .'** Alessandro Luzio, *Isabella d'Este e i Borgia*, Archivo Storico Lombardo (Milan, 1916), Serie Quinta, Book 1, p. 747.

p. 340 **'I will not live in the same . . .'** Cited Nigel Cawthorner, *Sex Lives of the Popes* (London, 1996), p. 219.

p. 340 **'a respectable and accomplished . . .'** See Roberto Gervasio, *I Borgia* (Milan, 1977) pp. 375–80.

ILLUSTRATIONS

Section one

Bronze medal depicting Pope Innocent VIII, attributed to Niccolò
Fiorentino, *c.* 1480/1486 (*Samuel H. Kress Collection, National Gallery
of Art, Washington D.C., USA*)

Portrait of Pope Alexander VI (*The Picture Art Collection/Alamy Stock
Photo*)

Pope Alexander VI, detail from Bernardino Pinturicchio's fresco of
the Resurrection in the Borgia Apartments of the Vatican (*Granger
Historical Picture Archive/Alamy Stock Photo*)

Ferdinand I of Aragon, painted marble bust, 15th century (*DeAgostini/
Getty Images*)

Posthumous portrait of Lorenzo de' Medici, 1560 (*Universal Images
Group North America LLC/Alamy Stock Photo*)

Portrait of Pope Julius II (*GL Archive/Alamy Stock Photo*)

Scenes from the life of Pius II, fresco by Bernardino Pinturicchio,
1503–1508 (*Sergio Anelli/Electa/Mondadori Portfolio via Getty Images*)

View of Rome, woodcut from the *Nuremberg Chronicle*, 1493
(*Wikimedia Commons*)

Wedding portrait of King Ferdinand of Aragon and Queen Isabella of
Castile, 15th century (*The Picture Art Collection/Alamy Stock Photo*)

Portrait of Federigo da Montefeltro by Piero Della Francesca, 1466
(*Hirarchivum Press/Alamy Stock Photo*)

Pope Pius II arrives in Ancona between 1502 and 1508 by Bernardino Pinturicchio (*The Picture Art Collection/Alamy Stock Photo*)

Portrait of Cesare Borgia (*The Picture Art Collection/Alamy Stock Photo*)

'Studies of the Head of Cesare Borgia from Three Points of View' by Leonardo da Vinci, *c.* 1480 (*Heritage Image Partnership Ltd/ Alamy Stock Photo*)

Plan of Imola by Leonardo da Vinci, 1502 (*PAINTING/Alamy Stock Photo*)

Section two

Portrait of Lucrezia Borgia by Bartolomea da Venezia (*GL Archive/ Alamy Stock Photo*)

Lucrezia Borgia, detail from Bernardino Pinturicchio's fresco in the Borgia Apartments of the Vatican (*The History Collection/Alamy Stock Photo*)

Portrait of Charles VIII (*World History Archive/Alamy Stock Photo*)

Portrait of King Louis XII (*Matthew Corrigan/Alamy Stock Photo*)

Portrait of Sancia of Aragon (*The Picture Art Collection/Alamy Stock Photo*)

Portrait of Cardinal d'Amboise (*Art Collection 4/Alamy Stock Photo*)

Portrait of Caterina Sforza by Lorenzo di Credi (*The Picture Art Collection/Alamy Stock Photo*)

Bust of Cardinal Guillaume d'Estouteville (*Peter Horree/Alamy Stock Photo*)

Portrait of Guidobaldo da Montefeltro, *c.* 1506 (*Heritage Image Partnership Ltd/Alamy Stock Photo*)

The Borgia Apartments (*© 2019 Veronica Costache/fotoLibra*)

Posthumous portrait of Niccolò Machiavelli by Santi di Tito (*Science History Images/Alamy Stock Photo*)

Portrait of Girolamo Savonarola by Alessandro Bonvicino (*DeAgostini/ Getty Images*)

The Borgia fortress at Nepi (*Lucky Team Studio/Shutterstock*)

Portrait of the Duke Alfonso I d'Este (*Heritage Image Partnership Ltd/ Alamy Stock Photo*)

INDEX

Aguerre, Ménaut, 133
d'Albret, Alain, 195
d'Albret, Cardinal Amanieu, 191
d'Albret, Charlotte, 167, 168, 195,
    198, 262, 302, 335
d'Albret, Jean, King of Navarre,
    333, 335
d'Alègre, Yves, 179, 184–5, 190, 223
Alexander the Great, 11, 14
Alexander VI, Pope, 4, 11–12, 26,
    77, 79–80
    ambitions, 12–14, 33, 84, 94,
        98–100, 129, 139–40, 150–60,
        165–6, 168–9, 189, 269–70
    appearance and personality, 8,
        27, 35–6, 68, 86, 216
    depravity/immorality, 8–9, 54–6,
        57, 59–60, 85, 129, 142–3, 237,
        259, 278
    early life and education, 33–6
    relationship with Cesare, 94,
        106, 126–7, 139, 149, 158–60,
        171–2, 183, 187, 189, 208, 222,
        263, 268–70, 283, 300
    relationship with children, 94–8,
        102–6, 126–33
    relationship with Juan, 94,
        130–32
    relationship with Lucrezia, 133,
        136–7, 142–3, 166, 174, 227–30
    spirituality and piety, 189, 237
    superstitious nature, 189, 201–2,
        237, 304
    wealth and greed, 49–50, 75, 80,
        84, 153–4, 191, 226–7, 245,
        329–30
    1431: birth, 33
    1455: appointed Bishop of Valencia,
        27–8, 37
    1456: appointed cardinal, 30, 36–7;
        appointed papal legate to
        Ancona, 37
    1457: appointed vice-chancellor
        to Callixtus III, 9, 30, 38–9;
        appointed Captain-General of
        Papal Forces, 40–41
    1458: death of Callixtus III, 32,
        43–4; papal conclave, 44–7;

appointed vice-chancellor to
Pius II, 48–50

1459: attends Congress of Mantua,
51–2

1460: attends 'party' in Seina, 54;
admonished by Pius II, 54–6

1461: supports Pius II's crusade, 58

1462: birth of Pedro Luis, 57

1464: travels to Ancona, 59; catches
plague, 60; death of Pius II,
60; papal conclave, 60–61;
appointed vice-chancellor to
Paul II, 61–2

1467: birth of Isabella, 64

1469: birth of Girolama, 64

1471: death of Paul II, 64; papal
conclave 64–5; appointed
vice-chancellor to Sixtus IV, 65

1472: travels to Spain on diplomatic mission, 66–8, 70

1473: shipwrecked, 69

1474: returns to Rome, 69; takes
Vanozza de' Cattanei as
mistress, 9, 70–71

1475: birth of Cesare, 71; sent to
greet King Ferrante, 73–4

1476: birth of Juan, 71

1477: appointed papal legate to
Naples, 74–5; lends money to
Sixtus IV, 75–6

1480: birth of Lucrezia, 71

1482: birth of Jofrè, 71

1484: death of Sixtus IV, 80; papal
conclave, 81–2; appointed
vice-chancellor to Innocent
VIII, 82, 84

1488: death of Pedro Luis, 94–5

c.1491: takes Giulia Farnese as
mistress, 91–2

1492: death of Innocent VIII, 4–10,
86–7; elected as pope, 10–11,
89; transforms Rome, 89–90;
coronation, 90–91; moves
family and Giulia Farnese to
Vatican, 91–4; birth of Laura,
93

1493: marriage of Lucrezia to
Giovanni Sforza, 95–8;
appoints twelve nephew-cardinals, 98

1494: Treaty of Tordesillas, 99–100;
French army occupy Rome,
110–11

1495: surrenders Sultan Cem to
Charles VIII, 111; appoints
Cesare as papal legate to
Charles VIII, 112; has secret
negotiations with Milan,
Venice and Spain, 114; refuses
to recognize Charles as ruler
of Naples, 115; suspected of
poisoning Cem, 116; establishes
Holy League; 118–20; flees
Rome, 120–21; bans Savonarola
from preaching, 124; Rome
floods, 124–5

1496: excommunicates Orsini
and Colonna, 125; summons
Lucrezia and Jofrè to Rome,
127–8; summons Juan to Rome,

130; sends papal force against the Orsini, 131

1497: papal army defeated, 132; refuses to pay Montefeltro's ransom, 132; sends papal force against French at Ostia, 132–3; appoints Cesare as papal legate to Naples, 134; Juan murdered, 135–6; banishes Lucrezia for affair with Calderon, 138; reassesses family strategy, 139–40; seeks annulment of Lucrezia's marriage, 141–2; accused of incest with Lucrezia, 142

1498: birth of Giovanni (*Infans Romanus*), 143; marriage of Lucrezia to Duke of Bisceglie, 144; arrest and execution of Savonarola, 144–7; gives consent to Louis XII to marry, 148; Cesare resigns as cardinal, 149; forms alliance with Louis XII, 150–52, 154; confiscates Jewish property and goods, 156–7; sends Cesare to France to marry Carlotta of Naples, 152–3, 158–60

1499: Carlotta refuses Cesare, 165; Duke of Bisceglie flees Rome, 166; Sancia flees Rome, 166; sends Lucrezia and Jofrè to Spoletto, 166–7; Cesare marries Charlotte d'Albret, 167; Giulia Farnese returns to Vatican,

172–3; Lucrezia reunited with Duke of Bisceglie, 174; travels to Spoletto, 174; appoints Lucrezia governor of Nepi, 174; strengthens position in Rome, 175; baptism of grandson, 175–6; declares Romagna 'feudatories' forfeit, 177–8; Cesare leads papal forces against Romagna, 179–81; Caterina Sforza's plot fails, 182

1500: receives Cesare back in Rome, 186–8; appoints Cesare captain-general of papal forces, 188–9; releases Caterina Sforza from prison, 189–90; modernizes Rome in Jubilee Year, 190–93; plans second Romagna campaign, 196; raises funds for a crusade, 196–7; makes Cardinal d'Amboise papal legate to France, 197; survives accident, 201–2; Duke of Bisceglie attacked and murdered, 204–8; crusader fleet sets sail, 215

1501: appoints Cesare Duke of Romagna, 217; excommunicates King Federigo, 223; combined Papal and French force march on Naples, 223–4; Naples campaign successful, 226; departs Rome leaving Lucrezia in charge, 227; legitimizes *Infans Romanus*, 229–30;

negotiates marriage of Lucrezia to Alfonso d'Este, 230–32; departs Rome with Cesare to inspect fortresses, 234–5; 'Banquet of Chestnuts', 237

1502: travels to Civitavecchia, 248; celebrates news of Lucrezia's pregnancy, 259; meetings with Cesare at Camerino, 268–70; orders Cesare to take Bologna, 270; furious over San Leo uprising, 273; raises funds for Cesare, 276; promises Cardinal Orsini papacy in return for support, 278; celebrates Cesare's promised return to Rome, 287–8

1503: imprisons Cardinal Orsini, 294–5; irate at Cesare's action against Siena, 296–7; threatens to excommunicate Cesare, 298, raises funds for Cesare, 300–301; negotiates over Naples, 302–3; son Rodrigo born, 304; taken ill, 305; death, 313–4; burial, 316

Alfonso II, King of Naples, 22, 28–9, 31, 34, 43, 66, 104, 108, 114–5, 141, 225

Alfonso V, King of Aragon, 18–20, 50

Alfonso of Aragon, Duke of Bisceglie, 141, 144, 166, 173, 175, 204–8, 233, 246, 333

d'Aliffe, Count, 141, 158

Alphonse, Duke of Calabria, 78

d'Amboise, Georges, Archbishop of Rouen, 148, 158, 160, 163, 168, 197, 320, 322

America, 99–100

Ancona, Italy, 37, 40, 59

Anjou, House of, 50, 53

Anne of Brittany, 147–8, 159, 162, 167

Aragon, Spain, 17, 66–8
House of, 235

Aranda, Pedro, Bishop of Calahorra, 156

Arezzo, Italy, 249, 253–4

Ascoli, Italy, 37

Astorre III Manfredi, 212, 216–7

Athens, Greece, 14, 51

d'Aubigny, 4th Lord (Bernard Stewart), 220, 223, 225

Aut Caesar aut nihil ('Either Caesar or nothing'), 180

Avignon, France, 160–61

Baglioni, Gian Paolo, 209, 213, 220, 249, 251, 254, 270–71, 287, 295, 317, 325

'Banquet of Chestnuts', 237

Barbo, Cardinal Marco, 69

Barbo, Cardinal Pietro, see Paul II

Barcelona, Spain, 67

Basanello, Italy, 9, 92–3

Bayezid II, Ottoman Sultan 99, 111, 115–6, 223

de Beaumonte, Louis, 2nd Count of Lerin, 335–6

de Beaumonte, Luis, 336

Belgrade, Serbia, 28

Bellonci, Maria, 207, 260, 309, 311

Bembo, Pietro, 307, 309–11, 339–40

Beneimbene, Camillo, 70

Bentivoglio, Ermes, 218, 272, 274

Bentivoglio, Giovanni, 218, 254, 268, 270, 274, 281

Bernardi, Andrea, 185, 261

Bessarion, Cardinal Basilios, 22–3, 45, 47, 60–61, 64, 69

de Bichis, Giovanni, 54

de Bierra, Baron, 283

Bologna, Italy, 35–6, 118, 218, 221, 270

University of, 27, 35

'Bonfire of the Vanities', 123–4,

Borgia family, 6, 12, 17–8, 33–4, 116, 129, 136, 157–8, 341

suspected Jewish ancestry, 157

Borgia, Camilla Lucrezia, 322

Borgia, Cesare, 11, 13, 14, 92, 229

appearance and personality, 104–6, 113, 126–7, 140–41, 150, 152–3, 158, 162–3, 186, 211–2, 238–9, 241–2, 252, 281–2, 324–6

appreciation of the arts, 170

as Duke of Romagna, 266–8, 275–85, 317–20

bullfights, 200–201

depravity/cruelty, 97, 137, 141, 198–9, 207–8, 211, 225, 236–9

early life, 94, 104–5

education, 77

exercise regime, 149–50, 200

relationship with Caterina Sforza, 185–8, 190

relationship with father, 94, 106, 126–7, 139, 149, 171–2, 183, 208, 268–9, 300

relationship with Juan, 130–31, 132, 134–5

relationship with Leonardo da Vinci, 170–71, 251–2, 266–7, 282, 299

relationship with Louis XII, 151–3, 163, 167–8, 172, 177, 253–5, 261–5, 296, 319, 332, 335

relationship with Lucrezia, 129–30, 133, 137–8, 184, 203–4, 207, 209, 238, 285–6

spirituality and piety, 238–9

syphilis, 141, 153, 161, 211–2, 234–5, 241–2, 281–2, 300, 336

wealth, 326–7, 329–30, 335

1475: birth, 71

1490: appointed Bishop of Pamplona, 94, 104–5

1492: appointed Archbishop of Valencia, 94, 105

1493: humiliated at Lucrezia's wedding, 96; appointed cardinal, 94, 98, 106

1495: taken hostage by Charles VIII, 112; escapes to Spoleto, 112–13; takes revenge on Swiss soldiers, 114

1496: has affair with Sancia of Aragon, 128, 130

1497: appointed papal legate to Naples, 134; suspected of Juan's murder, 135–6; crowns King Federigo, 139; proposes marriage to Carlotta of Naples, 139–40; contracts syphilis, 141

1498: suspected of murder of Calderon and Pantasilea, 138; master of ceremonies at Lucrezia's wedding, 144; resigns as cardinal, 149; becomes Duke of Valentinois, 149, 151; travels to French court to marry Carlotta of Naples, 152–3, 158–64

1499: accompanies Louis XII on trip through Loire Valley, 164–5; Carlotta refuses to marry him, 165; marries Charlotte d'Albret, 167, 168; accompanies Louis XII on campaign against Milan, 168–9; visits Leonardo da Vinci, 170–71; plans campaign in Romagna and the Marches, 170–71; secretly visits Rome, 179; leads papal forces against Romagna, 179–81; siege of Forli, 181–4

1500: returns to Rome with Caterina Sforza, 185–8; appointed captain-general of papal forces, 188–9; birth of daughter Louise, 195; affair with Fiammetta de' Michaelis, 199; plans second Romagna campaign, 202–3; has Duke of Bisceglie attacked and murdered, 204–8; embarks on second Romagna campaign, 209–10; takes Pesaro, 210; takes Rimini and Cesena, 212; lays siege to Faenza, 213; winters at Cesena, 214

1501: Faenza surrenders, 216–7; appointed Duke of Romagna, 217; negotiates peace treaty with Bologna, 218; marches into Florence, 218–9; lays siege to Piombino, 220; leads combined papal and French force to Naples, 224; takes Capua, 224–5; rewarded for success of Naples campaign, 226; helps negotiate marriage of Lucrezia to Alfonso d'Este, 232; departs Rome with father to inspect fortresses, 234–5; plans third Romagna campaign, 235, 242

1502: sets off on third Romagna campaign, 249; attacks Urbino, 250; meets with representatives of Florence, 250–51; hires Leonardo da Vinci, 252; ransacks Urbino, 252; flees Urbino to meet with Louis XII, 253–5; visits Lucrezia in

Ferrara, 255, 260–61; visits court of Louis XII in Milan, 261; leaves Milan, 264–5; visits sick Lucrezia, 265; plans governance for new dukedom in Imola, 266; Leonardo tours dukedom, 266; meetings with father at Camerino, 268–70; returns to Imola, 270; condottieri conspire against him, 270–74; raises troops to fight rebellion, 276–8; makes agreements with conspirators, 280–81; plans attack on Sinigalia, 281–3; French troops depart for Milan, 283; hosts ball in Cesena, 284; de Lorca murdered, 284–5; learns about conspiracy, 285; marches to Sinigalia, 286–7, 289; takes Sinigalia, 289–92; defeats conspirators, 292–4

1503: executes Vitellozzo and Oliverotto, 293–4; executes Orsini brothers, 295; marches to Siena, 296–8; lays siege to Ceri, 299; briefly returns to Rome, 300; Ceri surrenders, 301; returns to Rome to reinforce army, 303; taken ill, 305; reacts to death of father, 314–15; leaves Vatican and heads to Nepi, 318–20; returns to Rome, 321; reappointed as captain general of papal forces

by Julius II, 321, 324; marches to Ostia, 325; arrested and returned to Rome, 325; pope builds case against him, 327–8

1504: under house arrest, 330; promises to surrender Romagna fortresses, 331; travels to Ostia and is released, 331; heads to Naples, 332; imprisoned in Castel Nuovo, 332; surrenders Forli, 333; exiled to Spain, 333; imprisoned in Chinchilla, 333

1505: moved to La Motta, 334–5

1506: escapes from La Motta, 334–5; travels to Navarre, 335

1507: leads Navarese troops, 336; killed in battle, 336

Borgia, Francesco, Bishop of Cosenza, 175

Borgia, Giovanni (Infans Romanus), 175, 229–30, 260–61, 319, 322
    appointed Lord of Camerino, 268
    birth, 143, 172,
    inherits duchy of Nepi, 245
    legitimized by Alexander VI, 229

Borgia, Girolama (daughter of Rodrigo), 64, 82, 92

Borgia, Girolamo (son of Cesare), 322

Borgia, Isabella (daughter of Rodrigo), 64, 92

Borgia, Isabella (mother of Rodrigo), 25, 33, 64, 66

Borgia, Jofrè (father of Rodrigo), 33

Borgia, Jofrè, Prince of Squillace,
115, 259, 319
  appearance, 128
  bad behaviour, 166
  early life, 92, 94, 104
1482: born, 71
1494: marriage to Sancia of
  Aragon, 95, 98, 104, 128
1496: returns to Rome after French
  invasion, 127–8
1499: wife flees Rome, 166; sent to
  Spoletto, 166
1504: greets Cesare in Naples, 332

Borgia, Juan, 2nd Duke of Gandia,
92, 333
  appearance and personality,
  103–4, 130, 133
  early life, 94–5, 103
  relationship with Cesare Borgia,
  130–31, 132, 134–5, 188
  relationship with father, 94,
  130–32
1476: birth, 71
1488: becomes Duke of Gandia,
  103
1493: gives Lucrezia away at her
  wedding, 96; marries Maria
  Enriquez, 95, 103–4
1496: returns to Rome, 130; sent
  on campaign against the Orsini,
  131–2
1497: defeated by the Orsini, 132;
  leads papal force against French
  at Ostia, 132–3; made Duke of

Benevento, 134; murdered in
  Rome, 135–6

Borgia, Juan (great-nephew of
  Rodrigo), 173, 175, 180

Borgia, Laura (daughter of
  Rodrigo), 93

Borgia, Louise(daughter of Cesare),
  195, 198, 262, 302, 323

Borgia, Lucrezia, 92, 127–30,
  340–41
  and *Infans Romanus*, 143,
  229–30
  appearance and personality, 102,
  127, 128–9, 137, 228–9, 236–7,
  246–8, 309
  early life, 95, 102–3
  relationship with Cesare,
  129–30, 133, 137–8, 203–4,
  207, 209, 236–7, 333
  relationship with father, 103,
  133, 136–7, 142–3, 160, 174,
  184, 207, 210, 227–30, 237
  relationship with Pietro Bembo,
  310–11
  sexual proclivity, 136–8, 143,
  184, 229–30, 285–6, 309–11,
  339–40
  spirituality and piety, 237–8, 339
1480: birth, 71
1493: marries Giovanni Sforza,
  95–8, 102–3
1496: returns to Rome after French
  invasion, 127–8
1497: abandoned by Sforza, 133;
  has affair with Pedro Calderon,

138; proposed marriage to Alfonso, Duke of Bisceglie, 141; accused of paternal incest, 142; marriage to Sforza annulled, 142; proclamation of virginity, 143

1498: rumoured to have given birth, 143; marries Alfonso, Duke of Bisceglie, 144

1499: abandoned by Duke of Bisceglie, 166; appointed governor of Spoletto, 166–7; reunited with husband at Spoletto, 174; sent to fortress at Nepi, 174; gives birth to Rodrigo, 175

1500: Duke of Bisceglie attacked and murdered, 204–7; returns to Nepi, 207; returns to Rome, 209–10

1501: left in charge of papal matters in Rome, 227–9; plans marriage to Alfonso d'Este, 232–3; proxy marriage takes place in Rome, 242–4

1502: travels to Ferrara, 244–8; wedding takes place, 248; life in Ferrara, 257–9; becomes pregnant, 259; falls ill, 260; visited by Cesare, 260–61; gives birth to stillborn child, 265; Cesare pays short visit, 265

1503: learns of poisoning of Cesare and death of her father, 307–8, 311–12; sends troops to aid Cesare, 319–20

1504: petitions for Cesare's release, 333

1507: learns of Cesare's death, 339

1508: gives birth to Ercole, 339

1519: death, 341

Borgia, Pedro Luis, 1st Duke of Gandia, 92, 94–5, 172
 early life, 66, 71

1462: birth, 57

1485: betrothed to Maria Enriquez, 94

1488: death, 94–5

Borgia, Pedro Luis (brother of Rodrigo), 27, 30, 31–2, 34–6, 40–41, 44, 49

Borgia, Rodrigo, see Alexander VI

Borgia, Rodrigo (son of Rodrigo), 304

Borgia-Lanjol, Cardinal Juan, 304

de Borja family, see Borgia family

de Borja, Alonso, see Callixtus III

Borja, Spain, 17

Bossi, Lauro, 190

Botticelli, Sandro, 2, 6, 66, 80

Bracciano, siege of, 131–2

Bradford, Sarah, 102, 105, 185

bullfighting, 200

Buonaccorsi, Biagio, 219

Burchard, Johann, 96–7, 112–3, 130, 135, 138, 149, 158, 173, 177–8, 182, 192, 206, 217, 227–8, 234, 243, 248, 259, 278, 297, 315

Burckhardt, Jacob, 101

Byzantine Empire, 14, 23, 28, 51, 58

Caesar, Julius, 11, 180
Caetani family, 174, 234
Calandrini, Cardinal, Bishop of Bologna, 45–6
Calderon, Pedro ('Perotto'), 138, 143, 229
Callixtus III, Pope, 9, 17, 23–8, 30, 36–8, 42–3, 157
  as Bishop of Valencia, 19–20, 34
  as Cardinal, 19–20, 22, 34
  as secretary to Alfonso V, 18–19
  crusade, 28–31, 34, 40
  death, 32, 43–4
  early life, 17–18
  elected as Pope, 23–4
Camerino, Italy, 249–50, 253, 268
Campo de' Fiori, Rome, 25
Canale, Carlo, 71
cantarella (poison), 305
Capello, Paolo, 202
Capranica, Cardinal Angelo, 69
Capranica, Cardinal Domenico, 42, 44–5
Capua, Italy, 224–5
Carafa, Cardinal Oliviero, 70
de Cardenas, 334
Carlotta of Naples, 140, 150, 152, 158, 165, 167–8, 168
Carnival (Rome), 64, 186, 242–3, 288, 300
  horse races, 64, 242–4
Carvajal, Cardinal Juan, 331, 336

de Casanova, Cardinal Jaime, 315
Castel Nuovo, Naples, 332–3
Castel Sant'Angelo, Rome, 21, 27, 32, 36, 44, 63, 81, 110, 125, 190, 322
Castile, 66–8
Catalans, 23, 27, 31–2, 39, 43, 45, 67, 157
de' Cattanei, Vanozza, 9, 70–71, 92, 94, 106, 113–14, 134, 198, 318–19
Cem, Sultan, 99, 111, 115–6
de Centelles, Querubí Joan, 102
Cerignola, Battle of, 301
Cesena, Italy, 3, 212, 214, 252, 282, 284–5, 317–8, 320, 325, 330
Charlemagne, 111
Charles VIII, King of France, 9, 11, 100, 123, 125, 146, 147, 158
  and crusade, 111, 115–6, 119
  appearance, 108
  invasion of Italy, 109–21
  sexual appetite, 108, 115
Chinchilla, Spain, 333
Chinon, France, 162–4
Cibo, Cardinal Giovanni, see Innocent VIII
Città di Castello, Italy, 317
City states of Italy, 4, 28, 79, 84, 98, 100, 118–19
Civita Castellana, Italy, 234
Civitavecchia, Italy, 32, 44, 48, 110, 248
Clement VIII, 'anti-pope', 19
College of Abbreviators, 59, 61, 63

College of Cardinals, 5, 6, 9, 30, 44,
   61–2, 65, 149, 175, 228
Collenuccio, Pandolfo, 210–12
Colonna family, 24, 27, 110, 125–6,
   166, 174, 225, 234, 297–8, 317
Colonna, Cardinal Prospero, 47–9
Colonna, Fabrizio, 224–5
Colonna, Prospero, 225, 318–19,
   332–3
Columbus, Christopher, 15, 99, 117
conclaves
   1455, 22–3
   1458, 44–8
   1464, 60–1
   1471, 64–5
   1484, 81
   1492, 6–11, 87, 89
   September 1503, 316–7, 318,
      320
   October 1503, 322–3
consistory, 9, 42
Constantinople, Turkey, 22, 25, 28,
   30
de' Conti, Sigismondo, 85–6
conversos, 155
Copernicus, Nicolaus, 35
da Córdoba, Gonsalvo, 132, 133,
   215, 226, 301, 328, 332, 334
da Corella, Miguel, 203, 206–7,
   209, 246, 273–4, 276, 287–8,
   291, 293, 315, 318–9, 325, 327,
   329–30
Cornero, Cardinal Marco, 197
da Corneto, Cardinal Adriano,
   304–5, 314

Corte Vecchio, Italy, 170
Cosenza, Bishop of, 175
da Costa, Cardinal Jorge, 227–8
courtesans, 198–9
Curia, 30, 31, 38, 44, 49

Da Vinci, Leonardo, 2, 80, 84, 258
   employed by Cesare, 170–71,
      251–3, 266–7, 279–80, 282,
      293, 299–300
   employed by Ludovico Sforza,
      164, 170, 192
Dante Alighieri, 35, 310
Della Rovere family, 65, 93, 281,
   293
Della Rovere, Cardinal Francesco,
   see Sixtus IV
Della Rovere, Cardinal Giuliano,
   4–7, 9–11, 73–4, 80–82, 86–7,
   100, 106, 108, 111–2, 160–62,
   169, 197, 254, 320–23
   as Pope Julius II, 323–5, 327–33,
      335, 340
Della Rovere, Francesco (ruler of
   Sinigalia), 281, 287, 323
Della Rovere, Giovanni, 73
Diaz, Bartholomew, 99
Domesday Book, 280

Eleanora of Naples, Duchess of
   Ferrara, 258–9, 308
England, 28
Enrique IV, King of Castile, 68
Enriquez, Maria, 94–5, 103, 130,
   136

Erasmus of Amsterdam, 35

Ercole I d'Este, Duke of Ferrara, 230–32, 235–6, 242, 244, 247, 257–8, 265, 308–9, 312, 319, 333

Ercole II d'Este, Duke of Ferrara, 339

d'Este, Alfonso, 230–2, 247–8, 257, 260, 311–2, 319, 340–41

d'Este, Cardinal Ippolito, 307

d'Este, Ferrante, 245

d'Este, Isabella, Marquesa of Mantua, 258–9, 262, 308, 340

d'Este, Niccolò Maria, Bishop of Adria, 242

d'Este, Sigismund, 245

d'Estouteville, Guillaume, Cardinal of Rouen, 8, 45–7, 54, 64, 75, 80

de Estúñiga, Lope, 310

Eugenius IV, Pope, 19, 21, 22, 61

Faenza, Italy, 196, 318
    siege of, 212–3, 217

Farnese, Angelo, 93

Farnese, Cardinal Alessandro, 93, 98

Farnese, Giulia, 9, 91–4, 96, 110, 127, 129, 143, 172–3, 229

Federigo, King of Naples, 134, 139–40, 150, 152, 165, 173, 223, 225–6

Ferdinand II, King of Aragon, 15, 66–8, 70, 95, 100, 114, 132, 147, 332–4

Ferdinand, Duke of Calabria, 226

da Fermo, Oliverotto, see Oliverotto

Ferrante I, King of Naples, 4, 9–10, 12, 20, 29, 32, 50, 53, 58, 73–5, 78, 79, 83, 95, 98, 101, 104, 107–8

Ferrantino II, King of Naples, 114–5, 134

Ferrara, Italy, 84, 118, 210–11, 231–2, 244–8, 255, 257–60, 308–9, 339–40

First Italian War (1494–98), 108–21

Florence, 2, 3, 4, 12, 14, 21, 22, 76–8, 83–4, 101, 109, 123–4, 192, 221,
    and First Italian War, 109, 118
    and Savonarola, 144–7
    and Second Italian War, 215–6
    and second Romagna campaign, 218–21
    and third Romagna campaign, 248–50
    Signoria, 220–21

de Foix, Mademoiselle, 231

Forli, Italy, 180–81, 190, 214, 332–3

Fornovo, Battle of, 121, 148

Fortini, Pietro, 198

Fossombrone, Italy, 273

Fracastro, Girolamo, 117

France, 28, 50, 100, 109–10, 133, 147–8, 150, 165, 167, 173, 177, 196–7, 216

Gaeta, Italy, 328
  siege of, 302–3, 317
Galen, 80
Genoa, Italy, 9, 84, 177, 264,
  329–30, 335
Ghirlandaio, Domenico, 6, 80
Giovio, Paolo, 241, 295, 305
Giustinian, 283, 300–301, 321, 326,
  331
Gonzaga, House of, 65
Gonzaga, Cardinal Francesco, 65–6
Gonzaga, Federigo, 262
Gonzaga, Francesco, Duke of
  Mantua, 106, 121, 243–4, 254,
  258–9, 263–4, 339–40
Gonzaga, Isabella, 246
gout, 26, 48
Gran Cavallo ('Great Horse'),
  170
Great Schism, 19, 20–21, 25
Greece, 14, 23, 29, 51
Guicciardini, Francesco, 2, 8, 10,
  37, 107, 115, 117, 217, 225,
  267, 323
Guy XVI, Count of Laval, 140
de Guzman, 333

Henry the Navigator, Prince, 99
Henry VII, King of England, 118
Heywood, Colin, 79
Holy League, 118–21, 125–6, 148,
  153
Holy Roman Empire, 28
horse races, 64, 106, 242–3
Hundred Years War, 28

Hungary, 28, 29
Hunyadi, János, 29

Imola, Italy, 275, 278, 282, 318,
  320, 325
incest, 136, 137, 142–3, 184, 230
indulgences, 83
Infans Romanus, see Borgia,
  Giovanni
Infessura, Stefano, 10, 91, 97–8
Inghirami, Giovanni, 42
Innocent VIII, Pope, 1–7, 81–2,
  83–7
Innocent X, Pope, 341
Isabella I, Queen of Castile, 15,
  66–8, 70, 95, 132, 136, 334
Isabella of Naples, 150
Isabelle of Clermont, 20

Jacopo IV Appiano, 220
janissaries 149
Jerusalem, 19, 109, 111, 115–6
Jews, 154, 155–7
Joan of France, 148, 159, 162
Joana la Beltraneja, 68
Joanna II, Queen of Naples, 18–19,
  50
Joanna of Aragon, Queen of
  Naples, 74
John III, King of Navarre, 167
Johnson, Marion, 11
Juan II, King of Aragon, 66–8
Juan, Prince of Asturias, 74
Jubilee year 1475, 64, 73
Jubilee year 1500, 190–91, 200

Julius II, Pope, see Della Rovere,
    Cardinal Giuliano

Kefalonia, Greece, 215
Knights of St John, 99

La Magione, Italy, 271–2
La Motta, Spain, 334–5
Landucci, Luca, 250
Lascelles, Christopher, 83
Last Supper, The (Da Vinci), 164,
    170, 251
Lateran (Basilica of San Giovanni
    in Laterano), Rome, 24, 90
Lerida, University of, 18
Levant, 14, 30
Lippi, Raphael Brandolinus, 204,
    206
Little Ice Age, 3
Lives of the Popes (Platina), 63, 66
de Llançol, Jofrè, see Borgia, Jofré
Lopez, Cardinal Bernardino, 201–2
de Lorqua, Ramiro, 185, 203, 212,
    232, 246, 267, 274, 284–6, 293
Louis of Orléans, 121
Louis XI, King of France, 69
Louis XII, King of France, 158–60,
    162–5, 193, 220, 231–2, 251,
    263–4, 283, 294, 320
  alliance with Borgias, 149–51,
    160, 195–7
  and Anne of Brittany, 159, 162
  and Cesare Borgia, 151–3, 163,
    167–8, 172, 177, 253–5, 261–5,
    296, 319, 332, 335

and Joan of France, 147–8, 159,
    162
  and Second Italian War, 168–70,
    177, 197–8, 225–6
  loses Naples, 301
Luther, Martin, 314

Machiavelli, Niccolò, 12–4, 68–9,
    178–9, 206–7, 210, 221,
    250–51, 253, 263, 264, 268,
    271, 275–7, 281–7, 291, 293–4,
    299, 322, 324–5, 330–31, 337
malady of San Lazzaro, 161
malaria, 41–2, 303–4, 314
Malatesta family, 212
Malatesta, Sigismondo Pandolfo,
    Lord of Rimini, 53–4, 57–8, 79,
    169, 212, 317
Mallett, Michael, 37, 93
Manfredi family, 212
Manfredi, Giovanni, 216, 217
Mantua, Italy, 65, 263–4
  Congress of, 51–2, 65
Marches, 37, 79, 169–70, 269
Marescotti, Cleofe, 284
Marranos, 155–7
Martin V, Pope, 19, 21
Matarazzo, Francesco, 213, 237
Maximilian I, Holy Roman
    Emperor, 118, 145, 169
Medici Bank, 76–7, 83
Medici family, 76–8, 221
de' Medici, Cardinal Giovanni, 3,
    11, 77, 100, 104–5, 109
de' Medici, Giuliano, 78

de' Medici, Lorenzo (the
  Magnificent), 3–4, 76–8, 83–4,
  98
de' Medici, Piero, 100–101, 105,
  109, 249
Mehmed the Conqueror, Ottoman
  Sultan, 28–9, 51, 58, 79, 99
de Mendoza, Pedro González,
  Bishop of Sigüenza, 68
Meyer, G. J., 34, 50, 67, 120, 207
de' Michaelis, Fiammetta, 198–9
Michelangelo, 6, 84
Michiel, Cardinal Giovanni,
  300–301, 305
de Milà, Adriana, 72, 92, 102, 110,
  127
de Milà, Cardinal Luis Juan, 6,
  34–8, 72
Milan, 4, 12, 84, 95, 134, 142, 183,
  185, 192, 196
  and First Italian War, 109, 114
  and Second Italian War, 168–70,
  177
de Moncada, Ugo, 273–4
da Montefeltro, Federigo, Duke of
  Urbino, 54, 58, 73, 77, 131, 178
da Montefeltro, Giovanna, 73
da Montefeltro, Guidobaldo, Duke
  of Urbino, 131–2, 136, 154,
  246, 250, 254, 259, 264, 272–3,
  277–8, 280–81, 317, 325–7
Moors, 155
Mystras, Greece, 23, 51, 58

da Naldo, Dionigi, 183–4

Naples, 4, 17, 19–20, 31–2, 34, 50,
  53, 74–5, 84, 104, 108–9, 134,
  193, 301, 328, 332
  and First Italian War, 114–20
  and outbreak of syphilis, 117–8
  and Second Italian War, 197–8,
  204, 205, 223–6
  coronation of Federigo, 139–41
  partition of, 215, 276–7
Navarre, 335–6
nephew-cardinals, 62, 65, 98
Nepi, Italy, 75–6, 207, 209
  Castle, 174
Nicholas V, Pope, 22, 25, 30, 35, 41
Nietzsche, Friedrich, 13
Noel, Gerard, 45, 46, 48
Norwich, John Julius, 35, 63, 81

Oliverotto da Fermo, 219, 249, 271,
  287, 291–3, 295
'ordeal by fire', 146–7
Orsi family, 181
Orsini family, 20, 24, 27, 90 ,110,
  125–6, 131–2, 174, 202, 234,
  292–3, 297–9, 317
Orsini, Cardinal Giambattista, 203,
  254, 271, 278, 287, 293, 294–5,
  299
Orsini, Carlo, 131
Orsini, Francesco, 289, 291, 293
Orsini, Giangiordano, 298
Orsini, Giulio, 203, 209, 218,
  221, 224–5, 249, 253–4, 268,
  270–73, 287, 299, 301
Orsini, Niccolò, 298

Orsini, Orsino, 9, 92–3
Orsini, Paolo, 203, 209, 221, 224–5,
    249, 253–4, 268, 270–73, 287,
    289, 291–3, 277–9
Orsini, Roberto, 289, 291, 293
Orsini, Virginio, 125
Orthodox Catholic Church, 22–3
Ostia, Italy, 11, 44, 110, 133, 324–5
Otranto, Italy, 79
Ottoman Empire, 14, 22–3, 28–30,
    51, 58, 70, 79, 99, 111, 215, 223

Palazzo San Marco, Rome, 62–3
Pallavicini, Cardinal Sforza, 141
Pantasilea (Lucrezia's maid), 138
papal bulls, 35, 78–80, 83
Papal States, 21, 49, 53, 179, 196,
    231, 302
Paracelsus, 35
Parker, Geoffrey, 96–7
Pasha, Gedik Ahmed, 79
von Pastor, Ludwig, 55, 85–6, 196–7
Paul II, Pope, 7, 61–4, 65
Pazzi family, 76–8
Pedro of Atares, 235
Perotto, see Calderon, Pedro
Perugia, Italy, 213–4, 317
Perugino, Pietro, 84
Pesaro, Italy, 184–5, 210, 246, 287
Petrarch, 35, 310
Petrucci, Pandolfo, 272, 295, 297–8
Piccolomini, Cardinal Aeneas, see
    Pius II
Piccolomini, Cardinal Francesco,
    see Pius III

Pinturicchio, 126
Piombino, Italy, 220, 248
Pisa, 69–70, 77, 219, 248, 330
    University of, 77, 104–5, 284
de Pistoia, Antonio, 31
Pius II, Pope, 7, 8–9, 48–52, 5
    3–60
    as Bishop of Siena, 40, 45, 54
    as Cardinal, 38–40, 43–8
    crusade, 58–60
    death, 60
    elected Pope, 44–8
Pius III, Pope, 320–22
plague, 42, 59–60, 304
Platina, Bartolomeo, 63, 66
Plato, 22–3
poisoning, 116, 133, 300, 305,
    313–4
del Pollaiuolo, Antonio, 87
Ponte Sisto, Rome, 80
Pope Joan, 24
Portugal, 99–100
Poto, Gaspare, 201
Prince, The (Machiavelli), 13, 263,
    269, 294, 337
Procida, Don Gaspar de, 102, 141
di Prosperi, Bernardo, 308–9
Pucci, Puccio, 92
da Puglia, Francisco, 146

Ramirez, Diego, 327
Ramirez, Pedro, 319, 327
Ramiro I, King of Aragon, 18, 235
Raphael, 84, 179
Ravenna, Battle of, 340

Renaissance, 2, 4, 14–5, 22, 25, 80, 84, 192–3

Réné, Count of Anjou, 58

Rexach, Juan, 25

Riario family, 73

Riario, Cardinal Raffaele, 78

Riario, Francesco Salviati, 77–8

Riario, Girolamo, 81, 181

di Rignano, Domenico, 71

Rimini, Italy, 53, 54, 57, 169, 196, 212, 317

Rodrigo of Aragon, Duke of Bisceglie, 175–6, 244–5, 319, 322

de Rohan, Cardinal, 231

Romagna territories, 49, 53, 57, 79, 203, 224
    first Romagna campaign, 169–70, 178, 188–9
    second Romagna campaign, 196–7, 209–22
    third Romagna campaign, 235, 249–55, 262
    under Cesare Borgia, 266–8, 275–301, 317–20

Roman Catholic Church, 22–3
    Great Schism, 19, 20–21
    Orthodox Catholic Church, 22–3

Roman Empire, 14, 20

Rome, 3, 4, 9, 11–2, 20–26, 35, 41–2, 56, 64, 75, 79, 83–4
    anarchy and riots of 1484, 80–81
    and First Italian War, 109–11, 113–4, 116

Carnival season, 64, 186, 242–3, 288, 300
    flood of 1495, 124–5
    improvements in Jubilee of 1500, 190–92
    outbreaks of malaria, 41–2, 303–4
    outbreaks of plague, 42, 304
    under Alexander VI, 89–90

de Roo, Peter, 34, 74, 118

Rota (Church's supreme court), 49

Rovere, della, see Della Rovere

St Francis Borgia, 341

St Peter's, Rome, 21

Sala del Pappagallo, 187

di Saluzzo, Giorgio, Bishop of Lausanne, 36

Salviati Bank, 76

di San Genesio, Giacomo, 1–2, 4

San Leo, Italy, 273

San Sisto convent, 138, 142, 229

Sancia of Aragon, 115, 127–8, 144, 166, 205–6, 232, 259, 319, 332
    affair with Cesare Borgia, 128, 130, 135
    appearance and personality, 104, 128
    marriage to Jofrè Borgia, 95, 104,
    relationship with Rodrigo Borgia, 259

Sansavino, Antonio di Monte, 267, 279–80

Santa Maria Sopra Minerva church, 317

Santa Marie delle Grazie monastery, 170

Santi Quattro Coronati, Rome, 22

Sanuto the younger, Marino, 138, 185, 245

Savelli family, 27, 234, 297–8

Savonarola, Girolamo, 4, 101, 107, 109, 118, 123–4, 144–7, 173

Scalona, Gian Carlo, 4, 128

Scotland, 39–40

'Scourge of God', 4, 109, 118, 121, 123

Second Italian War (1499–1504), 168–70, 177, 197–8, 204, 205, 223–6

Setton, Kenneth, 226

Sforza Pallavicini, Cardinal Francesco, 120

Sforza, Anna, 230

Sforza, Cardinal Ascanio, 10, 12, 95, 142, 169, 174–5

Sforza, Caterina, Countess of Forli, 81, 181–6, 188–90

Sforza, Francesco, Duke of Milan, 30, 50, 54, 58, 170

Sforza, Giovanni, Lord of Pesaro, 184–5, 210, 317
  annulment of marriage, 141–3, 312
  marriage to Lucrezia, 95–8, 102–3, 127, 133–4, 136–8

Sforza, Ludovico, Duke of Milan, 12, 95, 108–9, 114, 142, 148, 161, 164, 168–70, 174, 181, 183, 185, 189–91, 252

Sicily, 19

siege machines, 299–300

Siena, 8, 54–5, 129, 215, 296–8

Sigismondo of Foligno, 217

Sinigalia, Italy, 281, 283, 286–8, 289–95

Sistine Chapel, 6, 10–11, 66, 80, 81

Sixtus IV, Pope, 6, 7, 65–71, 73–81, 94, 181

slavery, 79

Smyrna, Turkey, 70

Soderini, Francesco, Bishop of Volterra, 250–51

Soderini, Piero, 221, 250–51, 274, 281, 324, 330

Spain, 15, 17, 20, 35, 66–8, 70, 94, 99–100, 147, 165, 167, 202, 277, 302

Spanish Inquisition, 3, 79, 83, 155

Spannocchi Bank, 11

Strozzi, Ercole, 309, 311

syphilis, 60, 117–18, 141, 153, 161, 211

Tordesillas, Treaty of, 100

Torella, Gaspar, 141, 153, 161, 242, 260

de Torquemada, Tomás, 3, 83, 155

Trabzon, Turkey, 58

Trastevere, Rome, 27

Trevisano, Cardinal Ludovico, 21, 28–9

da Trezzo, Antonio, 30

Trivulzio, Gian Giacomo, 168–9

Umbria, Italy, 213–4
Urbino, Italy, 54, 77, 178–9, 246,
    250–53, 273–4, 278–81, 317

Valencia, Spain, 8, 18, 34
da Varano, Giulio, 249, 253–4
Vatican apartments, 126, 187
Vatican Library, 25, 66, 80
Velletri, Italy, 112
Venice, 4, 12, 28, 59–60, 84, 119,
    180, 192, 196, 210, 276–7,
    302–3
    crusade, 215
de Vera, Cardinal Juan, 331
da Verona, Gaspare, 35
Vesalius, Andreas, 80
vice-chancellorship (papal), 49–50

Villa Belvedere, Rome, 87
Villari, Pasquale, 145
'Virtù e Fortuna', 13, 68–9, 165–6,
    263, 322
Visconti family, 148
Vitellozzo, Vitelli, 203, 209, 220,
    221, 224, 249–51, 254, 268,
    270–71, 273–4, 277–8, 285,
    287, 289, 291–3, 295, 317
da Volterra, Jacopo, 8

witchcraft, 3, 83

Xàtiva, Spain, 33, 34

Zambotti, Bernardino, 213, 247
Zeno, Cardinal Giovanni, 226–7

A NOTE ABOUT THE AUTHOR

Paul Strathern studied philosophy at Trinity College, Dublin. He has lectured in philosophy and mathematics. He is a Somerset Maugham Award-winning novelist and the author of two series of books – 'Philosophers in 90 Minutes' and 'The Big Idea: Scientists Who Changed the World'. His other works include *The Medici; The Artist, the Philosopher and the Warrior; The Spirit of Venice* and *Death in Florence.*